Signet Classics

OTHER VOICES, OTHER VISTAS

A SUPERB COLLECTION OF CONTEMPORARY MULTICULTURAL FICTION

Chinua Achebe

Nadine Gordimer

Wang Anyi

Chen Rong

Anita Desai

R. K. Narayan

Kōbō Abe

Yukio Mishima

Isabel Allende

Gabriel García Marqu

and 15 other outstan
literary voices

Short Stories from Africa, China, India, Japan, and Latin America
Edited and with an Introduction by Barbara H. Solomon

$8.95 U.S.
$10.99 CAN.

ISBN 978-0-451-52840-7

9 780451 528407

50895

EAN

THE TOMOSHIBI by Sawako Ariyoshi

The whiskey is Western, but the condiments, the waitresses, and the sensibilities are very Japanese in a subtle psychological drama set in a small bar on the Ginza.

PIGEONS AT DAYBREAK by Anita Desai

The elderly married couple following the routines of an unremarkable day could live in Miami or Brooklyn, but Mr. Basu is struggling with his asthma and his irritation at his wife, Otima, in the hot Indian city of Darya Ganj.

CLARISA by Isabel Allende

Rich, deep, and satiric, this life of a "saint" is as South American in character as the unnamed city of its setting—both sacred and profane and filled with the grotesque, the magical, the unexpected.

SKETCHES FROM THE "CATTLE SHED" by Ding Ling

Imprisoned herself during the Cultural Revolution, the author's brief "sketches" of a woman's life in a cell are so moving as to be painful . . . but also more powerful in their cry for freedom than a political tract could ever be.

AND 21 MORE OUTSTANDING STORIES THAT ARE PASSPORTS TO OTHER WORLDS

Barbara H. Solomon is a professor of English and women's studies at Iona College in New Rochelle, New York. She is also Director of Writing for the Department of English. Among the anthologies she has edited are the Signet/Mentor editions of *Bernice Bobs Her Hair and Other Stories of F. Scott Fitzgerald; Rediscoveries: American Short Stories by Women, 1832–1916; Herland and Selected Stories of Charlotte Perkins Gilman; The Haves and Have-Nots; American Families;* and *The Awakening and Selected Stories of Kate Chopin.* She is currently researching contemporary American stories about the lives of women.

OTHER VOICES, OTHER VISTAS

Short Stories from Africa,
China, India, Japan,
and Latin America

EDITED AND WITH
AN INTRODUCTION BY
Barbara H. Solomon

SIGNET CLASSICS

This book is dedicated to the memory
of my father, Lothar Hochster.

Even to the utmost ...
A kind and good Father
—WORDSWORTH

SIGNET CLASSICS
Published by New American Library, a division of
Penguin Group (USA) Inc., 375 Hudson Street,
New York, New York 10014, USA
Penguin Group (Canada), 90 Eglinton Avenue East, Suite 700, Toronto,
Ontario M4P 2Y3, Canada (a division of Pearson Penguin Canada Inc.)
Penguin Books Ltd., 80 Strand, London WC2R 0RL, England
Penguin Ireland, 25 St. Stephen's Green, Dublin 2,
Ireland (a division of Penguin Books Ltd.)
Penguin Group (Australia), 250 Camberwell Road, Camberwell, Victoria 3124,
Australia (a division of Pearson Australia Group Pty. Ltd.)
Penguin Books India Pvt. Ltd., 11 Community Centre, Panchsheel Park,
New Delhi - 110 017, India
Penguin Group (NZ), 67 Apollo Drive, Rosedale, North Shore 0632,
New Zealand (a division of Pearson New Zealand Ltd.)
Penguin Books (South Africa) (Pty.) Ltd., 24 Sturdee Avenue,
Rosebank, Johannesburg 2196, South Africa

Penguin Books Ltd., Registered Offices:
80 Strand, London WC2R 0RL, England

Published by Signet Classics, an imprint of New American Library, a division of
Penguin Group (USA) Inc. Previously published in a Mentor edition.

First Signet Classics Printing, June 2002
20 19 18

PERMISSIONS
"Civil Peace" from *Girls at War and Other Stories* by Chinua Achebe, copyright © Chinua Achebe, 1972, 1973. Used by permission of Doubleday, a
division of Bantam Doubleday Dell Publishing Group, Inc.

"Africa Emergent" from *Livingstone's Companions* by Nadine Gordimer.
Copyright © Nadine Gordimer, 1971. Reprinted by permission of the pub-
lisher, Viking, a division of Penguin Group (USA) Inc.

(The following pages constitute an extension of this copyright page.)

Contents

Contents

LATIN AMERICAN STORIES

ACKNOWLEDGMENTS

I would like to express my appreciation to the members of Iona College's Department of English Seminar on Non-Western Literature: Helen Bauer, Peter Chetta, George Little, John Mahon, Michael Palma, Thomas Pendleton, and Cedric Winslow. Special thanks are due to Carol Parikh who supplied numerous sources for Indian literature. A great deal of assistance was provided at Ryan Library by Adrienne Franco, Anthony Todman, and Doris Viacava, as well as at the Secretarial Services Center by Mary A. Bruno and her staff: Teresa Alifante, Lisa Allocco, Patti Besen, Nancy Girardi, Theresa Martin, and Maureen McSweeney. I would also like to thank Ruth DiStefano, Susan Pavliscak, and Cathleen Sullivan, Department of English Student Assistants. To Iona College I am indebted for a faculty fellowship during 1988.

Introduction

When people say that the world is shrinking, they mean, of course, that we have a new or different perception of the distance between countries and even between continents. A number of economic and technological changes in recent decades have contributed to our altered perspective. Students who once left home to travel to college campuses several hundred miles away now casually elect to spend a semester or a year studying abroad. Middle-class Americans who once vacationed in Florida now compare the cuisine of Chinese restaurants in Hong Kong with that of Chinese restaurants in Shanghai. Large and small companies now regularly calculate the salability of their products around the globe and try to compete in the international marketplace. Investors—far from being fazed by distant enterprises—build factories, buy real estate, or even open fast-food restaurants in other countries. They find the challenge of new territories and populations to be invigorating as well as lucrative. Environmentalists, too, have made us conscious of a new kind of proximity. If we carelessly dump radioactive waste into the world's oceans, eventually the fish we eat will poison us. If one nation allows its smokestacks to pollute the air, the resulting acid rain may well fall on the innocent neighboring countryside as well as on the offending factories, and if we destroy the earth's ozone layer, the resulting damaging rays of the sun will observe no international boundaries.

Perhaps the most obvious influences on our realization that this is, indeed, a small world are connected to the advanced communication technology which has put us in touch, almost instantaneously, with other people around the world. If we have an important letter to send to Calcutta or Nairobi, we simply fax it and seconds later we receive notification that our message has arrived. Similarly, when we need to get information from places such as the London or Tokyo stock markets, we access a computer terminal and find out the closing price, an hour or two earlier, of a stock or the exchange rate for a nation's currency. If we need to speak to someone a few thousand miles away, we can make a telephone call with little more effort than is required to phone the next-door neighbor. Most important for many Americans have been the TV satellites that make it possible to witness and, in a sense, share in our living-room experiences across the globe. As a result of the vivid images on our TV screens, we have been horrified by the treatment of black people on the streets of Johannesburg. We have identified with the Chinese students who were crushed because they were demonstrating for democracy and had constructed their own version of the Statue of Liberty in Tiananmen Square. We were moved by the emotional reunions between East and West Germans as the Berlin Wall was dismantled. And most dramatically, we followed the events of the war in the Persian Gulf at the moment they occurred, seeing the sky over Baghdad illuminated by falling bombs and antiaircraft guns.

Watching these historic events on television, thoughtful people find themselves more curious than ever about life from someone else's perspective. What does it feel like to grow up in Beijing, Bombay, or Buenos Aires? Increasingly, we have become fascinated by the details of daily existence in other cultures and curious about the lives of those whose circumstances and pressures seem so different from our own. As always, fiction provides a window through which we can view the inner lives of others. It can clarify issues, dramatize themes, and reveal insights about an individual or a group.

In recent years, teachers of literature have increasingly attempted to expand their horizons to accommodate their perception that world literature ought indeed to be world literature and not essentially Western literature as it has generally been presented to students. As a result of this desire to explore several non-Western literary traditions with a view toward personal growth as well as of introducing non-Western authors in appropriate classes, my colleagues at Iona College and I formed a non-Western literature seminar several years ago. We created a reading list and, with the financial help of college administrators, invited several guest speakers. Each faculty member selected, researched, and analyzed several novels, plays, or epic poems, and chaired the discussions of those particular works. Thus, I was introduced to R. K. Narayan and the exotic world of his fictional Indian city Malgudi, and to the mountaintop retreat of Anita Desai's reclusive Nanda Kaul in *Fire on the Mountain*, and to the ways of the Ibo people in Chinua Achebe's *Things Fall Apart*. One result of having had the thoroughly enjoyable and enriching experiences of a year of literary discoveries has been this collection of stories from Africa, China, India, Japan, and Latin America.

Perhaps it might be well here to describe the guidelines I followed in choosing the stories for *Other Voices, Other Vistas*. They were all written by major authors who had published fiction after World War II. The majority of these authors continued to write during the 1980s and into the 1990s. A further consideration was to choose short stories by authors whose work is available in English translations so that when readers found stories they particularly enjoyed, they would be able to locate additional stories or novels by that writer. Finally, I found it necessary to observe strict geographical boundaries because of the wealth of material available for inclusion. For example, since I could reprint only a few selections from the considerable array of stories from China, I decided it would be too limiting to try to provide Chinese stories from Taiwan, or Hong Kong, or Singapore as well. Similarly, the story selection from Latin America does not include works by Caribbean authors.

As I began to make my selections, I found that the stories that attracted me generally succeeded in doing two things. First, they depict situations or scenes in which we glimpse the houses, streets, fields, villages, and cities of distant parts of the world and gain insight into the values, pressures, behavior, and conflicts of people living in cultures far different from our own. We discover what it feels like to travel on the overcrowded trolleys of a

Chinese city or to eat a meal with numerous family members in a small room. We are made to understand the
inexorable financial pressures on families in Africa struggling to find the tuition to send their children to schools
in nations where education, often, is not free; nations
where poor black parents know that having an education
is the only way their children will escape the grinding
poverty which has imprisoned them all of their lives.

The second quality that characterizes many of the stories in *Other Voices, Other Vistas* is that although they
reflect a particular time and a particular place, they also
transcend the individual situation and the specific location, touching upon universal human traits, relationships,
needs, and dreams. Although the characters' lives may
be dramatized against a backdrop of details of daily existence that is totally foreign or exotic to us, we recognize
an essential human condition with which we can identify
and a kinship that causes us to empathize with the sor-
rows of these characters and to celebrate their joys.

As I read fiction from the five areas I had selected, I
discovered a pattern of significant, recurring themes. A
number of the stories included in this collection depict
family relationships, particularly those between parent
and child or between husband and wife. These relationships in non-Western areas of the world tend to be complicated by the presence and importance of the extended
family. For example, in Charles Mungoshi's "Who Will
Stop the Dark?" the young boy, Zakeo, prefers his
grandfather's household to that of his parents where his
crippled father and angry mother insist on his going to
school. The boy is determined to learn the wisdom of his
ancestors and the skills of hunting and fishing from his
grandfather. Zakeo's mother is determined that her son
will be prepared for the future; Zakeo's grandfather is
concerned that his grandson be prepared for manhood
with the heritage of the past.

In Chinese stories in which family relationships are a
central theme, the tensions or conflicts between individuals are exacerbated not only by the emphasis of the culture on familial harmony, but by the physical closeness
forced on family members by a lack of housing. In "The
Destination" by Wang Anyi, twenty-eight-year-old Chen

Xin has been allowed to transfer back home to live with his mother, two brothers, sister-in-law, and young nephew in Shanghai. During the Cultural Revolution he had been forced to move to the countryside because only one son from each family would be given a job in the city. The lack of living space is both oppressive to family members and a divisive force. Chen Xin must live in a hut in the courtyard that his family has constructed. He must bathe either at the public bathhouse or in the bathroom of the factory where he works. Whether or not he marries is clearly contingent upon whether or not he has a room for his wife. A young woman brought to the house as a prospective bride for Chen Xin has little to recommend her except for the fact that her parents have a spare room. Chen Xin, who is not at all attracted to her, asserts: " 'I'm marrying a girl, not a room.' " His relationship with his older, married brother is threatened when this brother applies to the authorities to have the largest room in the house, a twenty-two-meter room, assigned for his use instead of dividing it with Chen Xin. Thus both brothers feel guilty about pursuing comfort and happiness at the expense of one another.

In "Kite Streamers" by Wang Meng, the young lovers Susu and Jiayuan have long-term as well as temporary problems of shelter. Their request for a flat so that they can marry has been rejected by the Housing Administration Department because married couples with children also lack housing. Even their night out together is marked by a desperate search for a place to stay. Because the restaurants and wonton canteens are crowded and it has begun to snow, they take shelter in the only place they can think of, a recently completed high-rise apartment house that is not yet inhabited.

Additionally, Susu feels that patriarchal scrutiny and the emphasis on family background is suffocating as her father questions her about Jiayuan:

"What's his name, his original name, any other names he's ever used? His family background, his own background? What was their economic situation before and after land reform? His personal history since he was three months old? His political record? Are

there any members of his family or immediate relatives who were sentenced to death or imprisonment,
put under surveillance, or were landlords, rich peasants, counter-revolutionaries, bad elements, Rightists?
When were they labelled as Rightists? And when were
the labels removed? How did he act in past political
movements? His and his family members' incomes and
expenditures, bank deposits and balances . . . ?"

Whereas in stories of Chinese family life the sharing
of household space and the resulting lack of autonomy
is often a matter of necessity, in stories of Indian family
life, the sharing of households by extended families and
the resulting lack of privacy or independence is clearly a
matter of preference, especially among wealthy families
in which the parents of married children have strong,
traditional values. In Ruth Prawer Jhabvala's "The Interview," the narrator who is married and has children has
always lived with his relatives: his mother, brother, sister-in-law, wife, and the children of both couples. He is
perfectly contented with this arrangement, and remi-
nisces about the way his mother insisted on serving his
meals even after his marriage. When she became too old
to perform this task, the narrator's sister-in-law took over
the responsibility, and he notes with satisfaction that he
continues to get the special tidbits that make his meals
so pleasant. His wife, who had not gotten along very well
with her mother-in-law, pleads: " 'Take me away, let us
go and live somewhere alone, only you and I and our
children.' " But the narrator knows that he will never
leave behind the comfortable accommodation and prefer-
ential treatment bestowed on him.
    Individuals who live within close proximity to their
families have, of course, to deal with the opinions and
pressures of the various members of the household. The
pervasive influence of the family is clearly shown in the
numerous stories of India in which characters frequently
identify themselves not merely with their family, but with
the religion, economic class, and caste of that family. In
spite of many changes in modern India, the tenacious
hold of the caste system is often apparent, particularly in
rural areas. In Mahasweta Devi's "Dhowli," an untouch-

able Dusad girl, a widow at nineteen, is pregnant with the child of Misrilal, the youngest son of a wealthy Brahman family. The opposition of his family to Misrilal's relationship with Dhowli is clearly overwhelming. The members of the Misra family conspire to separate the two and marry Misrilal to a suitable Brahman girl. Furthermore, they reduce Dhowli, her mother, and, later, even her illegitimate son, to destitution by refusing to employ either woman and causing even sympathetic villagers to fear giving offense to the Misra family should they hire Dhowli or her mother. When the former lovers meet after Misrilal has been married, he tells Dhowli, " 'What I've done I was forced to do. I did not do it of my own wish.' " She replies: " 'So you follow others' wishes in marrying, in starting your shop, and you follow your own wish only when it comes to destroying the poor and helpless.' " Even the girl's mother has little sympathy for her because through Dhowli's passion she has brought them to the brink of starvation.

Clearly, poverty is another overwhelming pressure often brought to bear on family relationships in "Dhowli" as well as in several other stories in this collection. These stories depict the efforts of individuals to support themselves and their families in a world in which it is difficult to find work and in which the laborer is paid subsistence wages. In R. K. Narayan's comic tale "A Horse and Two Goats," for example, an elderly Tamil villager, Muni, and his wife face a bleak and hungry day when the shopowner who often supplies their needs on credit refuses to give them anything further without payment. Once the affluent owner of a flock of about forty sheep and goats, Muni is dismayed by the prospect of eating the boiled and salted leaves from the tree that stands before his house. When he tells his wife that he fancies having the leaves cooked in sauce, but returns from the store emptyhanded, she tells him:

> "You are getting no sauce today, nor anything else. I can't find anything to give you to eat. Fast till the evening, it'll do you good. Take the goats and be gone now," she cried and added, "Don't come back before the sun is down." He knew that if he obeyed her she

would somehow conjure up some food for him in the evening. Only he must be careful not to argue and irritate her. Her temper was undependable in the morning but improved by evening time. She was sure to go out and work—grind corn in the Big House, sweep or scrub somewhere, and earn enough to buy foodstuff and keep a dinner ready for him in the evening.

Poverty, however, is not the only obstacle to satisfying familial relationships. A mother's longing for a normal family experience for her two children is the subject of "The Silent Traders" by Yūko Tsushima. The father of her children, a ten-year-old daughter and five-year-old son, is a married man who has two legitimate children and who has shown no interest in his illegitimate offspring. When the woman persuades him to share a day's outing to a museum with her and their children, she discovers the emptiness of his gesture:

I was becoming desperate for something to say. And weren't there one or two things he'd like to ask me? Such as how the children had been lately. But to bring that up, unasked, might imply that I wanted him to watch me as they grew. I'd only been able to ask for this meeting because I'd finally stopped feeling that way. Now it seemed we couldn't even exchange such polite remarks as "They've grown" or "I'm glad they're well" without arousing needless suspicions.

One interesting question I have posed when reading these non-Western stories is whether or not with a few changes of detail they might well describe an American experience. A few such as Anita Desai's "Pigeons at Daybreak," Carlos Fuentes's "The Cost of Living," Bessie Head's "The Collector of Treasures," Kōbō Abe's "The Magic Chalk," and Jorge Luis Borges's "The Book of Sand" certainly could be transformed.

In "Pigeons at Daybreak," Desai depicts a fairly routine day in the lives of a middle-aged couple, Mr. Basu and his wife, Otima. Although they experience minor problems and Mr. Basu, who suffers from asthma, is impatient with his wife, they are essentially comfortable with one another. If one were to situate them on a Florida patio or New Jersey backyard instead of an Indian balcony, it would be entirely possible to transfer the story to America. Of course, Desai's vivid details of the couple's meals, clothes, and possessions are particularly Indian and delightful to readers.

Salvador Rentería in Carlos Fuentes's "The Cost of Living" is a teacher and member of a union who has taken an additional part-time job as a taxi driver. With a sick wife and imminent teachers' strike, he needs to earn extra money. The violent experience he subsequently has is an everyday occurrence in American cities as well as in numerous places around the world.

Bessie Head's "The Collector of Treasures" would require a considerable number of changes in order to become a description of American events. It furnishes the reader with insights about the relationships between neighbors in a small African village where tribal values have been destroyed by colonialism. However, in its depiction of the reactions of a wife, Dikeledi Mokopi, to the attitudes and behavior of her husband, the tale dramatizes a situation all too familiar to American audiences. Garesego Mokopi had abandoned his wife, leaving her with three sons to raise. Now, he lives with another woman and her children and has no intention of giving Dikeledi any money to enable his oldest son to attend secondary school. The situation that helped to form the character of Garesego may be particularly African. His actions are not.

Perhaps the two most easily transferred stories in this collection are Kōbō Abe's "The Magic Chalk" and Jorge Luis Borges's "The Book of Sand." Abe is considered by readers in Japan as a writer whose work totally lacks distinctive Japanese qualities. The events of this story might easily have occurred any place in the world and during almost any era. Argon is a starving artist who frequently depends on a friend's willingness to give him half a lunch to sustain him. His damp room furnished with a single chair reflects the depth of his poverty. The unusual properties he discovers in a piece of red chalk might well have been explored in a Paris garret or a Greenwich Village walk-up.

Similarly, in "The Book of Sand," the astonishing qualities of the book purchased by the narrator in his Buenos Aires apartment from a traveling salesman are unrelated to the location of the transaction or the nationality of the characters. Curiously, in both stories a work of art empowers its owner to transcend the ordinary boundaries of reality.

On the other hand, a number of stories in this anthology could not be changed to a different setting or cultural milieu. "Africa Emergent" by Nadine Gordimer, "Papito's Story" by Luisa Valenzuela, "Sketches from the 'Cattle Shed' " by Ding Ling, and "Regarding the Problem of Newborn Piglets in Winter" by Chen Rong all have essential elements of plot and circumstance that would prove incomprehensible outside of the contexts in which they were created. They also dramatize a second major theme within this collection, the effects of governmental oppression on individuals.

The first-person narrator of Gordimer's "Africa Emergent" is a white man, a citizen of South Africa who is a successful architect. He has become a friend of two black men as a result of their participation in a traveling theater troupe. Even their most innocent activities are scrutinized or restricted by intrusive policing policies:

> We had to remember to write out "passes" at night so that our actors could get home without being arrested for being out after the curfew for blacks, we had to spend hours at the Bantu Affairs Department trying to arrange local residence permits for actors who were being "endorsed out" of town back to the villages to which, "ethnically," apparently, they belonged although they'd never set eyes on them, and we had to decide which of us could play the sycophant well enough to persuade the Bantu Commissioner to allow the show to go on the road from one Group Area, designated by color, to another, or to talk some town clerk into getting his council to agree to the use of a "white" public hall by a mixed cast. The black actors' lives were in our hands, because they were

black and we were white, and could, must, intercede for them.

Although one of his black friends, a sculptor named Elias Nkomo, has fled to America, the narrator finds that this successful artist's escape is merely illusory.

In Valenzuela's "Papito's Story," the terrifying sounds which the narrator, Julio, hears in the apartment next door are a literary mirror of events in Argentina between 1976–1983, the era known as *El Proceso* (the Process of National Reorganization). During that period of military rule, more than 10,000 Argentine people—including many women and children—disappeared, first imprisoned in police cells or concentration camps, and, later, executed and buried in mass graves. Only after the return of civilian rule in the country, did Argentine citizens begin to discover the extent of the slaughter. This story, like much of Valenzuela's short fiction, captures the violence and terror with which ordinary people must live. The police have come in the middle of the night to arrest Papito, Julio's next-door neighbor. Ruthless and all-powerful, they are filled with fury when Papito refuses to unlock the door, and clearly his life means nothing to them. The narrator comments: "I wouldn't open my door to see the cops' faces, drugged with loathing. The loathing of those who believe they are right is one step beyond reason, and I'd rather not confront it." Certainly the reader understands Julio's identification with Papito. On the nights to follow, who will the police arrest next?

Similarly, a searing glimpse of life in modern China is dramatized in "Sketches from the 'Cattle Shed' " by Ding Ling. She, like numerous others under the Communist Party's rule, was imprisoned. In fact, four of the five Chinese writers whose stories appear in this volume have shared similar experiences. They have been denounced by their government (and often by their frightened friends or colleagues) as traitors to the ideals of the Communist regime then in power, punished through long years of prison or exiled to hard labor in remote provinces, and eventually "rehabilitated" or reinstated when the regime was discredited. The pattern of their treatment is not coincidental, because it would be difficult, if not impossible, to find a group of writers or intellectuals in contemporary China untouched by governmental oppression as the result of recurring "anti-Rightist" or "anti-Party" campaigns that have swept across China since the collapse of Chiang Kai-shek's Kuomintang in 1949.

"Sketches from the 'Cattle Shed' " is narrated by a sixty-five-year-old woman who has been imprisoned for almost ten months. A political prisoner, she is kept in solitary confinement, locked in a small room where she is not allowed to have paper or a pen, books, or newspaper and can speak only to the "warder" assigned to watch her. She has been beaten, denounced, and interrogated over a period of time. Even before this imprisonment, she and her husband had been subjected to brutal treatment at the poultry-raising commune where they had been exiled to do manual labor. She recalls that their room "had been raided dozens of times," that they had suffered being humiliated and beaten and "had spent so many days and nights in terror." Although in America an innocent individual occasionally is mistakenly convicted of a crime and imprisoned unjustly, it would be very difficult to transfer Ding Ling's story to an American setting. Her characters suffer imprisonment for their idealism and because of extremist political factions seizing power over an entire nation.

A far less grim commentary on the workings of the Chinese government is Chen Rong's gentle satire of Communist bureaucracy in "Regarding the Problem of Newborn Piglets in Winter." The onset of cold weather sets in motion the party's elaborate and obviously unnecessary apparatus for accomplishing a simple task, the protection of piglets. Secretary Zhang Dingfan places a telephone call to Chief Jiao of Agriculture and Forestry. He gives the Chief an order:

> "First, notify every district in the county by telephone. Proceed level by level this very night. Don't let any piglet die from the cold. Then you may follow up by memorandum. Work on the draft right away."

At the end of this long line of messages and directives are the simple, illiterate family members who have carefully and successfully reared pigs for their entire lives. So much for party regulations!

Two additional stories, "Act of Worship" by Yukio Mishima and "The Wog" by Khushwant Singh, could not easily be relocated because the relationships between the male and female characters in each are understandable only in the context of the specific culture in which they are set. Both stories are based on a thorough-going acceptance of a class-conscious hierarchy and female inferiority. In "Act of Worship," Tsuneko is a forty-five-year-old widow and Professor Fujimiya is a poet and scholar who has employed her as his housekeeper for a period of ten years. The Professor, a fastidious sixty-year-old bachelor, holds a Chair of Japanese literature at Seimei University. Revered by some of his students who have become his disciples, Fujimiya is a domestic as well as an academic tyrant. Tsuneko has learned to perform her tasks unobtrusively and with the exactness the Professor requires.

A woman of some education who writes poetry, Tsuneko strives for an unattractive, older appearance so that her presence as a servant in the Professor's house will not lead to rumors about him. In her eyes, this self-centered and somewhat ridiculous pedant "occupied a middle ground between heaven and earth. Sometimes, even, she saw herself as a shrine maiden in a sort of secret religious community centering around his person." Both the nature of the relationship between the housekeeper and the Professor and the central action of the story, a pilgrimage to worship at three distant shrines, reflect very traditional Japanese attitudes toward social status and women.

Like Professor Fujimiya, Srijut Santosh Sen in Khushwant Singh's "The Wog" considers himself a preeminent gentleman who must protect his dignity. A "first class gazetted" government administrator in Delhi, he has taken a traditional Hindu bride to please his mother. Although Mr. Sen comes from a Hindu family, he scorns and rejects Indian culture, preferring instead the British tastes and standards he acquired at an Anglo-Indian school and, later, at Oxford University.

His wife, Kalyani, who was chosen by his relatives and

had never spoken to him before their marriage, is totally repugnant to Sen because of her Hindu customs. He is ashamed of the way she speaks English, her eating habits, and her appearance. Mrs. Sen is the victim of both her husband's snobbery and her culture's attitudes toward a failed wife. On the other hand, Mr. Sen might be viewed as a victim of a colonial system that fostered contempt for his own culture.

Of course all of the stories in this collection do a great deal more than transport us for a short time to the homes and streets of unfamiliar lands. They satisfy our appetite for narratives, for those artistic creations that convey something of the vast array of human experience wherever it occurs. They are food for our imagination, sustenance for our intellects, and they stimulate our senses. We taste for a little while the steaming dishes set on a table in Shanghai, hear the traffic of Bombay, and are touched by the toils and problems, the happiness and misery of others, who become less and less of the other and more and more of the self.

—BARBARA H. SOLOMON
Iona College
New Rochelle, New York

AFRICAN
STORIES

Chinua Achebe
(b. 1930)

Born in Ogidi, Nigeria, into a devout Christian family in
which Igbo was spoken, Albert Chinua (Iumogu) Achebe
learned English at the age of eight. He attended Government College, Umuahia, and University College of Iba-
dan where he was among the first graduates to earn a
B.A. From 1954 to 1966, he worked for the Nigerian
Broadcasting Corporation where he founded and directed the Voice of Nigeria, becoming director of external broadcasting. A senior Research Fellow at the
Institute of African Studies at Nsukka and, later, professor of literature at the University of Nigeria, Nsukka, he
has taught at the University of Massachusetts—Amherst,
University of Connecticut, and UCLA, as well as at Nigerian universities. For a two-year period, 1967–1969,
during the Nigerian Civil War, he served on diplomatic
missions for Biafra. From 1962–1972 he served as editor
of the African Writers Series, which he founded with
William Heinemann publishers. A short-story writer,
novelist, poet, essayist, author of children's books, as
well as editor, Achebe draws upon the proverbs, folklore, and customs of his native Ibo tribe in his fiction.
His first novel, *Things Fall Apart* (Heinemann, 1958;
repr. Fawcett, 1988), is set in the Ibo village of Umuo-
fia in the late nineteenth century as English administrators and missionaries arrive. A chronicle of the daily
life of the villagers and their traditional leader, Okon-
kwo, as the conflicts emerge between European influences and African culture, it has been translated into
more than forty-five languages. In his essay "The Novelist as Teacher," Achebe has described his literary
mission as follows:

to help my society regain belief in itself and to put away the complexes of the years of denigration and self-abasement. And it is essentially a question of education, in the best sense of that word. Here, I think, my aims and the deepest aspirations of society meet.

Founder and president from 1981–1986 of the Association of Nigerian Authors, Achebe has received the Margaret Wrong Memorial Prize, a Rockefeller Fellowship, the Nigerian National Trophy, the Jock Campbell/*New Statesman* Award, a Neil Gunn International Fellowship, a UNESCO Fellowship, and numerous honorary doctorates. His novels include *No Longer at Ease* (Heinemann, 1960; repr. Fawcett, 1988), *Arrow of Gold* (Heinemann, 1964; repr. John Day, 1967), *A Man of the People* (John Day, 1966; repr. Doubleday, 1967), *Anthills of the Savannah* (Anchor Books, 1988), *The Voter* (Viva Books, 1994), and *Home and Exile* (Oxford University Press, 2000). Some of his poetry is collected in *Beware, Soul-Brother, and Other Poems* (Doubleday, 1972; revised edition, Heinemann, 1972), and *Christmas in Biafra and Other Poems* (Doubleday, 1973). His stories are collected in *The Sacrificial Egg and Other Stories* (Onitsha, Nigeria, 1962) and *Girls at War* (Heinemann, 1973; repr. Fawcett, 1988).

CIVIL PEACE

Jonathan Iwegbu counted himself extraordinarily lucky. "Happy survival!" meant so much more to him than just a current fashion of greeting old friends in the first hazy days of peace. It went deep to his heart. He had come out of the war with five inestimable blessings—his head, his wife Maria's head and the heads of three out of their four children. As a bonus he also had his old bicycle—a miracle too but naturally not to be compared to the safety of five human heads.

The bicycle had a little history of its own. One day at the height of the war it was commandeered "for urgent military action." Hard as its loss would have been to him he would still have let it go without a thought had he not had some doubts about the genuineness of the officer. It wasn't his disreputable rags, nor the toes peeping out of one blue and one brown canvas shoes, nor yet the two stars of his rank done obviously in a hurry in biro, that troubled Jonathan; many good and heroic soldiers looked the same or worse. It was rather a certain lack of grip and firmness in his manner. So Jonathan, suspecting he might be amenable to influence, rummaged in his raffia bag and produced the two pounds with which he had been going to buy firewood which his wife, Maria, retailed to camp officials for extra stock-fish and corn meal, and got his bicycle back. That night he buried it in the little clearing in the bush where the dead of the camp, including his own youngest son, were buried. When he dug it up again a year later after the surrender all it needed was a little palm-oil greasing. "Nothing puzzles God," he said in wonder.

He put it to immediate use as a taxi and accumulated a small pile of Biafran money ferrying camp officials and their families across the four-mile stretch to the nearest tarred road. His standard charge per trip was six pounds and those who had the money were only glad to be rid of some of it in this way. At the end of a fortnight he had made a small fortune of one hundred and fifteen pounds.

Then he made the journey to Enugu and found another miracle waiting for him. It was unbelievable. He rubbed his eyes and looked again and it was still standing there before him. But, needless to say, even that monumental blessing must be accounted also totally inferior to the five heads in the family. This newest miracle was his little house in Ogui Overside. Indeed nothing puzzles God! Only two houses away a huge concrete edifice some wealthy contractor had put up just before the war was a mountain of rubble. And here was Jonathan's little zinc house of no regrets built with mud blocks quite intact! Of course the doors and windows were missing and five sheets off the roof. But what was that? And anyhow he

had returned to Enugu early enough to pick up bits of
old zinc and wood and soggy sheets of cardboard lying
around the neighborhood before thousands more came
out of their forest holes looking for the same things. He
got a destitute carpenter with one old hammer, a blunt
plane and a few bent and rusty nails in his tool bag to
turn this assortment of wood, paper and metal into
door and window shutters for five Nigerian shillings or
fifty Biafran pounds. He paid the pounds, and moved
in with his overjoyed family carrying five heads on their
shoulders.

His children picked mangoes near the military cemetery and sold them to soldiers' wives for a few pennies—
real pennies this time—and his wife started making
breakfast akara balls for neighbors in a hurry to start life
again. With his family earnings he took his bicycle to
the villages around and bought fresh palm-wine which he
mixed generously in his rooms with the water which had
recently started running again in the public tap down the
road, and opened up a bar for soldiers and other lucky
people with good money.

At first he went daily, then every other day and finally
once a week, to the offices of the Coal Corporation
where he used to be a miner, to find out what was what.
The only thing he did find out in the end was that that
little house of his was even a greater blessing than he
had thought. Some of his fellow ex-miners who had nowhere to return at the end of the day's waiting just slept
outside the doors of the offices and cooked what meal
they could scrounge together in Bournvita tins. As the
weeks lengthened and still nobody could say what was
what Jonathan discontinued his weekly visits altogether
and faced his palm-wine bar.

But nothing puzzles God. Came the day of the windfall
when after five days of endless scuffles in queues and
counter-queues in the sun outside the Treasury he had
twenty pounds counted into his palms as ex-gratia award
for the rebel money he had turned in. It was like Christmas for him and for many others like him when the pay-
ments began. They called it (since few could manage its
proper official name) *egg-rasher*.

As soon as the pound notes were placed in his palm

Jonathan simply closed it tight over them and buried fist and money inside his trouser pocket. He had to be extra careful because he had seen a man a couple of days earlier collapse into near-madness in an instant before that oceanic crowd because no sooner had he got his twenty pounds than some heartless ruffian picked it off him. Though it was not right that a man in such an extremity of agony should be blamed yet many in the queues that day were able to remark quietly on the victim's carelessness, especially after he pulled out the innards of his pocket and revealed a hole in it big enough to pass a thief's head. But of course he had insisted that the money had been in the other pocket, pulling it out too to show its comparative wholeness. So one had to be careful.

Jonathan soon transferred the money to his left hand and pocket so as to leave his right free for shaking hands should the need arise, though by fixing his gaze at such an elevation as to miss all approaching human faces he made sure that the need did not arise, until he got home.

He was normally a heavy sleeper but that night he heard all the neighborhood noises die down one after another. Even the night watchman who knocked the hour on some metal somewhere in the distance had fallen silent after knocking one o'clock. That must have been the last thought in Jonathan's mind before he was finally carried away himself. He couldn't have been gone for long, though, when he was violently awakened again.

"Who is knocking?" whispered his wife lying beside him on the floor.

"I don't know," he whispered back breathlessly.

The second time the knocking came it was so loud and imperious that the rickety old door could have fallen down.

"Who is knocking?" he asked then, his voice parched and trembling.

"Na tief-man and him people," came the cool reply. "Make you hopen de door." This was followed by the heaviest knocking of all.

Maria was the first to raise the alarm, then he followed and all their children.

"Police-o! Thieves-o! Neighbors-o! Police-o! We are

*lost! We are dead! Neighbors, are you asleep? Wake up!
Police-o!"*

This went on for a long time and then stopped suddenly. Perhaps they had scared the thief away. There
was total silence. But only for a short while.

"You done finish?" asked the voice outside. "Make
we help you small. Oya, everybody!"

*"Police-o! Tief-man-o! Neighbors-o! we done loss-o!
Police-o! . . ."*

There were at least five other voices besides the
leader's.

Jonathan and his family were now completely paralyzed by terror. Maria and the children sobbed inaudibly
like lost souls. Jonathan groaned continuously.

The silence that followed the thieves' alarm vibrated
horribly. Jonathan all but begged their leader to speak
again and be done with it.

"My frien," said he at long last, "we don try our best
for call dem but I tink say dem all done sleep-o . . . So
wetin we go do now? Sometaim you wan call soja? Or
you wan make we call dem for you? Soja better pass
police. No be so?"

"Na so!" replied his men. Jonathan thought he heard
even more voices now than before and groaned heavily.
His legs were sagging under him and his throat felt like
sandpaper.

"My frien, why you no de talk again. I de ask you say
you wan make we call soja?"

"No."

"Awrighto. Now make we talk business. We no be bad
tief. We no like for make trouble. Trouble done finish.
War done finish and all the katakata wey de for inside.
No Civil War again. This time na Civil Peace. No be
so?"

"Na so!" answered the horrible chorus.

"What do you want from me? I am a poor man. Everything I had went with this war. Why do you come to me?
You know people who have money. We . . ."

"Awright! We know say you no get plenty money. But
we sef no get even anini. So derefore make you open dis
window and give us one hundred pound and we go com-

mot. Orderwise we de come for inside now to show you
guitar-boy like dis . . ."

A volley of automatic fire rang through the sky. Maria
and the children began to weep aloud again.

"Ah, missisi de cry again. No need for dat. We done
talk say we na good tief. We just take our small money
and go nwayorly. No molest. Abi we de molest?"

"At all!" sang the chorus.

"My friends," began Jonathan hoarsely. "I hear
what you say and I thank you. If I had one hundred
pounds . . ."

"Lookia my frien, no be play we come play for your
house. If we make mistake and step for inside you no go
like am-o. So derefore . . ."

"To God who made me; if you come inside and find
one hundred pounds, take it and shoot me and shoot my
wife and children. I swear to God. The only money I
have in this life is this twenty pounds *egg-rasher* they
gave me today . . ."

"OK. Time de go. Make you open dis window and
bring the twenty pound. We go manage am like dat."

There were now loud murmurs of dissent among the
chorus: "Na lie de man de lie; e get plenty money . . .
Make we go inside and search properly well . . . Wetin
be twenty pound? . . ."

"Shurrup!" rang the leader's voice like a lone shot in
the sky and silenced the murmuring at once. "Are you
dere? Bring the money quick!"

"I am coming," said Jonathan fumbling in the darkness
with the key of the small wooden box he kept by his side
on the mat.

At the first sign of light as neighbors and others assem-
bled to commiserate with him he was already strapping
his five-gallon demijohn to his bicycle carrier and his
wife, sweating in the open fire, was turning over akara
balls in a wide clay bowl of boiling oil. In the corner his
eldest son was rinsing out dregs of yesterday's palm-wine
from old beer bottles.

"I count it as nothing," he told his sympathizers, his
eyes on the rope he was tying. "What is *egg-rasher*? Did

I depend on it last week? Or is it greater than other things that went with the war? I say, let *egg-rasher* perish in the flames! Let it go where everything else has gone. Nothing puzzles God."

Nadine Gordimer
(b. 1923)

Born in Springs, a small town, near Johannesburg, South Africa, Nadine Gordimer is the daughter of a British mother and Jewish emigrée father. Attending private schools and the University of the Witwatersand, she experienced a typical white, middle-class, colonial childhood in a nation divided by apartheid. A prolific writer who published her first story when she was fifteen, Gordimer was described by Maxwell Geismar in the *Saturday Review* as "the literary voice and conscience of her society." The tensions, politics and betrayals of contemporary South African life recur among the subjects of her fiction. For a time some of her books were banned in South Africa, but when the novel *Burger's Daughter* became her third banned book, Gordimer discovered she could request copies of the anonymous opinions of the censors, which she published, along with letters of protest from distinguished authors around the world, in a pamphlet titled *What Happened to Burger's Daughter*; or, *How South African Censorship Works*. The publication of the pamphlet, which was widely distributed in bookstores, led South Africa's Publications Control Board to review its decision and release the book. In recent years, Gordimer has been active in opposing government restrictions on newspaper, radio, and television news coverage, helping to organize the Anti-Censorship Action Group in South Africa. She is a member of the African National Congress and one of the founders of the Congress of South African Writers, an organization that helps black writers to publish their work. In America, she has taught creative writing at Columbia, Princeton, Harvard, Tulane, and Northwestern Universities, and received honorary degrees from City College (CUNY),

Mount Holyoke College, Smith College, Yale, Harvard, and the New School for Social Research. Among her novels are *The Lying Days* (Simon & Schuster, 1953; repr. Virago, 1983), *Occasion for Loving* (Viking, 1963; repr. Virago, 1983), *The Late Bourgeois World* (Viking, 1966; repr. Penguin, 1982), *A Guest of Honor* (Viking, 1970; repr. Penguin, 1988), *The Conservationist* (J. Cape, 1974; repr. Viking, 1975), *Burger's Daughter* (Viking, 1979), *July's People* (Viking, 1981), *A Sport of Nature* (Knopf, 1987), *My Son's Story* (Farrar, Straus & Giroux, 1990), *None to Accompany Me* (Farrar, Straus & Giroux, 1994), *Harold, Claudia, and Their Son Duncan* (Bloomsbury, 1996), and *The House Gun* (Farrar, Straus & Giroux, 1998). She has published numerous collections of stories, including *The Soft Voice of the Serpent and Other Stories* (Simon & Schuster, 1952), *Friday's Footprint and Other Stories* (Viking, 1960), *Not for Publication and Other Stories* (Viking, 1965), *Livingstone's Companions* (Viking, 1971), *Selected Stories* (J. Cape, 1975; repr. Viking, 1976), *A Soldier's Embrace* (Viking, 1980), *Something Out There* (Viking, 1984), and *Crimes of Conscience* (Heinemann, 1991). Stories from *Six Feet of the Country* (Simon & Schuster, 1956; Penguin, 1982) were dramatized for a television series with that title. In 1991, she received the Nobel Prize for literature.

AFRICA EMERGENT

He's in prison now, so I'm not going to mention his name. It mightn't be a good thing, you understand. — Perhaps you think you understand too well; but don't be quick to jump to conclusions from five or six thousand miles away: if you lived here, you'd understand something else—friends know that shows of loyalty are all right for children holding hands in the school playground; for us they're luxuries, not important and maybe dangerous. If I said, I was a friend of so-and-so, black man awaiting trial for treason, what good would it do him?

And, who knows, it might draw just that decisive bit more attention to me. *He*'d be the first to agree.

Not that one feels that if they haven't got enough in my dossier already, this would make any difference; and not that he really was such a friend. But that's something else you won't understand: everything is ambiguous, here. We hardly know, by now, what we can do and what we can't do; it's difficult to say, goaded in on oneself by laws and doubts and rebellion and caution and—not least—self-disgust, what is or is not a friendship. I'm talking about black-and-white, of course. If you stay with it, boy, on the white side in the country clubs and garden suburbs if you're white, and on the black side in the locations and beerhalls if you're black, none of this applies, and you can go all the way to your segregated cemetery in peace. But neither he nor I did.

I began mixing with blacks out of what is known as an outraged sense of justice, plus strong curiosity, when I was a student. There were two ways—one was through the white students' voluntary service organization, a kibbutz-type junket where white boys and girls went into rural areas and camped while they built school classrooms for African children. A few colored and African students from their segregated universities used to come along, too, and there was the novelty, not without value, of dossing down alongside them at night, although we knew we were likely to be harboring Special Branch spies among our willing workers, and we dared not make a pass at the colored or black girls. The other way—less hard on the hands—was to go drinking with the jazz musicians and journalists, painters and would-be poets and actors who gravitated toward whites partly because such people naturally feel they can make free of the world, and partly because they found an encouragement and appreciation there that was sweet to them. I tried the VSO briefly, but the other way suited me better; anyway, I didn't see why I should help this Government by doing the work it ought to be doing for the welfare of black children.

I'm an architect and the way I was usefully drawn into the black scene was literally that: I designed sets for a mixed color drama group got together by a white director. Perhaps there's no urban human group as intimate, in the end, as a company of this kind, and the color problem made us even closer. I don't mean what *you* mean, the how-do-I-feel-about-that-black-skin stuff; I mean the daily exasperation of getting round, or over, or on top of the color bar laws that plagued our productions and our lives. We had to remember to write out "passess" at night, so that our actors could get home without being arrested for being out after the curfew for blacks, we had to spend hours at the Bantu Affairs Department trying to arrange local residence permits for actors who were being "endorsed out" of town back to the villages to which, "ethnically," apparently, they belonged although they'd never set eyes on them, and we had to decide which of us could play the sycophant well enough to persuade the Bantu Commissioner to allow the show to go on the road from one Group Area, designated by color, to another, or to talk some town clerk into getting his council to agree to the use of a "white" public hall by a mixed cast. The black actors' lives were in our hands, because they were black and we were white, and could, must, intercede for them. Don't think this made everything love and light between us; in fact it caused endless huffs and rows. A white woman who'd worked like a slave acting as PRO-cum-wardrobe-mistress hasn't spoken to me for years because I made her lend her little car to one of the chaps who'd worked until after the last train went back to the location, and then he kept it the whole weekend and she couldn't get hold of him because, of course, location houses rarely have telephones and once a black man has disappeared among those warrens you won't find him till he chooses to surface in the white town again. And when this one did surface, he was biting, to me, about white bitches' "patronage" of people they secretly still thought of as "boys." Yet our arguments, resentments and misunderstandings were not only as much part of the intimacy of this group as the good times, the parties and the love-making we had, but were more—the defining part, because we'd got close enough to admit argument, resentment and misunderstanding between us.

He was one of this little crowd, for a time. He was a dispatch clerk and then a "manager" and chucker-out at a black dance club. In his spare time he took a small part in our productions now and then, and what he really was good at was front-of-house arrangements. His tubby charm (he was a large young man and a cheerful dresser) was just the right thing to deal with the unexpected moods of our location audiences when we went on tour—sometimes they came stiffly encased in their church-going best and seemed to feel it was vulgar to laugh or respond to what was going on, on stage; in other places they rushed the doors, tried to get in without paying, and were dominated by a *tsotsi*, street urchin, element who didn't want to hear anything but themselves. He was the particular friend—the other, passive half—of a particular friend of mine, Elias Nkomo.

And here I stop short. How shall I talk about Elias? I've never even learned, in five years, how to think about him.

Elias was a sculptor. He had one of those jobs—messenger "boy" or some such—that literate young black men can aspire to in a small gold-mining and industrial town outside Johannesburg. Somebody said he was talented, somebody sent him to me—at the beginning, the way for every black man to find himself seems inescapably to lead through a white man. Again, how can I say what his work was like? He came by train to the black people's section of Johannesburg central station, carrying a bulky object wrapped in that morning's newspaper. He was slight, round-headed, tiny-eared, dunly dressed, and with a frown of effort between his eyes, but his face unfolded to a wide, apologetic yet confident smile when he realized that the white man in a waiting car must be me—the meeting had been arranged. I took him back to my "place" (he always called people's homes that) and he unwrapped the newspaper. What was there was nothing like the clumps of diorite or sandstone you have seen in galleries in New York, London, or Johannesburg marked "Africa Emergent," "Spirit of the Ancestors." What was there was a goat, or a goat-like creature, in the way that a centaur is a horse-like, man-like creature, carved out of streaky knotted wood. It was delightful (I wanted to put out my hand to touch it), it was moving in its somehow concretized diachrony, beast-man, coarse wood-fine workmanship, and there was also something exposed about it (one would withdraw the hand, after all). I asked him whether he knew Picasso's goats? He had heard of Picasso but never seen any of his work. I showed him a photograph of the famous bronze goat in Picasso's own house; thereafter all his beasts had sex organs as joyful as Picasso's goat's udder, but that was the only "influence" that ever took, with him. As I say, a white man always intercedes in some way, with a man like Elias; mine was to keep him from those art-loving ladies with galleries who wanted to promote him, and those white painters and sculptors who were willing to have him work under their tutelage. I gave him an old garage (well, that means I took my car out of it) and left him alone, with plenty of chunks of wood.

But Elias didn't like the loneliness of work. That garage never became his "place." Perhaps when you've lived in an overcrowded yard all your life the counterstimulus of distraction becomes necessary to create a tension of concentration. No—well all I really mean is that he liked company. At first he came only at weekends, and then, as he began to sell some of his work, he gave up the messenger job and moved in more or less permanently—we fixed up the "place" together, putting in a ceiling and connecting water and so on. It was illegal for him to live there in a white suburb, of course, but such laws breed complementary evasions in people like Elias and me and the white building inspector didn't turn a hair of suspicion when I said that I was converting the garage as a flat for my wife's mother. It was better for Elias once he'd moved in; there was always some friend of his sharing his bed, not to mention the girls who did; sometimes the girls were shy little things almost of the kitchenmaid variety, who called my wife "madan" when they happened to bump into her, crossing the garden, sometimes they were the bewigged and painted actresses from the group who sat smoking and gossiping with my wife while she fed the baby.

And *he* was there more often than anyone—the plump and cheerful front-of-house manager; he was married, but as happens with our sex, an old friendship was a more important factor in his life than a wife and kids—

if that's a characteristic of black men, then I must be black under the skin, myself. Elias had become very involved in the theater group, anyway, like *him*; Elias made some beautiful *papier mâché* gods for a play by a Nigerian that we did—"spirits of the ancestors" at once amusing and frightening—and once when we needed a singer he surprisingly turned out to have a voice that could phrase a madrigal as easily as whatever the forerunner of Soul was called—I forget now, but it blared hour after hour from the garage when he was working. Elias seemed to like best to work when the other one was around; *he* would sit with his fat boy's legs rolled out before him, flexing his toes in his fashionable shoes, dusting down the lapels of the latest thing in jackets, as he changed the records and kept up a monologue contentedly punctuated by those soft growls and sighs of agreement, those sudden squeezes of almost silent laughter—responses possible only in an African language— that came from Elias as he chiselled and chipped. For they spoke in their own tongue, and I have never known what it was they talked about.

In spite of my efforts to let him alone, inevitably Elias was "taken up" (hadn't I started the process myself, with that garage?) and a gallery announced itself his agent. He walked about at the opening of his one-man show in a purple turtle-necked sweater I think his best friend must have made him buy, laughing a little, softly, at himself, more embarrassed than pleased. An art critic wrote about his transcendental values and plastic modality, and he said, "Christ, man, does he dig it or doesn't he?" while we toasted his success in brandy chased with beer— brandy isn't a rich man's sip in South Africa, it's made here and it's what people use to get drunk on. He earned quite a bit of money that year. Then the gallery owner and the art critic forgot him in the discovery of yet another interpreter of the African soul, and he was poor again, but he had acquired a patroness who, although she lived far away, did not forget him. She was, as you might have thought, an American lady, very old and wealthy according to South African legend but probably simply a middle-aged widow with comfortable stock holdings and a desire to get in on the cultural ground floor of some form of art collecting not yet overcrowded. She had bought some of his work while a tourist in Johannesburg. Perhaps she did have academic connections with the art world; in any case, it was she who got a foundation to offer Elias Nkomo a scholarship to study in America.

I could understand that he wanted to go simply in order to go: to see the world outside. But I couldn't believe that at this stage he wanted or could make use of formal art school disciplines. As I said to him at the time, I'm only an architect, but I've had experience of the academic and even, God help us, the frenziedly non-academic approach in the best schools, and it's not for people who have, to fall back on the jargon, found themselves.

I remember he said, smiling, "You think I've found myself?"

And I said, "But you've never been lost, man. That very first goat wrapped in newspaper was your goat."

But later, when he was refused a passport and the issue of his going abroad was much on our minds, we talked again. He wanted to go because he felt he needed some kind of general education, general cultural background that he'd missed, in his six years at the location school. "Since I've been at your place, I've been reading a lot of your books. And man, I know nothing. I'm as ignorant as that kid of yours there in the pram. Right, I've picked up a bit of politics, a few art terms here and there—I can wag my head and say 'plastic values' all right, eh? But man, what do I know about life? What do I know about how it all works? How do I know *how* I do the work I do? Why we live and die? —If I carry on here I might as well be carving walking sticks," he added. I knew what he meant: there are old men, all over Africa, who make a living squatting at a decent distance from tourist hotels, carving fancy walking sticks from local wood; only one step in sophistication below the "Africa Emergent" school of sculptors so rapturously acclaimed by gallery owners. We both laughed at this, and following the line of thought suggested to me his question to himself: "How do I know how I do the work I do?"—although in me it was a different line of thought from his—

I asked him whether in fact there was any sort of traditional skill in his family? As I imagined, there was not—he was an urban slum kid, brought up opposite a municipal beerhall among paraffin-tin utensils and abandoned motor-car bodies which, perhaps curiously, had failed to bring out a Duchamp in him but from which, on the contrary, hé had sprung, full-blown, as a classical expressionist. Although there were no rural walking-stick carvers in his ancestry, he did tell me something I had no idea would have been part of the experience of a location childhood—he had been sent, in his teens, to a tribal initiation school in the bush, and been circumcised according to rite. He described the experience vividly.

Once all attempts to get him a passport had failed, Elias's desire to go to America became something else, of course: an obsessive resentment against confinement itself. Inevitably, he was given no reason for the refusal. The official answer was the usual one—that it was "not in the public interest" to reveal the reason for such things. Was it because "they" had got to know he was "living like a white man"? (Theory put to me by one of the black actors in the group.) Was it because a critic had dutifully described his work as expressive of the "agony of the emergent African soul"? Nobody knew. Nobody ever knows. It is enough to be black; blacks are meant to stay put, in their own ethnically apportioned streets in their own segregated areas, in those parts of South Africa where the government says they belong. Yet—the whole way of our lives are maneuvered, as I say, is an unanswered question—Elias's best friend suddenly got a passport. I hadn't even realized that *he* had been offered a scholarship or a study grant or something, too; *he* was invited to go to New York to study production and the latest acting techniques (it was the time of the Method rather than Grotowski). And *he* got a passport, "first try" as Elias said with ungrudging pleasure and admiration; when someone black got a passport, then, there was a collective sense of pleasure in having outwitted we didn't quite know what. So they went together, *he* on his passport, and Elias Nkomo on an exit permit.

* * *

An exit permit is a one-way ticket, anyway. When you are granted one at your request but at the government's pleasure, you sign an undertaking that you will never return to South Africa or its mandatory territory, South West Africa. You pledge this with signature and thumbprint. Elias Nkomo never came back. At first he wrote (and he wrote quite often) enthusiastically about the world outside that he had gained, and he seemed to be enjoying some kind of small vogue, not so much as a sculptor as a genuine, real live African Negro who was sophisticated enough to be asked to comment on this and that: the beauty of American women, life in Harlem or Watts, Black Power as seen through the eyes, etc. He sent cuttings from *Ebony* and even from *The New York Times Magazine*. He said that a girl at *Life* was trying to get them to run a piece on his work; his work?—well, he hadn't settled down to anything new, yet, but the art center was a really swinging place, Christ, the things people were doing, there! There were silences, naturally; we forgot about him and he forgot about us for weeks on end. Then the local papers picked up the sort of news they are alert to from all over the world. Elias Nkomo had spoken at an anti-apartheid rally. Elias Nkomo, in West African robes, was on the platform with Stokely Carmichael. "Well, why not? He hasn't got to worry about keeping his hands clean for the time when he comes back home, has he?" —My wife was bitter in his defense. Yes, but I was wondering about his work—"Will they leave him alone to work?" I didn't write to him, but it was as if my silence were read by him: a few months later I received a cutting from some university art magazine devoting a number to Africa, and there was a photograph of one of Elias's wood sculptures, with his handwriting along the margin of the page—*I know you don't think much of people who don't turn out new stuff but some people here seem to think this old thing of mine is good*. It was the sort of wry remark that, spoken aloud to me in the room, would have made us both laugh. I smiled, and meant to write. But within two weeks Elias was dead. He drowned himself early one morning in the river of the New England town where the art school was. It was like the refusal of the passport; none of us knew why. In the usual arrogance one has in the face of such happenings, I even felt guilty about the letter. Perhaps, if one were thousands of miles from one's own "place," in some sort of a bad way, just a small thing like a letter, a word of encouragement from someone who had hurt by being rather niggardly with encouragement in the past . . . ? And what pathetic arrogance, at that! As if the wisp of a letter, written by someone between other preoccupations, and in substance an encouraging lie (how splendid that your old work is receiving recognition in some piddling little magazine) could be anything round which the hand of a man going down for the second time might close. Because before Elias went under in that river he must have been deep in forlorn horrors about which I knew nothing, nothing. When people commit suicide they do so apparently out of some sudden self-knowledge that those of us, the living, do not have the will to acquire. That's what's meant by despair, isn't it— what they have come to know? And that's what one means when one says in extenuation of oneself, *I knew so little about him, really.* I knew Elias only in the self that he had presented at my "place"; why, how out of place it had been, once, when he happened to mention that as a boy he had spent weeks in the bush with his circumcision group! Of course we—his friends—decided out of the facts we knew and our political and personal attitudes, why he had died: and perhaps it is true that he was sick to death, in the real sense of the phrase that has been forgotten, sick unto death with homesickness for the native land that had shut him out forever and that he was forced to conjure up for himself in the parody of "native" dress that had nothing to do with his part of the continent, and the shame that a new kind of black platform-solidarity forced him to feel for his old dependence, in South Africa, on the friendship of white people. It was the South African government who killed him, it was culture shock—but perhaps neither our political bitterness nor our glibness with fashionable phrases can come near what combination of forces, within and without, led him to the fatal baptism of that early morning. *It is not in the private interest that this should be revealed.* Elias never came home. That's all.

* * *

But his best friend did, towards the end of that year. *He* came to see me after he had been in the country some weeks—I'd heard he was back. The theater group had broken up; it seemed to be that, chiefly, he'd come to talk to me about: he wanted to know if there was any money left in the kitty for him to start up a small theatrical venture of his own, he was eager to use the know-how (his phrase) he'd learned in the States. He was really plump now and he wore the most extraordinary clothes. A Liberace jacket. Plastic boots. An Afro wig that looked as if it had been made out of a bit of karakul from South West Africa. I teased him about it—we were at least good enough friends for that—asking him if he'd really been with the guerrillas instead of Off-Broadway? (There was a trial on at home, at the time, of South African political refugees who had tried to "infiltrate" through South West Africa.) And felt slightly ashamed of my patronage of his taste when he said with such good humor, "It's just a fun thing, man, isn't it great?" I was too cowardly to bring the talk round to the point: Elias. And when it couldn't be avoided I said the usual platitudes and he shook his head at them—"Hell, man," and we fell silent. Then he told me that that was how he had got back—because Elias was dead, on the unused portion of Elias's air ticket. *His* study grant hadn't included travel expenses and he'd had to pay his own way over. So he'd had only a one-way ticket, but Elias's scholarship had included a return fare to the student's place of origin. It had been difficult to get the airline to agree to the transfer; he'd had to go to the scholarship foundation people, but they'd been very decent about fixing it for him.

He had told me all this so guilelessly that I was one of the people who became angrily indignant when the rumor began to go around that, he was a police agent: who else would have the cold nerve to come back on a dead man's ticket, a dead man who couldn't ever have used that portion of the ticket himself, because he had taken an exit permit? And who could believe the story, anyway? Obviously, *he* had to find some way of explaining why he, a black man like any other, could travel freely back and forth between South Africa and other countries. He had a passport, hadn't he? Well, there you were. Why should *he* get a passport? What black man these days had a passport?

Yes, I was angry, and defended him, by proof of the innocence of the very naïveté with which—a black man, yes, and therefore used to the necessity of salvaging from disaster all his life, unable to afford the nice squeamishness of white men's delicacy—he took over Elias's air ticket because he was alive and needed it, as he might have taken up Elias's coat against the cold. I refused to avoid him, the way some members of the remnant of our group made it clear they did now, and I remained stony-faced outside the complicity of those knowing half-smiles that accompanied the mention of his name. We had never been close friends, of course; but he would turn up from time to time. He could not find theatrical work and had a job as a travelling salesman in the locations. He took to bringing three or four small boys along when he visited us; they were very subdued and whisperingly well-behaved and well-dressed in miniature suits—our barefoot children stared at them in awe. They were his children plus the children of the family he was living with, we gathered. He and I talked mostly about his difficulties—his old car was unreliable, his wife had left him, his commissions were low, and he could have taken up an offer to join a Chicago repertory company if he could have raised the fare to go back to America—while my wife fed ice-cream and cake to the silent children, or my children dutifully placed them one by one on the garden swing. We had begun to be able to talk about Elias's death. He had told me how, in the weeks before he died, Elias would get the wrong way on the moving stairway going down in the subway in New York and keep walking, walking up. "I thought he was foolin' around, man, you know? Jus' climbin' those stairs and goin' noplace?"

He clung nostalgically to the American idiom; no African talks about "noplace" when he means "nowhere." But he had abandoned the Afro wig and when we got talking about Elias he would hold his big, well-shaped head with its fine, shaven covering of his own wool propped between his hands as if in an effort to think

more clearly about something that would never come
clear; I felt suddenly at one with him in that gesture,
and would say, "Go on." He would remember another
example of how Elias had been "acting funny" before he
died. It was on one of those afternoon visits that he said,
"And I don't think I ever told you about the business
with the students at the college? How that last weekend—before he did it, I mean—he went around and invited everybody to a party, I dunno, a kind of feast he
said it was. Some of them said he said a barbecue—you
know what that is, same as a *braaivleis*, eh? But one of
the others told me afterwards that he'd told them he was
going to give them a real African feast, he was going to
show them how the country people do it here at home
when somebody gets married or there's a funeral or so.
He wanted to know where he could buy a goat."

"A goat?"

"That's right. A live goat. He wanted to kill and roast
a goat for them, on the campus."

It was round about this time that *he* asked me for a
loan. I think that was behind the idea of bringing those
pretty, dressed-up children along with him when he visited; he wanted firmly to set the background of his
obligations and responsibilities before touching me for
money. It was rather a substantial sum, for someone of
my resources. But he couldn't carry on his job without
a new car, and he'd just got the opportunity to acquire
a really good second-hand buy. I gave him the money in
spite of—because of, perhaps—new rumors that were
going around then that, in a police raid on the house of
the family with whom he had been living, every adult
except himself who was present on that night had been
arrested on the charge of attending a meeting of a
banned political organization. His friends were acquitted
on the charge simply through the defense lawyer's skill
at showing the *agent provocateur*, on whose evidence the
charge was based, to be an unreliable witness—that is to
say, a liar. But the friends were promptly served with
personal banning orders, anyway, which meant among
other things that their movements were restricted and
they were not allowed to attend gatherings.

He was the only one who remained, significantly, it

seemed impossible to ignore, free. And yet his friends let him stay on in the house; it was a mystery to us whites—and some blacks, too. But then so much becomes a mystery where trust becomes a commodity on sale to the police. Whatever my little show of defiance over the loan, during the last year or two we have reached the stage where if a man is black, literate, has "political" friends and white friends, *and* a passport, he must be considered a police spy. I was sick with myself— that was why I gave him the money—but I believed it, too. There's only one way for a man like that to prove himself, so far as we're concerned: he must be in prison.

Well, *he* was at large. A little subdued over the fate of his friends, about which he talked guilelessly as he had about the appropriation of Elias's air ticket, harassed as usual about money, poor devil, but generally cheerful. Yet our friendship, that really had begun to become one since Elias's death, waned rapidly. It was the money that did it. Of course; he was afraid I'd ask him to begin paying back and so he stopped coming to my "place," he stopped the visits with the beautifully dressed and well-behaved black infants. I received a typed letter from him, once, solemnly thanking me for my kind cooperation and, etc., as if I were some business firm, and assuring me that in a few months he hoped to be in a position, etc. I scrawled a note in reply, saying of course I darned well hoped he was going to pay the money he owed, sometime, but why, for God's sake, in the meantime, did this mean we had to carry on as if we'd quarreled? Damn it all, he didn't have to treat me as if I had some nasty disease, just because of a few rands.

But I didn't see him again. I've become too busy with my own work—the building boom of the last few years, you know; I've had the contract for several shopping malls, and a big cultural center—to do any work for the old theater group in its sporadic comings-to-life. I don't think he had much to do with it anymore, either; I heard he was doing quite well as a salesman and was thinking of marrying again. There was even a—yet another— rumor, that he was actually building a house in Dube, which is the nearest to a solid, bourgeois suburb a black can get in these black dormitories outside the white man's city, if you can be considered to be a bourgeois without having freehold. I didn't need the money, by then, but you know how it is with money—I felt faintly resentful about the debt anyway, because it looked as if now *he* could have paid it back just as well as *I* could say I didn't need it. As for the friendship; he'd shown me the worth of that. It's become something the white man must buy just as he must buy the cooperation of police stool pigeons. Elias has been dead five years; we live in our situation as of now, as the legal phrase goes; one falls back on legal phrases as other forms of expression become too risky.

And then, two hundred and seventy-seven days ago, there was a new rumor, and this time it was confirmed, this time it was no rumor. *He* was fetched from his room one night and imprisoned. That's perfectly legal, here; it's the hundred-and-eighty-day Detention Act. At least, because he was something of a personality, with many friends and contacts in particular among both black and white journalists, the fact has become public. If people are humble, or of no particular interest to the small world of white liberals, they are sometimes in detention for many months before this is known outside the eyewitness of whoever happened to be standing by, in house or street, when they were taken away by the police. But at least we all know where *he* is: in prison. They say that charges of treason are being prepared against him and various others who were detained at the same time, and still others who have been detained for even longer— three hundred and seventy-one days, three hundred and ten days—the figures, once finally released, are always as precise as this—and that soon, soon they will be brought to trial for whatever it is that we do not know they have done, for when people are imprisoned under the Detention Act no one is told why and there are no charges. There are suppositions among us, of course. Was he a double agent, as it were, using his *laissez-passer* as a police spy in order to further his real work as an underground African nationalist? Was he just unlucky in his choice of friends? Did he suffer from a dangerous sense of loyalty in place of any strong convictions of his own? Was it all due to some personal, unguessed-at bond it's none of our business to speculate about? Heaven knows—those police spy rumors aside—nobody could have looked more unlikely to be a political activist than that cheerful young man, second-string, always ready to jump up and turn over the record, fond of Liberace jackets and aspiring to play Le Roi Jones Off-Broadway.

But as I say, we know where he is now; inside. In solitary most of the time—they say, those who've also been inside. Two hundred and seventy-seven days he's been there.

And so we white friends can purge ourselves of the shame of rumors. We can be pure again. We are satisfied at last. He's in prison. He's proved himself, hasn't he?

Bessie Head
(1937–1986)

Bessie Amelia Emery was born in Pietermaritzburg, South Africa, the daughter of a Scottish mother from an affluent family and an African stable hand. The penalty imposed on this upper-class mother was that her family had her permanently committed to a mental hospital, in which her illegitimate child was born. Bessie was raised by two foster families. Because the first, an Afrikaner family, rejected her for being insufficiently white and the second, a "colored" family, was deemed inadequate, she was sent to a mission orphanage when she was thirteen. During her twenties, she worked as a journalist and elementary schoolteacher. In 1963, after her divorce from Harold Head, she and her son left South Africa to settle permanently in Botswana. At Bamangwato Development Farm she supported herself and her son by raising vegetables and making guava jam to sell. Comforted and inspired by Botswana village life in Serowe, she began to write again in spite of the physical hardships she experienced. Betty Fradkin, who visited her, noted that because the novelist's house lacked electricity, Head typed at night using six candles for light. She published three novels, *When Rain Clouds Gather* (Simon & Schuster, 1969), *Maru* (Mc Call, 1971), and *A Question of Power* (Davis Poynter, 1973, repr. Pantheon, 1974). In the highly autobiographical *A Question of Power*, Head dramatizes a year in the life of Elizabeth, a woman struggling to maintain her sanity. She is a perpetual outsider in her village because of mixed racial parentage. Lacking a sense of identity, tortured by exhausting nightmares, Elizabeth craves African acceptance, yet must resist internalizing the disparaging racial stereotypes about Africans that surround her. Nancy Topping Barzin, in *Black*

52

Scholar, has pointed out that Head's fiction often depicts Africa's sexism as well as racism and is particularly sensitive to women's societal and family problems. Two of Head's other works, *Serowe: Village of the Rain Wind* (Heinemann, 1981) and *A Bewitched Crossroad: An African Saga* (Donker—Craighall, 1984; repr. Paragon House, 1986) might be described as historical chronicles, because they combine sociological and historical accounts with folklore, and *The Collector of Treasures and other Botswana Village Tales* (Heinemann, 1977) is a volume of connected short stories.

THE COLLECTOR OF TREASURES

The long-term central state prison in the south was a whole day's journey away from the villages of the northern part of the country. They had left the village of Puleng at about nine that morning and all day long the police truck droned as it sped southwards on the wide, dusty cross-country track-road. The everyday world of plowed fields, grazing cattle, and vast expanses of bush and forest seemed indifferent to the hungry eyes of the prisoner who gazed out at them through the wire mesh grating at the back of the police truck. At some point during the journey, the prisoner seemed to strike at some ultimate source of pain and loneliness within her being and, overcome by it, she slowly crumpled forward in a wasted heap, oblivious to everything but her pain. Sunset swept by, then dusk, then dark and still the truck droned on, impersonally, uncaring.

At first, faintly on the horizon, the orange glow of the city lights of the new independence town of Gaborone, appeared like an astonishing phantom in the overwhelming darkness of the bush, until the truck struck tarred roads, neon lights, shops and cinemas, and made the

bush a phantom amidst a blaze of light. All this passed
untimed, unwatched by the crumpled prisoner; she did
not stir as the truck finally droned to a halt outside the
prison gates. The torchlight struck the side of her face
like an agonizing blow. Thinking she was asleep, the policeman called out briskly:

"You must awaken now. We have arrived."

He struggled with the lock in the dark and pulled open
the grating. She crawled painfully forward, in silence.

Together, they walked up a short flight of stairs and
waited awhile as the man tapped lightly, several times,
on the heavy iron prison door. The night-duty attendant
opened the door a crack, peered out and then opened
the door a little wider for them to enter. He quietly and
casually led the way to a small office, looked at his colleague and asked: "What do we have here?"

"It's the husband murder case from Puleng village,"
the other replied, handing over a file.

The attendant took the file and sat down at a table on
which lay open a large record book. In a big, bold scrawl
he recorded the details: Dikeledi Mokopi. Charge: Man-
slaughter. Sentence: Life. A night-duty wardress appeared and led the prisoner away to a side cubicle, where
she was asked to undress.

"Have you any money on you?" the wardress queried,
handing her a plain, green cotton dress which was the
prison uniform. The prisoner silently shook her head.

"So, you have killed your husband, have you?" the
wardress remarked, with a flicker of humor. "You'll be
in good company. We have four other women here for
the same crime. It's becoming the fashion these days.
Come with me," and she led the way along a corridor,
turned left and stopped at an iron gate which she opened
with a key, waited for the prisoner to walk in ahead of
her and then locked it with the key again. They entered
a small, immensely high-walled courtyard. On one side
were toilets, showers, and a cupboard. On the other, an
empty concrete quadrangle. The wardress walked to the
cupboard, unlocked it and took out a thick roll of clean-
smelling blankets which she handed to the prisoner. At
the lower end of the walled courtyard was a heavy iron
door which led to the cell. The wardress walked up to

this door, banged on it loudly and called out: "I say, will you women in there light your candle?"

A voice within called out: "All right," and they could hear the scratch-scratch of a match. The wardress again inserted a key, opened the door and watched for a while as the prisoner spread out her blankets on the floor. The four women prisoners already confined in the cell sat up briefly, and stared silently at their new companion. As the door was locked, they all greeted her quietly and one of the women asked: "Where do you come from?"

"Puleng," the newcomer replied, and seemingly satisfied with that, the light was blown out and the women lay down to continue their interrupted sleep. And as though she had reached the end of her destination, the new prisoner too fell into a deep sleep as soon as she had pulled her blankets about her.

The breakfast gong sounded at six the next morning. The women stirred themselves for their daily routine. They stood up, shook out their blankets and rolled them up into neat bundles. The day-duty wardress rattled the key in the lock and let them out into the small concrete courtyard so that they could perform their morning toilet. Then, with a loud clatter of pails and plates, two male prisoners appeared at the gate with breakfast. The men handed each woman a plate of porridge and a mug of black tea and they settled themselves on the concrete floor to eat. They turned and looked at their new companion and one of the women, a spokesman for the group said kindly:

"You should take care. The tea has no sugar in it. What we usually do is scoop the sugar off the porridge and put it into the tea."

The woman, Dikeledi, looked up and smiled. She had experienced such terror during the awaiting-trial period that she looked more like a skeleton than a human being. The skin creaked tautly over her cheeks. The other woman smiled, but after her own fashion. Her face permanently wore a look of cynical, whimsical humor. She had a full, plump figure. She introduced herself and her companions: "My name is Kebonye. Then that's Otsetswe, Galeboe, and Monwana. What may your name be?"

"Dikeledi Mokopi."

"How is it that you have such a tragic name," Kebonye observed. "Why did your parents have to name you *tears?*"

"My father passed away at that time and it is my mother's tears that I am named after," Dikeledi said, then added: "She herself passed away six years later and I was brought up by my uncle."

Kebonye shook her head sympathetically, slowly raising a spoonful of porridge to her mouth. That swallowed, she asked next:

"And what may your crime be?"

"I have killed my husband."

"We are all here for the same crime," Kebonye said, then with her cynical smile asked: "Do you feel any sorrow about the crime?"

"Not really," the other woman replied.

"How did you kill him?"

"I cut off all his special parts with a knife," Dikeledi said.

"I did it with a razor," Kebonye said. She sighed and added: "I have had a troubled life."

A little silence followed while they all busied themselves with their food, then Kebonye continued musingly:

"Our men do not think that we need tenderness and care. You know, my husband used to kick me between the legs when he wanted that. I once aborted with a child, due to this treatment. I could see that there was no way to appeal to him if I felt ill, so I once said to him that if he liked he could keep some other woman as well because I couldn't manage to satisfy all his needs. Well, he was an education-officer and each year he used to suspend about seventeen male teachers for making school girls pregnant, but he used to do the same. The last time it happened the parents of the girl were very angry and came to report the matter to me. I told them: 'You leave it to me. I have seen enough.' And so I killed him."

They sat in silence and completed their meal, then they took their plates and cups to rinse them in the washroom. The wardress produced some pails and a broom. Their sleeping quarters had to be flushed out with water; there was not a speck of dirt anywhere, but that was a prison routine. All that was left was an inspection by the director of the prison. Here again Kebonye turned to the newcomer and warned:

"You must be careful when the chief comes to inspect. He is mad about one thing—attention! Stand up straight! Hands at your sides! If this is not done you should see how he stands here and curses. He does not mind anything but that. He is mad about that."

Inspection over, the women were taken through a number of gates to an open, sunny yard, fenced in by high, barbed-wire where they did their daily work. The prison was a rehabilitation center where the prisoners produced goods which were sold in the prison store; the women produced garments of cloth and wool; the men did carpentry, shoe-making, brick-making, and vegetable production.

Dikeledi had a number of skills—she could knit, sew, and weave baskets. All the women at present were busy knitting woollen garments; some were learners and did their work slowly and painstakingly. They looked at Dikeledi with interest as she took a ball of wool and a pair of knitting needles and rapidly cast on stitches. She had soft, caressing, almost boneless, hands of strange power—work of a beautiful design grew from those hands. By mid-morning she had completed the front part of a jersey and they all stopped to admire the pattern she had invented in her own head.

"You are a gifted person," Kebonye remarked, admiringly.

"All my friends say so," Dikeledi replied smiling. "You know, I am the woman whose thatch does not leak. Whenever my friends wanted to thatch their huts, I was there. They would never do it without me. I was always busy and employed because it was with these hands that I fed and reared my children. My husband left me after four years of marriage but I managed well enough to feed those mouths. If people did not pay me in money for my work, they paid me with gifts of food."

"It's not so bad here," Kebonye said. "We get a little money saved for us out of the sale of our work, and if you work like that you can still produce money for your children. How many children do you have?"

"I have three sons."

"Are they in good care?"

"Yes."

"I like lunch," Kebonye said, oddly turning the conversation. "It is the best meal of the day. We get samp and meat and vegetables."

So the day passed pleasantly enough with chatter and work and at sunset the women were once more taken back to the cell for lock-up time. They unrolled their blankets and prepared their beds, and with the candle lit continued to talk a while longer. Just as they were about to retire for the night, Dikeledi nodded to her new-found friend, Kebonye:

"Thank you for all your kindness to me," she said, softly.

"We must help each other," Kebonye replied, with her amused, cynical smile. "This is a terrible world. There is only misery here."

And so the woman Dikeledi began phase three of a life that had been ashen in its loneliness and unhappiness. And yet she had always found gold amidst the ash, deep loves that had joined her heart to the hearts of others. She smiled tenderly at Kebonye because she knew already that she had found another such love. She was the collector of such treasures.

There were really only two kinds of men in the society. The one kind created such misery and chaos that he could be broadly damned as evil. If one watched the village dogs chasing a bitch on heat, they usually moved around in packs of four or five. As the mating progressed one dog would attempt to gain dominance over the festivities and oust all the others from the bitch's vulva. The rest of the hapless dogs would stand around yapping and snapping in its face while the top dog indulged in a continuous spurt of orgasms, day and night until he was exhausted. No doubt, during that Herculean feat, the dog imagined he was the only penis in the world and that there had to be a scramble for it. That kind of man lived near the animal level and behaved just the same. Like the dogs and bulls and donkeys, he also accepted no responsibility for the young he procreated and like the dogs and bulls and donkeys, he also made females abort. Since that kind of man was in the majority in the society, he needed a little analyzing as he was responsible for the complete breakdown of family life. He could be analyzed over three time-spans. In the old days, before the colonial invasion of Africa, he was a man who lived by the traditions and taboos outlined for all the people by the forefathers of the tribe. He had little individual freedom to assess whether these traditions were compassionate or not—they demanded that he comply and obey the rules, without thought. But when the laws of the ancestors are examined, they appear on the whole to have been vast, external disciplines for the good of the society as a whole, with little attention given to individual preferences and needs. The ancestors made so many errors and one of the most bitter-making things was that they relegated to men a superior position in the tribe, while women were regarded, in a congenital sense, as being an inferior form of human life. To this day, women still suffered from all the calamities that befall an inferior form of human life. The colonial era and the period of migratory mining labor to South Africa was a further affliction visited on this man. It broke the hold of the ancestors. It broke the old, traditional form of family life and for long periods a man was separated from his wife and children while he worked for a pittance in another land in order to raise the money to pay his British Colonial poll-tax. British Colonialism scarcely enriched his life. He then became "the boy" of the white man and a machine-tool of the South African mines. African independence seemed merely one more affliction on top of the afflictions that had visited this man's life. Independence suddenly and dramatically changed the pattern of colonial subservience. More jobs became available under the new government's localization program and salaries sky-rocketed at the same time. It provided the first occasion for family life of a new order, above the childlike discipline of custom, the degradation of colonialism. Men and women, in order to survive, had to turn inwards to their own resources. It was the man who arrived at this turning point, a broken wreck with no inner resources at all. It was as though he was hideous to himself and in an effort to flee his own inner emptiness, he spun away from himself in a dizzy kind of death dance of wild destruction and dissipation.

One such man was Garesego Mokopi, the husband of Dikeledi. For four years prior to independence, he had worked as a clerk in the district administration service, at a steady salary of R50.00 a month. Soon after independence his salary shot up to R200.00 per month. Even during his lean days he had had a taste for womanizing and drink; now he had the resources for a real spree. He was not seen at home again and lived and slept around the village, from woman to woman. He left his wife and three sons—Banabothe, the eldest, aged four; Inalame, aged three; and the youngest, Motsomi, aged one—to their own resources. Perhaps he did so because she was the boring, semi-literate traditional sort, and there were a lot of exciting new women around. Independence produced marvels indeed.

There was another kind of man in the society with the power to create himself anew. He turned all his resources, both emotional and material, towards his family life and he went on and on with his own quiet rhythm, like a river. He was a poem of tenderness.

One such man was Paul Thebolo and he and his wife, Kenalepe, and their three children, came to live in the village of Puleng in 1966, the year of independence. Paul Thebolo had been offered the principalship of a primary school in the village. They were allocated an empty field beside the yard of Dikeledi Mokopi, for their new home.

Neighbors are the center of the universe to each other. They help each other at all times and mutually loan each other's goods. Dikeledi Mokopi kept an interested eye on the yard of her new neighbors. At first, only the man appeared with some workmen to erect the fence, which was set up with incredible speed and efficiency. The man impressed her immediately when she went around to introduce herself and find out a little about the newcomers. He was tall, large-boned, slow-moving. He was so peaceful as a person that the sunlight and shadow played all kinds of tricks with his eyes, making it difficult to determine their exact color. When he stood still and looked reflective, the sunlight liked to creep into his eyes and nestle there; so sometimes his eyes were the color of shade, and sometimes light brown.

He turned and smiled at her in a friendly way when she introduced herself and explained that he and his wife were on transfer from the village of Bobonong. His wife and children were living with relatives in the village until the yard was prepared. He was in a hurry to settle down as the school term would start in a month's time. They were, he said, going to erect two mud huts first and later he intended setting up a small house of bricks. His wife would be coming around in a few days with some women to erect the mud walls of the huts.

"I would like to offer my help too," Dikeledi said. "If work always starts early in the morning and there are about six of us, we can get both walls erected in a week. If you want one of the huts done in woman's thatch, all my friends know that I am the woman whose thatch does not leak."

The man smilingly replied that he would impart all this information to his wife, then he added charmingly that he thought she would like his wife when they met. His wife was a friendly person; everyone liked her.

Dikeledi walked back to her own yard with a high heart. She had few callers. None of her relatives called for fear that since her husband had left her she would become dependent on them for many things. The people who called did business with her; they wanted her to make dresses for their children or knit jerseys for the winter time and at times when she had no orders at all, she made baskets which she sold. In these ways she supported herself and the three children but she was lonely for true friends.

All turned out as the husband had said—he had a lovely wife. She was fairly tall and thin with a bright, vivacious manner. She made no effort to conceal that normally, and every day, she was a very happy person. And all turned out as Dikeledi had said. The work-party of six women erected the mud walls of the huts in one week; two weeks later, the thatch was complete. The Thebolo family moved into their new abode and Dikeledi Mokopi moved into one of the most prosperous and happy periods of her life. Her life took a big, wide up-

ward curve. Her relationship with the Thebolo family
was more than the usual friendly exchange of neighbors.
It was rich and creative.

It was not long before the two women had going one
of those deep, affectionate, sharing-everything kind of
friendships that only women know how to have. It
seemed that Kenalepe wanted endless amounts of dresses
made for herself and her three little girls. Since Dikeledi
would not accept cash for these services—she protested
about the many benefits she received from her good
neighbors—Paul Thebolo arranged that she be paid in
household goods for these services so that for some years
Dikeledi was always assured of her basic household
needs—the full bag of corn, sugar, tea, powdered milk,
and cooking oil. Kenalepe was also the kind of woman
who made the whole world spin around her; her attractive personality attracted a whole range of women to her
yard and also a whole range of customers for her dress-
making friend, Dikeledi. Eventually, Dikeledi became
swamped with work, was forced to buy a second sewing-
machine and employ a helper. The two women did everything together—they were forever together at weddings,
funerals, and parties in the village. In their leisure hours
they freely discussed all their intimate affairs with each
other, so that each knew thoroughly the details of the
other's life.

"You are a lucky someone," Dikeledi remarked one
day, wistfully. "Not everyone has the gift of a husband
like Paul."

"Oh yes," Kenalepe said happily. "He is an honest
somebody." She knew a little of Dikeledi's list of woes
and queried: "But why did you marry a man like Garesego? I looked carefully at him when you pointed him
out to me near the shops the other day and I could see
at one glance that he is a butterfly."

"I think I mostly wanted to get out of my uncle's
yard," Dikeledi replied. "I never liked my uncle. Rich
as he was, he was a hard man and very selfish. I was
only a servant there and pushed about. I went there when
I was six years old when my mother died, and it was not
a happy life. All his children despised me because I was
their servant. Uncle paid for my education for six years,

then he said I must leave school. I longed for more because as you know, education opens up the world for one. Garesego was a friend of my uncle and he was the only man who proposed for me. They discussed it between themselves and then my uncle said: 'You'd better marry Garesego because you're just hanging around here like a chain on my neck.' I agreed, just to get away from that terrible man. Garesego said at that time that he'd rather be married to my sort than the educated kind because those women were stubborn and wanted to lay down the rules for men. Really, I did not ever protest when he started running about. You know what the other women do. They chase after the man from one hut to another and beat up the girlfriends. The man just runs into another hut, that's all. So you don't really win. I wasn't going to do anything like that. I am satisfied I have children. They are a blessing to me."

"Oh, it isn't enough," her friend said, shaking her head in deep sympathy. "I am amazed at how life imparts its gifts. Some people get too much. Others get nothing at all. I have always been lucky in life. One day my parents will visit—they live in the south—and you'll see the fuss they make over me. Paul is just the same. He takes care of everything so that I never have a day of worry . . ."

The man Paul, attracted as wide a range of male friends as his wife. They had guests every evening; illiterate men who wanted him to fill in tax forms or write letters for them, or his own colleagues who wanted to debate the political issues of the day—there was always something new happening every day now that the country had independence. The two women sat on the edge of these debates and listened with fascinated ears, but they never participated. The following day they would chew over the debates with wise, earnest expressions.

"Men's minds travel widely and boldly," Kenalepe would comment. "It makes me shiver the way they freely criticize our new government. Did you hear what Petros said last night? He said he knew all those bastards and they were just a lot of crooks who would pull a lot of dirty tricks. Oh dear! I shivered so much when he said that. The way they talk about the government makes you feel in your bones that this is not a safe world to be in, not like the old days when we didn't have governments. And Lentswe said that ten percent of the population in England really control all the wealth of the country, while the rest live at starvation level. And he said communism would sort all this out. I gathered from the way they discussed this matter that our government is not in favor of communism. I trembled so much when this became clear to me . . ." She paused and laughed proudly. "I've heard Paul say this several times: 'The British only ruled us for eighty years.' I wonder why Paul is so fond of saying that?"

And so a completely new world opened up for Dikeledi. It was so impossibly rich and happy that, as the days went by, she immersed herself more deeply in it and quite overlooked the barrenness of her own life. But it hung there like a nagging ache in the mind of her friend, Kenalepe.

"You ought to find another man," she urged one day, when they had one of their personal discussions. "It's not good for a woman to live alone."

"And who would that be?" Dikeledi asked, disillusioned. "I'd only be bringing trouble into my life whereas now it is all in order. I have my eldest son at school and I can manage to pay the school fees. That's all I really care about."

"I mean," said Kenalepe, "we are also here to make love and enjoy it."

"Oh I never really cared for it," the other replied. "When you experience the worst of it, it just puts you off altogether."

"What do you mean by that?" Kenalepe asked, wide-eyed.

"I mean it was just jump on and jump off and I used to wonder what it was all about. I developed a dislike for it."

"You mean Garesego was like that!" Kenalepe said, flabbergasted. "Why, that's just like a cock hopping from hen to hen. I wonder what he is doing with all those women. I'm sure they are just after his money and so they flatter him . . ." She paused and then added earnestly: "That's really all the more reason you should find another man. Oh, if you knew what it was really like, you would long for it, I can tell you! I sometimes think I enjoy that side of life far too much. Paul knows a lot about all that. And he always has some new trick with which to surprise me. He has a certain way of smiling when he has thought up something new and I shiver a little and say to myself: 'Ha, what is Paul going to do tonight!' "

Kenalepe paused and smiled at her friend, slyly.

"I can loan Paul to you if you like," she said, then raised one hand to block the protest on her friend's face. "I would do it because I have never had a friend like you in my life before whom I trust so much. Paul had other girls you know, before he married me, so it's not such an uncommon thing to him. Besides, we used to make love long before we got married and I never got pregnant. He takes care of that side too. I wouldn't mind loaning him because I am expecting another child and I don't feel so well these days . . ."

Dikeledi stared at the ground for a long moment, then she looked up at her friend with tears in her eyes.

"I cannot accept such a gift from you," she said, deeply moved. "But if you are ill I will wash for you and cook for you."

Not put off by her friend's refusal of her generous offer, Kenalepe mentioned the discussion to her husband that very night. He was so taken off-guard by the unexpectedness of the subject that at first he looked slightly astonished, and burst out into loud laughter and for such a lengthy time that he seemed unable to stop.

"Why are you laughing like that?" Kenalepe asked, surprised.

He laughed a bit more, then suddenly turned very serious and thoughtful and was lost in his own thoughts for some time. When she asked him what he was thinking he merely replied: "I don't want to tell you everything. I want to keep some of my secrets to myself."

The next day Kenalepe reported to her friend.

"Now whatever does he mean by that? I want to keep some of my secrets to myself?"

"I think," Dikeledi said smiling, "I think he has a conceit about being a good man. Also, when someone loves someone too much, it hurts them to say so. They'd rather keep silent."

Shortly after this Kenalepe had a miscarriage and had to be admitted to hospital for a minor operation. Dikeledi kept her promise "to wash and cook" for her friend. She ran both their homes, fed the children and kept everything in order. Also, people complained about the poorness of the hospital diet and each day she scoured the village for eggs and chicken, cooked them, and took them to Kenalepe every day at the lunch-hour.

One evening Dikeledi ran into a snag with her routine. She had just dished up supper for the Thebolo children when a customer came around with an urgent request for an alteration on a wedding dress. The wedding was to take place the next day. She left the children seated around the fire eating and returned to her own home. An hour later, her own children asleep and settled, she thought she would check the Thebolo yard to see if all was well there. She entered the children's hut and noted that they had put themselves to bed and were fast asleep. Their supper plates lay scattered and unwashed around the fire. The hut which Paul and Kenalepe shared was in darkness. It meant that Paul had not yet returned from his usual evening visit to his wife. Dikeledi collected the plates and washed them, then poured the dirty dishwater on the still-glowing embers of the outdoor fire. She piled the plates one on top of the other and carried them to the third additional hut which was used as a kitchen. Just then Paul Thebolo entered the yard, noted the lamp and movement in the kitchen hut and walked over to it. He paused at the open door.

"What are you doing now, Mma-Banabothe?" he asked, addressing her affectionately in the customary way by the name of her eldest son, Banabothe.

"I know quite well what I am doing," Dikeledi replied happily. She turned around to say that it was not a good thing to leave dirty dishes standing overnight but her mouth flew open with surprise. Two soft pools of cool liquid light were in his eyes and something infinitely sweet passed between them; it was too beautiful to be love.

"You are a very good woman, Mma-Banabothe," he said softly.

It was the truth and the gift was offered like a nugget of gold. Only men like Paul Thebolo could offer such gifts. She took it and stored another treasure in her heart. She bowed her knee in the traditional curtsey and walked quietly away to her own home.

Eight years passed for Dikeledi in a quiet rhythm of work and friendship with the Thebolos. The crisis came with the eldest son, Banabothe. He had to take his primary school leaving examination at the end of the year. This serious event sobered him up considerably as like all boys he was very fond of playtime. He brought his books home and told his mother that he would like to study in the evenings. He would like to pass with a "Grade A" to please her. With a flushed and proud face Dikeledi mentioned this to her friend, Kenalepe.

"Banabothe is studying every night now," she said. "He never really cared for studies. I am so pleased about this that I bought him a spare lamp and removed him from the children's hut to my own hut where things will be peaceful for him. We both sit up late at night now. I sew on buttons and fix hems and he does his studies . . ."

She also opened a savings account at the post office in order to have some standby money to pay the fees for his secondary education. They were rather high—R85.00. But in spite of all her hoarding of odd cents, toward the end of the year, she was short on R20.00 to cover the fees. Midway during the Christmas school holidays the results were announced. Banabothe passed with a "Grade A." His mother was almost hysterical in her joy at his achievement. But what to do? The two youngest sons had already started primary school and she would never manage to cover all their fees from her resources. She decided to remind Garesego Mokopi that he was the father of the children. She had not seen him in eight years except as a passer-by in the village. Sometimes he waved but he had never talked to her or inquired about her life. Then this unpleasant something turned up at his office one day, just as he was about to leave for lunch. She had heard from village gossip, that he had eventually settled down with a married woman who had a brood of children of her own. He had ousted her husband, in a typical village sensation of brawls, curses, and abuse. Most probably the husband did not care because there were always arms outstretched toward a man, as long as he looked like a man. The attraction of this particular woman for Garesego Mokopi, so her former lovers said with a snicker, was that she went in for heady forms of love-making like biting and scratching.

Garese go Mokopi walked out of his office and looked irritably at the ghost from his past, his wife. She obviously wanted to talk to him and he walked toward her, looking at his watch all the while. Like all the new "success men," he had developed a paunch, his eyes were bloodshot, his face was bloated, and the odor of the beer and sex from the previous night clung faintly around him. He indicated with his eyes that they should move around to the back of the office block where they could talk in privacy.

"You must hurry with whatever you want to say," he said impatiently. "The lunch-hour is very short and I have to be back at the office by two."

Not to him could she talk of the pride she felt in Banabothe's achievement, so she said simply and quietly: "Garesego, I beg you to help me pay Banabothe's fees for secondary school. He has passed with a 'Grade A' and as you know, the school fees must be produced on the first day of school or else he will be turned away. I have struggled to save money the whole year but I am short by R20.00."

She handed him her post office savings book, which he took, glanced at and handed back to her. Then he smiled, a smirky know-all smile, and thought he was delivering her a blow in the face.

"Why don't you ask Paul Thebolo for the money?" he said. "Everyone knows he's keeping two homes and that you are his spare. Everyone knows about that full bag of corn he delivers to your home every six months so why can't he pay the school fees as well?"

She neither denied this, nor confirmed it. The blow glanced off her face which she raised slightly, in pride. Then she walked away.

As was their habit, the two women got together that afternoon and Dikeledi reported this conversation with her husband to Kenalepe who tossed back her head in anger and said fiercely: "The filthy pig himself! He thinks every man is like him, does he? I shall report this matter to Paul, then he'll see something."

And indeed Garesego did something but it was just up his alley. He was a female prostitute in his innermost being and like all professional prostitutes, he enjoyed publicity and sensation—it promoted his cause. He smiled genially and expansively when a madly angry Paul Thebolo came up to the door of his house where he lived with *his* concubine. Garesego had been through a lot of these dramas over those eight years and he almost knew by rote the dialogue that would follow.

"You bastard!" Paul Thebolo spat out. "Your wife isn't my concubine, do you hear?"

"Then why are you keeping her in food?" Garesego drawled. "Men only do that for women they fuck! They never do it for nothing."

Paul Thebolo rested one hand against the wall, half dizzy with anger, and he said tensely: "You defile life, Garesego Mokopi. There's nothing else in your world but defilement. Mma-Banabothe makes clothes for my wife and children and she will never accept money from me so how else must I pay her?"

"It only proves the story both ways," the other replied, vilely. "Women do that for men who fuck them."

Paul Thebolo shot out the other hand, punched him soundly in one grinning eye and walked away. Who could hide a livid, swollen eye? To every surprised inquiry, he replied with an injured air:

"It was done by my wife's lover, Paul Thebolo."

It certainly brought the attention of the whole village upon him, which was all he really wanted. Those kinds of men were the bottom rung of government. They secretly hungered to be the President with all eyes on them. He worked up the sensation a little further. He announced that he would pay the school fees of the child of his concubine, who was also to enter secondary school, but not the school fees of his own child, Banabothe. People half liked the smear on Paul Thebolo; he was too good to be true. They delighted in making him a part of the general dirt of the village, so they turned on Garesego and scolded: "Your wife might be getting things from Paul Thebolo but it's beyond the purse of any man to pay the school fees of his own children as well as the school fees of another man's children. Banabothe wouldn't be there had you not procreated him, Garesego, so it is your duty to care for him. Besides, it's your fault if your wife takes another man. You left her alone all these years."

So that story was lived with for two weeks, mostly because people wanted to say that Paul Thebolo was a part of life too and as uncertain of his morals as they were. But the story took such a dramatic turn that it made all the men shudder with horror. It was some weeks before they could find the courage to go to bed with women; they preferred to do something else.

Garesego's obscene thought processes were his own undoing. He really believed that another man had a stake in his hen-pen and like any cock, his hair was up about it. He thought he'd walk in and reestablish his own claim to it and so, after two weeks, once the swelling in his eye had died down, he espied Banabothe in the village and asked him to take a note to his mother. He said the child should bring a reply. The note read: "Dear Mother, I am coming home again so that we may settle our differences. Will you prepare a meal for me and some hot water that I might take a bath. Gare."

Dikeledi took the note, read it and shook with rage. All its overtones were clear to her. He was coming home for some sex. They had no differences. They had not even talked to each other.

"Banabothe," she said. "Will you play nearby? I want to think a bit then I will send you to your father with the reply."

Her thought processes were not very clear to her. There was something she could not immediately touch upon. Her life had become holy to her during all those years she had struggled to maintain herself and the children. She had filled her life with treasures of kindness and love she had gathered from others and it was all this that she wanted to protect from defilement by an evil man. Her first panic-stricken thought was to gather up the children and flee the village. But where to go? Garesego did not want a divorce, she had left him to approach her about the matter, she had desisted from taking any other man. She turned her thoughts this way and that and could find no way out except to face him. If she wrote back, don't you dare put foot in the yard I don't want to see you, he would ignore it. Black women didn't have that kind of power. A thoughtful, brooding look came over her face. At last, at peace with herself, she went into her hut and wrote a reply: "Sir, I shall prepare everything as you have said. Dikeledi."

It was about midday when Banabothe sped back with the reply to his father. All afternoon Dikeledi busied herself making preparations for the appearance of her husband at sunset. At one point Kenalepe approached the yard and looked around in amazement at the massive preparations, the large iron water pot full of water with a fire burning under it, the extra cooking pots on the fire. Only later Kenalepe brought the knife into focus. But it was only a vague blur, a large kitchen knife used to cut meat and Dikeledi knelt at a grinding-stone and sharpened it slowly and methodically. What was in focus then was the final and tragic expression on the upturned face of her friend. It threw her into confusion and blocked their usual free and easy feminine chatter. When Dikeledi said: "I am making some preparations for Garesego. He is coming home tonight," Kenalepe beat a hasty retreat to her own home terrified. They knew they were involved because when she mentioned this to Paul he was distracted and uneasy for the rest of the day. He kept on doing upside-down sorts of things, not replying to questions, absent-mindedly leaving a cup of tea until it got quite cold, and every now and again he stood up and paced about, lost in his own thoughts. So deep was their sense of disturbance that toward evening they no longer made a pretense of talking. They just sat in silence in their hut. Then, at about nine o'clock, they heard those wild and agonized bellows. They both rushed out together to the yard of Dikeledi Mokopi.

* * *

He came home at sunset and found everything ready for him as he had requested, and he settled himself down to enjoy a man's life. He had brought a pack of beer along and sat outdoors slowly savoring it while every now and then his eye swept over the Thebolo yard. Only the woman and children moved about the yard. The man was out of sight. Garesego smiled to himself, pleased that he could crow as loud as he liked with no answering challenge.

A basin of warm water was placed before him to wash his hands and then Dikeledi served him his meal. At a separate distance she also served the children and then instructed them to wash and prepare for bed. She noted that Garesego displayed no interest in the children whatsoever. He was entirely wrapped up in himself and thought only of himself and his own comfort. Any tenderness he offered the children might have broken her and swerved her mind away from the deed she had carefully planned all that afternoon. She was beneath his regard and notice too for when she eventually brought her own plate of food and sat near him, he never once glanced at her face. He drank his beer and cast his glance every now and again at the Thebolo yard. Not once did the man of the yard appear until it became too dark to distinguish anything any more. He was completely satisfied with that. He could repeat the performance every day until he broke the mettle of the other cock again and forced him into angry abuse. He liked that sort of thing.

"Garesego, do you think you could help me with Banabothe's school fees?" Dikeledi asked at one point.

"Oh, I'll think about it," he replied casually.

She stood up and carried buckets of water into the hut, which she poured into a large tin bath that he might bathe himself, then while he took his bath she busied herself tidying up and completing the last of the household chores. Those done, she entered the children's hut. They played hard during the day and they had already fallen asleep with exhaustion. She knelt down near their sleeping mats and stared at them for a long while, with an extremely tender expression. Then she blew out their lamp and walked to her own hut. Garesego lay sprawled across the bed in such a manner that indicated he only thought of himself and did not intend sharing the bed with anyone else. Satiated with food and drink, he had fallen into a deep, heavy sleep the moment his head touched the pillow. His concubine had no doubt taught him that the correct way for a man to go to bed, was naked. So he lay, unguarded and defenseless, sprawled across the bed on his back.

The bath made a loud clatter as Dikeledi removed it from the room, but still he slept on, lost to the world. She reentered the hut and closed the door. Then she bent down and reached for the knife under the bed which she had merely concealed with a cloth. With the precision and skill of her hardworking hands, she grasped hold of his genitals and cut them off with one stroke. In doing so, she slit the main artery which ran on the inside of the groin. A massive spurt of blood arched its way across the bed. And Garesego bellowed. He bellowed his anguish. Then all was silent. She stood and watched his death anguish with an intent and brooding look, missing not one detail of it. A knock on the door stirred her out of her reverie. It was the boy, Banabothe. She opened the door and stared at him, speechless. He was trembling violently.

"Mother," he said, in a terrified whisper. "Didn't I hear father cry?"

"I have killed him," she said, waving her hand in the air with a gesture that said—well, that's that. Then she added sharply: "Banabothe, go and call the police."

He turned and fled into the night. A second pair of footsteps followed hard on his heels. It was Kenalepe running back to her own yard, half out of her mind with her fear. Out of the dark Paul Thebolo stepped toward the hut and entered it. He took in every detail and then he turned and looked at Dikeledi with such a tortured expression that for a time words failed him. At last he said: "You don't have to worry about the children, Mma-Banabothe. I'll take them as my own and give them all a secondary school education."

Charles Mungoshi
(b. 1947)

Born in Manyene near Chivhu, Zimbabwe (Rhodesia at that time), Charles Mungoshi was educated at All Saints School, Daramombe School, and St. Augustine's Secondary School. He has worked as a research assistant for the Forestry Commission, a bookstore clerk, an editor at the Literature Bureau, and, in recent years, has served as literary director of Zimbabwe Publishing House and as writer-in-residence at the University of Zimbabwe. His short fiction often depicts the family tensions and strained relationships that are exacerbated as individuals struggle to maintain their allegiance to traditional, rural values and responsibilities that conflict with their desire and need to succeed in the bewildering urban centers of modern education and work. Doris Lessing has described his stories as "brilliant, subtle, sad, alive," while Nadine Gordimer has observed that "Charles Mungoshi writes with power, poignancy, and gentle humor; his characters confide intimately the secrets of their lives." In 1970 the Rhodesian African Literature Bureau published a novel of his written in Shona, an African language, but his work was also, at times, banned in Rhodesia. Many stories from his first collections, *Coming of the Dry Season* (Oxford University Press, 1972; repr. Zimbabwe Publishing House, 1981) and *Some Kinds of Wounds and Other Stories* (Mambo Press, 1980), have been collected in *The Setting Sun and The Rolling World* (Beacon Press, 1989). He won Rhodesian PEN awards in 1976 and 1981. Some of his poetry is collected in *The Milkman Doesn't Only Deliver Milk: Selected Poems* (published by the Poetry Society of Zimbabwe in 1981), and his novel *Waiting for the Rain*, first published in the Heinemann African Writers Series in 1972 and printed, after independence, in Zimbabwe in 1981, has become recommended reading at many schools there. It has been translated into French, Bulgarian, German, and Hungarian. Charles Mungoshi's other titles are *Stories from a Shona Childhood* (Baobab Books, 1989), *One Day Long Ago: More Stories from a Shona Childhood* (Baobab Books, 1991), and *Walking Still* (Baobab Books, 1997).

WHO WILL
STOP THE DARK?

The boy began to believe what the other boys at school said about his mother. In secret he began to watch her—her face, words and actions. He would also watch his father's bare arched back as he toiled at his basket-weaving from day to day. His mother could go wherever she wanted to go. His father could not. Every morning he would drag his useless lower limbs out of the hut and sit under the *muonde* tree. He would not leave the tree till late in the evening when he would drag himself again back into the hut for his evening meal and bed. And always the boy felt a stab of pain when he looked at the front of his father's wet urine-stiffened trousers.

The boy knew that his mother had something to do with this condition of his father. The tight lines round her mouth and her long silences that would sometimes erupt into unexpected bursts of red violence said so. The story was that his father had fallen off the roof he had been thatching and broken his back. But the boy didn't believe it. It worried him. He couldn't imagine it. One day his father had just been like any other boy's father in their village, and the next day he wasn't. It made him wonder about his mother. He felt that it wasn't safe in their house. So he began to spend most of his time with the old man, his grandfather.

"I want you in the house," his mother said, when she could afford words, but the boy knew she was saying it all the time by the way she tightened her mouth and lowered her looking-away-from-people eyes.

The boy remembered that his grandfather had lived under the same roof with them for a long time. He couldn't remember how he had then come to live alone in his own hut half-a-mile from their place.

"He is so childish," he heard his mother say one day.

"He is old," his father said, without raising his head from his work.

"And how old do you think my mother is?" The lines round his mother's mouth drew tighter and tauter.

"Women do not grow as weak as men in their old age," his father persisted.

"Because it's the men who have to bear the children— so they grow weak from the strain!" His mother's eyes flashed once—so that the boy held his breath—and then she looked away, her mouth wrinkled tightly into an obscene little hole that reminded the boy of a cow's behind just after dropping its dung. He thought now his father would keep quiet. He was surprised to hear him say, "A man's back is the man. Once his back is broken—" another flash of his mother's eye silenced him and the boy couldn't stand it. He stood up to go out.

"And where are you going?" his mother shouted after him.

"To see grandfather."

"What do you want there with him?"

The boy turned back and stayed round the yard until his mother disappeared into the house. Then he quietly slid off for his grandfather's place through the bush. His father pretended not to see him go.

The old man had a way of looking at the boy: like someone looking into a mirror to see how badly his face had been burned.

"A, Zakeo," the old man said when the boy entered the yard. He was sitting against the wall of his hut, smoking his pipe quietly, looking into the distance. He hadn't even looked in Zakeo's direction.

"Did you see me this time?" Zakeo asked, laughing. He never stopped being surprised by the way his grandfather seemed to know everyone by their footfalls and would greet them by their names without even looking at them.

"I don't have to look to know it's you," the old man said.

"But today I have changed my feet to those of a bird," the boy teased him.

"No," the old man shook his head. "You are still the cat in my ears."

The boy laughed over that and although the old man smoked on without changing his expression, the boy knew that he was laughing too.

"Father said to ask you how you have spent the day," the boy said, knowing that the old man would know that it was a lie. The boy knew he would be forgiven this lie because the old man knew that the boy always wished his father would send him with such a message to his own father.

"You don't have to always protect him like that," the old man growled, almost to himself.

"Sekuru?" the boy didn't always understand most of the grown-up things the old man said.

"I said get on with the work. Nothing ever came out of a muscular mouth and snail-slime hands."

The boy disappeared into the hut while the old man sat on, smoking.

Zakeo loved doing the household chores for his grandfather: sweeping out the room and lighting the fire, collecting firewood from the bush and fetching water from the well and cooking. The old man would just look on, not saying anything much, just smoking his pipe. When he worked the boy didn't talk. Don't use your mouth and hands at the same time, the old man had told him once and whenever he forgot the old man reminded him by not answering his questions. It was a different silence they practiced in the old man's house, the boy felt. Here, it was always as if his grandfather was about to tell him a secret. And when he left his parent's place he felt he must get back to the old man at the earliest opportunity to hear the secret.

"Have you ever gone hunting for rabbits, boy?" his grandfather asked him one day.

"No, *Sekuru.* Have you?"

The old man didn't answer. He looked away at the darkening landscape, puffing at his pipe.

"Did you like it?" the boy asked.

"Like it? We lived for nothing else, boy. We were born hunters, stayed hunters all our life and most of us died hunters."

"What happened to those who weren't hunters?"

"They became tillers of the land, and some, weavers of bamboo baskets."

"You mean Father?"

"I am talking of friends I used to know."

"But didn't you ever teach Father to hunt, *Sekuru?*" The boy's voice was strained, anxious, pained. The old man looked at him briefly and then quickly away.

"I taught him everything a man ought to know," he said distantly.

"Basket-weaving too?"

"That was his mother," the old man said and then silently went on, *his mother, your grandmother, my wife, taught your father basket-weaving. She also had been taught by a neighbor who later gave me the lumbago.*

"You like basket-weaving?" he asked the boy.

"I hate it!" The old man suddenly turned, surprised at the boy's vehemence. He took the pipe out of his mouth for a minute, looking instantly at the boy, then he looked away, returning the pipe to his mouth.

"Do you think we could go hunting together, *Sekuru?*" the boy asked.

The old man laughed.

"Sekuru?" the boy was puzzled.

The old man looked at him.

"Please?"

The old man stroked the boy's head. "Talk of fishing," he said. "Or mouse-trapping. Ever trapped for mice?"

"No."

"Of course, you wouldn't have." He looked away. "You go to school these days."

"I don't like school!" Again, the old man was taken by surprise at the boy's violence. He looked at his grandson. The first son of his first son and only child. The boy's thirteen-year-old fists were clenched tightly and little tears danced in his eyes. *Could he believe in a little snotty-arse boy's voice? He looks earnest enough. But who doesn't, at the I-shall-never-die age of thirteen?* The old man looked away as if from the sight of the boy's death.

"I tell you I *hate* school!" the boy hissed.

"I hear you," the old man said quietly but didn't look at him. He was aware of the boy looking at him, begging him to believe him, clenching tighter his puny fists, his big ignorant eyes daring him to try him out on whatever milk-scented dream of heroics the boys might be losing sleep over at this difficult time of his life. The old man felt desolate.

"You don't believe me, do you, *Sekuru?*"

"Of course. I do!"

The boy suddenly uncoiled, ashamed and began to wring his hands, looking down at the ground.

That was unnecessarily harsh, the old man felt. So he stroked the boy's head again. *Thank you, ancestors, for our physical language that will serve our sons and daughters till we are dust.* He wished he could say something in words, something that the boy would clearly remember without it creating echoes in his head. He didn't want to give the boy an echo which he would later on mistake for the genuine thing.

"Is mouse-trapping very hard, *Sekuru?*" the boy asked, after some time.

"Nothing is ever easy, boy. But then, nothing is ever really hard for one who wants to learn."

"I would like to try it. Will you teach me?"

Physically, the old man didn't show anything, but he recoiled inwardly, the warmth in the center of him turned cold. *Boys' pranks, like the honey-bird luring you to a snake's nest. If only it were not this world, if only it were some other place where what we did today weren't our future, to be always there, held against us, to always see ourselves in . . .*

"And school?" he asked, as if he needed the boy to remind him again.

It was the boy's turn to look away, silent, unforgiving, betrayed.

As if stepping on newly-laid eggs, the old man learned a new language: not to touch the boy's head any more.

"There is your mother," he said, looking away, the better to make his grandson realize the seriousness of what he was talking about. From the corner of his eye he watched his grandson struggling with it, and saw her dismissed—not quite in the old way—but in a way that filled him with regrets for opportunities lost and a hopeless future.

"And if she doesn't mind?" the boy asked mischievously.

"You mean you will run away from school?" The old man restrained from stroking the boy's head.

"Maneto ran away from school and home two weeks ago. They don't know where he is right now."

Echoes, the old man repeated to himself. "But your mother is your mother," he said. *After all is said and done, basket-weaving never killed anyone. What kills is the rain and the hailstorms and the cold and the hunger when you are like this, when the echoes come.*

"I want to learn mouse-trapping, *Sekuru*," the boy said. "At school they don't teach us that. It's always figures and numbers and I don't know what they mean and they all laugh at me."

The grandfather carefully pinched, with right forefinger and thumb, the ridge of flesh just above the bridge of his nose, closed his eyes and sighed. The boy looked at him eagerly, excited, and when he saw his grandfather settle back comfortably against the wall, he clapped his hands, rising up. The old man looked at him and was touched by the boy's excitement and not for the first time, he wondered at the mystery that is called life.

"Good night, *Sekuru*," the boy said.

"Sleep well, Zakeo. Tell her that I delayed you if she asks where you have been." But the boy had already gone. The old man shook his head and prepared himself for another night of battle with those things that his own parents never told him exist.

They left the old man's hut well before sunrise the following day.

The boy had just come in and dumped his books in a corner of the room and they had left without any questions from the old man.

The grandfather trailed slowly behind the boy who ran

ahead of him, talking and gesticulating excitedly. The old man just listened to him and laughed with him.

It was already uncomfortably warm at this hour before sunrise. It was October. The white cowtracks spread out straight and flat before them, through and under the new thick flaming *musasa* leaves, so still in the morning air. Through patches in the dense foliage the sky was rusty-metal blue, October-opaque: the end of the long dry season, towards the *gukurahundi*, the very first heavy rains that would cleanse the air and clean the cowdung threshing floors of chaff, change and harden the crimson and bright-yellow leaves into hard green flat blades and bring back the stork, the millipede and the centipede, the fresh water crickets and the frogs, and the tiny yellow bird— *jesa*—that builds its nest on the river-reeds with the mouth of the nest facing down.

The air was harsh and still, and the old man thought, with renewed pleasure, of how he had almost forgotten the piercing whistle of that October-thirst bird, the *non-ono*, and the shrill jarring ring of the *cicada*.

The cowtracks fell toward the river. They left the bush and came out into the open where the earth, bare and black from the *chirimo* fires, was crisscrossed with thousands of cattle-tracks which focused on the water-holes. The old man smelt wet river clay.

"It's hot," the boy said.

"It's October, *Gumiguru*, the tenth and hottest month of the year." The old man couldn't resist telling the boy a bit of what he must be going through.

The boy took off his school shirt and wound it round his waist.

"With a dog worth the name of dog—when dogs were still dogs—a rabbit goes nowhere in this kind of terrain," the old man said, seeing how naturally the boy responded to—blended in with—the surroundings.

"Is that why people burn the grass?"

"Aa, so you know that, too?"

"Maneto told me."

"Well, it's partly why we burn the grass but mainly we burn it so that new grass grows for our animals."

Finally, the river, burnt down now by the long rainless months to a thin trickle of blood, running in the shallow, sandy bottom of a vlei. But there were still some fairly deep water-holes and ponds where fish could be found.

"These ponds are great for *muramba*," the old man said. "You need fairly clean flowing water for *magwaya*—the flat short-spear-blade fish."

They dug for worms in the wet clay on the river banks. The old man taught the boy how to break the soft earth with a digging stick for the worms.

"Worms are much easier to find," the old man said. "They stay longer on the hook. But a maggot takes a fish faster." Here the old man broke off, suddenly assailed with a very vivid smell of three-day-old cowdung, its soft cool feel and the entangled wriggling yellow mass of maggots packed in it.

"Locusts and hoppers are good too, but in bigger rivers, like Munyati where the fish are so big they would take another fish for a meal. Here the fish are smaller and cleverer. They don't like hoppers."

The old man looked into the coffee tin into which they were putting the worms and said, "Should be enough for me one day. There is always some other place we can get some more when these are finished. No need to use more than we should."

"But if they should get finished, *Sekuru?* Look, the tin isn't full yet." Zakeo looked intently at his grandfather. He wanted to fit in all the fishing that he would ever do before his mother discovered that he was playing truant from school. The old man looked at him. He understood. But he knew the greed of thirteen-year-olds and the retribution of the land and the soil when well-known laws were not obeyed.

"There will always be something when we get where these worms run out."

They walked downstream along the bank, their feet kicking up clouds of black and white ash.

The sun came up harsh and red-eyed upstream. They followed a tall straight shadow and a short stooped one along the stream until they came to a dark pool where the water, though opaque, wasn't really dirty.

"Here we are. I will get us some reeds for fishing rods while you prepare the lines. The hooks are already on the lines."

The old man produced from a plastic bag a mess of tangled lines and metal blue-painted hooks.

"Here you are. Straighten these out."

He then proceeded to cut some tall reeds on the river bank with a pocket knife the boy had seen him poking tobacco out of his pipe with.

"Excellent rods, look." He bent one of the reeds till the boy thought it was going to break, and when he let go, the rod shot back like a whip!

"See?" the old man said.

The boy smiled and the old man couldn't resist slapping him on the back.

The boy then watched the old man fasten the lines to the rods.

"In my day," the old man said, "there were woman knots and men knots. A woman knot is the kind that comes apart when you tug the line. A knot worth the name of whoever makes it shouldn't fall apart. Let the rod break, the line snap, but a knot, a real man's knot, should stay there."

They fished from a rock by a pool.

"Why do you spit on the bait before you throw the line into the pool, *Sekuru?*"

The old man grinned. "For luck, boy, there is nothing you do that fate has no hand in. Having a good hook, a good line, a good rod, good bait or a good pool is no guarantee that you will have good fishing. So little is knowledge, boy. The rest is just mere luck."

Zakeo caught a very small fish by the belly.

"What's this?" he asked.

"A very good example of what I call luck! They aren't usually caught by the belly. You need several all-way facing hooks in very clear water even without bait—for you to catch them like that!"

The boy laughed brightly and the old man suddenly heard the splash of a kingfisher as it flew away, fish in beak, and this mixed with the smell of damp-rotting leaves and moisty river clay, made the old man think: nothing is changed since our time. Then, a little later: except me. Self-consciously, with a sly look at the boy to make sure he wasn't seeing him, the old man straightened his shoulders.

The boy's grandfather hooked a frog and dashed it against a rock.

"What's that?" the boy asked.

"Know why I killed that—that—criminal?" he asked the boy.

"No, *Sekuru*."

"Bad luck. Throw it back into the pool and it's going to report to the fish."

"But what is it?"

"Uncle Frog."

"A frog!" The boy was surprised.

"Shhh," the old man said. "Not a frog. Uncle Frog. You hear?"

"But why Uncle Frog, *Sekuru*?"

"Just the way it is, boy. Like the rain. It comes on its own."

Once again, the boy didn't understand the old man's grown-up talk. The old man saw it and said, "That kind of criminal is only good for dashing against the rock. You don't eat frogs, do you?"

The boy saw that the old man was joking with him. "No," he said.

"So why should we catch him on our hook when we don't eat him or need him?"

"I don't know, *Sekuru*." The boy was clearly puzzled.

"He is the spy of the fish," the old man said in such a way that the boy sincerely believed him.

"But won't the fish notice his absence and wonder where he has gone to?"

"They won't miss him much. When they begin to do we will be gone. And when we come back here, they will have forgotten. Fish are just like people. They forget too easily."

It was grown-up talk again but the boy thought he would better not ask the man what he meant because he knew he wouldn't be answered.

They fished downriver till they came to where the Chambara met the Suka River.

"From here they go into Munyati," the old man said to himself, talking about his old hunting grounds; and to the boy, talking about the rivers.

"Where the big fish are," the boy said.

"You know that too?" the old man said, surprised.

"Maneto and his father spent days and days fishing the Munyati and they caught fish as big as men," the boy said seriously.

"Did Maneto tell you that?"

"Yes. And he said his father told him that *you, Sekuru,* were the only hunter who ever got to where the Munyati gets into the big water, the sea. Is that true?"

The old man pulled out his pipe and packed it. They were sitting on a rock. He took a long time packing and lighting the pipe.

"Is it true?" the boy asked.

"I was lost once," the old man said. "The Munyati goes into just another small water—but bigger than itself—and more powerful."

The boy would have liked to ask the man some more questions on this one but he felt that the old man wouldn't talk about it.

"You aren't angry, *Sekuru?*" the boy asked, looking up earnestly at his grandfather.

The old man looked at him, surprised again. *How do these milk-nosed ones know what we feel about all this?*

"Let's get back home," he said.

Something was bothering the old man, the boy realized, but what it was he couldn't say. All he wanted him to tell him was the stories he had heard from Maneto—whether they were true or not.

They had caught a few fish, enough for their supper, the boy knew, but the old man seemed angry. And that, the boy couldn't understand.

When they got back home the boy lit the fire, and with directions from the old man helped him to gut and salt the fish. After a very silent supper of sadza and salted fish the boy said he was going.

"Be sure to come back tomorrow," the old man said.

And the boy knew that whatever wrong he had done the old man, he would be told the following day.

Very early the following morning the boy's mother paid her father-in-law a visit. She stood in front of the closed door for a long time before she knocked. She had to collect herself.

"Who is there?" the old man answered from within

the hut. He had heard the footsteps approaching but he did not leave his blankets to open up for her.

"I would like to talk to you," she said, swallowing hard to contain her anger.

"Ah, it's Zakeo's mother?"

"Yes."

"And what bad winds blow you this way this early, *muroora?*"

"I want to talk to you about my son."

"Your son?"

She caught her breath quickly. There was a short silence. The old man wouldn't open the door.

"I want to talk about Zakeo," she called.

"What about him?"

"Please leave him alone."

"You are telling me that?"

"He must go to school."

"And so?"

She was quiet for a minute, then she said, "Please."

"What have I done to him?"

"He won't eat, he won't listen to me, and he doesn't want to go to school."

"And he won't listen to his father?" the old man asked.

"He listens to *you.*"

"And you have come here this early to beat me up?"

She swallowed hard. "He is the only one I have. Don't let him destroy his future."

"He does what he wants."

"At his age? What does he know?"

"Quite a lot."

She was very angry, he could feel it through the closed door.

She said, "He will only listen to you. Please, help us."

Through the door the old man could feel her tears coming. He said, "He won't even listen to his father?"

"His father?" he heard her snort.

"Children belong to the man, *you* know that," the old man warned her.

And he heard her angry feet as she went away.

Zakeo came an hour after his mother had left the old man's place. His grandfather didn't say anything to him.

He watched the boy throw his school bag in the usual corner of the hut, then after the usual greetings, he went out to bring in the firewood.

"Leave the fire alone," the old man said. "I am not cold."

"Sekuru?" The boy looked up, hurt.

"Today we go mouse-trapping in the fields."

"Are we going right now?"

"Yes."

"I'll make the fire if you like. We can go later."

"No. Now." The old man was quiet for some time, looking away from the boy.

"Are you all right, *Sekuru?"*

"Yes."

"We will go later when it's warm if you like."

The old man didn't answer him.

And as they came into the open fields with the last season's corn crop stubble, the boy felt that the old man wasn't quite well.

"We can do it some other day, *Sekuru.*"

His grandfather didn't answer.

They looked for the smooth mouse-tracks in the corn stubble and the dry grass. Zakeo carried the flat stones that the old man pointed out to him to the places where he wanted to set up the traps. He watched his grandfather setting the traps with the stone and two sticks. The sticks were about seven inches long each. One of them was the male and the other the female stick. The female was in the shape of a Y and the male straight.

The old man would place the female stick upright in the ground with the forked end facing up. The male would be placed in the fork parallel to the ground to hold up one end of the stone across the mousepath. The near end of the male would have a string attached to it and at the other end of the string would be the "trigger"—a match-stick-sized bit of straw that would hold the bait-stick against the male stick. The stone would be kept one end up by the delicate tension in the string and if a mouse took the bait the trigger would fly and the whole thing fall across the path onto the unfortunate victim.

The boy learned all this without words from the old

man, simply by carefully watching him set about ten traps all over the field that morning. Once he tried to ask a question and he was given a curt, "Mouths are for women." Then he too set up six traps and around noon the old man said, "Now we will wait."

They went to the edge of the field where they sat under the shade of a *mutsamwi* tree. The old man carefully, tiredly, rested his back against the trunk of the tree, stretched himself out, sighed, and closing his eyes, took out his pipe and tobacco pouch and began to load. The boy sat beside him, looking on. He sensed a tension he had never felt in his grandfather. Suddenly it wasn't fun any more. He looked away at the distant hills in the west. Somewhere behind those hills the Munyati went on to the sea, or the other bigger river which the old man hadn't told him about.

"Tell me a story, *Sekuru*," Zakeo said, unable to sit in his grandfather's silence.

"Stories are for the night," the old man said without opening his mouth or taking out the pipe. "The day is for watching and listening and learning."

Zakeo stood up and went a little way into the bush at the edge of the field. Tears stung his eyes but he would not let himself cry. He came back a little later and lay down beside the old man. He had hardly closed his eyes in sleep, just at that moment when the voices of sleep were beginning to talk, when, he felt the old man shaking him up.

"The day is not for sleeping," the old man said quietly but firmly. He still wasn't looking at Zakeo. The boy rubbed the sleep out of his eyes and blinked.

"Is that what they teach you at school?"

"*Sekuru?*"

The old man groaned in a way that told Zakeo what he thought of school.

The boy felt ashamed that he had hurt his grandfather. "I am sorry."

The grandfather didn't answer or look at him. Some time later he said, "Why don't you go and play with the other boys of your own age?"

"Where?"

"At school. Anywhere. Teach them what you have learned."

The boy looked away for some time. He felt deserted, the old man didn't want him around any more. Things began to blur in his eyes. He bit his lip and kept his head stiffly turned away from his grandfather.

"You can teach them all I have taught you. Huh?"

"I don't think they would listen to me," the boy answered, still looking away, trying to control his voice.

"Why?"

"They never listen to me."

"Why?"

"They—they—just don't." He bit his lower lip harder but a big tear plopped down on his hand. He quickly wiped away the tear and then for a terrible second they wouldn't stop coming. He was ashamed in front of his grandfather. The old man, who had never seen any harm in boys crying let him be.

When the boy had stopped crying he said, "Forget them."

"Who?"

"Your friends."

"They are not my friends. They are always laughing at me."

"What about?"

"O, all sorts of silly things."

"That doesn't tell me what sort of things."

"O, O, *lots of things!*" The boy's face was contorted in an effort to contain himself. Then he couldn't stop himself, "They are always at me saying your father is your mother's horse. Your mother rides hyenas at night. Your mother is a witch. Your mother killed so-and-so's child. Your mother digs up graves at night and you all eat human flesh which she hunts for you." He stopped. "O, lots of things I don't know!" The boy's whole body was tensed with violent hatred. The old man looked at him, amused.

"Do they really say that, now?"

"Yes and I know I could beat them all in a fight but the headmaster said we shouldn't fight and father doesn't want me to fight either. But I know I can lick them all in a fight."

The old man looked at the boy intensely for some time, his pipe in his hand, then he looked away to the side and spat out brown spittle. He returned the pipe to his mouth and said, "Forget them. They don't know a thing." He then sighed and closed his eyes once more and settled a little deeper against the tree.

The boy looked at him for a long time and said, "I don't want to go to school, Sekuru."

"Because of your friends?"

"They are not *my friends!*" He glared blackly at his grandfather, eyes flashing brilliantly and then, ashamed, confused, rose and walked a short distance away.

The old man looked at him from the corner of his eyes and saw him standing, looking away, body tensed, stiff and stubborn. He called out to him quietly, with gentleness, "Come back Zakeo. Come and sit here by me."

Later on the boy woke up from a deep sleep and asked the old man whether it was time yet for the traps. He had come out of sleep with a sudden startled movement as if he were a little strange animal that had been scared by hunting dogs.

"That must have been a very bad dream," the old man said.

Zakeo rubbed the sleep out of his eyes and blinked. He stared at the old man, then the sun which was very low in the west, painting everything with that ripe mango hue that always made him feel sad. Tall dark shadows were creeping eastward. He had that strange feeling that he had overslept into the next day. In his dream his mother had been shouting at him that he was late for school. A rather chilly wind was blowing across the desolate fields.

"Sit down here beside me and relax," the old man said. "We will give the mice one more hour to return home from visiting their friends. Or to fool themselves that it's already night and begin hunting."

Zakeo sat beside his grandfather and then he felt very relaxed.

"You see?" the old man said. "Sleep does you good when you are tired or worried. But otherwise don't trust sleeping during the day. When you get to my age you will learn to sleep without sleeping."

"How is that?"

"Never mind. It just happens."

Suddenly, sitting in silence with the old man didn't bother him any more.

"You can watch the shadows or the setting sun or the movement of the leaves in the wind—or the sudden agitation in the grass that tells you some little animal is moving in there. The day is for watching and listening and learning."

He had got lost somewhere in his thoughts when the old man said, "Time for the traps."

That evening the old man taught him how to gut the mice, burn off the fur in a low-burning flame, boil them till they were cooked and then arrange them in a flat open pan close to the fire to dry them so that they retained as little moisture as possible which made them firm but solidly pleasant on eating.

After supper the old man told him a story in which the hero seemed to be always falling into one misfortune after another, but always getting out through his own resourcefulness only to fall into a much bigger misfortune—on and on without the possibility of a happily ever after. It seemed as if the old man could go on and on inventing more and more terrible situations for his hero and improvising solutions as he went on till the boy thought he would never hear the end of the story.

"The story had no ending," the old man told him when he asked. He was feeling sleepy and he was afraid his mother would put a definite stop to his visits to the old man's place, even if it meant sending him out to some distant relative.

"Carry her these mice," the old man said when Zakeo said good night and stood up to go. "I don't think she will beat you tonight. She loves mice," he said with a little laugh.

But when he got home his mother threw the mice to the dog.

"What did I tell you?" she demanded of him, holding the oxhide strop.

Zakeo didn't answer. He was looking at his mother without blinking, ready to take the strop like Ndatofa, the hero in the old man's story. In the corner of his eye he saw his father working at his baskets, his eyes watering from the guttering smoking lamp he used to give him light. The crow's feet round his eyes made him appear as if he were wincing from some invisible pain.

"Don't you answer when I am talking to you?" his mother said.

The boy kept quiet, sitting erect, looking at his mother. Then she made a sound which he couldn't understand, a sound which she always uttered from some unliving part of her when she was mad. She was blind with rage but the boy held in his screams right down there where he knew screams and sobs came from. He gritted his teeth and felt the scalding lashes cutting deep into his back, right down to where they met the screams, where they couldn't go any farther. And each time the strop cut into him and he didn't scream his mother seemed to get madder and madder. His father tried to intervene but he quickly returned to his basket-weaving when the strop cracked into *his* back twice in quick merciless succession. It was then that Zakeo almost let out a deafening howl. He closed his eyes so tightly that veins stood out in his face. He felt on fire.

"I could kill you—you—you!" He heard his mother scream and he waited, tensed, for the strop and then suddenly as if someone had told him, he knew it wasn't coming. He opened his eyes and saw that his mother had dropped the strop and was crying herself. She rushed at him and began to hug him.

"My Zakeo! My own son. What are you doing this to me for? Tell me. What wrong have I done to you, ha? O, I know! I know very well who is doing this to you. He never wanted your father to marry me!"

He let her hug him without moving but he didn't let her hugging and crying get as far as the strop lashes. *That* was his own place. He just stopped her hugs and tears before they got *there*. And when he had had enough, he removed her arms from round him and stood up. His mother looked at him, surprised, empty hands that should have contained his body becoming emptier with the expression on her face.

"Where are you going, Zakeo?" It was as if *he* had slapped her.

"Do you care?"

"Zakeo! I am *your* mother! Do you know that? No one here cares for you more than I do! Not *him*!" pointing at his father. "And *not* even him!"—indicating in the direction of his grandfather's hut.

"You don't know anything," Zakeo said, without understanding what he meant by that but using it because he had heard it used of his classmates by the old man.

"You don't know anything," he repeated it, becoming more and more convinced of its magical effect on his mother who gaped at him as if she was about to sneeze.

As he walked out he caught sight of his father who was working furiously at his baskets, his head almost touching his knees and his back bent double.

The old man was awake when Zakeo walked in.

"Put another log on the fire," the old man said.

Zakeo quietly did so. His back ached but the heat had gone. He felt a little relaxedly cool.

"You didn't cry today."

The boy didn't answer.

"But you will cry one day."

The boy stopped raking the coals and looked at the old man, confused.

"You will cry one day and you will think your mother was right."

"But—" the boy stopped, lost. The night had turned suddenly chilly, freaky weather for October. He had been too involved with something else to notice it when he walked the half-mile between their place and the old man's. Now he felt it at his back and he shivered.

"Get into the blankets, you will catch a cold," the old man said.

Zakeo took off his shirt and left the shorts on. He got into the blankets beside the old man, on the side away from the fire.

"One day you will want to cry but you won't be able to," the old man said.

"Sekuru?"

"I said get into the blankets."

The boy lay down on his left side, facing the wall, away from the old man and drew up his knees with his hands between them. He knew he wouldn't be able to sleep on his back that night.

"Thirteen," the old man said, shaking his head.

"*Sekuru?*"

"Sleep now. I must have been dreaming."

Zakeo pulled the smoke-and-tobacco-smelling ancient blankets over his head.

"Who doesn't want to cry a good cry once in a while but there are just not enough tears to go round all of us?"

"*Sekuru?*"

"You still awake?"

"Yes."

"You want to go school?"

"No."

"Go to sleep then."

"I can't."

"Why?"

"I just can't."

"Try. It's good for you. Think of fishing."

"Yes, *Sekuru.*"

"Or mouse-trapping."

"And hunting?"

"Yes. Think all you like of hunting."

"You will take me hunting some day, won't you *Sekuru?*"

"Yes," the old man said and then after some time, "When the moon becomes your mother's necklace."

"You spoke, *Sekuru?*"

"I said yes."

"Thank you, *Sekuru.* Thank you very much."

"Thank you, *Sekuru,* thank you very much," the old man mimicked the boy, shook his head sadly—knowing that the following day the boy would be going to school. Soon, he too was fast asleep, dreaming of that mountain which he had never been able to climb since he was a boy.

Ngugi wa Thiong'o
(James T. Ngugi)
(b. 1938)

Born James Thiong'o in Limuru, Kenya, the author changed his name in 1977, replacing James, which to him had connotations of Christianity and colonial oppression, with a name in the major language of Kenya, Gikuyu. A critic of British colonial influences in Kenya and the disappointing, new black Kenyan ruling class that gained power upon Kenya's independence from Great Britain, Ngugi (as he is known throughout East Africa) has consistently employed his literary talent to depict the conditions of the people against a background of corrupt politicians and greedy businessmen. Educated at Makerere University where he received a B.A. and the University of Leeds in England, Ngugi became a professor at the University of Nairobi. There, he and several colleagues convinced the school's administrators to transform the English Department into the Department of African Languages and Literature. As a novelist, dramatist, essayist, and literary critic, Ngugi expressed such searing criticism of the Kenyan government, that he was arrested and imprisoned without a trial for a year by the authorities. In 1982, fearing for his safety after his theater group had been banned by the government, Ngugi left Kenya for London where he continued to write in self-imposed exile. In his first novel *Weep Not, Child*, he depicted the impact of the Mau Mau rebellion against the British administration in the 1950s on the lives of a young boy and his family. In a 1964 interview Ngugi commented:

> . . . in the novel I have tried to show the effect of the
> Mau Mau war on the ordinary man and woman who

were left in the villages. I think the terrible thing about the Mau Mau war was the destruction of family life, the destruction of personal relationships. You found a friend betraying a friend, father suspicious of the son, a brother doubting the sincerity or the good intentions of a brother, and above all these things the terrible fear under which all these people lived.

His four novels written in English, published by Heinemann and reprinted in the United States by Collier Books, are: *Weep Not, Child* (1964), *The River Between* (1965), *A Grain of Wheat* (1967), and *Petals of Blood* (1977); *Devil on the Cross* (Zimbabwe Publishing, 1983) was written in Gikuyu and translated by the author. A number of his stories are collected in *Secret Lives and Other Stories* (Heinemann, 1974; repr. Lawrence Hill, 1975). Among his plays are *The Black Hermit* (Heinemann, 1968), *This Time Tomorrow* (East African Literature Bureau, 1970), and *I Will Marry When I Want*, coauthored and translated with Ngugi wa Mirii (Heinemann, 1982). His works of nonfiction include *Writers in Politics: Essays* (Heinemann, 1981), *Detained: A Writer's Prison Diary* (Heinemann, 1981), *Barrel of a Pen: Resistance to Repression in Neo-Colonial Kenya* (New Beacon, 1983), *Decolonising the Mind: The Politics of Language in African Literature* (Heinemann, 1986), *Writing Against Neocolonialism* (Vita, 1986), and *Moving the Center: The Struggle for Cultural Freedoms* (Heinemann, 1992).

A MEETING IN THE DARK

He stood at the door of the hut and saw his old, frail but energetic father coming along the village street, with a rather dirty bag made out of a strong calico swinging by his side. His father always carried this bag. John knew what it contained: a Bible, a hymn-book and probably a notebook and a pen. His father was a preacher. He knew it was he who had stopped his mother from telling him stories when he became a man of God. His mother had stopped telling him stories long ago. She would say to him, "Now, don't ask for any more stories. Your father may come." So he feared his father. John went in and warned his mother of his father's coming. Then his father entered. John stood aside, then walked toward the door. He lingered there doubtfully, then he went out.

"John, hei, John!"

"Baba!"

"Come back."

He stood doubtfully in front of his father. His heart beat faster and there was that anxious voice within him asking: Does he know?

"Sit down. Where are you going?"

"For a walk, Father," he answered evasively.

"To the village?"

"Well-yes-no. I mean, nowhere in particular." John saw his father look at him hard, seeming to read his face. John sighed, a very slow sigh. He did not like the way his father eyed him. He always looked at him as though John was a sinner, one who had to be watched all the time. "I am," his heart told him. John guiltily refused to meet the old man's gaze and looked past him appealingly to his mother who was quietly peeling potatoes. But she seemed oblivious of everything around her.

"Why do you look away? What have you done?"

John shrank within himself with fear. But his face remained expressionless. He could hear the loud beats of his heart. It was like an engine pumping water. He felt no doubt his father knew all about it. He thought: "Why does he torture me? Why does he not at once say he knows?" Then another voice told him: "No, he doesn't know, otherwise he would have already jumped at you." A consolation. He faced his thoughtful father with courage.

"When is the journey?"

Again John thought: Why does he ask? I have told him many times.

"Next week, Tuesday," he said.

"Right. Tomorrow we go to the shops, hear?"

"Yes, Father."

"Then be prepared."

"Yes, Father."

"You can go."

"Thank you, Father." He began to move.

"John!"

"Yes?" John's heart almost stopped beating.

"You seem to be in a hurry. I don't want to hear of you loitering in the village. I know young men, going to show off just because you are going away? I don't want to hear of trouble in the village."

Much relieved, he went out. He could guess what his father meant by not wanting trouble in the village.

"Why do you persecute the boy so much?" Susana spoke for the first time. Apparently she had carefully listened to the whole drama without a word. Now was her time to speak. She looked at her tough old preacher who had been a companion for life. She had married him a long time ago. She could not tell the number of years. They had been happy. Then the man became a convert. And everything in the home put on a religious tone. He even made her stop telling stories to the child. "Tell him of Jesus. Jesus died for you. Jesus died for the child. He must know the Lord." She, too, had been converted. But she was never blind to the moral torture he inflicted on the boy (that was how she always referred to John), so that the boy had grown up mortally afraid of his father. She always wondered if it was love for the son. Or could it be a resentment because, well, they two had "sinned" before marriage? John had been the result of that sin. But that had not been John's fault. It was the boy who ought to complain. She often wondered if the boy had . . . but no. The boy had been very small when they left Fort Hall. She looked at her husband. He remained mute though his left hand did, rather irritably, feel about his face.

"It is as if he was not your son. Or do you . . ."

"Hm, Sister." The voice was pleading. She was seeking a quarrel but he did not feel equal to one. Really, women could never understand. Women were women, whether saved or not. Their son had to be protected against all evil influences. He must be made to grow in the footsteps of the Lord. He looked at her, frowning a little. She had made him sin but that had been a long time ago. And he had been saved. John must not tread the same road.

"You ought to tell us to leave. You know I can go away. Go back to Fort Hall. And then everybody . . ."

"Look, Sister," he hastily interrupted. He always called her sister. Sister-in-Lord, in full. But he sometimes wondered if she had been truly saved. In his heart he prayed: Lord, be with our sister Susana. Aloud, he continued, "You know I want the boy to grow in the Lord."

"But you torture him so! You make him fear you!"

"Why! He should not fear me. I have really nothing against him."

"It is you. You. You have always been cruel to him . . ." She stood up. The peelings dropped from her frock and fell in a heap on the floor. "Stanley!"

"Sister." He was startled by the vehemence in her voice. He had never seen her like this. Lord, take the devil out of her. Save her this minute. She did not say what she wanted to say. Stanley looked away from her. It was a surprise, but it seemed he feared his wife. If you had told the people in the village about this, they would not have believed you. He took his Bible and began to read. On Sunday he would preach to a congregation of brethren and sisters.

Susana, a rather tall, thin woman, who had once been beautiful, sat down again and went on with her work. She did not know what was troubling her son. Was it the coming journey? Still, she feared for him.

Outside, John was strolling aimlessly along the path that led from his home. He stood near the wattle tree which was a little way from his father's house and surveyed the whole village. They lay before his eyes, crammed, rows and rows of mud and grass huts, ending in sharply defined sticks that pointed to heaven. Smoke was coming out of various huts. It was an indication that many women had already come from the shambas. Night would soon fall. To the west, the sun—that lone daytime traveller—was hurrying home behind the misty hills. Again, John looked at the crammed rows and rows of huts that formed Makeno Village, one of the new mushroom "towns" that grew up all over the country during the Mau Mau war. It looked so ugly. A pain rose in his heart and he felt like crying—I hate you, I hate you! You trapped me alive. Away from you, it would never have happened. He did not shout. He just watched.

A woman was coming toward where he stood. A path into the village was just near there. She was carrying a big load of Kuni which bent her into an Akamba-bow shape. She greeted him. "Is it well with you, Njooni (John)?"

"It is well with me, Mother." There was no trace of bitterness in his voice. John was by nature polite. Everyone knew this. He was quite unlike the other proud, educated sons of the tribe—sons who came back from the other side of the waters with white or Negro wives who spoke English. And they behaved just like Europeans! John was a favorite, a model of humility and moral perfection. Everyone knew that though a clergyman's son, John would never betray the tribe. They still talked of the tribe and its ways.

"When are you going to—to—"

"Makerere?"

"Makelele." She laughed. The way she pronounced the name was funny. And the way she laughed, too. She enjoyed it. But John felt hurt. So everyone knew of this.

"Next week."

"I wish you well."

"Thank you, Mother."

She said quietly, as if trying to pronounce it better "Makelele." She laughed at herself again but she was tired. The load was heavy.

"Stay well, Son."

"Go well and in peace, Mother."

And the woman who all the time had stood, moved on, panting like a donkey, but she was obviously pleased with John's politeness.

John remained long, looking at her. What made such a woman live on day to day, working hard, yet happy? Had she much faith in life? Or was her faith in the tribe? She and her kind, who had never been touched by ways of the whiteman, looked as though they had something to cling to. As he watched her disappear, he felt proud that they should think well of him. He felt proud that he had a place in their esteem. And then came the pang. *Father will know. They will know.* He did not know what he feared most; the action his father would take when he found out, or the loss of the little faith the simple villagers had placed in him, when they knew. He feared to lose everything.

He went down to the small local tea-shop. He met many people who wished him well at the college. All of them knew that the priest's son had finished all the whiteman's learning in Kenya. He would now go to Uganda. They had read this in the *Baraza*, the Swahili Weekly. John did not stay long at the shop. The sun had already gone to rest and now darkness was coming. The evening meal was ready. His tough father was still at the table reading his Bible. He did not look up when John entered. Strange silence settled in the hut.

"You look unhappy." His mother first broke the silence.

John laughed. It was a nervous little laugh. "No, Mother," he hastily replied, nervously looking at his father. He secretly hoped that Wamuhu had not blabbed.

"Then I am glad."

She did not know. He ate his dinner and went out to his hut. A man's hut. Every young man had his own hut. John was never allowed to bring any girl visitor in there. Stanley did not want "trouble." Even to be seen standing with one was a crime. His father could easily thrash him. He feared his father, though sometimes he wondered why he feared him. He ought to have rebelled like the other educated young men. He lit the lantern. He took it in his hand. The yellow light flickered dangerously and then went out. He knew his hands were shaking. He lit it again and hurriedly took his big coat and a huge Kofia which were lying on the unmade bed. He left the lantern burning, so that his father would see it and think he was in. John bit his lower lip spitefully. He hated himself for being so girlish. It was unnatural for a boy of his age.

Like a shadow, he stealthily crossed the courtyard and went on to the village street.

He met young men and women lining the streets. They were laughing, talking, whispering. They were obviously enjoying themselves. John thought, they are more free

than I am. He envied their exuberance. They clearly
stood outside or above the strict morality that the educated ones had to be judged by. Would he have gladly
changed places with them? He wondered. At last, he
came to the hut. It stood at the very heart of the village.
How well he knew it—to his sorrow. He wondered what
he should do! Wait for her outside? What if her mother
came out instead? He decided to enter.

"Hodi!"

"Enter. We are in."

John pulled down his hat before he entered. Indeed
they were all there—all except she whom he wanted. The
fire in the hearth was dying. Only a small flame from a
lighted lantern vaguely illuminated the whole hut. The
flame and the giant shadow created on the wall seemed
to be mocking him. He prayed that Wamuhu's parents
would not recognize him. He tried to be "thin," and to
disguise his voice as he greeted them. They recognized
him and made themselves busy on his account. To be
visited by such an educated one, who knew all about the
whiteman's world and knowledge and who would now go
to another land beyond, was not such a frequent occurrence that it could be taken lightly. Who knew but he
might be interested in their daughter? Stranger things
had happened. After all, learning was not the only thing.
Though Wamuhu had no learning, yet she had charms
and could be trusted to captivate any young man's heart
with her looks and smiles.

"You will sit down. Take that stool."

"No!" He noticed with bitterness that he did not call
her "Mother."

"Where is Wamuhu?"

The mother threw a triumphant glance at her husband.
They exchanged a knowing look. John bit his lip again
and felt like bolting. He controlled himself with
difficulty.

"She has gone out to get some tea leaves. Please sit
down. She will cook you some tea when she comes."

"I am afraid . . ." he muttered some inaudible words
and went out. He almost collided with Wamuhu.

In the hut: "Didn't I tell you? Trust a woman's eye!"

"You don't know these young men."

"But you see John is different. Everyone speaks well of him and he is a clergyman's son."

"Y-e-e-s! A clergyman's son! You forget your daughter is circumcised." The old man was remembering his own day. He had found for himself a good virtuous woman, initiated in all the tribe's ways. And she had known no other man. He had married her. They were happy. Other men of his Rika had done the same. All the girls had been virgins, it being a taboo to touch a girl in that way, even if you slept in the same bed, as indeed so many young men and girls did. Then the white men had come, preaching a strange religion, strange ways, which all men followed. The tribe's code of behavior was broken. The new faith could not keep the tribe together. How could it? The men who followed the new faith would not let the girls be circumcised. And they would not let their sons marry circumcised girls. Puu! Look at what was happening. Their young men went away to the land of the whitemen. What did they bring? White women. Black women who spoke English. Aaa—bad. And the young men who were left just did not mind. They made unmarried girls their wives and then left them with fatherless children.

"What does it matter?" his wife was replying. "Is Wamuhu not as good as the best of them? Anyway, John is different."

"Different! Different! Paul! They are all alike. Those coated with the white clay of the whiteman's ways are the worst. They have nothing inside. Nothing—nothing here." He took a piece of wood and nervously poked the dying fire. A strange numbness came over him. He trembled. And he feared; he feared for the tribe. For now he saw it was not only the educated men who were coated with strange ways, but the whole tribe. The old man trembled and cried inside mourning for a tribe that had crumbled. The tribe had nowhere to go to. And it could not be what it was before. He stopped poking and looked hard at the ground.

"I wonder why he came. I wonder." Then he looked at his wife and said, "Have you seen strange behavior with your daughter?"

His wife did not answer. She was preoccupied with her own great hopes.

John and Wamuhu walked on in silence. The intricate streets and turns were well known to them both. Wamuhu walked with quick light steps; John knew she was in a happy mood. His steps were heavy and he avoided people, even though it was dark. But why should he feel ashamed? The girl was beautiful, probably the most beautiful girl in the whole of Limuru. Yet he feared being seen with her. It was all wrong. He knew that he could have loved her; even then he wondered if he did not love her. Perhaps it was hard to tell but, had he been one of the young men he had met, he would not have hesitated in his answer.

Outside the village he stopped. She, too, stopped. Neither had spoken a word all through. Perhaps the silence spoke louder than words. Both of them were only too conscious of each other.

"Do they know?" Silence. Wamuhu was probably considering the question. "Don't keep me waiting. Please answer me," he implored. He felt weary, very weary, like an old man who had suddenly reached his journey's end.

"No. You told me to give you one more week. A week is over today."

"Yes. That's why I came!" John whispered hoarsely.

Wamuhu did not speak. John looked at her. Darkness was now between them. He was not really seeing her; before him was the image of his father—haughtily religious and dominating. Again he thought: I, John, a priest's son, respected by all and going to college, will fall, fall to the ground. He did not want to contemplate the fall.

"It was your fault." He found himself accusing her. In his heart he knew he was lying.

"Why do you keep on telling me that? Don't you want to marry me?"

John sighed. He did not know what to do. He remembered a story his mother used to tell him. *Once upon a time there was a young girl . . . she had no home to go to and she could not go forward to the beautiful land*

*and see all the good things because the Irimu was on
the way . . .*

"When will you tell them?"

"Tonight."

He felt desperate. Next week he would go to the college. If he could persuade her to wait, he might be able
to get away and come back when the storm and consternation had abated. But then the government might withdraw his bursary. He was frightened and there was a sad
note of appeal as he turned to her and said, "Look,
Wamuhu, how long have you been pre- . . . I mean, like
this?"

"I have told you over and over again, I have been
pregnant for three months and mother is being suspicious. Only yesterday she said I breathed like a woman
with a child."

"Do you think you could wait for three weeks more?"

She laughed. Ah! the little witch! She knew his trick.
Her laughter always aroused many emotions in him.

"All right," he said. "Give me just tomorrow. I'll
think up something. Tomorrow I'll let you know."

"I agree. Tomorrow. I cannot wait any more unless
you mean to marry me."

Why not marry her? She is beautiful! Why not marry?
Do I love her or don't I?

She left. John felt as if she was deliberately blackmailing him. His knees were weak and lost strength. He could
not move but sank on the ground in a heap. Sweat
poured profusely down his cheeks, as if he had been
running hard under a strong sun. But this was cold sweat.
He lay on the grass; he did not want to think. Oh, no!
He could not possibly face his father. Or his mother. Or
Reverend Carstone who had had such faith in him. John
realized that, though he was educated, he was no more
secure than anybody else. He was no better than Wamuhu. Then why don't you marry her? He did not know.
John had grown up under a Calvinistic father and learnt
under a Calvinistic headmaster—a missionary! John tried
to pray. But to whom was he praying? To Carstone's
God? It sounded false. It was as if he was blaspheming.
Could he pray to the God of the tribe? His sense of guilt
crushed him.

He woke up. Where was he? Then he understood. Wamuhu had left him. She had given him one day. He stood up; he felt good. Weakly, he began to walk back home. It was lucky that darkness blanketed the whole earth and him in it. From the various huts, he could hear laughter, heated talks or quarrels. Little fires could be seen flickering red through the open doors. Village stars, John thought. He raised up his eyes. The heavenly stars, cold and distant, looked down on him impersonally. Here and there, groups of boys and girls could be heard laughing and shouting. For them life seemed to go on as usual. John consoled himself by thinking that they, too, would come to face their day of trial.

John was shaky. Why! Why could he not defy all expectations, all prospects of a future, and marry the girl? No. No. It was impossible. She was circumcised and he knew that his father and the church would never consent to such a marriage. She had no learning—or rather she had not gone beyond standard four. Marrying her would probably ruin his chances of ever going to a university.

He tried to move briskly. His strength had returned. His imagination and thought took flight. He was trying to explain his action before an accusing world—he had done so many times before, ever since he knew of this. He still wondered what he could have done. The girl had attracted him. She was graceful and her smile had been very bewitching. There was none who could equal her and no girl in the village had any pretense to any higher standard of education. Women's education was very low. Perhaps that was why so many Africans went "away" and came back married. He too wished he had gone with the others, especially in the last giant student airlift to America. If only Wamuhu had learning . . . and she was uncircumcised . . . then he might probably rebel.

The light still shone in his mother's hut. John wondered if he should go in for the night prayers. But he thought against it; he might not be strong enough to face his parents. In his hut the light had gone out. He hoped his father had not noticed it.

John woke up early. He was frightened. He was normally not superstitious, but still he did not like the dreams of the night. He dreamt of circumcision; he had just been initiated in the tribal manner. Somebody—he could not tell his face, came and led him because he took pity on him. They went, went into a strange land. Somehow, he found himself alone. The somebody had vanished. A ghost came. He recognized it as the ghost of the home he had left. It pulled him back; then another ghost came. It was the ghost of the land he had come to. It pulled him forward. The two consented. Then came other ghosts from all sides and pulled him from all sides so that his body began to fall into pieces. And the ghosts were insubstantial. He could not cling to any. Only they were pulling him and he was becoming nothing, nothing . . . he was now standing a distance away. It had not been him. But he was looking at the girl, the girl in the story. She had nowhere to go. He thought he would go to help her; he would show her the way. But as he went to her, he lost his way . . . he was all alone . . . something destructive was coming toward him, coming, coming . . . He woke up. He was sweating all over.

Dreams about circumcision were no good. They portended death. He dismissed the dream with a laugh. He opened the window only to find the whole country clouded in mist. It was perfect July weather in Limuru. The hills, ridges, valleys and plains that surrounded the village were lost in the mist. It looked such a strange place. But there was almost a magic fascination in it. Limuru was a land of contrasts and evoked differing emotions at different times. Once John would be fascinated and would yearn to touch the land, embrace it or just be on the grass. At another time he would feel repelled by the dust, the strong sun and the pot-holed roads. If only his struggle were just against the dust, the mist, the sun and the rain, he might feel content. Content to live here. At least he thought he would never like to die and be buried anywhere else but at Limuru. But there was the human element whose vices and betrayal of other men were embodied in the new ugly villages. The last night's incident rushed into his mind like a flood, making him weak again. He got out of his blankets and went out. Today he would go to the shops. He was uneasy. An odd feeling was coming to him—in fact had been coming—that his relationship with his father was perhaps unnatural. But he dismissed the thought. Tonight would be the day of reckoning. He shuddered to think of it. It was unfortunate that his scar had come into his life at this time, when he was going to Makerere and it would have brought him closer to his father.

They went to the shops. All day long, John remained quiet as they moved from shop to shop buying things from the lanky but wistful Indian traders. And all day long, John wondered why he feared his father so much. He had grown up fearing him, trembling whenever he spoke or gave commands. John was not alone in this.

Stanley was feared by all.

He preached with great vigor, defying the very gates of hell. Even during the Emergency, he had gone on preaching, scolding, judging and condemning. All those who were not saved were destined for hell. Above all, Stanley was known for his great and strict moral observances—a bit too strict, rather pharisaical in nature. None noticed this; certainly not the sheep he shepherded. If an elder broke any of the rules, he was liable to be expelled, or excommunicated. Young men and women, seen standing together "in a manner prejudicial to church and God's morality" (they were one anyway) were liable to be excommunicated. And so, many young men tried to serve two masters by seeing their girls at night and going to church by day. The alternative was to give up church-going altogether.

Stanley took a fatherly attitude to all the people in the village. You must be strict with what is yours. And because of all this he wanted his house to be a good example of this to all. That is why he wanted his son to grow upright. But motives behind many human actions may be mixed. He could never forget that he had also fallen before his marriage. Stanley was also a product of the disintegration of the tribe due to the new influences.

The shopping did not take long. His father strictly observed the silences between them and neither by word nor by hint did he refer to last night. They reached home and John was thinking that all was well when his father called him.

"John."

"Yes, Father."

"Why did you not come for prayers last night?"

"I forgot . . ."

"Where were you?"

Why do you ask me? What right have you to know where I was? One day I am going to revolt against you. But, immediately, John knew that this act of rebellion was something beyond him—unless something happened to push him into it. It needed someone with something he lacked.

"I-I-I mean, I was . . ."

"You should not sleep so early before prayers. Remember to turn up tonight."

"I will."

Something in the boy's voice made the father look up. John went away relieved. All was still well.

Evening came. John dressed like the night before and walked with faltering steps toward the fatal place. The night of reckoning had come. And he had not thought of anything. After this night all would know. Even Reverend Carstone would hear of it. He remembered Reverend Carstone and the last words of blessing he had spoken to him. No! he did not want to remember. It was no good remembering these things; and yet the words came. They were clearly written in the air, or in the darkness of his mind. "You are going into the world. The world is waiting even like a hungry lion, to swallow you, to devour you. Therefore, beware of the world. Jesus said, Hold fast unto . . ." John felt a pain—a pain that wriggled through his flesh as he remembered these words. He contemplated the coming fall. Yes! He, John, would fall from the Gates of Heaven down through the open waiting Gates of Hell. Ah! He could see it all, and all that people would say. All would shun his company, all would give him oblique looks that told so much. The trouble with John was that his imagination magnified the fall from the heights of "goodness" out of all proportion. And fear of people and consequences ranked high in the things that made him contemplate the fall with so much horror.

John devised all sorts of punishment for himself. And when it came to thinking of a way out, only fantastic and impossible ways of escape came into his head. He simply could not make up his mind. And because he could not, and because he feared Father and people and did not know his true attitude to the girl, he came to the agreed spot having nothing to tell her. Whatever he did looked fatal to him. Then suddenly he said:

"Look, Wamuhu. Let me give you money. You might then say that someone else was responsible. Lots of girls have done this. Then that man may marry you. For me, it is impossible. You know that."

"No. I cannot do that. How can you, you . . ."

"I will give you two hundred shillings."

"No!"

"Three hundred."

"No!" She was almost crying. It pained her to see him so.

"Four hundred, five hundred, six hundred." John had begun calmly but now his voice was running high. He was excited. He was becoming more desperate. Did he know what he was talking about? He spoke quickly, breathlessly, as if he was in a hurry. The figure was rapidly rising—nine thousand, ten thousand, twenty thousand . . . He is mad. He is foaming. He is quickly moving toward the girl in the dark. He has lain his hands on her shoulders and is madly imploring her in a hoarse voice. Deep inside him, something horrid that assumes the threatening anger of his father and the village seems to be pushing him. He is violently shaking. Wamuhu, while his mind tells him that he is patting her gently. Yes, he is out of his mind. The figure has now reached fifty thousand shillings and is increasing. Wamuhu is afraid. She extricates herself from him, the mad, educated son of a religious clergyman, and runs. He runs after her and holds her, calling her by all sorts of endearing words. But he is shaking her, shake, shake, her, her—he tried to hug her by the neck, presses. . . . She lets out one horrible scream and then falls on the ground. And so all of a sudden, the struggle is over, the figures stop, and John stands there trembling like the leaf of a tree on a windy day.

Soon everyone will know that he has created and then killed.

SELECTED AFRICAN ANTHOLOGIES

Achebe, Chinua and C. L. Innes, eds. *African Short Stories*. London: Heinemann, 1985.

Bruner, Charlotte H., ed. *Unwinding Threads: Writing by Women in Africa*. London and Exeter, NH: Heinemann, 1983.

Gordiner, Nadine and Lionel Abrahams, eds. *South African Writing Today*. Harmondsworth: Penguin Books, 1967.

Gray, Stephen, ed. *The Penguin Book of Southern African Stories*. Harmondsworth: Penguin Books, 1985.

Komey, Ellis Ayitey and Ezekiel Mphahlele, eds. *Modern African Stories*. London: Faber and Faber, 1964.

Larson, Charles R., ed. *African Short Stories: A Collection of Contemporary African Writing*. New York: Collier Books, 1970.

Malan, Robin, ed. *Ourselves in Southern Africa: An Anthology of Southern African Writing*. New York: St. Martin's Press, 1989.

Mutloatse, Moothobi, ed. *Africa South: Contemporary Writings*. London: Ravan Press/Heinemann, 1980 and 1981.

Obradovic, Nadezda, ed. *Looking for a Rain God: An Anthology of Contemporary African Short Stories*. New York: Simon & Schuster/Fireside, 1990.

Rive, Richard, ed. *Modern African Prose*. London: Heinmann, 1964 and 1970.

Schanlon, Paul A., ed. *Stories from Central and Southern Africa*. London: Heinemann, 1983.

Wright, David, ed. *South African Stories*. London: Faber and Faber, 1960.

CHINESE
STORIES

Wang Anyi
(b. 1954)

The daughter of a famous woman writer and member of the Communist Party, Ru Zhijuan, and a father who was denounced as a Rightist when she was three years old, Wang Anyi writes that she was "born and raised in a lane of Shanghai's wealthiest and most prosperous thoroughfare, Huaihai Road." As a result of the Cultural Revolution, however, she was not permitted to continue her education beyond the junior high school level. Instead, at age fifteen, she was assigned as a farm laborer to a commune in Anhui, an impoverished area near the Huai River, which was plagued by famine. Transferred in 1972 to a cultural troupe in Xuzhou, in 1976 she began to publish short stories. One story that grew out of this experience, "Life in a Small Courtyard," recounts the housekeeping details, marriage customs, and relationships of a group of actors assigned to very limited space where they live and rehearse between their professional engagements. She was allowed to return home to Shanghai in 1978 to work as an editor of the magazine *Childhood*. In 1980 she received additional professional training from the Chinese Writers' Association, and her fiction achieved national prominence, winning literary awards in China. A novella and six of her stories have been translated and collected in *Lapse of Time* (China Books, 1988). In his preface to that collection, Jeffrey Kinkley notes that Anyi is a realist whose stories "are about everyday urban life" and that the author "does not stint in describing the brutalizing density, the rude jostling, the interminable and often futile waiting in line that accompany life in the Chinese big city." Tillie Olsen has commented on Anyi's work:

In these wonderful stories, Wang Anyi has done even
more than create a vivid gallery of how some human
beings intensely lived through years of enormous
upheaval. . . . Through the magic of art, she has en-
meshed us in these lives and carried us into understanding the circumstances, humanity, pain, and
promise of those years.

Two novels of her controversial trilogy, *Three Loves*,
have been translated into English: *Love in a Small Town*,
published in China in 1986 (Renditions Paperbacks,
1988) and *Love on a Barren Mountain* (Renditions Paperbacks, 1990); *Baotown* was published in 1989 by
Norton.

THE DESTINATION

Over the loudspeaker came the announcement, "The
train is arriving at Shanghai terminal. . . ."

Dozing passengers opened their eyes. "We're arriving
in Shanghai."

"We're nearing the terminal."

The impatient ones removed their shoes and climbed
onto their seats to reach for their luggage.

A group of middle-aged men from Xinjiang began
making plans. "We'll take a bath as soon as we check
into a hotel. Then we'll call the heavy-machinery plant
and go out to a Western-style restaurant."

"Right. We'll have Western food." Their spirits rose.
They had gone to work in Xinjiang after their university
years in Beijing, Fuzhou and Jiangsu. Though they retained their accents, their appearance and temperament
were "Xinjiangized," weatherbeaten and blunt. When
Chen Xin asked casually about Xinjiang after he got on
the train at Nanjing, they gave him a detailed and enthu-

siastic account of the region: the humor and wit of Xinjiang's different ethnic minorities, the beautiful songs they sang, the graceful dances and lively girls. They also described their own life there, how they fished and hunted. Expressive and eloquent, they painted an appealing picture.

"How long will you be in Shanghai?" one of the group, a man from Beijing, asked, patting Chen Xin on the shoulder.

With a smile, he turned around from gazing out the window. "I've come back for good."

"Got a transfer?"

"Right."

"Bringing your wife and children?"

"I haven't any," he blushed. "I couldn't have come back if I'd been married."

"My, you must be determined." Chen Xin's shoulder received a heartier slap. "You Shanghainese can't survive away from Shanghai."

"It's my home," Chen Xin said, justifying himself.

Chen Xin smiled.

"One should be able to find interesting things anywhere. You skate in Harbin, swim in Guangzhou, eat big chunks of mutton with your hands in Xinjiang and Western food in Shanghai. . . . Wherever fate lands you, you look for something interesting and enjoy it as best you can. Maybe that's what makes life interesting."

Chen Xin only smiled. Absentmindedly he kept his eyes on the fields flitting past his window, fields carefully divided into small plots and planted like squares of embroidery—there were patches of yellow, dark and light green and, beside the river, purple triangles. To eyes used to the vast, fertile soil of the north, the highly utilized and carefully partitioned land struck him as narrow and jammed. But he had to admit that everything was as fresh and clean as if washed by water. This was the south, the outskirts of Shanghai. Oh, Shanghai!

The train hurtled past the fields and low walls and entered the suburbs. Chen Xin saw factories, buildings, streets, buses and pedestrians. . . . Shanghai became closer and tangible. His eyes moistened and his heart thumped. Ten years ago, when classes were suspended during the Cultural Revolution, he and other sent-down youth left for the countryside. At that time, as Shanghai faded into the distance, he had not expected to return. No. He probably had thought about it. In the countryside, he plowed, planted, harvested wheat, dredged rivers, and tried to get a job or admittance to a university. . . . He finally enrolled in a teachers' college. After graduation he was assigned to teach in a middle school in a small town. Able to earn his own living at last, his struggles should have ended; he could start a new life. But he felt he had not arrived at his destination. Not yet. He was still unsettled and expectant, waiting for something. He only realized what he had been waiting for, what his destination really was, when large numbers of school-leavers returned to Shanghai after the fall of the Gang of Four.

In the past decade, he had been to Shanghai on holiday and on business. But with every visit he only felt the distance between him and Shanghai grow. He had become a stranger, an outsider, whom the Shanghainese looked down upon. And he found their superiority and conceit intolerable. The pity and sympathy of his friends and acquaintances were as unbearable. For at the back of that lay pride. Still he was forced to admire Shanghai's progress and superiority. The department stores were full of all kinds of goods and people dressed in the latest fashions. Clean, elegant restaurants. New films at the cinemas. Shanghai represented what was new in China. But above all there was his home, his mother, brothers, and dead father's ashes. . . . He smiled, his eyes brimming with tears. He would make any sacrifice to return. He had acted as soon as he learned that his mother was retiring and that one of her children could take her job. He had gone here and there to get his papers stamped, a troublesome and complicated business. He had fought a tense and energetic battle, but he had won.

The train pulled into the station. As Chen Xin opened the window, a cool breeze—a Shanghai breeze—rushed in. He saw his younger brother, now grown tall and handsome. Seeing him, the youth ran beside the train calling happily, "Second brother!" Chen Xin's heart shrank with regret. He calmed down, remembering how, ten years earlier, his elder brother had run beside the train too at his departure.

The train came to a halt. His younger brother caught up, panting. Chen Xin was too busy talking to him and handing him his luggage to notice that the cheerful group of middle-aged men were bidding him farewell.

"Elder brother, his wife, and Nannan are here too. They're outside. We only got one platform ticket with your telegram, saying you were coming. Have you got a lot of luggage?"

"I can manage. How's Mom?"

"She's OK. She's getting dinner ready. She got up at three this morning to buy food for you."

A lump rose in his throat; he lowered his head in silence. His brother fell silent too.

They moved quietly out of the long station. At the exit his elder brother, his wife, and son, Nannan, took his suitcases from him. They struggled under the weight for a few steps and then gave them back to him. Everybody laughed. His elder brother clasped him around his shoulders while his younger brother took his arm. His sister-in-law followed, carrying Nannan.

"Have you got all the necessary papers?" his elder brother inquired. "Tomorrow I'll ask for leave and take you to the labor bureau."

"I can take him. I haven't got anything to do," offered his younger brother.

Chen Xin's heart trembled again. He turned to him with a smile. "OK. No. 3 can take me."

It took three buses to reach home. His mother greeted him, lowering her head to wipe away tears. The three sons were at a loss for words, not knowing how and also too shy to express their feelings. All they could say was, "What's there to cry about?" It was his sister-in-law who knew how to stop her. She said, "This calls for a celebration, Mum. You should be rejoicing."

The tension lifted. "Let's eat," they said to one another. The table was moved from his mother's six-square-meter room to the big room his elder brother and his wife occupied. Chen Xin looked around. The room where he and his two brothers had once lived had a different appearance. The light green wallpaper was decorated with an oil painting and a wall light. Smart new furniture had been made to fit the room. The color was special too.

"What do you call this color?" asked Chen Xin.

"Reddish brown. It's the fashion," answered his younger brother with the air of an expert.

Nannan moved a stool over to a chest of drawers, climbed on it, and turned on the cassette player. The strong rhythm of the music raised everybody's spirits.

"You live well!" The excitement in Chen Xin's voice was obvious.

His elder brother smiled apologetically. After a long pause he said, "I'm glad you're finally back."

His sister-in-law carried in some food, "Now that you're back, you should find a sweetheart and get married."

"I'm old and ugly. Who'd want me?"

That made everyone laugh.

More than ten different dishes were placed on the table: diced pork and peanuts, braised spareribs, crucian carp soup. . . . Everybody piled food onto Chen Xin's plate. Even Nannan copied them. They went on serving him even when his plate was like a hill, as if to compensate for the ten hard years he had spent away from home. His elder brother almost emptied the stir-fried eel, Chen Xin's favorite dish, onto his plate. Though younger by three years, Chen Xin had always been his brother Chen Fang's protector. Chen Fang, tall and slender, had been nicknamed String Bean. His school marks were high, but outside of school he was poor at sports and had slow reflexes. His legs always got caught in the rope when it was his turn to jump. When playing cops and robbers, the side he was on was sure to lose. Chen Xin always fought for him when no one wanted him. "If you don't want my brother, I won't play either. And if I don't play, I'll make sure there'll be no game." And he meant what he said, so the boys compromised, fearing the terrible havoc he'd wreak on the one hand and hating to lose a popular, funny playmate on the other. Later, when Chen Fang had to wear glasses, he looked so scholarly that his nickname became Bookworm. For some reason Chen Xin considered this even more insulting than the previous one. He brought an end to it by bashing anyone who dared to utter it. When classes were suspended during the Cultural Revolution, he had finished junior middle and his brother senior middle school. The government's policy was clear; only one son could work in Shanghai, the other must go to the countryside. His heartbroken mother had mumbled tearfully, "The palm and the back of my hand. . . . They are both my flesh and blood." Feeling sorry for her, Chen Xin volunteered, "I'll go to the countryside. Brother's a softy; he'll get bullied. Let him stay in Shanghai. I'll go. . . ." when he set out, Chen Fang had seen him off at the station, standing woodenly behind a group of friends, not daring to meet his eyes. As the train pulled out, Chen Fang moved forward to grasp Chen Xin's hand and run beside the train even after the speeding locomotive pulled them apart.

Chen Xin had finally returned. Overcome by all sorts of emotions, no one was particularly good at expressing them, so they transformed them into action. After supper his elder brother served tea while his wife made up a bed in the hut they had constructed in the courtyard. His younger brother stood in a queue for Chen Xin to go to the public bathhouse. When Chen Xin had eaten his fill and bathed, he lay on the double bed he was to share with his younger brother, feeling as relaxed as if he were drunk. The clean, warm bedding had a pleasant smell. The lamp on the desk beside the bed gave the simple hut a soft glow. Someone had placed a stack of magazines beside his pillow; the family knew and had remembered that he always read himself to sleep. Oh, home. This was home! He had returned home after ten years. Feeling a peace that he had never felt before, he closed his eyes and dozed off without reading. At dusk he woke up. Someone had come in and turned off the light. He opened his eyes in the darkened room and peacefully drifted back to slumber.

Early in the morning Chen Xin and his younger brother went to the labor bureau to start the formalities. The triangular lot beside the bus stop was filled with tailors' stalls and sewing machines. A young man with a measuring tape hanging round his neck accosted them.

"Do you want something made?" They shook their heads and walked away. Curious, Chen Xin turned to look back at the young man who was dressed up like a model, soliciting customers.

His brother tugged at him. "The bus's coming. They're all school-leavers waiting for jobs. Shanghai's full of them." Chen Xin was astonished. His brother, shoving his way onto a bus, stopped at the door and called out to him, "Come on, Second Brother."

"Let's wait for the next one." The bus filled to bursting and the crowd at the bus stop made Chen Xin hesitate.

"More people will come. Get on quick." His brother's voice seemed to come from afar.

Chen Xin was strong. He could push. He shoved and squeezed until he caught the door handle and placed his feet on the steps. Then he mustered his strength and, amid cries and curses, pushed deeper into the bus to stand beside a window where he could hang on to the back of the seat. But he was crammed in and uncomfortable, bumping against people's heads or backs, having a hard time fitting in. All round him the passengers grumbled.

"Look at the way you're standing!"

"Just like a door plank."

"Outsiders are always so awkward on buses."

"Who're you calling an outsider?" An indignant No. 3 squeezed his way over, ready to pick a quarrel. Chen Xin tugged him. "Don't mind them. It's so crowded. Don't fight."

Softly, No. 3 gave him a tap. "Turn this way. Right. Hold the seat with your left hand. That's better. See?"

It was true. Chen Xin heaved a long sigh. He finally fitted in with his chest pressed against a back and his back against someone else's chest. At least his feet touched the floor. He turned his head to look and noticed a silent understanding among the passengers. Facing in the same direction, they all stood in a straight line, one behind the other. This way, the bus could fill to capacity. He thought of the remote town he had lived in where passengers squeezed in any old way, no scientific method at all. The bus held fewer people while the crowding and discomfort were the same. Shanghainese could adapt themselves to smaller spaces better.

The female conductor's voice came through a loud-speaker in Beijing and Shanghai dialects: "The next stop is Xizang Zhong Road. Those who're getting off please get ready." With royal airs, these women looked proud and disdainful, like strict disciplinarians. But these announcements helped passengers. He recalled again the buses and women conductors in that little town: battered, dusty buses shooting off before their doors were closed; unenthusiastic conductors never announcing stops, closing doors on passengers and catching their clothes in them. They had no rules at all. Things were shipshape in Shanghai. In that sort of environment, you had to do things properly.

When they got off the bus, No. 3 took Chen Xin down a street to one of the city's free markets. There were vegetables, fish, poultry, woollen sweaters, sandals, purses and hair clips, and stalls with fried food and meat dumplings. Below a placard announcing folk toys were paper lanterns and clay dolls. Seeing a market like that, Chen Xin had to laugh. What a strong contrast with Shanghai's wealthy, modern Nanjing Road.

"There are a lot of markets like this in Shanghai," explained No. 3. "The government encourages school-leavers to be self-employed."

The mention of the unemployed youth made Chen Xin frown. After pausing, he asked, "What was the matter with you, No, 3? Why did you fail the university entrance exam again?"

"No. 3 lowered his head. "I don't know. I guess I'm stupid."

"Will you take it again next year?"

After a long silence, No. 3 said haltingly, "I might fail a third time."

That made Chen Xin angry. "You've no confidence in yourself."

No. 3 smiled honestly. "I'm not cut out to study. I forget what I learn."

"Your elder brother and I didn't have the chance to continue our studies. You're the only one in the family who can attend a university. But you've no ambition."

No. 3 fell silent.

"What are your plans then?"

No. 3 gave a laugh but said nothing. Just then someone called out behind them, "Chen Xin!"

They turned to face a woman leading a handsome little boy. She was in her thirties, with long permed hair and stylish clothes. Chen Xin couldn't place her.

"Have I grown so old that you don't recognize me?"

"Why, it's you, Yuan Xiaoxin! You don't look older, just prettier," Chen Xin laughed.

Yuan laughed with him. "Come on. We were in the same group in the countryside for two years, and yet you couldn't place me. What a poor memory!"

"No. It was just that I didn't expect to see you. Weren't you among the first batch to get a job? Are you still at Huaibei Colliery?"

"No. I came back to Shanghai last year."

"How come?"

"It's a long story. How about you?"

"I returned yesterday."

"Oh." She didn't show surprise. "Zhang Xinhu and Fang Fang are back too."

"Good," Chen Xin said excitedly. "So half the group has returned. We must get together sometime. Our hard times are finally over."

She gave a faint smile, revealing fine wrinkles at the corners of her eyes.

"Uncle," chirped the little boy. "You've got white hair like my grandpa."

Chen Xin laughed, bending down to take the boy's hand. "This is your son?" he addressed Yuan.

"He's my sister's son," she explained blushing. "I'm not married. If I were I couldn't have come back."

"Oh." Chen Xin was surprised. Having graduated the same year as Chen Fang, Yuan must be thirty-three or thirty-four. "But why didn't you marry after your return?"

"Well, how shall I put it? One has to wait for an opportunity."

Chen Xin said nothing.

Caressing the little boy's fluffy hair she said softly, "Sometimes I felt that the sacrifices I made to return to Shanghai weren't worth it."

Chen Xin tried to console her, "Don't say that. It's good to be back."

"We'll be late for the film, Aunty," cried the boy.

"Right, we ought to be going." She looked up and smiled at Chen Xin. "Sorry if I dampened your spirits. But you're different. You're a man, and you're young. You'll find happiness."

Chen Xin's heart grew heavy as he watched her disappear into the crowd.

No. 3 commented, "She's a dead crab."

"What do you mean?"

"She's over thirty and hasn't got a boyfriend. She's like a dead crab. No hope."

"It isn't that she can't find one. She said she was waiting for someone to come along. Don't you see?"

Whether he understood or not, he answered disapprovingly, "Whatever you say, she's got a big problem. Men in their thirties are married, or else handicapped or ineligible. Eligible ones are hard to please and like young, beautiful girls. There are handfuls of twenty-year-old girls up for grabs."

Chen Xin meant to say that some people were waiting for love. But then he had second thoughts. That was beyond No. 3. Youngsters like him were so different from his generation. Throwing a sidelong glance at his brother, he said instead, "You really know a lot."

No. 3 looked very proud. The sarcasm was lost on him. Feeling apologetic, Chen Xin added in a kinder tone, "What do you do every day?"

"Nothing much except watch television, listen to the radio and sleep."

"What are your plans?"

He said nothing. When they were walking up the steps of the labor bureau, No. 3 confided, "I'd like to get a job."

Chen Xin halted. No. 3 turned to urge him, "Come on." His eyes were frank and sincere. Still Chen Xin avoided them.

He started work at his mother's factory, which was a long way away. It took him an hour and twenty minutes and three buses to get there. Assigned to work at a lathe, he had to learn from scratch; mockingly, he called himself a thirty-year-old apprentice. What he found hard was not the lathe but the adjustments to the new life and the fast pace. He had to run from the first bus to catch the second and then the third. . . . He mustn't miss any of the connections, which meant no smoking or daydreaming. He also found it hard to adjust to three rotating shifts. After a week on night shift it took more than two weeks to catch up on his sleep; as a result he was always tired. Within two months his face grew thinner. People said he looked better that way for the weight he had gained before he came home was not healthy. It was the result of the flour and stodge he had eaten in the North, whereas in Shanghai people ate rice.

Still he was glad he had returned to Shanghai even though his contentment was marred by a feeling of emptiness. Something was missing. The longing of the past ten years, an ache that had affected his sleep and appetite, had come to an end. But it had given him a goal to fight for. Now he was at a loss and felt empty. Maybe he was too happy being back? He must start a new life even though he had not given much serious thought to what it should be like. Things were only just beginning.

Ending the early shift, he dragged his legs, numb after eight hours' standing, to the bathroom, had a bath, changed, and left the factory. At the bus stop passengers spilled from the pavement onto the middle of the street. At least three buses were late. He waited for ten minutes but there was no sign of a bus. The passengers complained, assuming there must have been an accident. Losing patience, Chen Xin started to walk the few stops to catch the second bus. Li, a worker a year younger than he, had once shown him a shortcut. Relying on his memory, he went along a lane to a narrow cobbled street where people on both sides were washing honey buckets, cooking, knitting, reading, doing homework, playing chess or Ping-Pong, or sleeping on door planks, making the little street even narrower. The houses lining it resembled pigeon coops or the squares of a harmonica. Through the small, low windows he saw only beds, large and small, two bunks and camp beds. So, recreation, work, other activities, all had to take place outdoors.

What would they do when all those at work came home, or on rainy and snowy days? Suppose a grown-up son found a wife? If . . . behind the colorful shop windows, dazzling billboards, glamorous clothes and the latest film posters, there existed streets that narrow, rooms that crowded, lives that miserable. Shanghai was not as wonderful as one imagined.

It took him half an hour to reach the second bus stop. He shoved in and fitted his six-foot-high body into the smallest space as he had now learned to do, so that he wouldn't be taken for an outsider. It was already six when he got home, hungry and tired, expecting to find steaming hot food waiting for him, but supper was not ready. His mother had been shopping on Huaihai Avenue and had got home late, as it was impossible to rush through the teeming crowds on the streets, in stores, on buses. His sister-in-law had started to cook when she returned home from work. His mother helped wash and chop the vegetables.

"No. 3 does nothing but sleep and listen to his transistor radio," his mother said, showing her annoyance. "You could have sliced the meat for me, you layabout."

Frustrated, Chen Xin went over to his dark hut. A transistor radio was buzzing jarringly, half-talking and half-singing between two stations. He jumped in fright when, groping over toward his bed, he almost fell over a leg. His brother sat up and said, "You're back, Second Brother?"

Chen Xin turned on the desk lamp. "You're too lazy, No. 3. Why don't you give Mother a hand when you've nothing to do?" he stormed.

"I bought the rice and mopped the floor this afternoon," No. 3 said, defending himself.

"So what? When I was your age I was ploughing and harvesting in the countryside."

No. 3 fell silent.

"You're twenty this year. You should use your brains and do something useful. Get up. How can you while away your time doing nothing? Pull yourself together and act like a man."

No. 3 walked out silently. Chen Fang, just back from work, joined in. "You're an adult, No. 3. You should behave like one. We all need some rest when we come home from work. You should've helped."

Chen Xin added from the hut, "If you were studying for the university entrance exam, we wouldn't blame you, but would let you have as much time as you needed. . . ."

No. 3 remained silent. His mother interrupted to make peace. "It's all my fault. I didn't tell him what to do before I left. Supper'll soon be ready. Eat some biscuits first. Go and buy some vinegar for me, No. 3." When No. 3 had left, she told her two elder sons, "I'd rather he stayed at home and didn't roam around and get into trouble. Of all these unemployed youngsters, he's one of the nicest."

Supper was at last ready at half past seven. They ate in his mother's small room. No one felt like talking after the episode with No. 3, and with no chatting, no one enjoyed the meal. In an attempt to liven up the atmosphere, the sister-in-law broke the silence by saying, "My bureau has set up a club to help young bachelors who want to get married. Shall I get a form for you to fill in, Chen Xin?"

Chen Xin forced a smile. "Certainly not. I don't want to get married."

"Nonsense," his mother piped up. "Everyone gets married. With your looks, I'm sure you'll find a wife."

"Tall men like you are very popular nowadays with young girls," said a smiling No. 3, who had forgotten all about the reproaches he had received. He was still young.

"Getting married's no joke," his sister-in-law added. "You need to have at least a thousand yuan."

"We'll help even if we go bankrupt. Right, Chen Fang?" his mother asked.

"Hmm," his elder brother mumbled stupidly.

"But even if you've money, but no room, it's still hopeless," his sister-in-law went on.

"If we can't find a room I'll move out and sleep in the lane if he's getting married. Right, Chen Fang?" his mother asked again.

"Sure," his elder brother agreed.

"You mean what you say, Mum?" asked his sister-in-law, smiling.

His mother laughed. "Haven't I always meant what I said?"

"What sort of a joke is that?" Chen Xin put down his bowl. Although three of them smiled, he sensed they were serious and full of hints. It was highly unpleasant.

He watched television in his brother's room. Before long he felt drowsy and could hardly keep his eyes open. He had to get up very early to go to work so he rose and retired to his hut where No. 3 was already in bed listening to the transistor radio, laughing at a comedy show, looking happy and comfortable.

"Bed so early?" Chen Xin asked.

"The television program was awful," No. 3 answered, but only when the program ended in applause. He reluctantly turned off the radio.

As usual, Chen Xin read for a few minutes and then switched out the light. In the darkness he heard his brother say, "I wish Dad was still alive. Then you could take his place while I took Mum's. Dad had a better job, working in an office."

Chen Xin's nose tingled. He wanted to hold his brother in his arms but he only turned and said hoarsely, "You should have tried to go to university."

After a while No. 3 began to snore. But Chen Xin's urge to sleep had vanished.

No. 3 could have had his mother's job but for him. . . .

He had called long distance saying, "No. 3 is living in Shanghai. He'll have a way out somehow. This is my only chance. . . ." His mother was silent at the other end. He had repeated, "I left home at eighteen, Mum, and I've been alone for ten years. EIghteen, and I've been all alone for ten years. Ten whole years, Mum." Still silence. He knew that his mother must be weeping and repeating to herself, "The palm and the back of my hand . . . Oh, the palm and the back of my hand . . ." In the end, No. 3 gave him the chance, which was only natural. Ten years ago, he had done the same for his elder brother. Like him, his younger brother had not complained or grumbled but was nice to him. Turning in his sleep, No. 3 stretched one leg across him again. He did not push it away.

His brother was too lazy. Wouldn't everything be fine and everyone happy if he could enter the university? But not everyone could do that or go to a technical college. No. 3, ashamed at not having passed the exam, was amiable to everyone and never defended himself when he was criticized.

Chen Xin sighed. Life in Shanghai was not easy.

One evening, Aunt Shen, who worked in the same factory as Chen Xin's mother, was to bring a girl over to meet Chen Xin. As this had been arranged by his mother, he couldn't give a flat refusal although he found the situation awkward and silly. "You must start building a new life," said his elder brother. The statement had stunned him. When his new life became so concrete, he was not prepared for it and found it hard to accept. But, on second thought, he couldn't imagine a more significant and important new life. Maybe it just means marrying and having a child? Shaking his head, he smiled wryly, while an emptiness filled him. The ten years of longing for Shanghai, though gnawing, had been mixed with sweetness. It was like a dream, a yearning suffused with imagination. Anticipation was perhaps the best state. He remembered that when he was a child Saturday had always been better than Sunday.

But everyone in the family was full of enthusiasm. Preparations started after lunch. His sister-in-law swept and dusted her room, while his elder brother bought cakes and fruit. They planned to put Nannan to bed early in case he made a faux pas. It had happened once before when his grandmother was matchmaking and the young couple met at their place. Having always been present when grown-ups talked and not really understanding what it all was about, he suddenly pointed at the young man and girl and asked his mother, "Are they getting married, Mum?" It had been very embarrassing.

No. 3 was the busiest of all. He suggested that his mother cook lentil soup and offered Chen Xin his best clothes to wear. Chen Xin was annoyed by his excitement, which was just because he had nothing better to do.

His enthusiasm dampened, No. 3 still helped cook a large pot of lentil soup and made Chen Xin put on his bell-bottom trousers.

The girl arrived at seven-thirty; hiding shyly behind Aunt Shen and moving quickly over to an armchair in a corner, where she picked up a book to read. With her head lowered in the darkness, no one could see her features clearly.

"Chen Xin is a promising young man. The workers at the factory are very pleased with him. The ten years he spent in the small town in the countryside gave him a lot of experience. He's not irresponsible like new school-leavers," began Aunt Shen.

"Yes, it was hard for him, having to stay far away so long," said his mother, her eyes glancing over to the girl in the corner.

"How do you like working at a lathe, Chen Xin?" Aunt Shen turned to him. "Standing on your feet for eight hours is quite tiring."

"It's OK. I don't mind it. I did all kinds of work in the countryside," replied Chen Xin, his attention fixed on the corner. He could see nothing except her profile, short hair and wide shoulders.

"Where's your son, Chen Fang? He must be a lively boy."

"He's sleeping. He's a nice boy," Chen Fang answered absentmindedly.

"He isn't so nice," countered his wife. "He's a little scamp. I don't want him."

"Don't talk like that. No one can take him away from you. Naughty boys are clever boys."

"That's true. . . ." Chen Xin's sister-in-law moved over to the corner. "Come and have some lentil soup."

Someone quicker had got to the corner first and switched on the standard lamp, saying, "You need some light to read." It was No. 3 who had slipped in unnoticed. Chen Xin was ready to throw him out, but he was grateful for his clever intervention.

The girl was bathed in light. All stopped talking and turned to her. Then all turned back to look at one another with disappointed expressions. After a while, his sister-in-law collected herself and said, "Don't read now. Come and have some lentil soup."

Very embarrassed, the girl finished her bowl of soup, wiped her mouth with a handkerchief and announced that she was leaving. No one made any attempt to stop her. After some polite remarks— "Please come again," "Take care of yourself"—they all rose to see her to the door, while Aunt Shen saw her out of the lane alone. This was the custom and all scrupulously obeyed it. Chen Xin, recently back, didn't know the rules. But No. 3 stood beside him, showing him what to do.

His mother asked, "How did you like her, Chen Xin?"

He laughed in reply.

"She's no good. Her cheekbones are too high. It's a sign that her husband'll die early," said No. 3.

"Don't be silly. No one's asking you."

"She's a bit short on looks," commented his elder brother.

"She's not pretty. I wonder what sort of person she is," said his mother.

The comments stopped when Aunt Shen returned. She addressed Chen Xin with a smile, "She seemed to like you. It all depends on what you think now."

Chen Xin remained silent smiling.

Realizing something was wrong, she added, "She's a nice girl, honest and simple. She's twenty-eight. Her parents are well-to-do. They don't mind whether the young man is well off or not, provided that he's nice. If he has no room, he can live with them. They have a spare room. . . . You'd better talk it over and give me a reply as soon as possible. . . . You must trust me, Chen Xin. I won't let you down. I've known you since you were a kid."

The whole family saw her to the entrance of the lane.

When they returned, his elder brother asked, "What's your impression of her?"

Chen Xin gave a frank reply. "Not good."

"Looks aren't important. You can date her for a while," suggested his sister-in-law.

"Looks are very important. Otherwise, my elder

brother wouldn't have married you," Chen Xin teased her, causing general laughter.

His sister-in-law punched him on the shoulder, half laughing and half angry.

"I too think you could date her, Chen Xin. You mustn't go by looks alone," said his elder brother.

"Looks are very important when two people are introduced to each other. What would I fall in love with if not with her looks?" Chen Xin had his reasons.

"She doesn't have to be a beauty, but at least presentable." No. 3 had to voice his opinion.

"I think she's OK, Mum," his sister-in-law said, turning to his mother. "Besides, she has a room. That's very important in Shanghai."

Chen Xin retorted, "I'm marrying a girl, not a room."

"But it's an important factor. She's not ugly except that her face is a bit wide. Her eyes and eyebrows are all right."

"Forget the eyes and brows. For one thing, she doesn't attract me at all."

No. 3 laughed. This was something new to him.

"It's all for your own good. You can't live on attraction," said his sister-in-law.

"I agree," his elder brother added.

His mother broke in, "Let him decide for himself."

"Yes, yes," his elder brother seconded.

"Well, let's leave it at that," cried Chen Xin. It was all so pointless. "Don't bother about it any more, Mum. I'll find my own wife. If I can't find a good wife, I'll remain a bachelor all my life." He retired to his hut.

In his dreams, a pair of eyes smiled at him, a pair of jade black eyes, in the shape of a new moon, eyes that smiled sweetly and gently. He woke up. From his window, only one-foot square, he saw a new moon.

Ah, eyes like a new moon. Where was she? Who was she? In the school where he had taught, every morning on his way to breakfast in the canteen he saw a girl on an old-fashioned bicycle taking a shortcut from the back gate to the front. Elegant and petite, she always turned to look at him with those eyes. . . . He was confident that if he had asked, where are you going? she would have replied. He had never asked, and he would never

know where she came from and where she was bound.
Many people took a shortcut through his school. The
front gate led to a hospital, cultural center, cultural
troupe, and a machinery plant. At the back gate were a
department store, playground, and cotton mill. She had
passed by him hundreds, thousands of times and he had
let her go even though he liked her and the sight of her
made him happy. But his mind was set on Shanghai, his
sole destination. He had finally returned to Shanghai,
while she had become something in his past, something
that would never return, leaving only a beautiful memory. He had few regrets as Shanghai carried more weight
than a girl. Still he was a little sorry.

He remembered his school with its big garden, bigger
than any school in Shanghai. The campus had a boulevard and a grove. In summer he iced melons in the well
in front of his room. Several students used to bring food
to him. But he had left these loyal students without saying good bye, afraid of complicating matters. He missed
that school. That part of his life had touched his heart.

One morning his elder brother surprised them by telling his mother that his family wanted a separate residence card. He stammered, "Then . . . we can have . . .
two rations of eggs. . . . Two rations of everything."

He avoided his mother's eyes when she looked up silently. Chen Xin wondered why he stuttered, as if it were
something very embarrassing. After all it was a bright
idea to get extra rations, which were given according to
residence cards. He laughed. "What a brainstorm. How
did you ever think of it?"

But his joke had made his brother flee in shame. His
mother fixed her eyes on him, saying nothing.

Chen Xin left for work. Following behind him, No. 3
whispered as if it were a secret, "You know why elder
brother wanted to have another residence card?"

"He wanted more eggs. . . ."

"Of course not," No. 3 cut him short. "He's after the
room."

"The room?" Chen Xin halted, puzzled.

"Right," No. 3 affirmed. "The twenty-two-meter room

belongs to him once he has his own residence card. It must be our sister-in-law's idea."

"Let him have it," Chen Xin moved on. "You don't put your brains to good use, yet you're very quick in such matters."

That day, Chen Xin was preoccupied, his brother's suggestion recurring in his mind. He had a feeling it implied something more. Then his younger brother's words rang in his ears: "He's after the room." He also recalled how his sister-in-law had harped about his marrying a girl with a room. Did it really mean that? Instinctively he waved his hand to deny it. "It can't be," he said almost aloud, scaring himself. Then he had to laugh.

When he returned home after work, he heard his mother saying to his elder brother, "You can't separate from us. Chen Xin has a right to that room too. He has been away working in the countryside for ten years. If he marries, you must divide it. Isn't that right?" His mother asked again when he didn't answer, "Isn't that right?" Only then did he echo, "Right." Bringing in a dish, his wife banged it loudly on the table. By coincidence?

A heavy cloud hung over the dinner table. His elder brother and wife sulked while his mother apologetically piled food in their bowls. No. 3 kept throwing meaningful glances at Chen Xin. "See?" he seemed to say. Disgusted, Chen Xin turned away, looking at no one. Luckily Nannan brightened the atmosphere by standing up and sitting down on the chair asking for this and that. He had thrown away his spoon and was grabbing with his fingers. His grandmother caught his hand and spanked him lightly on the palm. No. 3 made a face and cried "Hurrah!" while Nannan declared proudly, "It didn't hurt at all."

Everybody laughed. But Nannan's mother dragged him down from his chair and scolded, "You rude boy. You don't appreciate favors. You should thank your lucky stars that you're not kicked out." The laughter froze as everyone wondered whether to continue laughing or look solemn. "Oh, boy!" No. 3 said softly to ease the embarrassment.

Chen Xin's mother's face fell. "What do you mean?"

"Nothing," his sister-in-law countered.

"I know what you were driving at." His mother brought it into the open. "It's the room."

"No. I don't care about the room. But when my son grows up, I won't let him marry a girl if he doesn't have a room."

"Don't rub it in. I may be poor but I love all my sons and treat them all equally. The palm and the back of my hand, they're all my flesh. Chen Xin had to leave home because of Chen Fang. You shouldn't be so ungrateful." The old lady wept.

"Ungrateful? When other girls marry, they all get a suite of furniture including chairs and a standard lamp. When I married Chen Fang what did he have? Have I ever complained? And we never failed to send Chen Xin parcels and money every festival. What complaints can you have about such a daughter-in-law?" She wept too.

Chen Fang was stunned, not knowing whom to console.

No. 3 fled. He was useless, disappearing whenever a real crisis occurred.

"Don't cry." Chen Xin stood up. He was disturbed and agitated. "I don't want the room, Mother. I'm not marrying. I'm quite happy just back in Shanghai."

His mother was even sadder. Stealing a glance at him, his sister-in-law wept more softly.

At night, when everybody had retired to bed, his elder brother entered the hut smoking a cigarette. "Don't mind your sister-in-law," he said. "She's not mean, though she likes to grumble. I had no savings when we married. We had nothing except a bed and she's never complained. These last years, by scrimping and scraping, we bought some furniture and decorated the room. She was content with the improvement and wants to keep it. She's not bad and knows we should divide the room into two for you but just finds it hard to accept. I'll talk her round gradually."

"Forget it, Brother," Chen Xin stopped him. "I meant what I said. I swear I don't want the room. Please reassure her. Just don't separate from us. The old lady likes to have her whole family together."

His brother broke down, putting his arms around Chen Xin's shoulders. Though Chen Xin wanted to take him into his arms, he pushed him away and pulled the quilt over his head. Ten years had toughened him.

It was not easy to live in Shanghai.

Chen Xin, used to a carefree life, was very disturbed. The following morning, his day off, he got up at daybreak and went out, telling no one. He wanted to take a walk. Accustomed to the vast spaces in the north, he found Shanghai oppressive. High-rise buildings blocked out the breeze and the crowds made the air stale. Where could he go? He would go to the Bund.

He got off the bus and moved ahead. He could see the ships anchored in the Huangpu River on the other side of the road. On the bank there were green trees and red flowers, and old people doing taijiquan exercises, children playing and young people strolling and taking photos. He felt lighter. He crossed over to the river, the symbol of Shanghai. It was not blue, as he recalled, but muddy and stinking. Everything should be viewed from a distance, perhaps. A closer look only brought disappointment.

He came to the Bund Park, bought a ticket and went in. A fountain cascaded down a rock into a pool, rippling the water. He recalled that long, long ago, the water didn't fall directly into the pool but onto a statue of an umbrella under which a smiling mother and two children were sheltered. He had liked the sculpture so much when he first saw it as a child that he had stared at it refusing to be led away. It was like a symbol of his life. His father had died early and his mother had brought up her three sons, overcoming many difficulties. By sticking together, they had given one another warmth in hard times. When a typhoon hit Shanghai, the four of them had huddled together on the bed. The lightning, thunder, and howling wind had frightened and excited them. His younger brother had made exaggerated shrieks, his mother playfully blamed the sky, and Chen Xin, acting as a protector, sat beside the light switch, which his elder brother, having just learned something about electricity, was scared of. The storm was frightening and exhilarating. And there was a warmth. It was this that had attracted and drawn him home.

Water, falling on the pond, caused monotonous, empty ripples. A drop fell on his hand. He suddenly realized that it was from his eyes. What was the matter with him? When he had left home and his mother had sobbed her heart out, he hadn't shed a tear. Today . . . he experienced a tremendous disappointment, as if a most precious thing had suddenly been shattered. He turned and left the park.

The stores were opening and salespeople were removing the shutters outside the shop windows, which displayed a dazzling array of goods. The pedestrians on the street, so well dressed they looked like models, made his head spin. Unconsciously he stopped outside a shop window: Plump dolls with enormous heads were shooting down a slide, two others were swinging in each other's arms. In the background several Young Pioneers were flying model planes, which circled in a blue sky.

He couldn't move. It all reminded him of his childhood, his youth and the golden memory he had when he left Shanghai. He had mistaken this memory for Shanghai, to which he had struggled to return. Back home, he found he could never recapture the past.

The pedestrians increased, edging from the pavement onto the street. They seemed to be walking in file, and it was hard to move quickly. Life in such a compressed world was difficult. He remembered the struggles on buses. In restaurants, he had to stand beside tables for seats, and then others waited for him to leave while he ate. In the parks three couples sat on one bench and in the Yu-yuan park lined up to have a picture taken on a rock mountain. Humans created not only wonders, but also problems. Why must he squeeze in? Why?

People rubbed shoulders, toes touched heels. Though they lived so closely, they were all strangers. Not knowing or understanding one another, they were proud and snobbish. He remembered a song his brother had recorded a few days ago: "People on earth are thronged like stars in the sky. Stars in the sky are as distant as people on earth."

A town was different. It was calm, maybe a little too deserted. One could run and stroll at ease on the streets and breathe freely. And in a small town, the same people meeting constantly knew one another by sight, nodding to and greeting all acquaintances, creating a warm, friendly feeling. So a big city had its drawbacks, while a small town its advantages.

He moved with the stream of people, not caring where he was heading. He was dazed. The bittersweet yearning in the past decade disappeared, and with it the fullness he had felt in the past ten years. He had arrived at his destination. What was his next step? One must have a destination. Should he follow the new trend and equip himself with Western-style clothing, leather shoes, bell-bottom trousers, and a cassette recorder . . . then find a sweet-heart and get married? . . . Yes. He could start doing that though it required effort and hard work. But would he find happiness if fashionable clothes concealed a heavy miserable heart? If he married for the sake of getting married and the wife he chose was not under-standing, wouldn't he be adding a burden to his life? Again he missed the new-moon eyes and the chances he had lost. A man's destination must be happiness, not misery. He suddenly felt that the destination he sought ought to be something bigger. Yes, bigger.

His spirits lifting, the dark clouds parted slightly to let through a dim light. Dim and hazy, it was still a light.

"Chen Xin."

He halted. Someone had called him.

"Chen Xin:" He turned and saw a bus plowing slowly through the crowds on the street. His elder brother was leaning halfway out the window, reaching out to him. Behind him was his sister-in-law. They seemed agitated.

Shocked, he chased the bus. His elder brother grabbed his hands and gazed at him speechless and wooden, as he had done ten years ago when he ran after the train. Chen Xin was touched. His sister-in-law grabbed him too. "Chen Xin, you mustn't do anything drastic." She broke down.

"What nonsense!" Chen Xin laughed, tears rolling down his face.

"Come home," said his brother.

"Yes. I'll come home." Home was, after all, home. Quarrels were caused by poverty. I made you suffer, my loved ones. He was suddenly ashamed of having used the ten years as a trump card. His mother, two brothers and sister-in-law had also endured those difficult years. And besides, life meant joy, fun, pleasure. For instance, the boulevard, tree groves, the well, innocent pupils, and eyes like a new moon. . . . He had overlooked them all. But ahead of him there would be another ten, twenty and thirty years, a long, long time. He must give his future some serious thought.

Another train was leaving the station. Where was it bound? He knew that his destination would be farther, greater, and he would have to wander more than a decade, maybe two or three decades, a lifetime. He might never settle down. But he believed that once he arrived at his true destination, he would have no doubts, troubles, or sense of rootlessness.

Translated by Yu Fanqin

Ding Ling
(1904–1986)

Born Jiang Bingzhi (also transliterated as Chiang Pin-chin) in China's Hunan Province, Ding Ling early repudiated traditional Chinese family practices by refusing to marry her cousin who had been chosen to become her husband. She rejected the commonly accepted view that parents as the source of the child's body are its owners, and she asserted that she owned and controlled her own body. She joined the Communist Party in 1932, a year after her husband, Hu Yepin, an impoverished worker, poet, and Communist activist, had been executed in jail by the Kuomintang. By then, Ding Ling had become well known as the author of "Miss Sophie's Diary" (1928), a story that frankly depicted a young woman's sexual feelings and, therefore, shocked its Chinese audience, which had semifeudal attitudes. Deeply committed to the Communist revolutionary cause, she was placed under house arrest in Shanghai by the Kuomintang for a three-year period from 1933–1936. Ironically, long after the defeat of Chiang Kai-Shek's Nationalist government she suffered even harsher treatment throughout her literary career because of shifting Communist Party politics and power struggles. Always a political activist, in 1957 she was denounced as a "Rightist" and her fiction and essays were banned. She spent five years in jail during the 'Cultural Revolution' and was sentenced to do manual labor on a farm for twelve years before being "rehabilitated" in 1978. In her introduction to *Miss Sophie's Diary and Other Stories* (Panda Books, 1985), Ding Ling explains her indebtedness to the writers of other cultures:

I can say that if I have not been influenced by Western literature I would probably not have been able to write fiction, or at any rate not the kind of fiction included in this collection. It is obvious that my earliest stories followed the path of Western realism. . . . A little later, as the Chinese revolution developed, my fiction changed with the needs of the age and of the Chinese people. . . . Literature ought to join minds together . . . turning ignorance into mutual understanding. Time, place and institutions cannot separate it from the friends it wins. . . . And in 1957, a time of spiritual suffering for me, I found consolation in reading much Latin American and African literature.

A few years before her death, she was allowed to travel to the United States where she was a guest at the University of Iowa's International Writing Program. In spite of the years she spent as a farm laborer and those in solitary confinement, she authored more than 300 works. After her "rehabilitation" many of her previously banned books, such as her novel *The Sun Shines over the Sanggan River* (China Books, 1984) were republished and translated into numerous languages. Some of her short works, spanning a fifty-year period, are collected in *I Myself Am a Woman: Selected Writings of Ding Ling* (Beacon Press, 1989).

SKETCHES FROM
THE "CATTLE SHED"

A shrill whistle shrieked through the air, resounding along the full length of the corridor and out into the square beyond the windows. The ear-piercing sound rent the curtain of darkness, and the misty, blue light of dawn crept quietly into my prison cell. The naked electric light bulb hanging from the ceiling seemed yellower than ever.

My warder, Tao Yun, pushed aside her quilt, climbed down from the brick bed and hurried out of the room, pulling the door shut behind her and fixing the lock firmly. I listened intently. Outside a low rumble of footsteps could be heard moving down the corridor. I listened even more attentively, hoping to detect a light and often rapid footstep, a slight cough and a low, sweet greeting. "Oh! What are they taking from the end of the corridor? Ah! They are taking brooms. They are going to do a major clean-up and they're going to sweep the square outside my window." As if a stone had been cast into a tranquil pool, my heart began to pulsate. I dressed quickly and began to pace up and down beside the brick bed. I was waiting for Tao Yun, waiting for her to come back. Maybe they would let me go out and sweep the ground. Even if they would just let me sweep inside the main door beside the stairs and along the corridor I wouldn't mind. Ah! Even if they would just let me sweep those places and not go on to the square, even if my waist was sore and my back ached, even if . . . I could still feel that we were laboring together, and yearning for each other in the midst of our labor, and. . . . Ah! Such extravagant longings! When the crowd of you came back from sweeping the square and I was still in the corridor, we could watch one another surreptitiously, we could gaze at each other, letting our eyes tell how we had missed one another. You would give a tranquil smile of warm sincerity that no one else could detect and, just as thirty years ago, those eyes filled with the freshness of the morning sun would give me boundless encouragement. That dauntless confidence in the future, those unquenchable hopes, that healthy optimism, the strength to defy all difficulties, and obstacles. . . . How I longed for that silent, vitalizing support, and, now that I was facing the possibility of mental collapse at any moment, it was a thousand times more necessary, a thousand times more important to me than it had been thirty years ago!

There was no hope. Tao Yun hadn't come back. With a sudden, agile movement, I leaped on to the brick bed, and trembling with fear, stood watching out from behind the window. An old uniform hanging from the upper window frame concealed my face. Through a narrow gap in the cloth I silently combed the square, searching through the crowd of sweepers: here, there, at the front, below my window, group after group. . . . Then, in the early morning light, on the frost-covered square, among the moving crowds, I found in the distance, right in the center of my window, that figure that seemed small and thin even in its padded cotton clothing, and those large, bright eyes under that thick, heavy fur hat. I lightly pushed aside the uniform that hung at the window and a ray of sunshine shone on to my face. I watched him intently as he raised his great bamboo broom. He—he had seen me. Taking huge paces, he swept rapidly to his right and left, coming in a straight line toward me. Raising his head, he gazed intently at the familiar face partially revealed inside the window. He opened his mouth as if he wanted to speak, as if he was saying something. What audacity! My heart began to pound rapidly and I hastily pulled the uniform back over the window, leaving just a narrow slit to peep through. I wanted him to come closer so that I could have a clearer view of him: was he thinner and older, or fatter and even more rosy-cheeked? I didn't discover whether anyone was shadowing him or whether anyone had noticed me. . . . But suddenly I heard the lock on my door rattle: Tao Yun was about to come in. I thought of ignoring her—it did not intimidate me that she would vent her fury on me—but could I really afford it? I couldn't let her know, must safeguard my secret, my happy secret. Otherwise they would be sure to paint the two upper panes of my window with a thick coating of lime as well, parting me permanently from the bright blue sky, the snow-covered countryside, the thick tangle of tree branches where crows and magpies often came to roost, and that vital, living, outside world of people coming and going. Most of all, I would no longer be able to savor those unspoken words and the boundless feeling in those gazes. So with a movement lighter and quicker than any cat, I slid down into a sitting position on the brick bed, as if I had just wakened from a deep sleep and although I had got dressed, was still reluctant to leave the world of dreams. She opened the door and came in, detecting nothing out of the ordinary.

All she said was, "Get up! Wash your face, rake the stove and sweep the room!"

Thus a false alarm was averted, but my heart was still thumping wildly. I could no longer search for that lost shadow. The siren shrieked again to indicate that early morning stint was over. They would now return to that big room of theirs in preparation for starting their day's labor.

These perilous activities of mine behind the window also brought me a few fleeting seconds of happiness three times a day when the prisoners went *en masse* to collect their meals from the communal kitchen. At every meal they had to line up in a long queue, and after muttering political incantations, confessing their errors and asking for punishment, passed in single file beneath my window on the way to the canteen. After collecting their food they would return in a line to their large "cattle shed." Each time Tao Yun left to fetch my food for me (I had no right to fetch my own—probably because they were afraid that I might see somebody, or somebody might see me), I would dodge behind the window, waiting. Tao Yun always walked behind the ranks of the prisoners with a crowd of other wardens, so as the inmates went to and fro, I could stand behind my covered window, surreptitiously push aside the old uniform and reveal my face, then, a moment later, once more conceal myself behind the uniform. This way, crafty Tao Yun and the horde of brutal, so-called "rebel soldiers" were never able to wrest from me those few seconds of rapture that I enjoyed a few times each day. These paltry pleasures supported me through my most difficult years with their days of misery and their long, sleepless nights. What an inspiration they were to my will to live.

Letters

Tao Yun had at first been quite sympathetic toward me. At public condemnation meetings, at denunciation parades, and during manual labor, she had found all sorts of ways to give me a little protection. She even acted contrary to the wishes for the multitude by frequently

buying me good food and urging me to eat more. I was
often deeply moved by these acts of goodwill on her part.
But ever since several people had come from Beijing
under the signboard of the Military Control Commission,
and interrogated me day and night for a month, Tao Yun
had shown an intense hatred of me and kept me locked
in my small room under heavy surveillance. I was followed closely even when I went to the toilet. She was
almost illiterate, yet she would examine at length anything I had written and order me to read it to her. Later
she simply confiscated all my paper and my ballpoint
pen, and would question me harshly without the slightest
provocation. No longer did I see the softer side of her.

I had not a single book and not a single newspaper, and
apart from her, I never saw even the shadow of another
person inside that tiny room. All I could do was sit
blankly like a mute, or pace up and down the floor.
How were these endless days and sleepless nights to be
endured? Under these circumstances, now when I
thought of the tiny seven-meter-square thatched room in
our home area where we had once lived—that room that
had been raided dozens of times, where he had suffered
to the full humiliations and beatings and where I had
spent so many days and nights in terror—I was filled with
nostalgia for that shining little paradise. Even if we were
battered by violent storms, at least the two of us were
together! At least it was our home. It was the place
where we two sat in silent watch on the small brick bed,
where we ate at the tiny table, where we exchanged looks
of silent understanding. Two people, hands clasped
tightly together, hearts beating together, together coping
with the nocturnal visits of those brutal, malignant, destructive hooligans. . . . What precious evenings and
deep nights! We supported one another, each drawing
strength from the other, dispelled all doubts and suspicions and strengthened our mutual trust. In the midst of
difficulties we sought existence, and in our blind alley we
sought the road to life. But now I had left all of it. Only
evil seeped its way into my lonely soul. A loneliness like
death itself was choking the last feeble breath out of me.
When would I once more gaze in delight at your radiantly
happy face? When would I again hear your deep, strong

voice? At present, even if I had a pair of powerful wings, I could not burst out of this cage which imprisoned me so securely. Even if I held the most ardent hopes, I had no way of embracing even a ray of sunshine! All I could do was quietly recite to myself a poem from the days of the underground struggle that we used to like to sing: "Prisoners, prisoners of the times. We have committed no crime. We are here from the front lines, from the firing line of class struggle. No matter how it is repressed, blood is still boiling . . ."

One day while I was out in the corridor attending to the built-in stove, a shrill whistle rent the air, and out of the large room next door surged a crowd of "demons and monsters." As they moved rapidly toward the main door, I gingerly raised my head to watch them, but all I could see were the outlines of a crowd of men with pieces of white cloth pinned to their backs. None of them turned to look at me, and the passageway was very dark, so I could not distinguish one from the other and did not find the figure I was hoping to. But suddenly I felt something fall lightly to the ground beside my foot. I instinctively stood on it, my heart beginning to race. What a wonderful opportunity, Tao Yun was out. I quickly felt it with my fingers: it was a crumpled ball of paper, no larger than one's fingertip. Without stopping to give the matter further thought, I hastily thrust it into my blouse, then sauntered casually into my prison room and slipped it underneath my bedding. Then I quietly returned to the corridor and finished raking the stove. I finished all the tasks I was supposed to do, and calmly and sedately lay down on the bed. But in fact my heart was burning like a fire, that tiny ball of paper underneath me was baking me, burning me. Superficial tranquillity could not conceal the excitement that was churning through my heart. "Ah, how could you have imagined, how could you have known the frame of mind I have been in lately? You really are a bold one! Don't you know that it's against the rules? I'm really elated, I welcome your audacity! What piddling law is it anyway? We ought to revolt! We have no choice but to do this, we ought to do this . . ."

Shortly afterwards Tao Yun came in. With a grim look

on her face she silently inspected the room, but could find nothing in its single table and chair to arouse her slightest suspicions. Seeing my look of exhaustion, she roared, "Got another headache?" I grunted in the affirmative, at which she stopped observing me, turned and walked out, locking the door behind her. I didn't move. The room was perfectly still and through the two upper panes of my window, two shafts of sunlight shone on to the gray mud floor beyond the brick bed. Tao Yun! There's no need to spy on me through that little hole in the door. I won't let you see anything. I understand you.

Only when I was absolutely certain that I was alone in the room and unobserved did I smooth out that little ball of paper. It was a brightly colored piece of a cigarette packet. The creased, white inner side of the paper was covered thickly with black speckles that resembled a nest of ants. Only by looking very closely could I recognize them as characters. You are also in a "cattle shed," living in the eye of the public. How it must have taxed your ingenuity to write this!

He had written: "You must steadfastly believe in the Party, believe in the masses, believe in yourself and believe in time. History will draw the final conclusion. You must live on! Take a long-term view of things, live for the realization of Communism, live for the sake of our children, live for our future! I love you for ever."

Almost all the intimate sentiments on the letter had been expressed to me many times before, yet now they seemed so fresh and forceful that I felt as if I were hearing them for the first time. This letter had been sent to me in the face of great peril. In the present circumstances, what else could he have said to me? . . . I was determined to do as the letter exhorted, and do my utmost to make a success of it. He could be reassured of that. It was just that . . . what in fact could I do? Apart from cudgelling my brains all day in this dark little room, what else could I do? All I could do was wait, wait, go out each morning to rake the stove, clean out the cinders and wait to discover another crumpled ball of paper, wait for another ball of paper to land on the ground beside me.

As I'd anticipated, sometimes I would discover a withered maize leaf beside the stove, or perhaps the corner of an old newspaper, or a discarded matchbox. What boundless happiness these ingenious ruses brought me! They were my only spiritual nourishment. They acted as a replacement for newspapers, books and everything that could brighten my room with a little life. They comforted me, encouraged me, brought me hope. I wanted to keep them, keep them for ever; they were poetry, they were fiction, they were eternal keepsakes. Often, when I was certain that no one was watching me, I would pull them out and fondle them, arrange them neatly in order and in a low voice recite them over and over again, or I would lay them at my breast to let them burn like a fire next to my heart. Below are some of those poetic exhortations that I recited so often and which became indelibly printed on my memory.

"They can wrest from you your bodily health, but they cannot deprive you of your healthy mind. You are a white sail on the deep ocean floating far into the distance. Hope lies in your struggle with the waves. I am watching closely as you chart your course, and the earnest hopes of the people are at one with mine."

"Being locked in a small room isn't so bad, you don't have to hear so many shameless lies; with no one to disturb you, you can become intoxicated with your own memories. Those heroes who once brought you hope of a glorious future, and whom you endowed with life, will achieve frame through your creation, and through them your name will live for ever. In the process of recollection, they will become richer, more mature, while you will attain boundless happiness."

"Forget the names of those people who harmed you; hold fast to the names of those who stretched out a helping hand in times of difficulty. Don't consider wolves and jackals to be people, and don't be disappointed in mankind because it includes such as they. You must look far ahead to the clouds of dawn; the day will come when they will shine with radiant glory."

"For you it is a matter of pride never to ask for pity, but there are always many who show great concern for your plight. I am not the only one who silently cries out

at the vicissitudes of your life. You belong to the people;
you must take good care of yourself."

"As the dark night passes, the light of dawn ap-
proaches. The bitter cold of winter turns to spring. Violent storms cannot beat down a tender stalk of grass, let
alone a tall and mighty tree! Your attainments were not
charitably bestowed upon you by anyone, nor can they
be assassinated, annihilated by the sinister talons of the
perverse and violent. Straighten your back; fearlessly live
on."

"We are not alone. Who can say how many talented
people who have contributed much to the revolution are
now suffering hardship? We are just a drop of water in
the ocean, not worth grieving over! Brace yourself, save
your energy, prepare for golden opportunities of the future. On no account become pessimistic."

" . . ."

These brief letters could be collated into a pamphlet,
into a small book. I tied them into a rool and carried
them like a treasure inside my blouse. They would accompany me through the world to the end of my days.

But alas! That day when I stood in handcuffs, that day
when I was stripped naked and given a body search, my
only wealth, my cherished poems, were destroyed as
pieces of waste paper. All my entreaties that these were
evidence of my crimes and must be preserved, came to
nothing. Gone were those poems more precious to me
than any priceless treasure. Those little pieces of paper
that had shared with me long hours of torment had left
me for ever. But, even so, those letters were eternally
buried in my heart, eternally imprinted on my memory.

Parting

The spring winds blew a green veil over the plains of the
Great Northern Wilderness. The weather grew warmer
day by day and, according to the season, the spring sowing had already started. The inhabitants of these large
and small rooms of ours diminished in number daily. I
heard that some people had already gone home to return
to their former work units, while others had been as-

signed to labor in production brigades. New hope sprang into everyone's heart.

On 14 May, just after breakfast, a uniformed man came to my room, and I sensed that a new chapter in my destiny was about to begin. I fervently hoped that I might be able to return to that seven-meter-square thatched room where we had once found the warmth of home. I fondly imagined that we might once more live the pitiful yet happy life of a couple of industrious, impoverished peasants.

I politely sat at one end of the brick bed, and invited the visitor to take a seat in the center. He looked me up and down for a moment, and then asked, "How old are you?"

"Sixty-five," I answered.

He asked further, "You seem to be in good shape, can you do manual labor?"

"I've always done manual labor," I replied.

"We intend to let you go and do manual labor. We think it will be better for you."

I didn't understand what he was getting at, so I made no reply.

"We're sending you to XX Brigade to work. You will be under the 'dictatorship of the revolutionary masses,' do you understand?"

My heart lurched. XX Brigade, I understood only too well. I could expect no gentle treatment at that place. I had already had some experience of a few of the people there. Group after group of people from XX Brigade had been to my home in the depths of the night; there was nothing they hadn't done. Yet I was not concerned: every place had a certain number of scoundrels, and would certainly also have good people. Furthermore, good people were always in the majority. I simply asked, "When do I leave?"

"Straight away."

"I'd like to sort out a change of clothes for the summer, may I go home first?" I was thinking of my little thatched room again. I'd been away from it for almost ten months and I'd heard that one night during the winter, someone had broken in through the window. Heaven only knew what state the empty room was in now.

"We'll send someone to collect them for you and have them sent to XX Brigade." He stood up as if he were about to leave.

I said hastily, "I'd like to request a meeting with C. There are a few things we must talk about. We have our household responsibilities."

As I spoke, I stood up and moved toward the door as if I wouldn't let him go until he had assented.

He muttered something to himself and surveyed me for a moment, then agreed to my request. I let him through the door and he went out closing it behind him.

How could they still refuse to let us go home? Why would they still not allow us to be together? After all, what crime had we committed? Since July last year when I had been seized from the poultry farm where I had been working and imprisoned here, I had been through beatings, denunciations and interrogations. Hadn't the two factions of the farm already formed an alliance? I'd heard that now they were running along the right track again, so why was there no end to this treatment of us? It was really incomprehensible!

In fact, C. and I had been separated since July last year when I had begun my solitary confinement in this little room. Only in October when this "prison in disguise" was enlarged to accommodate a great influx of people, did C. come to live in the large "cattle shed" next door to mine. Even though we were not permitted to speak to each other, we were at least living under the same roof and still met by chance occasionally. Sometimes we could even gaze at one another through the window, not to mention the fact that for the last few months I'd been receiving his brief, illegal letters. But now it seemed that even this life of bitter, mutual longing was to become the subject of nostalgic thoughts and sweet memories. I would go alone to XX Brigade, to a "tiger" brigade, to subject myself to the "dictatorship of the revolutionary masses." But where would he be sent? When would we see one another again? With a single blow, my life was about to be cut off from all joy, solicitude, comfort and the faintest gleam of brightness. All that would be left me was suffering, exhaustion, anger, yearning and disappointment. . . . I would have to fight those accursed devils. I must never surrender to them, never allow myself to be dragged down. Dying was relatively easy, it was living that was so difficult. Death would be quite comfortable, yet living was so painful! But I was a member of the Communist Party (even though I had been expelled from the Party at the end of 1957, over eleven years ago, I still considered myself a member, made demands on myself as one and regarded everything from the point of view of a Party member). All I could do was continue to tread this endless path beset with hardships and danger. In the face of death I must always seek life!

The door opened with a creak and C. walked in. The whole world took on a different look. Sunlight filled this tiny, dark prison cell. Understanding the preciousness of time, I rushed forward and grasped those firm, outstretched hands, gazed into that face it seemed I hadn't seen for decades. His expression betrayed a complexity of emotions: he was overjoyed at seeing me, yet agonized by our imminent separation. He wanted to encourage me to stand up to even greater trials, yet was worried by my thin, pallid face and white temples; he wanted to be gentle, but did not dare to dissolve the little courage I still possessed by his kindness; he wanted to embrace me fervently, but was afraid to trigger the release of uncontrollable emotions. We gazed at one another in silence, unable to prevent the hot tears stinging our eyelids, but suppressing them with a shake of the head and a forced bitter smile. He nodded and said in a low voice, "I know."

"Where will you be going?" I asked quietly.

"I still don't know," he shook his head.

He pulled a banknote from his pocket and lightly and discreetly placed it in my hand, I knew that this was his entire five *yuan* savings from his monthly living allowance of fifteen *yuan*, but I had no choice but to accept it. I only had a little over one *yuan* in my pocket.

He said, "Don't hesitate to use it. Don't skimp yourself on food and don't eat too badly. You musn't let yourself collapse physically. It won t be long before I find some way to . . ."

I said that I wanted to go home to pick up some clothes.

He said dejectedly, "Someone else has already moved in. Don't bother about that place any more. I'll go and sort out your clothes and have the things you need sent to you. Don't you worry about it. I'll write to you every month. If there's anything you need, I'll find some way of getting it to you."

I choked on my words, forcing back all those things I wanted to say most. And the words he most wanted to say, I could only read in his eyes. Our hands were locked tightly together, our eyes riveted on one another in a gaze that neither of us could break. We were facing immediate separation. Without even a reunion, we were once more to be torn apart. And who could know whether we would ever meet again?

Crash! The door was suddenly kicked open by a leather-booted foot, and a young man glared into the room.

"What do you want?" I asked.

"What do I want! It's getting late. Get your things and come straight away!"

He was obviously the "escort" sent from XX Brigade to fetch me. Whether he was Dong Chao or Xue Ba* made no difference, I now had to set off for the "forage farm" and a life of manual labor.

C. helped me to roll up my thin quilt and the gray cotton-padded mattress that had been issued to me by the Huabei Bureau in Zhangjiakou at the time of the victory over the Japanese. To make things easier for me, C. tied them and my extra clothing into two rolls, so that I could carry one on my back and one in front of me.

That done, he hesitated for a few moments, then said resolutely, "I'd better go. Take care of yourself, keep calm and if you run into problems, don't let them upset you. Even if you hear bad news, like . . . oh, nothing. All in all, you must prepare for all eventualities, especially bad ones. In any case, there's nothing to be afraid of, considering the situation we're already in, what else is there to be afraid of? I'm just worried that you . . ."

---

*Dong Chao and Xue Ba: two jailers under whose guard one of the heroes in the Chinese classical novel *Outlaws of the Marsh*, Lin Chong, was exiled.

His words struck me dumb with fear. I realized there was something he had been hiding from me that he now had no choice but to make me prepare for mentally. Ah! Just what was the bad news that he was keeping from me?

Seeing my stupefied, tear-filled eyes, he comforted me, saying, "Nothing has happened, it's just me being over-cautious. I'm afraid that if something unexpected happens you won't be able to take it in your stride. In short, this will all come to an end eventually. We must believe in ourselves. The situation isn't limited to just the two of us. Maybe it won't be long before everything changes. We must prepare to welcome back the good times when they come. It won't do to endure the hard times but not last out for the happy times afterwards." He sought to bring a smile to my face with his optimistic words, but I was already incapable of smiling. This ominous parting had already crushed my heart into fragments.

He left the room before me. I gathered up my belongings and followed my "escort" from that tiny room out into the square. The spring wind stroked my body, and in the distance, I could see a figure standing by a well under a scholar tree, waving his hand in my direction. He was drawing water for the boiler room. His arm was raised high, as if in carefree, joyous, warm farewell to a friend setting out on a journey to distant parts.

(March 1979, written in Youyi Hospital)

Translated by R. A. Roberts

Wang Meng
(b. 1934)

Born in Beijing where his parents were students, Wang
Meng joined the Communist Party in 1948 about a week
before his fourteenth birthday, working with the Communist Youth League before the peaceful liberation of
Beijing from the Chinese Nationalist government in 1949.
In 1956, he published a story titled "The Young Newcomer
in the Organization Department," a controversial work
criticizing Party corruption, which resulted in severe consequences for its author. The story was considered anti-
socialist and Wang Meng was denounced as a "Rightist,"
expelled from the Party, and sent to perform manual
labor on the outskirts of Beijing from 1958 to 1962. After
one year of teaching Chinese literature at the Beijing
Normal College in 1962, he spent the next sixteen years
exiled to do physical labor in Xinjiang, in western China.
For part of that time he lived as a member of the family
in the household of a Uygur peasant couple, and he also
served as a deputy chief in a commune production brigade. He became fluent in the language of the region
and translated several Uygur literary works into Chinese.
Of his love of language Wang Meng has remarked: "To
me, language is also an art form, a kind of music. It is a
key to other minds and other cultures. Studying another
language is like growing another set of sensory organs or
getting a whole new brain." In 1976, after the fall of the
Gang of Four, he was "rehabilitated," and began to publish fiction again. His lack of bitterness concerning his
long exile within China possibly is the result of the fondness he developed for the people of Xinjiang and of the
rich personal growth he and his wife experienced there.
Reinstated as a Party member in 1979, he traveled to
West Germany, America, Mexico, and Russia during the

next few years, and was appointed China's Minister of Culture in 1986. During this period, his work was awarded national prizes and he became vice-director of the Chinese branch of PEN as well as a member of the secretariat of the Chinese Writers' Association. His departure from public office coincided with the government's violent suppression of students demonstrating for democracy in Tiananmen Square in June 1989. Some of his work is collected in two volumes published in 1989 by the Foreign Language Press of Beijing, *The Strain of Meeting* and *Snowball*. These volumes contain the novels *The Movable Parts* and *The Strain of Meeting* together with short stories, fables, and literary criticism. A number of his stories appear in *The Butterfly and Other Stories* (Chinese Literature, 1983), *Tales from the Xinjiang Exile* (Bogos and Rosenberg, 1991), and *The Stubborn Porridge and Other Stories* (Braziller, 1994). In his most recent novel to be published in English, *Bolshevik Salute: A Modernist Chinese Novel* (University of Washington Press, 1989), Wang Meng, once again, courageously depicts characters who are openly critical of the Communist Party's harmful policies.

KITE STREAMERS

Beside the white-on-red slogan "Long Live the Great People's Republic of China," its exclamation mark squeezed tightly against it, towered a two-story-high advertisement for Triangle brand spoons, forks and knives. Together with its neighbors—advertising Xinghai brand pianos, Great Wall travelling cases, Snow Lily cashmere sweaters, Goldfish pencils—it received the meek kisses bestowed by the loyal lights and revealed a glossy, covetous smile. Lean and unyielding willows and two friendly cypresses, one large, the other small, used their random, elegant shadows to console a lawn robbed of its freshness by the west wind. Between the loud billboards and the solitary lawn Fan Susu stood in a relentless early winter night wind. She wore a trim apricot coat, well-ironed gray polyester pants and pert, low-heeled black leather shoes. Around her neck her snow-white gauze scarf resembled the down of a swallow and complimented eyes and hair which were blacker than the night.

"Let's meet by those upstarts," she had said to Jiayuan on the phone. She always referred to this row of billboards as "upstarts," endearing as well as enviable new idols which had all of a sudden sprung into being.

"The more you look, the more you think you too could have a piano," Jiayuan had said.

"Sure, and if you keep on saying, 'kill or be killed,' often enough, you become an animal yourself," she answered.

Twenty minutes had gone by, but Jiayuan had still not turned up. He was always late. Fool, have you been blackmailed again? Early one winter morning he had been cycling to the library. On his way he had seen an old woman groaning by the side of the road. Whoever had knocked her down had run away long before she knew what had happened. He had gone over and helped her up, asked her where she lived, locked his bicycle, left it by the roadside and taken her home. As a result, the old woman's family and neighbors had all come out and surrounded him, thinking he was the culprit. And that dim-sighted old woman, egged on and bombarded with questions, had insisted that it was Jiayuan who had run her down. Was it the confusion of old age? Was she driven by some negative intuition that regards all strangers as enemies? When he told the whole story, explaining that all he had done was to offer his help, a woman had shouted in a creaking voice, "Are you trying to tell us that you are a 'Lei Feng' sort of person?"* A guffaw burst from the crowd. That had happened in 1975, when everyone had studied Xunzi and believed that human nature was fundamentally bad.**

*Lei Feng was a young soldier who was singled out in the early 1960s as a model for people to emulate.

**Xunzi was a 3rd century B.C. philosopher known principally for his theory that human nature in its original state is evil.

He was always late, and always so busy he didn't even have time to clean the stains and dirt on his glasses. Before she met him Susu had never been busy. If a button on her coat was loose she didn't bother to fix it, but left it dangling instead. With the exception of her grandmother's warmth, everything about this city was cold and unwelcoming. When the city had thrown her out, she had only been sixteen. To say "thrown out" is not exactly fair. Salvoes of firecrackers had been set off, and brass bugles sounded to summon her to the vast countryside. In addition, there were red flags, red books, red armbands, red hearts and red oceans, a red world to be built. All the nine hundred million people in this world, from eight to eighty, formed a circle and recited quotations from Chairman Mao in unison shouting, "Kill to the left! Kill to the right! Kill! Kill! Kill!" Her longing for this kind of world had been stronger even than her earlier desire for a kite with two bells. However, she never saw this red world, she saw a green one instead: grass, crops. She had acclaimed this green world. Afterwards it became a yellow world: dead leaves, dirt, the bare land of winter. She became homesick. Then came a black world. That was when her eyesight was affected by a vitamin deficiency after seeing her companions pull strings to leave the countryside.

Her dream of a bright red world had been lost in the changing of green to yellow and then to black. She began to lose her appetite, started having stomach trouble and became emaciated. Aside from the red dream, there had been lots of other dreams of different colors which she had lost or discarded, which had been snatched away in uproar and chaos, or stolen stealthily. The white dream had been about a navy uniform and sea spray; a professor of medicine and a machinist; about Snow White. Why is every snowflake uniformly hexagonal and yet always changing? Doesn't Nature also have the character of an artist? The blue dream was about the sky, the bottom of the sea, starlight, steel, a champion fencer and parachute jumping; about chemistry flasks and spirit lamps. Oh, yes, and there had been an orange dream, a dream of love! Where was he? Tall, handsome, intelligent, kind-hearted, always smiling good-naturedly. . . . "Here I am!'' she once shouted to the Echoing Wall at the Temple of Heaven.

Dad and Mum had tried every means possible and asked as many people as they could to help get her back to the city which had bestowed, generously, so many dreams upon her. Her father had finally realized that it was unavoidable. The story of what he had gone through to get her back was another dream, strange and absurd. She no longer cared for that sort of dream, nor did she care for that kind of life or the title "Gallant Shepherd Girl." She seldom, if ever, brought up that name and those differently-colored sides of her life.

She returned having lost many colors but having gained strength, and added a number of odors: oil, mashed garlic, fried golden spring onion; drinkers' hiccups, steam, sheep's-head meat sliced thinner than paper. She now worked as a waitress in a Muslim canteen, though she was not a Muslim. Presenting flowers, congratulations, straight A grades, extraordinary good news, trains, cars, parades, tears of joy, Red Guards brandishing leather belts against class enemies, recitations of "the highest instructions," green and maroon horses, the look on the production team leader's face. . . . Was all this aimed at a plate containing three ounces of fried dough? One day she found a picture of herself which had been taken when she was seven. It was National Day, 1959. She was wearing plaits with two big butterfly bows which flew with her up to the sky. Along with her teacher she flew up to the rostrum in Tian An Men Square and presented flowers to Chairman Mao. Chairman Mao shook hands with her. She was small and had never shaken hands with anybody before. Chairman Mao's hand was big, thick, warm and strong. Chairman Mao seemed to say something but she didn't catch it. Afterwards she recalled vaguely that it was something like "little child." How lucky she was. She was Chairman Mao's "little child" and she would be happy for ever and ever.

But afterwards she was not sure whether it really was a picture of her. Had it actually happened? She couldn't recognize herself. Neither when she came back to the city in 1975 could she recognize Chairman Mao. In the past Chairman Mao used to stand straight and his movements were energetic. But now when she saw him on the newsreel's "News in Brief," it seemed that he had difficulty moving his feet, that he opened his mouth and was unable to shut it again for a long time. But all day the newspapers and radio kept publicizing noisily his ambiguous "latest instructions." She felt sad and wanted to go and see Chairman Mao and prepare a bowl of yam soup for him. When grandma fell ill, she had made her soup with white, velvety, finely cut chunks of yam, sweet hot, and tasty. It was a tonic for a weak old person. No, she didn't want to tell Chairman Mao about her anxieties and grievances, mustn't bother him. If she started crying in his presence, she would have to turn her face away.

But this was all impossible. Was she no longer fortunate? Had her luck run out at the age of seven? What had she come back to the city for? For mother? Ridiculous! For grandmother! No, that wasn't why. The papers said that everything you did was for Chairman Mao, but she couldn't see him! So Susu stopped dreaming. Nevertheless, she kept talking, tossing, sighing, grinding her teeth in her sleep. "Susu wake up!" said her mother. She woke up, lost, unable to remember her dream and felt only a cold sweat on her forehead and an ache all over, as though she had just been carried out of a contagious diseases ward.

She happened to be at the roadside the day the foolish Jiayuan was falsely accused for his kindness to the old woman, saw him surrounded and attacked. Jiayuan was not tall or good-looking, and always wore a naive smile which she seemed to have known long ago.

Afterwards a policeman came to the scene. This policeman was as clever as King Solomon. "Get two witnesses to testify that you didn't knock down the old woman," he said. "Otherwise you did." "Can you get two people to testify that you're not a KGB agent? If not, then you will be executed," Susu thought to herself although she didn't, in fact, utter a sound. All she was doing was watching an interesting scene before going to work. There was row upon row of watchers because it was free and more novel than the theater and cinema, where all you heard was "soaring to the heavens," "soaring to the empyrean" or "conquer the heavens," "shooting through the clouds and sky."* They could write of nothing but annoying the "sky."

"What do you want? Should I be punished just because I did her a good turn?" The naive smile became wide, agonized eyes. Susu felt a thorn pricking at her heart and wanted to vomit. She stumbled away, hoping that King Solomon was not chasing after her.

It so happened that that evening the young fool came to the canteen to have fried dough chips. He was all smiles again. He only ordered two ounces.

"Is two ounces enough for you?" Susu intuitively changed her practice of not chatting with customers.

"Well, I'll have two ounces to start with," said the young fool apologetically. He crooked the second finger of his right hand to push up his glasses which, in fact, did not seem to be slipping down his nose.

"If you haven't got enough money or grain coupons," she said without realizing why, "it doesn't matter. Eat now and pay for the rest tomorrow."

"What about the canteen regulations?"

"I'll pay for you. It's nothing to do with the regulations."

"Thank you. In that case I'll have some more. I didn't have enough to eat for lunch."

"Do you want a jin and a half?"

"Oh, no, six ounces will do."

"Okay." She got him four ounces more. When the chef found out Susu knew the customer, he ladled out an extra portion of diced mutton. Each piece of dough had been freshly fried and they glittered on the plate like gold beans. The light from the gold beans shone on the young man's face and his smile became even more attractive. For the first time Susu understood that fried dough chips were a great and powerful treasure.

"They said that I knocked her down while cycling and took away all my money and grain coupons."

"But you didn't, did you?"

"Of course not."

"Why did you give them the money? You shouldn't have given them a penny! What an insult!"

"Look, that old woman needed money and grain cou-

---

*Expressions popular during the "cultural revolution."

pons badly. Besides, I didn't want to waste my time getting angry." Customers across the room were calling. "Coming!" she shouted, and left, cloth in hand.

After she got home that night, she thought of telling her grandmother about that fool. But grandma had had an angina attack. Her father and mother couldn't decide whether or not they should send her to hospital immediately. "The emergency room of that hospital is stinking, unbearable. If anyone survives after lying there for five hours, it proves that their internal organs are made of iron," said Susu. Her father glared at her reproachfully for being so heartless about grandma. She turned and left for her room, a makeshift extra room.

That night Susu had a dream. It was a dream she'd often had years ago—about flying a kite. But each time it had been different. She hadn't had that kind of dream since 1966, and she had not had any dreams at all for the six years since 1970. Water filled the long-dried river bed. The long-blocked roads reopened to traffic, the dreams reappeared. But this time it was not from the lawn or the playground, but from horse-back that the kite was being flown. And it wasn't Susu flying it but the young man who had eaten six ounces of fried dough chips. The kite was simply made, shabby enough to make you cry! Long and rectangular, it was known locally as a "botty curtain." It flew up, higher even than the new wing of the Dongfeng Hotel, the pine trees on the hill and the eagles over the grassland. It flew higher too than the balloon saying "Long Live the Great Proletarian Cultural Revolution!" It flew and flew over mountains, rivers, rows of pines, groups of Red Guards, herds of horses and plates of fried dough chips. How wonderful! She too began to fly along after that "botty curtain," and became a long streamer trailing behind it.

She awoke from the dream. Dawn had not yet broken. She shone a torch looking for the photograph of that happiest of times. At the tenth anniversary of the founding of the People's Republic of China she had presented flowers to Chairman Mao. She thought herself a fortunate person. Humming the song "All Commune Members Are Sunflowers," she repaired the button which she had left loose and dangling for so long. Then she spontaneously wished Chairman Mao good health. She made some yam soup for her grandmother. The soup would have an almost magical effect. Her grandmother would feel better as soon as she drank it. By now it was getting brighter. Her family and neighbors were all up. She began to brush her teeth and wash with great delight, all the while making noises as if a train were rumbling through their courtyard. Her washing sounded like the legendary Nezha storming the ocean. She ate some left-over steamed bread together with hot pickled vegetables. Only when she drank a bowl of boiled water did she feel she was reentering the real world from the "botty curtain" and in the moment doubted whether the article "Boiled Water is the Best Drink" had really been attacking the "three red banners."* She tied her shoelaces and walked with a thumping sound as though iron nails had been driven into her heels or a peg was being hammered into a board to make a Czechoslovakian-style cabinet.

"What are you so happy about, Susu?" asked her father.

"I'm going to be promoted to director," Susu answered.

Her father was overjoyed. When, at the age of six, she had been selected as group leader in the kindergarten, her father had been so happy he kept telling everybody he met about it. When at nine, she was serving as a captain in the Young Pioneers he was in heaven. . . . When the steam whistle of the train tooted, he had suddenly burst into tears, his face convulsed, ghastly. All the children except Susu had cried too. Susu took it much more in her stride than her father. She seemed determined to find an outlet for her talent and resolved to become a great success.

"Hello! You're back. What would you like today?"

"First, let me settle my account. Here's four ounces worth of grain coupons and the money, twenty-eight fen."

"You take it so seriously."

---

*An article in the Beijing Evening News which was criticized for attacking the "three red banners," namely, "the General Line, the Great Leap Forward and People's Commune."

"I guess I'll have four ounces of fried dough chips again."

"Why don't you have something else for a change? We've got ravioli, seven to the ounce for fifteen fen; dumplings, two per ounce, eighteen fen; beancurd jelly with sesame cakes, only thirty fen for four ounces."

"I'll have whatever's quickest."

"Just a second. There's another customer. . . . I'll get you some dumplings then. Do you want six ounces again? . . . Here they are. Why are you so busy? Are you a student?"

"Do you think I'm capable of being that?"

"Then maybe you're a technician, an accordionist, or a new guy promoted to a top job."

"Is that what I look like?"

"Well, what do you do . . . ?"

"I don't have a job."

"Hold on a minute, here comes another customer. . . . If you don't have a job why are you so busy?"

"A jobless person is also a human being with a life to lead, youth, lots of things to do."

"What keeps you so busy then?"

"Reading."

"Reading? Reading what?"

"Optimization, paleontology, foreign languages."

"Are you going to take a university entrance exam?"

"Do universities admit students by entrance exam nowadays? Anyway, I'm not the kind of person who would turn in a blank exam paper."

"It's a pity Zhang Tiesheng's* way of getting into college doesn't work."

"We're still young. We should learn something useful, don't you think?" He finished his dumplings and hurried off, leaving the puzzle unsolved.

He was punctual, and came at the same time as before. This time he ordered beancurd jelly, the gray bean curd jelly with green chive flowers and mud-like sesame jam with red pepper spread on top of it. Why is it that people

---

*Zhang Tiesheng was a student who turned in a blank paper in a university entrance exam and was later admitted to college. He was held up by the "gang of four" as a hero who rebelled against the "old educational system."

in China and abroad know the name of the first emperor of the Qin Dynasty but not the name of the scientific genius who invented beancurd jelly?

"You lied to me."

"No, I didn't."

"You told me you didn't have a job."

"It's true. I came back from the north only three months ago. The reason I gave for leaving was 'personal business.' But I start a job next month."

"In a scientific research institute?"

"No, in a neighborhood service center. I'll be apprenticed to learn how to repair umbrellas."

"That's terrible!"

"No, it's not. If you've got a broken umbrella, bring it to me."

"What about your optimization methods, paleontology and foreign languages?"

"I'll go on studying."

"Are you going to repair umbrellas by the optimization method, or make an umbrella out of dinosaur bones?"

"Well, optimization could also be applied to umbrella repairing. The thing is, however. . . . I'd like another bowl of beancurd jelly, not too much pepper, please . . . you can see the perspiration on my forehead . . . thank you. You know, you take a job to make a living and also to do your duty. But a person should be more than just his trade. A job isn't everything, nor does it last for ever. Human beings should be the masters of the world and their work, and above all, masters of knowledge. Suppose both of us are umbrella repairers, and we each earn eighteen yuan a month. But then if you know about dinosaurs whereas I don't, you're better off and richer than I am. Am I right?"

"I don't know what you're talking about."

"Yes you do. In fact, you already did. Otherwise, why would you be talking to me? Look, that customer from Shandong over there is getting angry because he got some grit in his boiled peanuts and he's hurt his teeth. Goodbye!"

"Bye! See you tomorrow."

On uttering the word "tomorrow," Susu flushed. Tomorrow was, like the streamers tied to that "botty curtain," simple and unadorned, easy and unrestrained. It was like bamboos, clouds, dreams, ballet, a note from a G string, like autumn leaves and spring flowers. But it was a "botty curtain" only a poor, bare-bottomed child could afford to fly.

He didn't come the following day. Nor did he come the day after that. And looking for that foal, Susu lost her own way and moaned like a sad whinnying mare. It was as if her residence registration, grain certificates and ration cards had been revoked in one fell swoop.

"It's you! You're . . . back again!"

"My grandmother died."

Leaning against the wall, Susu felt as if she had fallen into an ice pit. It was some time before she realized that this bespectacled young fool's grandmother was not her own grandmother. Yet she still felt saddened and cold all over.

"One's life is short, and time is the most precious thing."

"But my most precious time is spent carrying plates." She smiled heavily and seemed to hear the distant sound of a galloping colt.

"You've carried plates for a lot of people. We should thank you. But it's more than that."

"What else? They don't really even need me to carry dishes. It wasn't easy for my dad and mum to get this job for me. They had to go to a lot of trouble."

"It's the same everywhere," he said with an understanding smile. "I suggest you learn some Arabic since this is a Muslim canteen."

"What's so special about a Muslim canteen? Anyhow, the Egyptian ambassador won't be coming here for fried dough chips."

"But you might be the ambassador to Egypt. Have you ever thought of that?"

"You're joking," she said. The colt raced into the Muslim canteen and trod on her feet. "That's just dreaming."

"Dreaming, joking, what's wrong with that? Otherwise life would be too dull, wouldn't it? Besides, you should be confident that you could develop the talents, the qualifications and abilities to be an ambassador to Egypt, or, better still, overtake him. You may not serve as an ambassador, but you should be able to surpass him. The key to achievement is study."

"You sound like a rather ambitious careerist."

"No. Like Adam."

"What is Adam?"

"It's the first Arabic word I am going to teach you. Adam means person. It's a beautiful word. Adam in the Garden of Eden. It is a transliteration. And Eve is pronounced *Hawa*, meaning sky. Human beings need the sky and the sky in turn needs human beings."

"So that's why from childhood onwards we fly kites?"

"See, you're an exceptional student."

Lesson one: Human beings. Adam needs Eve and Eve needs Adam. Human beings need the sky and the sky needs human beings. We need kites, balloons, airplanes, rockets and spaceships. That was how she started to learn Arabic. It made people roundabout a little uneasy. "You should keep your mind on carrying dishes. Be careful not to make a bad impression. Do you have any friends or relatives abroad? If the purification-of-class-ranks movement starts again, strange people, strange things and strange phenomena will be examined. You'll be placed under investigation as a special case." "I haven't dropped a single plate. I don't wish to be promoted to director. I know Muhammad, Sadat and Arafat. You are entirely welcome to be chief of my special-case examination group."

Besides, she was in love with Jiayuan. The news soon reached her father's ears. It was as though cameras and bugging devices, all shadowing the young girl, were omnipresent. "What's his name, his original name, any other names he's ever used? His family background, his own background? What was their economic situation before and after land reform? His personal history since he was three months old? His political record? Are there any members of his family or immediate relatives who were sentenced to death or imprisonment, put under surveillance, or were landlords, rich peasants, counterrevolutionaries, bad elements, Rightists? When were they labelled as Rightists? And when were the labels removed? How did he act in past political movements? His and his family members' incomes and expenditures, bank deposits and balances . . . ?"

To all of these questions, Susu had no answers. Her mother was so frightened she cried. "You're only twenty-four years and seven months old. You're not supposed to think about marriage for another five months yet. There are bad people around everywhere, you know." Dad was resolved to see the young man's neighborhood committee, his work unit, local police station, personnel department and file department, anywhere he might be known. To get things moving, he planned to give a hot-pot dinner for the relevant people and accordingly started to make preparations. His favorite Yixing teapot was flung to the ground and smashed into pieces.

"The way you are doing things, you might find counter-revolutionaries but you would never find a friend!" Susu shouted and then burst into tears.

The director, members of the management, group leader and instructor all raised questions like her father's and gave advice like her mother's. A proletarian love should grow out of a shared belief, a shared point of view and a shared ideology, and a mutual and deep understanding should be cultivated seriously, cautiously and sincerely over a long period. One must always be on the alert for enemy activities. The choice of one's love should follow the five conditions for a young revolutionary. She couldn't throw the restaurants' teapot on the floor since she had been trained since childhood to protect public property.

Chairman Mao passed away. Susu shook and cried bitterly. She had wanted to cry long ago, to cry for Chairman Mao, to cry for herself and for others.

"China is finished!" said her father, but instead it was the end of the "gang of four." Susu was close to Chairman Mao a second time when she paid respects to his remains. "I once came to present flowers to you," she said quietly and calmly.

She knew that everything was changing. She could openly and casually learn Arabic although the fact remained that admission to the Party and promotion came easier for those who spent the whole night playing poker than for those who studied foreign languages. She could walk hand-in-hand with Jiayuan, although some people went crazy at the sight of young men and women together. But they still couldn't find a place to talk. The chairs in the park were always occupied. After trying hard they eventually did find one but it turned out that there was a pool of vomit in front of it. They moved on to a large, ramshackle park where loudspeakers hung from the telegraph poles beside every bench. The loudspeakers were blaring out "Information for Visitors," ". . . Fifty fen to fifteen yuan fine," ". . . will be sent to the relevant law-enforcing authority," "conscientiously observe the regulations and obey the administrative personnel," etc. The regulations were so complicated a person wouldn't even know how to stroll in the park without first taking a week's training course. How could they possibly sit there and talk about their love? They left.

But where to? By the side of the moat was a place without loudspeakers, but it was somewhat out-of-the-way. Once, it was said, a courting young couple had been whispering there. All of a sudden, they heard "Don't move!" and a masked man appeared, dagger in hand. Next to him stood an accomplice. Their watches were stolen and the money taken from their pockets. Lovers are always powerless in the face of violence. The case was cracked by the police and the perpetrators arrested. Why do some people dislike the police department? No one could do without them.

What about going to a restaurant? Well, first you have to position yourself behind someone's chair and watch him eat, mouthful by mouthful, then light a cigarette and stretch himself. Not long after you take this hard-to-come-by seat and pick up your chopsticks, your newly-arrived successor places his foot on the rung of your chair. As he moved his leg, the diced meat and slices of tripe you're eating begin to dance in your throat. Should you want to go to a bar or a coffee shop, you won't be able to find one because those are decadent places. Taking a walk will keep you in trim and is a fashion in America. But in winter it's too cold. Of course they did go out together in that cold weather, twenty degrees below zero, wearing padded coats, fur hats, woolen scarves and face masks. Hygienic and infection-free. But what often happens to courting couples is that naughty children playing in the lanes burst out laughing, or curse and throw stones at them. It makes you wonder how these brats ever came into this world.

Jiayuan was easygoing about things. He didn't mind where they went. Whether it was leaning against a railing, or sitting beneath a parasol tree or on the riverbank, he just wanted to stop and sit awhile, speak in Arabic and English and snuggle up to Susu. But Susu was always dissatisfied, difficult to please. No, she didn't want to accept that kind of substitute, in the same way that the customer from Shandong couldn't tolerate the grit in his peanuts. For three years now they had spent their weekends looking for somewhere to sit down. They kept on looking and whole evenings disappeared. Oh, my boundless sky and vast land, on which tiny piece of you may young people court, embrace and kiss? All we need is a small, small place. You can hold great heroes, earth-shaking rebels, vicious destroyers and dissolute scoundrels. You can hold battlefields, demolition sites, city squares, meeting halls, execution grounds . . . why can't you find a place for Susu, 1.6 meters tall and 48 kilos in weight, and for Jiayuan, just under 1.7 meters and 54 kilos, who are head over heels in love?

Susu rubbed her burning eyes. Had she touched some pepper? Had she rubbed her eyes because they were burning or were her eyes burning because she'd rubbed them? "Can we find a place to stay this evening?" she wondered. Though the weather was getting colder, it wasn't yet necessary to wear a face mask. Jiayuan said that he would go to see the Housing Administration Department. They would get married as soon as they found a place. They wouldn't have to walk in the lanes any longer.

"Hey, Comrade Elder Sister, can you tell me where Dashi Street is?" asked a man with an accent, a big bundle on his back and dust all over his new clothes. He was actually much older than Susu.

"Dashi Street? This is Dashi Street," answered Susu, pointing to the intersection where the traffic lights were changing, and the cars, buses and bicycles were surging ahead, stopping and then rushing forward again like the tide.

"Is this really Dashi Street?" His back bent, the middle-aged man looked up and rolled his eyes, expressing doubt.

"It *is* Dashi Street," Susu repeated emphatically. She wished she could show this honest, skeptical person the department store and the big roast duck restaurant by holding them all in the palm of her hand. The man hesitantly took a few steps. He went to cross the street, but not at the pedestrian crossing. A white-uniformed traffic policemen shouted at him through a loudspeaker. Alarmed and confused by the tongue-lashing, the man halted in the middle of the road, surrounded by a whirlpool of automobiles. "Comrade Elder Brother," the man asked, tilting back his head, "where is Dashi Street?"

"Susu!" Jiayuan arrived, breathless, his hair dishevelled, his forehead dripping with sweat.

"Did you just burrow up out of the ground? I've been waiting ages for you. You don't show up and then all of a sudden you appear out of nowhere."

"I know how to make myself invisible. In fact, I've been following you."

"If only we both knew that trick. . . ."

"What do you mean?"

"Then nobody could see us if we danced in the park."

"Why are you talking so loudly? People are looking at you."

"Some people think dancing is vulgar because they're so ugly themselves."

"You're sounding more and more sarcastic. You weren't like this before."

"It must be the autumn wind sharpening up my tongue. We can't even find a place to shelter from it."

Jiayuan's eyes were dim and Susu lowered her head. Multitudes of lights, windows and houses were reflected in the lens of his glasses.

"No flat?"

"No. The Housing Administration Department refused to let us have one. They told me there are people who've been married for several years and have kids that still don't have a place."

"Well, where did they get married then? In a park? In the kitchen where the dough chips are made? In the traffic policemen's kiosk? That would be a good place with glass on all sides. Or maybe in a cage at the zoo? But that would send up the price of tickets."

"Don't get so touchy. What you . . ." He pushed back the glasses which were unlikely to slip off. "What you said is no doubt correct. But you can't expect houses to drop out of the sky. There are so many people who need houses. And some of them really are in a more difficult position than we are."

Susu was reduced to silence. Lowering her head, she began to kick a non-existent pebble.

"Well, have you had supper? I haven't." Jiayuan changed the subject.

"What did you say? Oh, I only remember serving meals, never whether I've eaten myself."

"I take it you haven't then. Let's go to that won ton canteen. You stand in the queue and I'll try to get a seat. Or I'll get a seat while you line up."

"You're repeating yourself. You sound like somebody making a speech at a meeting."

The won ton canteen was crowded. You would have thought the won ton was free, or better yet that you'd be paid to eat it instead of paying twenty fen per bowl. "Let's forget about the won ton and buy some sesame cakes instead. Oh, there's a queue for that too. Then let's go and get some buns from the store across the street." But just as they got there and reached out for the buns, the salesclerk was selling the last two to a little old man wearing a Qing-dynasty robe lined with badger fur. "Well, let's forget about the buns. But what can we do?"

"It would have been great if we just hadn't been born in the first place," Susu said coldly. "If Ma Yinchu's* new population theory hadn't been mistakenly criticized we would never have come into this world."

"Why are you in such a bad temper? Anyway, we actu-

*Ma Yinchu, ex-president of Beijing University, was criticized during the "cultural revolution" for his theories of family planning and population control, and was rehabilitated after the fall of the "gang of four."

ally came into the world before his population theory
existed. Since the fruit buns are sold out, let's buy a
couple of bags of biscuits. We have biscuits. We wait on
customers and repair umbrellas. We study, we do good
things and help people. And there can never be too many
good people—on the contrary, there aren't enough."

"What's the reward for being a do-gooder? To have
to hand over seven yuan and two jin's worth of grain
coupons to somebody who's having you on?"

"In any case, I still should've helped the old woman,
even if they had extorted seven hundred yuan. . . . I suppose you would've done the same thing, wouldn't you?
Susu!" Jiayuan suddenly shouted. Thunder and lightning.
The electricity wires and lights were swaying.

"Try one of my biscuits," said Jiayuan.

"They're the same as mine."

"No, mine are particularly good."

"Why?"

"Why not? Even two drops of water aren't exactly the
same."

"Try mine then,"

"Alright, I'll try yours."

"You try mine after I've tried yours."

They exchanged biscuits and then shared them one by
one. When they had eaten them all Susu laughed. Hungry people are worse-tempered than the well-fed.

There was a drastic change in the weather. Electricity
wires were whining. Billboards were roaring. The street
lights became hazy. A rustling cold wind dispersed the
pedestrians. In a matter of seconds, the street was broad
and empty. Traffic policemen retreated into the kiosks
Susu had reckoned were an idea bridal chamber.

"We must find some shelter!" Icy sleet, falling at an
angle, offered a stern caress. They held hands, unable to
hear each other speak. Against nature and against life
they were undefended. But the big hand and the smaller
hand were both warm. Their own inextinguishable fire
was all the property and power they had.

"Let's find somewhere to shelter," they mumbled,
chewing dust and rain. They started to run. Whether Jiayuan was pulling Susu, Susu was pulling Jiayuan, or the
wind was pushing the two of them was hard to tell. In

any case, a burst of energy pulled and shoved them forward. They made their way to a recently finished fourteen-story block. They had longed for a place in this newly-born row of high-rises. But they were strangers. And aversion to strangers was one of the characteristics of the old woman who'd been run down and the old man in the badger fur robe. What a look the old boy had given the two of them when they went to buy buns! As though he thought that any minute they would take out daggers.

There had been widespread criticism of this row of high-rises. A family living on a top floor had been unable to carry a wardrobe up to their flat. They then tried to hoist it up through the window. What a marvellous spectacle. The rope broke and the wardrobe fell and was smashed to pieces. A new *Arabian Nights* story. But Susu and Jiayuan thought otherwise. They always felt a little shy approaching the buildings, their longing being a kind of unrequited love.

The snow and rain gave them the courage to dash in. They climbed up story after story. The staircase was filthy. There were no lights. There were sockets but no bulbs. Fortunately the street lights were on all night and that was enough. After making numerous turns they eventually reached the corridor on the top floor. It seemed uninhabited. There was a smell of cement and fresh paint and it was warm. No wind, rain or snow. It was devoid of loudspeakers broadcasting instructions, people in masks, pedestrians and impatient customers jiggling your chair to make you leave. Here there were no parents who looked down on umbrella repairers and waitresses. No mischievous children who would, seeing a courting couple, use foul language, abuse and throw stones at them. From here, the lights of the twenty-five story Dongfeng Hotel were visible. The melodious chiming of the railroad station clock was audible and the electric clock on the customs building could be seen. Looking down, they saw green, orange and silver lights. Electric sparks flashed from the trolley wires. Headlights and red signal lights blinked on and off. They heaved a deep sigh of relief, as though they had reached paradise.

"Are you tired?"

"No, not at all."

"We've climbed fourteen stories."

"I could climb another fourteen."

"So could I."

"That man was a real idiot."

"Who?"

"That country bumpkin we met a while ago. He was at the bottom of Dashi Street but he was still wandering all over the place looking for it. I told him but he wouldn't believe me."

They began to speak in Arabic. Stammering, like their heartbeats, enthusiastic, unconventional. Jiayuan was going to take an entrance exam for graduate school. "We may not succeed," he urged the less-than-confident Susu, "but we should try our best." Jiayuan took her hand in his. It was tender and firm. Susu moved closer and nestled against his ordinary, strong shoulder. Her hair was like warm black rain. The lights—glimmering, flickering and twisting—formed the lines of a poem. An old German ballad goes: "There is a flower called 'forget-me-not,' its blossoms are blue." A Northern Shanxi ballad goes: "Words of love I have for you. Fearing the laughter of others, I hesitate to let you know." Blue flowers floated in the air. Waves washed over them. Why fear being laughed at? Youth is more fiery even than fire itself. It is a pigeon's whistle, fresh flowers, Susu and Jiayuan's tear-filled eyes.

Clatter . . . clack. . . .

"Who's there?" barked a loud voice. Jiayuan and Susu suddenly became aware of several people at either end of the corridor. Many of them were carrying things: rolling pins, spatulas, shovels. Man is a tool-using animal. You might have thought this was an uprising of primitive citizens.

A harsh and hostile interrogation began: "Who are you? What are you up to? Who are you looking for? Did you say you weren't looking for anyone? That you came here to take shelter from the wind and rain? Damn you! Sneaking around and hugging like that. I bet you were up to no good. Young people nowadays are just impossible. China will be destroyed by the likes of you. Where do you work? Your names? Your original names, any other names you've ever used? Have you got your resident's cards, employee's I.D. cards or letters of introduction? Why don't you stay home? Why don't you stay with your parents, your leaders or the broad masses? No, you can't leave. Did you think nobody would see you? Whose doors have you pried open? A public place? This public place is ours, not yours. Shame on you! Hooligans! Disgraceful! What? An insult? What do you mean insult? Don't you know we were given half-shaved heads? We were beaten. We were made to do the 'jet-plane.'* Get out of here or we'll show you what we can do. Get the ropes ready. . . ."

Susu and Jiayuan both kept calm. A moment earlier they had been happy. The two of them knew, though not well, several languages. But neither of them could understand this strange language spoken by their dear compatriots. If dinosaurs could talk, they would be more intelligible than this. Confused, they looked at each other and smiled.

"We're going to do something about this," a "dinosaur" plucked up enough courage to say. No sooner had he finished than he went and hid behind the others.

"We're really going to do something about this," others echoed and then shrank back. Jiayuan and Susu were still encircled and blocked, unable to get away.

Suddenly a brave man with a drainpipe in his hand shouted, "Aren't you Susu?"

Susu nodded. With a doubt.

The misunderstanding was cleared up. "Sorry. We apologize. We were afraid of the thief. People say there've been thefts in this building. We have to take precautions. There are some bad types about. We thought you were. . . . How stupid. Sorry."

Susu vaguely recognized the long-haired young man as a classmate from elementary school. He was white-skinned, plump, like a bun made from fine white flour, a food which should be popularized.

"Now that you're at my door. . . ." her schoolmate

---

*Punishments inflicted on "bad" elements during the "cultural revolution." In the "jet-plane" the victim was forced to bend down with arms forced upwards for long periods of time.

invited them in. "All right," Susu and Jiayuan winked at each other. They followed her schoolmate to the dazzlingly bright lift. Now they had a legitimate status as the guests of a resident. The door closed and the lift began to drone. Thanks to this kind-hearted schoolmate their security and dignity were assured. The Arabic numerals on the lift wall changed quickly, from 14 to 4, and now the ear shaped number 3 lit up. It stopped and the door opened. Leaving the lift, they turned one corner after another until they reached his flat. The serrated key, the real trouble-shooter, opened the door confidently with a click. A flicked switch and the lounge and kitchen lights were on. The white walls looked as though they were wearing too much powder. The bedroom door creaked open. A bluish light from the street lamps filled the room. Before Susu could ask her schoolmate not to switch on the light it was on. "Sit down." A twin bed, wardrobe, a red leatherette sofa, a chest of drawers, a tin of malt-and-milk extract, an unopened "ten-delicacy" tonic wine. Her schoolmate continued to introduce his new home: space, amenities, design. Water, heating, gas. Lighting, ventilation, sound-proofing. Fire-proofing, earthquake-proofing.

"You live here all by yourself?"

"Yes," rubbing his hands, the schoolmate was becoming prouder by the minute. "My dad got this place for me. My parents are really anxious for me to get married. I plan to take care of that next May Day. You must come. Good, that's settled. I've got someone to give a hand. He's my friend's uncle and he used to work as a cook at the French embassy. It's going to be both Chinese and foreign food. His best dish is sugar-coated yams. You can wind the sugar threads round and round and they won't break. Don't give me any presents, by the way. Don't buy me furniture or a desk lamp or bedding. I've got everything I need."

"What's your fiancee's name? Where does she work?"

"Oh, that hasn't been decided yet."

"Is she waiting to be assigned a job?"

"No, I mean I haven't made up my mind yet who I'm going to marry. But I'll get somebody before next May Day. No problem."

Susu picked up a balloon from a table and rubbed it vigorously against the leatherette sofa. She tossed it upwards and it clung firmly to the ceiling. Looking up, she delighted in a game she had loved since childhood.

"Oh, good heavens! Why doesn't it come down?" asked the schoolmate, his mouth agape in astonishment. "It's still up there!"

"It's a kind of magic," Susu replied, looking sideways at Jiayuan and pulling a face. They left. Flabbergasted, their hospitable host had yet to regain his composure as he saw them off at the lift. His mind was still on the balloon on the ceiling.

Susu and Jiayuan left their lovely high-rise. It was still snowing and a wind was still blowing. As it fell on their hands and on their faces and trickled down their necks, the damp snow seemed to express a kind of affection for them.

"It's all my fault," said Jiayuan. "I've got no way of getting that sort of place. I'm sorry I've put you in such a difficult position." Laughing, Susu covered his mouth with her hand. In her happiness, her smiling face would have put a blossoming pomegranate to shame.

Jiayuan understood. He began to laugh too. They both understood their own fortune. They knew that life and the world belonged to them. The laughter of the young couple seemed to halt the wind, snow and rain, and the glow of the night sky over the city was the sun.

Susu ran ahead and Jiayuan chased after her. Beneath the street lamp, the sheets of rain seemed even heavier and more dense.

"This is Dashi Street. It's right here!" shouted Susu at the top of her voice, pointing to the hotel building.

"Of course. I never doubted it."

"We've had a wonderfully happy evening. Now we should shake hands and say goodbye."

"Well, goodbye. We won't meet tomorrow. We must work hard. We both want to pass that entrance exam."

"Well, it's just possible that we will."

"Pleasant dreams!"

"Dreams about what?"

"Dreams about . . . a kite!"

What? A kite? How did he know about that? "You

know about the kite too, do you? Do you know about the streamers hanging from that kite?"

"Why, of course. How could I not?"

Susu ran back to embrace him and kissed him right there in the street. Then they each headed home, turning frequently, as the distance between them grew, to wave to one another.

Translated by Lu Binghong

Chen Rong
(b. 1935)

Born in Hankow, the daughter of a judge, Chen Rong (sometimes translated as Shen Rong) left school at the age of fifteen to become a salesgirl in a bookshop after the 1949 Revolution. In 1952 she joined the staff of the *Southwest Workers' Daily* in Chonquig, and two years later she moved to Beijing in order to study Russian. Her work there as a translator at the radio station was cut short when, because of poor health, she moved to Shanxi to live with a peasant family. Having returned to Beijing in 1964, she began writing plays and novels. In a country that practices strict censorship, she continues to write fiction that is critical of governmental oppression. A member of the Chinese Writers' Association, she published "At Middle Age" in 1980, translated and published in *Seven Contemporary Chinese Women Writers* (Panda Books, 1982). This novella achieved wide recognition in China for its honest and realistic depiction of a dedicated eye surgeon, a married woman who leads a frugal and stressful life. She lives in the single small room the authorities have assigned to her, her husband, and their two small children. In spite of the fact that she does her best, working diligently at the hospital as well as at home where she is responsible for housework and child care, she experiences guilt, fearing that she is not a good wife and mother. The film *At Middle Age*, based on the novella and directed by Wang Qimin, won China's Best Film Award for 1983. While Rong's short stories frequently explore tense family situations, her fiction often takes a comic turn. Stories such as "Ten Years Deducted" and "Regarding the Problem of Newborn Piglets in Winter" (reprinted here) ridicule the absurd directives of the communist bureaucracy.

REGARDING THE PROBLEM OF NEWBORN PIGLETS IN WINTER

1. "H'mm, have you considered . . . ?"

"Silent is the night over the military harbor . . ." On the color television screen gleamed the graceful white figure of Su Xiaoming singing in her low soft voice.

"Grandma, turn it louder," the six-year-old Babe issued a command from the large soft couch she was sprawled on.

"Loud enough!" Grandma nevertheless walked over and turned the volume up slightly.

Babe suddenly jumped up and knelt on the couch. "Grandpa, can you hear?" she cried over the back of the couch.

"Don't yell. Grandpa's resting."

"Let our sailors sleep in peace . . ." the song went on.

So Grandpa slept on.

Zhang Dingfan was resting; his eyes closed, his gray hair pillowed against the sofa back and his arm limp on the armrest. After a day's hard work his wrecked nerves found repose in the lull of his own snoring.

Suddenly, a wind blew up outside and the door and the window rattled. The green velveteen curtain gave a stir.

Zhang Dingfan turned his head and uttered a sound barely audible, "H'mm."

Madam Zhang, wife of the Secretary, rose to her feet and walked over to the door and the window for a quick inspection. Both were tightly shut. Then she touched the heater; it was toasty warm. Everything seemed to be in order so she fetched a light wool blanket from the bedroom and walked toward the Secretary. Just as she was about to cover him with the blanket, Zhang Dingfan sat up with a jerk and stopped her. He turned his face toward the door and called, "Little You."

Madam Zhang, startled for a second, piped up in unison, "Mr. You, Mr. You."

In reply, a young man in his thirties came in from the anteroom.

"Get me Chief Jiao of Agriculture and Forestry."

Mr. You stepped lightly toward the table in the corner. He turned the lamp on and dialed the telephone. After he was connected to the right party, he raised the receiver, turned round and said, "Comrade Dingfan."

Zhang Dingfan rose slowly and walked toward the telephone. He seated himself in a chair before he took the receiver in his hand.

"It's me," he coughed. "Looks like it's getting colder. H'mm . . ."

Quickly. Madam Zhang turned the volume of the television set to the lowest. Poor Su Xiaoming suddenly became mute, her red lips gaping and closing soundlessly.

"Grandma, I can't hear, I can't hear," Babe protested.

"Don't fuss, Grandpa is working."

Work is sacred; Babe stopped shouting.

"H'mm, have you considered—this sudden change in temperature and the problem of piglets in the winter— h'mm, we'd better do something. No, no, not by memorandum. First, notify every district in the county by telephone. Proceed level by level this very night. Don't let any piglet die from the cold. Then you may follow up by memorandum. Work on the draft right away."

He hung up the telephone, "These people, just like counters on an abacus—they only move when you give them a push. How can we ever achieve the Four Modernizations?"

"All right—it's all right now that you've alerted them," Madam Zhang comforted him.

"Grandma," Babe couldn't wait any longer.

The volume was once again adjusted. The singer had disappeared. With the tinkling of electronic music and sudden pop, eight modernized angels in their white tight-fitting costumes emerged on the color screen, dancing and twisting their slender waists.

"No, no, I want Su Xiaoming," Babe demanded, rolling in the sofa and kicking her feet in the air.

Zhang Dingfan bent down to pat his granddaughter's head and said cheerfully, "Why not this? The melody of youth. Very nice."

2. *"We'll have wonton tonight."*

Every light was burning in Chief Jiao's office, the Municipal Department of Agriculture and Forestry.

The young cadre had just finished a memorandum: "Regarding the Problem of Newborn Piglets in Winter" which he had been working on all evening. Now he was presenting it to the Chief for approval.

"No good, don't write this way." Chief Jiao quickly looked over the document and threw it on the desk. "Now, in writing a memorandum, you must avoid empty, boastful and irrelevant expressions."

He picked up the manuscript again and pointed at it, "Look here, 'After the winter solstice comes the Prelude of Cold,' who doesn't know that? And here, 'The development of a pig farm is a matter of great importance in promoting food production, supplies of meat to urban people, and reserve funds for the Four Modernizations of our country.' This is empty talk. Needless to say, more pigs means more money and more food. You have to use your brains to draft a memorandum."

The young cadre was totally lost—staring, wordless.

"Come here, sit down. Let's discuss this. A few concrete suggestions should make this memo more practical."

Burning the midnight oil was Chief Jiao's forté. He arose from his seat vigorously, while the young cadre sat down and opened his notebook.

"Regarding newborn piglets in winter—the first problem is to protect them from the cold. Isn't that right? The condition of winterization, in general, is not sufficient. Some pig farms are equipped with straw mats and curtains etc., but most are without even this minimum protection. Such conditions are contradictory to the objective of protecting newborn piglets. So the first and most important issue here is adequate winterization, and toward that end we must adopt every feasible and effective means." Chief Jiao rambled on, pacing the floor to and fro. He rolled his eyes and thought of more to say.

"The problem of piglets in the winter is mainly that of cold and hunger. Cold is an external cause, whereas hunger, an internal one—insufficient feeding will cause decline in body temperature, which in turn will cause decrease in resistance. Therefore, the second point is to keep the little piglets well fed. That's right. Be sure to include this point—increase the proportion of dietary nutrition in pigs' feed."

Chief Jiao made sure that the young cadre had jotted down what he had just said before he came to the third point:

"Furthermore, include the disease prevention. By the way, what is the most common disease that threatens pigs in the winter? As I remember we issued a special memo to that effect last time. You may repeat it here: how to prevent the premature death of newborn piglets."

Chief Jiao walked over to the file bureau, opened the door and gleefully produced a document, "Here is a good paragraph you may copy from: 'Report promptly any case of illness to the local Veterinary Disease Prevention Division. Meantime, take proper measures in treating the infected pig, in accordance with the rules and regulations currently in effect. In case of failure to report, a severe measure of action will be taken and the rule of accountability applies to all.' Add something to the effect that it is important to carry out the objective of prevention."

With an ache in his writing hand and a sense of relief in his heart, the young cadre peered at the Chief's thick babbling lips and could not help admiring him.

"The fourth point, emphasize the importance of political enlightenment. I need not provide you with the exact wording here. Also mention the material reward. You know that helps. Now, how many points do we have now? Four? H'mm . . ."

Chief Jiao stopped pacing the floor. The young cadre closed his notebook.

"Wait a minute. Last but not least: each level of the Party Committee should take the initiative by establishing the NEWBORN-PIGLETS-IN-THE-WINTER LEADERSHIP GROUP. Designate an assistant secretary to be in charge. Each related department should share the work responsibility. United we fight the problem. Report and follow up at regular intervals, and so on."

The young cadre bent down his head and wrote swiftly. One could hear the sound of his ball-point pen scratching the paper.

Chief Jiao stretched himself and heaved a deep breath. He cracked open his thick lips in a self-satisfied smile, "That's fine, now just add a little effort on your part—a bit of polishing up will do."

He looked at his watch. Eleven o'clock. "Let's go," he said while locking the desk drawer. "Time for our midnight snack. We'll have wonton tonight."

3. *"There'll be words aplenty at a memorial service."*

The cigarette butts piled up like a mound inside the ashtray. A ring of ashes scattered around it. The smoke, rising steadily from the tray, swirled around the room like a fog, dense and gray.

Ma Mingpeng, the Secretary of the County Committee, was leaning against the desk, holding a cigarette with his smoke-stained fingers. His small wearied eyes blinked in his dark and sullen face. Two little pouches hung under his eyes.

Since coming to the office early this morning, he had not stepped away except twice to go to the dining hall. The Committee meeting took up the whole morning, and the Study Group the afternoon. The evening was first occupied by the conference of Leadership Groups from the Security Promotion Committee, followed by the report of "No-Office Project" on the issues of disputes between a county chemical factory and a Production Group. Now sitting in front of him was an old cadre looking for a job. Every word the cadre uttered smashed like a nail on his numb and fatigued nerves.

"Secretary Ma, many years have gone by since the collapse of the Gang of Four. I am still wandering about like a desolate ghost, not a sign of work. Others have got their positions back. Why is it so hard in my case?"

"You're an old comrade, I'll be candid with you. We're having problems inside the Committee: more people than work. Every department is already staffed with seven or eight chiefs. People are talking: too many cooks but no broth. Where can I place you?"

"I need to work, even a doorman's job will do."

"That's what you think. Well, I know old comrades like you are dedicated to the Revolution, not your own interests. But what could I do? You were already a cadre before the Cultural Revolution. The authorities will have to place you in a proper position. Comrade, don't worry . . ."

"How can I help it? I'm reaching sixty."

The telephone rang. Ma Mingpeng picked up the receiver.

"What? Emergency notice from the City Committee— piglets in the winter. Erh . . . erh . . . well, very well." Ma Mingpeng rolled his eyes; procedures one after another turned up in his mind which he issued over the telephone as rapidly as an electronic computer, "First, telephone all the communes tonight and relate the message of the City Committee. Urge them to comply and adopt appropriate means. Second, as soon as you receive the memorandum from the City Committee, pass it on to the Regular Committee. Third, notify the Regular Committee to add one more agenda on Thursday's meeting—the problem of piglets in the winter. Fourth, request the people from the Cattle Office to draft a supplementary notice based on the ideas of the City Committee and present it for further discussion at the regular meeting. Fifth, ask the Cattle Office to send someone over to inspect and collect material for a further report. A report to the City Committee should be scheduled in a few days."

Putting the receiver down, Ma Mingpeng touched his temple with his smoke-stained fingers and closed his puffy eyelids.

"All these years, what am I? How could I justify myself to the people? Secretary Ma, just think one day I might drop dead and not even a memorial service in my honor . . ."

Ma Mingpeng opened his eyes and said with a half smile, "Rest assured Comrade, there'll be words aplenty in a memorial service."

4. *"The peasants, they can't live without a son."*

"It's getting late. I say, let's call it a day. I've made up my mind today not to waste any more electricity. Go to bed early."

In the Commune Conference Room the fire in the fireplace had been out for a long time. Light from the smoking pipes and hand-rolled cigarettes flickered now and then and made the room cozy and seemingly warmer. Shen Guigeng, the Secretary of the Commune, was conferring with the cadres from the Production Group and Political Group.

"How many working units did you say have joined the System of Contract and Accountability? The Production Group reported fifty-seven units, which I think is a blown-up figure. Nowadays the emphasis is on truthful reports. We don't need to pad the figure."

No one said anything. The Production Group Leader made a mark on his papers.

"The Safety Training Class for truck drivers will begin day after tomorrow. But the majority of units have not yet handed in the enrollment list. This calls for our immediate attention. Three people died from accidents in one month. It's a matter of life and death, not to be overlooked. Will you, Chief Yu, take charge of this matter? Send someone to check tomorrow. Those drivers know nothing about safety regulations and some don't even have a driver's license. They race down the street like mad men. If we don't do something, our commune will soon become notorious."

Secretary Shen rubbed his bloodshot eyes and changed the subject to a few "trivial matters" such as forthcoming visitors to the commune. He then turned to ask the committee members, "Is there anything you wish to say?"

The plump Big Sister Gu, a member from Planned Parenthood, asked, "What are we to do when we report to the County Committee about the enforced birthrate? The goal is set for an increase of eight out of one thousand, but ours is way over eighteen."

"That's no good. Planned parenthood should be enforced. One more is too much."

"I know, but we can't make them do it. Our people

from Planned Parenthood and doctors from the Public Health, they all dread going to the country. People point at their backs and curse them for doing such wicked things. Young wives scamper at the very sight of our white uniforms. The other day some woman hid in the closet for half a day, nearly died of suffocation."

"You should enlighten the masses."

"Enlighten them! How do you enlighten them? You just go and try. The peasants will tell you—without a son who would paint the house for me in the spring, harvest the grain for me in the autumn? These days, with the new bonus system, more labor means more money. Where would you be without manpower? They don't care if you restrict their rations, they want their son."

Secretary Shen sighed, "Ai, quite so. The peasants, they can't live without a son."

"What do you suggest we should do?"

"What to do, that's up to you. Why should we have Planned Parenthood if you ask me?"

Secretary Shen stood up, which meant the meeting was over. The roomful of people stretched and yawned and shuffled their respective chairs and stools. One after another they got up. At this moment Little Wang, the cadre of the Commune Office, entered the room.

"Secretary Shen, emergency telephone call from the County."

"Wait. Don't leave yet." Secretary Shen took the message from the cadre and looked at it. Then he said to Little Wang, "Telephone every group right away. Make sure they don't let any piglets die. Notify all of them tonight. If there is no answer by phone, you'll have to run over there. Every notice must be sent out before dawn."

Little Wang left. The roomful of people looked at one another and wondered why on earth the problem of piglets should become such a crisis.

"The County Committee telephoned to convey the message from the City Committee that we must deal with this issue of piglets in winter," Secretary Shen said as he seated himself again in his chair. "We'll have to discuss this problem and consume more electricity tonight. Let's see, all of you from the Production Group stay behind."

5. *"Those city girls . . ."*

The television program had already finished some time
ago but a few youngsters still remained in the office.
They were talking, eating watermelon seeds and teasing
Grandpa Cao.

"Hi, you, lift your feet, stop throwing seeds on the
floor, don't you see I'm sweeping behind you as fast as
I can?"

Grandpa Cao, holding a big broom, was sweeping the
floor which was strewn with cigarette butts, watermelon
seeds and dust. Panting hard, he looked fierce, as though
he was about to chase them out.

"Ya. This is our Group, not your home," a youngster
answered back.

"What? As long as I'm paid for doing the job, I'm in
charge here. Hey, move your butt over to the fireplace,
will you?"

The youngster swaggered over to the fireplace and spat
out a few more watermelon seeds, "What do you know?
Grandpa Cao is in charge here. Looking after a fourteen-
inch black and white television set so he can just sit and
watch it all day long."

"I watch television!" Grandpa Cao scoffed and glared.
"Pooh, what a disgrace. Nowadays, good-looking girls
strip themselves half naked. That's the kind of fashion
for you. I bet those city girls wear no pants. If I had a
daughter who exposes herself like that, I'd break her
neck."

The youngsters cracked up so hard that they almost
fell over.

"What's so funny? None of you has a streak of decency
left. You all want to follow the ways of those city
slickers."

"You're right. If I get a job in the city, what I'll do
first is buy myself a pair of bell-bottomed jeans and a
pair of sandals. Then I'll wear my hair long and put on
a pair of toad-like dark glasses. When I come to see you,
Grandpa Cao, you won't even recognize me."

"You, I could recognize you even if you were burned
to ashes! You good-for-nothing."

"Ah, you're as good as treasures from an excavation."

"What?" Grandpa Cao was shuffling the chairs around after the sweeping. The phrase "treasures from an excavation" sounded alien to his ears.

"He said you ought to keep company with the Emperors from the Ming Tombs," another youth explained, winking.

"I'm not that fortunate."

The roar of laughter nearly drowned out the ring of the telephone. Only the youth standing near the phone heard it. He picked up the receiver, "Yes, you want Old Cao? What do you have to say? Just tell me."

The other party refused.

"Tell you! You'd better step aside quick," Grandpa Cao smiled proudly. He rubbed his hands on his pants before he solemnly took the receiver, "Hello, the Commune, it's me. Are you Comrade Wang, still up? Ah, about piglets. Nothing wrong. We're expecting two litters—so I heard from the Guos. Any time now—what? Don't let any die from the cold. If there's any trouble, just ask for me—fine, good-bye."

Grandpa Cao replaced the telephone and looked at the young men in the room, "I say, who'll send a message to the Village Cadre?"

The young men grimaced and shrugged.

"Not me, I wouldn't dare. This is important business from the Commune Office. I can't be responsible."

"Whoever is paid should do the job."

"Then I'd better step aside."

Grandpa Cao glared at them, put on his old lamb wool tunic and left for the trip to the Village Cadre.

6. *"For the sake of the extra five dollars . . ."*

The wife of Xu Quan, the Village Cadre, was awakened by the pounding on the door. "What on earth is the matter? Scaring people like this in the middle of the night," she muttered.

Xu Quan was sitting in the chair with his quilted coat over his shoulders. He fished out his tobacco box from his pocket and rolled a cigarette. He slowly answered his wife. "A notice from the Commune: don't let any piglets die from the cold . . ."

"That's worrying for nothing. The pigs are contracted to the Guo family who are capable and clever people. Why should they let any pig die? You just come back to bed and get some sleep."

"No, I'll have to check the pigs," Xu Quan stretched an arm into the coat sleeve, "I heard this evening they're expecting piglets tonight. If anything should happen, I'll be the first one to blame."

"Look at yourself—so 'positive,' all for the sake of the extra five dollars a month. You think of it as something special, but not me," she suddenly sat up, pulling the quilt over her and becoming very agitated, "If you're really so 'positive,' try and earn more for your family. Look at our neighbor Old Du. After a couple of long trips and some secret deals, he's earned at least several thousand already and they're building a five-room brick house now."

"I won't do anything illegal."

"Is it illegal to contract the work of the rice field? Good for those who did. The price of rice is going up, plus the price for good production; one family can easily earn up to seven or eight hundred dollars. Only you, fool, hooked by the official title, have stuck with poverty. You can burn your eyes out with envy."

"It's a good thing for people to earn more. The policy nowadays is to let people prosper. What are you griping about?"

"I'm not unscrupulous. I'm only talking about you. If you were clever, you'd have put our name in at the time of signing the contract."

"Put my name in? How do I find the time? Half of my days are taken up by meetings. I'm only busy and concerned with the good of the public."

"Tut, tut, not that nonsense again. As a cadre for more than ten years, what have you done for your family? We're all in for misery with you. The good of the public indeed! You've got the whole village against you."

"You're envious. Why don't you work in the rice field yourself? Nobody's stopping you. You want to get rich by doing nothing but staying in bed. No such luck."

He pushed open the door and stepped over the threshold.

"Put on your dog-skin hat. If you get a cold, I've no money to buy medicine." A black furry object flew toward him and landed on the crook of his elbow.

He put the hat on his head and turned around, "Just leave me alone."

7. *"I'll make up words to suit*
Whatever tune the authority picks."

In the pig-farm lights were shining brightly. Xu Quan called once before he lifted the cotton curtain. A rush of warm air greeted him.

He held his hands together and looked around. Mammy Guo's second daughter was squatting in front of the fireplace, making a fire. Mammy Guo, in a blue apron and with sleeves rolled up high, was lifting the lid of a pot in which the rice broth was cooking.

"Newborn piglets?"

"Yes, a litter of twelve, every one alive." Mammy Guo wiped off the perspiration from her forehead with her elbow. She was all smiles. She replaced the lid and wiped her hands on the apron. She then led the cadre inside.

On the warm kang, twelve tiny piglets huddled together in a bundle of round, plump and quavering bodies. A little humming noise came out from the bundle.

"Our pig farm is doing well this time," Xu Quan complimented her cheerfully.

"The group trusts us to do the job and lets us contract the pig farm. Of course, we want to do our very best. We need all the help we can get so I sent for my father from the next village."

Xu Quan saw an old man in the far corner of the room, squatting in front of a broken table and drinking wine by himself.

"Come on, have a cup," Mammy Guo brought out a wine cup.

"Ha, have you moved here with the pigs?" Xu Quan, laughing, squatted down.

"I'm worried if I'm away. It's really more convenient

staying right here with the pigs, especially early mornings and late at night."

"Let's drink. What a day." The old man lifted his cup.

With a lightened heart and prompted by the warm hospitality, Xu Quan lifted his cup and finished the wine in a few gulps. A current of heat came over him. Just think, twelve piglets—Mammy Guo really knows what she's doing. He asked her about her past farm experience and her suggestions for the future.

"I just feed them—that's all. I can't read a single word; don't ask me about my experience," Mammy Guo said, quite pleased with herself.

Yes, what could she say? I have to make up my own report. H'mm—"To carry out the System of Accountability—if every member in the Commune shares the responsibility, the cadre can be assured of success,"—pretty good—but one sentence is not enough—this wine is not bad, must be at least sixty-five per cent alcohol, better than the one I bought last time—Mammy Guo is quite a capable woman, how she mobilizes everybody, old and young, the eighty-year-old father and the school-aged daughter—isn't this an "experience"? "Enlist all help, regardless of age or sex, in our care for the piglets"—sounds nice, but wait, how stupid can I get? This jingle is from the late fifties, no longer popular now. "Mass mobilization means massive achievement"—no good, you don't see such slogans on newspapers anymore. I have to use new expressions, such as "United in heart and spirit, we strive for the Four Modernizations"—that's better—one hears it broadcast eight times a day—but what category of modernization does Mammy Guo's work fit in?—I'd better stop drinking. Tomorrow I have to report to my superior—but what shall I say about "experience"? Pooh—never mind, when the time comes, I'll make up words to suit whatever tune the authority picks.

Translated by Chun-Ye Shih

Lu Wenfu
(b. 1928)

Born in a small village on the bank of the Yangtse River, Lu Wenfu was graduated from secondary school in Suzhou before he enlisted in the Communist guerrilla force then fighting the Kuomintang. At the age of twenty-five, after eight years as a journalist at the *Suzhou Daily*, his story "Honour" was published by the *Literary Monthly* and he began to consider himself a writer of fiction. As an author, his experiences with the Chinese government are typical and representative of the treatment of writers and intellectuals in China during the last three decades. He was twice denounced as a "Rightist" and an "anti-Party" element and severely punished for his artistic views. In 1957 he and a group of other young writers who were about to publish a magazine titled *Explorers* were banished from Nanjing and sent to do manual labor, ordered to examine their thinking and reform their ideas. After several years of working at a lathe in a machine plant, in 1960 Wenfu was deemed sufficiently reformed to be reassigned to Nanjing as a professional writer. In "A Writer's Life," an introductory essay in his fiction collection, Wenfu writes:

> My wits were sharper this time. I took care and knew my place. But it was hard to write when class struggle was everything. Heroes were robust giants, three or four times bigger than ordinary people. I couldn't really fall in with this; I was only 1.74 metres tall myself and had never seen such giants. Maybe they existed up in heaven, but I had never been up there, even on a plane. So I wrote about ordinary labourers, about their work and their outlook. Using my two years or

more in the factory, I broke fresh ground in my writing and was quite prolific.

But in 1965, a second round of denunciations and persecutions began. Wenfu was transferred to a cotton mill in Suzhou where he ceased all reading and writing and worked as a mechanic. He describes these days:

> During the Cultural Revolution I had an even harder time. I was "struggled against," forced to confess my crimes and paraded through the streets with a placard around my neck. I was already numb to the pain, and only worried about when this disaster for my country would end. Every step socialism made was difficult, while destruction was so easy. When would that happy society I had dreamt of as a boy be realized.

In 1969 Wenfu, his wife, and their two daughters were banished once again, this time to an impoverished area of Jiangsu, where he spent nine years as a farmer, living in a hut he had built himself. After thirteen years, during which he had done no writing, the downfall of the Gang of Four led to his reinstatement as a professional author and return to Suzhou. *A World of Dreams*, a novel, was published by the Chinese Literature Press in 1986 and some of his short fiction is collected in *The Gourmet and Other Stories of Modern China* (Reader's International, 1987).

THE MAN FROM A PEDDLERS' FAMILY

To couple peddlers and family heritage is a bit odd. Let's just say that there is a certain Zhu Yuanda whose people from generation to generation have been engaged in peddling. During which dynasty did his family begin to peddle? It has never been established. What things did they peddle? This too can't be said for certain. All I remember is that, thirty-two years ago, the day after I moved to this lane, just after dusk, I heard the sound of a bamboo clapper approaching from a distance. The rhythm was very marked, "Duo duo duo, duo duo, di di di duo, duo duo, di di duo." Although there were only two notes, there were many variations in modulation and in the strength of the tapping. Under the cover of night it seemed as though someone were calling or relating something.

I opened the long window facing the street, and looking down I spotted a light at the end of the alley. The light wavered on the white chalk walls, whizzing along like a spirit on night patrol. Gradually it became more distinct. It was a brightly lacquered *wonton* carrying-pole. Steam was rising above the pole, while sticks of firewood burned in the stove. The carrier was Zhu Yuanda. At the time he was perhaps seventeen or eighteen, tall and thin. Beside him shuffled an old gray-haired fellow—his father. His carrying days were over. He'd very recently passed the job on to his son. Now he went on ahead striking the bamboo clapper, leading his son along the bumpy road he'd followed throughout his life to keep on selling *wonton*.

In those days I was out of work. I relied entirely on helping several overworked Chinese language teachers, correcting students' composition exercise notebooks, getting a share of "classroom chalk dust" so as to make ends meet. This was not easy work and every night I was burning the midnight oil!

The "di di, duo duo" sound of that clapper passed nightly beneath my window. It would always depart at dusk and eventually return, most often just as the Beijing opera goers were leaving the theater.

Whoever works as I did through the long winter nights, dressed in a thin shirt, becomes frozen stiff, only his shrunken heart continuing to beat. Inside the room there is no stove, while outside the north wind cuts through the window lattice like a knife. The swirling night rain turns into ice crystals which dance on the roof tiles. After midnight the whole world becomes an icehouse. At that hour, a steaming hot bowl of *wonton* dumplings for five *fen* with which you can have extra helpings of soup and hot sauce is a powerful temptation and a delight!

Almost from the first day I became Zhu Yuanda's main customer. Later it became my habit that at the last sound of the Beijing opera gong, I would lift my eyes from the students' exercise books and wait to hear the warming sound of the clapper.

Zhu Yuanda's clapping was better than his father's. It was livelier and seemed at once both joyful and mischievous. Before long the clapper would be sounding beneath my window. "Eat, eat, come quickly and eat," it seemed to be calling. If I was a little slow, Zhu Yuanda would put down his pole and call up to me, "Mr. Geo, come down and warm yourself."

I would hurry downstairs to stand by his carrying-pole, watching him fan the fire in the small oven and put the *wonton* in the pot while I listened to Zhu talk of the evening's business. He was very talkative; the words would flow in a stream, so that while you waited for your *wonton* you didn't feel at all lonely or anxious.

"Tonight's business was very good," he would invariably begin, as though sales never went poorly. "When the opera ended at least twenty people gathered around my carrying-pole. And would you believe it, there wasn't enough meat stuffing. I'm not kidding you. The last few bowls had dumplings which were only half-stuffed. . . . Oh! Yours I set aside specially. They're stuffed with meat." He used a brass spoon to stir the *wonton* in the pot so as to prove this to me. "See, each one is bulging with meat."

I laughed as I said, "I don't care whether they're stuffed or not, just add a few more hot peppers!"

Zhu Yuanda didn't miss his chance to add, "It's so cold. Would you like another bowl?"

"Okay. But you're sold out of meat stuffing."

Zhu laughed heartily, his eyes winking slyly. "You'd be throwing away your money selling *wonton!* In business, always say there's a limited supply of your product. Then people will snap it up. If you tell them that there's no meat filling left, then the customers will want even the pastry sheets!" Saying this he withdrew from a little cupboard an earthenware bowl of meat which he thrust before me. "See if this isn't enough for you!" He laughed, thoroughly pleased with himself.

I began to laugh myself. It was just like watching a magician gaily and deliberately giving away the tricks of his trade.

At that time I didn't think that Zhu Yuanda was doing anything dishonest or that he was putting his profits ahead of everything else. I felt that the reason I wanted to correct more exercise books and he wanted to sell more *wonton* was because our lives were so difficult. Every night he brought me a little warmth. If I was able to buy for his sake one more bowl of *wonton*, we would be helping each other out—as two fish in a drying pool splash foam on one another.

After Liberation I got a job as a cadre in an educational department. Although I was still busy, I didn't have to stay up half the night. Although my salary wasn't much, I felt it was beneath me to be having *wonton* at five *fen* a bowl. If I was returning home late from a Beijing opera, I would rather have noodles and shredded pork at fifteen *fen*—to say nothing of sitting ostentatiously in a restaurant—than to be eating tiny *wonton*, standing with hunched shoulders by the seller's stall.

Although the sound of the clapper would still pass nightly beneath my window, it lost its sense of mischief and joy with the passage of time, though it still seemed to be calling, saying something. And I rarely ran into Zhu Yuanda. When he'd return home late at night striking his clapper, I would be deep in sleep. If I did by chance catch that "duo, duo" sound, it would still bring a feeling of warmth to my sleeping, though very faint and far away.

It was probably sometime after 1958 when, being obliged to wait in line at a noodle shop, I suddenly recalled what I hadn't heard for a long time—the sound of that clapper in the dead of night. It seemed a shame, as though I was missing something. But ever since the anti-Rightist campaign, I could hardly dare to keep such attachments. I had not only to convince myself of this, but others too. Socialism required a certain uniformity. It wasn't proper to have capitalist peddlers roaming the streets late at night. I was happy for Zhu Yuanda. He'd broken free of his shackles and leapt into the torrent of the Great Leap Forward.

But things turned out differently. Zhu was no longer beating his clapper but carrying willow wicker baskets through the streets and lanes sneakily and in a flurry. In the spring he sold red bayberries; in the autumn water chestnuts and lotus roots; in the summer it was watermelon. In the winter he would set up his stall beneath the eaves of a house and sell roasted sweet potatoes. Sometimes he would sell cabbage, soybean sprouts, live chickens, fish or shrimp. You never knew for certain what he would be selling. If someone in the courtyard had an unexpected guest, you'd hear the housewife quietly ordering her husband to "run down to Zhu Yuanda and see what he's selling." I never bought anything from him and I wouldn't allow my wife or children to go. I believed that buying his things was aiding the spontaneous rise of capitalism.

I recall that during the mid-autumn festival one year the anti-Rightist inclination campaign became particularly heated in my department. I had just been engaged in a war of words with someone with a Rightist inclination. When I reached home, the moon had already passed its zenith. The scent of osmanthus flowers was floating everywhere in the city. The moonlight was like water. It felt very strange—the struggle was so intense while all around one everything was so delicately beautiful. The world seemed out of joint.

As I was crossing a little stone bridge, I suddenly noticed Zhu Yuanda at the other end of the bridge setting up shop. One basket contained cherry-red water chestnuts, the other tender white lotus roots. I stopped immediately. I wanted to buy a few to take back with me. These are the traditional delicacies of the mid-autumn festival. I hadn't seen them for years. But I hesitated because before me wasn't a state-run fruit store, but a black market stall.

Zhu Yuanda came forward. "Comrade Gao. Why don't you buy a few to take away with you? See, they're very fresh. You can't get these at the state-run stores. They've a few but they can't compare with mine. You could hardly call theirs red water chestnuts. They'd break your teeth.. They're all shrivelled up and they stink!" He gave his basket of chestnuts a shake to show that his merchandise was as good as his words. He was as talkative as ever, still looking for ways to get his customers to buy.

But the moment I began to listen, something seemed wrong. His patter was exactly like that of the Rightists in my department. It was slandering socialism! I didn't want to enter into a "struggle" with Zhu Yuanda. But I had to say a few words to help better the man.

"You really should watch what you say in the future. You'd be wise to get out of these little business activities as soon as possible. They're the roots of capitalism and they're all to be swept away very shortly!"

He was startled. "What! They even want to arrest us peddlers?"

"They won't arrest you, but sooner or later everything that smacks of capitalism will be abolished."

He began to laugh. "Relax. It can't be destroyed. There are people who want to buy and those who want to sell. If the state-run stores won't sell things, how can you say capitalism will be abolished?"

"How can it be abolished! Chiang Kai-shek's armies of millions were swept away. What are a few little shops and stalls?" I had often used this gambit at "struggle" meetings. No one could resist its logic.

Zhu Yuanda made a sweeping bow. "Of course, Comrade Gao. Pardon my ignorance. I know nothing of the ways of the world. I'll take you as my guide from now on." Saying this, he quickly shouldered his baskets and left as though he feared I would arrest him.

As I watched him stagger away from me, I felt a little regret. There was a taste of ashes in my mouth. Those years ago standing by his carrying-pole eating wonton, how could I have thought that he would be swept away? We had formed a genuine affection. As Zhu Yuanda slowly disappeared, I simply couldn't understand how this great distance had come between us.

I longed to run into Zhu again, to smile and nod my head at him, to say a few pleasant words to him to show that our friendship was still alive. Unexpectedly, it was

he who came to see me. He carefully seated himself in
my rattan chair and eyed the furniture approvingly.

"Comrade Gao, you're doing all right now. I can remember that year when you were sick and you asked me
to bring up a bowl of *wonton* for you. All you had then
was a plank bed and a broken-down desk. It was pitiful!"

I remembered this, not without some grateful laughter.
But I was thinking to myself, "Why has he come to see
me?" To tell the truth, ever since the anti-Rightist movement, I had become afraid of keeping contact with almost
everyone, lest I stir up trouble where I would have difficulty defending myself.

But Zhu was very good at guessing your meaning from
your face, so he quickly explained his reason for coming.

"Comrade Gao, I had no other choice. You're the only
one I know who has a way with words. I've come to ask
you to write something for me."

"Write something!" I was even more afraid of putting
anything in writing.

"A self-criticism."

That was better. I could do that for him. "What are
you accused of?"

"Profiteering. What else could it be!" He said this very
easily as though it meant nothing to him.

I sighed, "And selling at exorbitant prices too?"

"Actually you could hardly call them exorbitant, I buy
my shrimps at forty *fen* a catty and sell them at sixty.
Take into account I'm up half the night running around
for sixty *li*, and all I earn is two or three yuan. I know
you won't like to hear this, but you earn more than I do
and all you do is sit around and shoot the breeze."

This made me very uncomfortable. "How can you
make a comparison like that. We serve the people. You
just earn money for yourself!"

He wasn't convinced. "I don't serve the people? If I
don't serve them, how is it that they have shrimps to
fry?"

My goodness! This strange reasoning had to be re-
futed. I stood up and, jabbing my finger at him, said—
"You serve the people when you sell at the proper price.
It's profiteering when you sell at high prices. This is a
very serious matter!"

Zhu suddenly woke up to the situation he'd gotten himself into. He was like a balloon with all the air gone out of it.

"Sure, Comrade. But you don't understand business. You don't understand prices. If you're talking about quality goods at fair prices, well, the vegetable market doesn't have any. Those list prices they hang up there are just to fool you. They're lies!"

"How dare you! . . ." I had learned my lesson from our last encounter so I did my best to keep myself under control, but in spite of myself I lunged forward blustering.

Zhu Yuanda immediately clasped his hands in the traditional manner of submission.

"Okay, okay. I won't say another word. Just please write the self-criticism for me."

For a moment I had him. "If you've done nothing wrong, what's there to criticize? I refuse to do it!"

Zhu grasped my sleeve; then from a pocket he pulled out a wrinkled sheet of paper.

"Don't be angry. I was mistaken. I'm a capitalist! Write what you like; dress it up a little! I've known you, old friend, since I was in my teens."

This softened me. I sat down at my desk and took up my pen. But I couldn't help asking him, "Can you guarantee that you won't break the law again?"

"I . . . I promise. I promise you I'll be a little smarter next time." He winked at me as slyly as he had in his youth.

I was compelled to put down my pen and say to him earnestly, "Look, you're very intelligent. You're a very capable worker and you can put up with a lot. Why don't you become a laborer or a shop assistant? Isn't that respectable work? Why do you have to slither about like a rat?"

His face darkened. He sat dumbly in the rattan chair, his arms folded across his chest. It was a while before he spat out, "I . . . I can't."

"Why can't you?" I drew my chair over toward him and began my analysis.

"Selfish thinking is the main cause of our trouble. It's the root of all evil. Capitalism rests on that. You have to be determined to reform. Naturally, it isn't easy to switch from doing everything for your own profit to looking after the common good. It will be a painful transition. Take us intellectuals for example; our reform is particularly painful."

He was startled. "You suffer too?"

"Painfully."

"No, no. Don't be polite. You and your wife are both cadres. You draw a hundred yuan a month. You don't have to worry about the weather. You get your salary every tenth of the month. If I could only exchange your sufferings for mine I'd be in seventh heaven!"

"Why . . . Why . . . Why don't you get a job? Workers . . . Cadres . . ." I was unprepared for his attack. I was babbling like an idiot.

"Get a job? Without knowing any of the tricks of the trade, how much money do you think I would earn in a month?"

"You'd earn about . . . about . . . about thirty or forty yuan."

Zhu jumped to his feet. "Comrade Gao, I have four children. And then there's my father and mother. Eight mouths to feed in all. What could I do with thirty or forty yuan? I'm not a despicable man, shamelessly thinking only of money, am I? You don't see my children crying from hunger. The old woman, her eyes full of tears. It cuts into your heart more painfully than a knife. I'm . . . I'm ashamed of myself. . . ." He choked back a sob and wiped away the tears running down his cheeks.

I felt as though cold water had been thrown in my face. It was as though I had been standing at the top of a high building looking out at the wide and beautiful universe when suddenly I noticed beneath me a dark swamp, destroying my lofty feelings and dirtying my beautiful picture. I didn't dare say anything more. All I could do was to erect a barrier in my mind: this was an individual and temporary problem. There was no way I could help this individual and temporary Zhu Yuanda. Nothing I could add by way of consolation. I was obliged to write a hurried and confused self-criticism and thrust it into his hands.

From then on I released my wife and children from their ban, allowing them to buy things from Zhu Yuanda.

I felt that Zhu couldn't become a capitalist. If I could be counted a member of the proletariat, then how could he, being poorer and more wretched than I, be considered a capitalist? During the difficult periods when the free markets were permitted, I rejoiced for Zhu Yuanda. At that moment I knew for certain that he couldn't be a capitalist. But right afterwards there was a movement to adhere to the principles of class struggle. Then I would be confused. He really was a capitalist! I was in a terrible muddle. And then a thunderclap split the earth. The bugles of the Cultural Revolution were sounded, announcing the end of all capitalism.

It was altogether unjust. Now it was my turn to be publicly criticized and denounced because I believed that one should work hard for one's monthly salary, not always be spouting jargon, and that each person must make up his own mind. This had become "pushing an extremely reactionary capitalist line." I was angry. Fine. From now on I would be indistinguishable from the masses. I would be like everyone else.

I mingled with the crowds. I read the wall posters, watched the searches and seizures, the public denunciations and parading the accused through the streets. The more I saw of this the more alarmed I grew.

This was no way to live. In the back lanes it was a little more peaceful. There life flowed on like a river. So every day I avoided the big streets and chose instead the byways.

Little by little the big-character wall posters began to appear there too. But they weren't very striking. The paper was rather small and the characters were all higgledy-piggledy. It cost so much effort to read these posters that one paid little attention to them. Later when I did look more closely I realized how odd their contents were. No mention of the usual "reactionary capitalist line" or "cruel suppression." They were quite down to earth. Who had beaten whom? Who had thrown dirty water into so-and-so's courtyard? Who had had a child out of wedlock and with whom? Who was having a love affair with whom? They employed the most spiteful language, larded with terms like "ruthless" and "shameful." . . . My heart sank as I read them. It was like watching people pulling at one another's hair and thrashing each other. And it was for nothing. Sooner or later there would be a verdict on the political questions, but how could all this feuding ever be settled? I had no appetite to continue reading. I turned and started east, passing in front of Zhu Yuanda's door.

It was wide open. There wasn't a rear window so the interior of the main room was dimly lit. I was suddenly given a terrible start. Standing on a bench in the poorly lit room was Zhu Yuanda, his arms hanging at his sides, his head lowered as though he were suspended there. His head was half shaved, his left cheek a dark purple, his eye above swollen to the size of a walnut. Next to the door had been stuck up a sheet of white paper on which was written, "Evil Den of Capitalism—Zhu Yuanda must bow his head and admit to his crimes! He has twenty-four hours to turn over the offending tools!"

He didn't notice me. I didn't dare watch him any longer because I didn't know to whom he was obliged to confess his crimes. Was it to me? Although I hadn't the skill to mend the heavens, I felt a twinge of conscience.

I skipped quickly passed Zhu's house. I looked about again and noticed the white sheets of paper next to the doorways of the flatbread seller, the hot water hawker, the itinerant barber and the cobbler. The contents of the texts were the same and they all bore the signature, "Combat Unit to Smash Dens of Evil." I felt that something terrible was in the air—that Zhu Yuanda had landed himself in a dreadful fix. If the Cultural Revolution was bent on digging away all the soil which nurtured capitalism, then Zhu Yuanda was rooted directly in its path.

My fears were confirmed. Twenty-four hours later along came the "evil den smashers." Some were carrying iron clubs. Others, like wandering knights of old, had at their waists great shining knives with pieces of red silk tied at the handles. The children of the lane followed closely at their heels shouting, "House search! Come and watch the house search!"

I hesitated a long while upstairs. Should I go and watch or not? According to the self-protective "principles" of the times, it was best not to get involved in questions of right and wrong. But I had to take a look. They were going to a poor peddler's house—what could they confiscate there?

By the time I arrived the combat unit had already gone into action. This wasn't like the search and seizure of a cadre's home or an intellectual's. When they searched those places the emphasis would be on the "four olds"—documents, letters, diaries, manuscripts. The work would be done under the guise of a solemn mission. And those whose homes were being searched would stand silently to one side, sadly and indignantly watching the work of a lifetime, precious keepsakes, the wisdom of mankind all go up in smoke.

But the search and seizure at Zhu Yuanda's house was altogether different. It was absolutely terrifying. Even from a distance you could hear the cries and the wailing, the sound of things being smashed and torn, and the shouting of morale-boosting slogans.

Zhu's house had become a battleground. Inside, the din was deafening. Outside clouds of dust were blowing. The willow wicker basket was tossed and hacked to pieces by the great knives. This was because it had been an instrument of crime. It had been used to sell chestnuts and lotus roots. Neither did the vegetable basket escape. It had been used to carry fish and shrimps. One after another, pots and basins flew out the door and were smashed to smithereens on the stone street. These things had all been used in making bean sprouts. For some unknown crime a tin bucket was battered by an iron club. Zhu's wife and children would shriek every time an item was snatched away. The wicker basket that the children clung to so desperately had kept them alive. Zhu's wife hugged the earthenware bowl. Inside were green beans she had been keeping to sell. There was a great cacophony as they fought, bleeding and rolling around on the ground. I couldn't believe my eyes. How could a noble theory produce such piracy as this!

Finally the *wonton* carrying-pole was dragged out. Zhu Yuanda was pursuing it like a madman. "Help! Spare that!"

How well I knew that *wonton* carrying-pole. It had always provided warmth and a full stomach. It had never

committed a single crime. On the contrary, it was a thing
of exquisite workmanship. It was a miniature portable
kitchen complete with cupboards, water tanks, wood
shed, water canisters kept hot by surplus heat and storage
compartments for salt, oil and spices. One could profit-
ably study it in designing a galley for an airplane. I actually thought of walking straight over there and rescuing
the priceless artifact. But I didn't have the courage. All
I could do was stand and watch as the bamboo splinters
flew under the blows of the great knives and the iron
clubs.

Once the capitalist den was no more, it was all over.
No one came and pestered Zhu Yuanda about a self-
criticism. The storm passed quickly. But no one knew
how he would make a living.

After dusk about three days later, I saw Zhu's wife
leading along their four children. There was a length of
string in each of their hands. At dawn the five of them
returned one after the other. Each had a great bundle of
waste paper tied to his or her back. Those accusing posters that had been posted up everywhere had been quickly
blown to the four winds and were being trampled into
waste paper. By picking up enough of it, you could earn
four or five yuan a day. So it's true—Heaven does allow
a way out! Who would have thought that those same
posters that had driven men insane and others to suicide
could rescue Zhu Yuanda? Life is truly a mystery!

While Zhu was nursing his wounds at home, I went to
see him. He was as talkative as ever. He spoke a lot
about the past. "Comrade Gao, I'm truly sorry. I should
have listened to you in those days. During the Great
Leap Forward my wife and I should have managed to
get into factory work. You wouldn't have to worry about
looking after the little ones, you just drag them to the
union office and beg for help. The Communist Party isn't
going to let you starve to death. Hell no! Why should I
care about losing a little face? The skin off this face can
hardly compare with money. Ai! I believed in myself too
much. I always believed in bringing up my children by
my own efforts. Things are fine now! My old woman and
the children are out picking up garbage in the streets. . . ."

Zhu's words poured out of him. It was as though he wanted to sum up his entire life for me.

There was nothing I could do but give him encouragement. "Calm down. First look after yourself. Later . . . oh yes, the *wonton* carrying-pole was destroyed. What a shame."

At that time the newspapers were filled with the slogan, "We have two good hands. Let's not loaf about in the city!" The rumor was that this was thought up by some city dweller. So why pay heed to it? Nevertheless I watched carefully to know if cadres might be sent with their families down to the countryside. I didn't want my name to be found on such lists. So I went scurrying about, looking for army representatives and workers' propaganda teams. This silent struggle was terrifying!"

Fortunately, I wasn't sent down. But Zhu Yuanda came to say goodbye, his eyes filled with tears. His entire family had been sent down to the most wretched place. It was then that I understood the meaning of "We have two good hands. Let's not loaf about in the city!" Who was it that was loafing about in the city? Of course those with no jobs. Zhu Yuanda could not be counted as having a job; he must then be in the loafing category. It was useless to try to appeal. The two of us sat in silence. He regarded me with envy, I him with shame. I could avoid disturbance. But for him there was no escape. Even if I couldn't avoid being sent down, my salary would remain the same.

Just before we parted, Zhu took something out of his bag and gave it to me. "Yesterday when I was cleaning up the mess I found this in a corner. It would be a shame if it were chopped up for firewood. I want to give it to you as a memento." As he said this he placed the bamboo clapper before me.

I received it in both hands. I studied it carefully. It was a semicircular bamboo clapper about eight inches long. It held no secrets. But in Zhu Yuanda's palms what wonderful sounds it produced. It had been caressed by generations of hands. The sweat and oil had penetrated the wood so that it now had a deep black sheen like a bronze mirror. Zhu gave it to me perhaps because he wanted me to remember that he had lived here and that he had done a little something for others.

Zhu and his family disappeared from the lane. Their departure was noisy. There was a great beating of gongs as the banner "Glorious Household" was pasted up at their door. How could an "Evil Den" be transformed into a "Glorious Household"? So, in the twinkling of an eye, an old chicken was turned into a duck.

Four other families in the lane disappeared at the same time. One was a cadre's, while the others were the hot water hawker's, the itinerant barber's and the cobbler's. All of them loafers. From then on you had to walk a mile to get hot water; it took twenty days to get your shoes mended. The old men had to wait in the streets for a haircut. The old women would curse, "Damn those who said they were loafing in the city. Now they've gone off to the countryside to loaf. You can forget about getting hot water to drink. Old man, don't bother about getting your haircut; just keep it in a pigtail!"

I heard no news of Zhu Yuanda for eight years. It wasn't until this spring that I heard that his two sons had been called back for work and had both been assigned to a nearby factory. Later I heard that Zhu had returned. He sent a message through someone explaining he wanted to ask something from me. The moment I heard this I knew it had to be the clapper he wanted. After all, at this time everyone was talking about "social service" and the "commercial network," "hot water vendors," "*won-ton* carrying-poles" and what have you. Zhu Yuanda had returned, so of course he'd be returning to his old line of work. I got the clapper out and wiped it clean. I held it in my hands. In the deep gleam of the wood it was as though I could see the kindling burning in the red earthenware stove. I thought I could hear the "duo duo" sound reverberating at the end of the alley in the dead of night. Then it seemed to pause before a lamp-lit window. Inside perhaps there was a university student, or a young worker devoted to his studies, or perhaps a weather-beaten old man. They all feel keenly how much time they've lost and how little knowledge they have stored up in them. Their efforts are not for themselves alone. Their lives, too, demand that there be others bringing them warmth and convenience. It had taken me more than twenty years to learn this elementary lesson.

It was dusk once again when Zhu Yuanda knocked at my door. My wife and he talked spiritedly as they climbed the stairs. The sound of their voices and of their footsteps was as joyful and as playful as the sound of his clapper in his younger days. Youth itself cannot last for ever, but its spirit can be recovered.

"*Aiya!* Comrade Gao. I've been back now for over a month. I've been busy finding a home and applying for a residence permit so I haven't had any time to come by and see you. And we couldn't be enjoying this day if we hadn't gotten rid of the Gang of Four!" His resounding voice and exuberant facial expression were completely out of keeping with his former self.

I was very happy. I felt that he really had managed to free himself from his awful burdens. "Sit down," I said quickly.

He took a seat in the rattan chair and took out a pack of good cigarettes. Each of us lit one up. He inhaled deeply. Then out poured the story of his eight years in the countryside. I knew too well. It had been no picnic. But as Zhu told it, it all came off sounding like a victory for him. Even though he'd sold off even the broken furniture, he'd got a good price for it. When he was finished he cast an appraising eye over my place. He shook his head disapprovingly. "It's all the same here. Why don't you make some changes?" There was a tone of contempt in his voice as he eyed my shabby furnishings.

I laughed. "Things haven't changed but the man has."

"That's obvious! If you don't change, then how can life go on?" Zhu straightened his new clothes. "Look. Haven't things really turned out well for me? My two sons are back. They're in state-run outfits. The two girls are in the country now. In collectively-owned units. Then there's my youngest—the fifth; I want to see him go to university. Four iron rice bowls and a golden one. Everything's just right. And that iron club can't smash them!" Zhu laughed heartily. He was thoroughly at ease and pleased with himself.

I quickly put the bamboo clapper in front of him.

"You'll be taking up your pole again. Congratulations on the reopening of your business!"

Zhu rolled his eyes as though he didn't get my meaning. Then his face reddened a little. He put the clapper I'd given him aside. "You . . . you . . . you're kidding me!" He was very embarrassed as if he were a new-made millionaire whose shady origins had just been exposed.

I added brightly, "No, not at all. It's permitted to go into business for yourself, now. You're needed. The people in the lane have been asking after you."

Zhu raised his head. "They still expect me to work my carrying-pole?"

I thought to myself: Of course that precious work of art had been destroyed long ago. You couldn't fashion a new one overnight. "Okay, then sell sweet potatoes. The old folk love that sort of thing. You can't get them nowadays."

Zhu Yuanda grinned and gave me a sly wink. "To tell the truth, the labor unit also approached me about going back to my old line. I humored them a little. I'm working in a factory although I'm a bit unhappy with the job. Originally I'd thought of being the doorman. But they sent me to the workshop to sweep iron filings. I do a little sweeping and I get by. It's far less trouble and worry than baking sweet potatoes." Telling me his little joke was just like the time he thrust that earthenware bowl of meat in my face.

I didn't feel the least amused. I just sighed. "Why? If you don't take up your carrying-pole then your son won't either. That would be a shame."

"A shame? Where's the shame in that?" He got up and straightened himself up. "From now on I'm not taking a backseat to anyone."

"But you never did. You were serving the people."

"Still 'Serving the People'? That was petty capitalism— it was to be abolished. I nearly gave my life for that 'den of evil'!" He'd become very excited all of a sudden. His voice was trembling. He shook as he took out the pack of cigarettes. "Come, let's have another smoke. Let's not talk about all those awful things. I came here today to ask you for some review materials to help my son, the fifth one, to prepare for the university entrance exams."

I was certainly not opposed to someone going to university. I got together some mimeographed materials and put them in Zhu Yuanda's hands.

He thanked me effusively, and then said he had to be going. He asked me over to his place sometime. "Come on. Don't worry that you'll eat us out of house and home. The five iron rice bowls are refilled every month!"

The door below creaked as it closed. Distractedly I opened the large window facing the street. Was I looking for some *wonton* peddler coming with his steaming wares? Did I want to hear that "duo duo duo" sound sweeping along? . . . There was nothing. Just Zhu Yuanda with the mimeographs tucked under his arm, slowly disappearing into the night. I had felt disappointed, but I hadn't dared say so in front of him. In these past years I and others had hurt him. We had stifled so much spirit. In the end all anyone wants is to hold an iron rice bowl in his hands, safe from trouble and worry. Each month that rice bowl may not be all that full. And there will certainly never be enough in the pot to go around.

1979

SELECTED CHINESE ANTHOLOGIES

Chinese Literature Press, ed. *Best Chinese Stories: 1949–1989*. Beijing: Chinese Literature Press, 1989.

———, ed. *Seven Contemporary Women Writers*. Beijing: Chinese Literature Press, 1982.

Hong, Zhu, trans. and ed. *The Chinese Western: Short Fiction from Today's China*. New York: Ballantine Books, 1988.

Hsia, C. T. with Joseph S. M. Lau, eds. *Twentieth-Century Chinese Stories*: New York and London: Columbia University Press, 1971.

Hsu, Kai-yu and Ting Wang, eds. *Literature of the Peoples Republic of China*. Bloomington: Indiana University Press, 1980.

Hsu, Vivian Ling, ed. *Born of the Same Roots: Stories of Modern Chinese Women*. Bloomington: Indiana University Press, 1981.

Issacs, Harold R., ed. *Straw Sandals: Chinese Short Stories: 1918–1933*. Cambridge: MIT Press, 1974.

Jenner, W.J.F. and Gladys Yang, eds. *Modern Chinese Stories*. Oxford: Oxford University Press, 1970.

Lau, Joseph, S. M., C. T. Hsia, and Leo Ou-Fan Lee, eds. *Modern Chinese Stories and Novellas: 1919–1949*. New York: Columbia University Press, 1981.

Link, Perry, ed. *Stubborn Weeds: Popular and Controversial Chinese Literature after the Cultural Revolution*. Bloomington: Indiana University Press, 1983.

———, ed. *Roses and Thorns: The Second Blooming of the Hundred Flowers in Chinese Fiction: 1979–1980*. Berkeley: University of California Press, 1984.

Liu, Nienling et al., trans. and ed. *The Rose Colored Dinner: New Works by Contemporary Chinese Women Writers*. Hong Kong: Joint Publishing (H.K) Co., 1988.

Nieh, Hua-ling, ed. *Eight Stories by Chinese Women*. Taipei: Heritage Press, 1962.

Roberts, R. A. and Angela Knox, trans. *One Half of the Sky: Stories from Contemporary Women Writers of China*. Oxford: Heinemann, 1987; reprt. New York: Dodd, Mead and Co., 1988.

Siu, Helen F. and Zelda Stern, eds. *Mao's Harvest: Voices from China's New Generation*. New York: Oxford University Press, 1983.

Tai, Jeanne, trans. and ed. *Spring Bamboo: A Collection of Contemporary Chinese Short Stories*. New York: Random House, 1989.

INDIAN
STORIES

Anita Desai
(b. 1937)

Born in Mussoorie, India, and educated at Delhi University, Anita Desai is the daughter of a Bengali father and German mother. The author of eight novels and children's books as well as short stories, she has been described as "one of the most gifted of contemporary Indian writers" (*The New Yorker*) and "a writer's writer" (*The Times Literary Supplement*). Married and the mother of four children, she was a Visiting Fellow at Girton College, Cambridge, and has taught creative writing at Mount Holyoke and Smith College. Desai has described her work as an attempt to reveal "the truth that is nine-tenths of the iceberg that lies submerged beneath the one-tenth visible portion we call Reality." *Fire on the Mountain* (Harper & Row, 1977), perhaps Desai's best-known novel, depicts an elderly widow, Nanda Kaul's, secluded life on a ridge in Kasauli. After a lifetime crowded with caring for "so many children" and entertaining "too many guests," in short living for and serving the needs of others, Nanda jealously guards the quiet freedom of her rustic retreat. Her way of life is irrevocably altered with the arrival of Raka, her erratic and destructive great-granddaughter. Typically in Desai's fiction, modern family life is filled with discord, and even violence. Among her early novels are *Cry, the Peacock* (P. Owen, 1963), *Voices in the City* (P. Owen, 1965), *Bye-Bye, Blackbird* (Hind Pocket Books, 1968), and *Where Shall We Go This Summer* (Vikas Publishing House, 1975). Two of her other novels, *Clear Light of Day* (Penguin, 1980) and *In Custody* (Harper & Row, 1984), were nominated for England's Booker Prize. Desai's *Baumgartner's Bombay* (Knopf, 1989; repr. Penguin, 1990) dramatizes the experiences of a Jewish refugee from Hitler's Germany who in his old age finds himself caught up in the very madness and violence he thought he had escaped as he becomes exposed to India's burgeoning drug culture. Her most recent novels are *Journey to Ithaca* (Knopf, 1995) and *Fasting, Feasting* (Houghton Mifflin, 2000). Desai's short stories, which have appeared in *Illustrated Weekly of India, Indian Literature, Femina, Thought, Envoy,* and *Harper's Bazaar,* are collected in *Games at Twilight and Other Stories* (Harper & Row, 1978).

PIGEONS AT DAYBREAK

One of his worst afflictions, Mr Basu thought, was not to be able to read the newspaper himself. To have them read to him by his wife. He watched with fiercely controlled irritation that made the corners of his mouth jerk suddenly upwards and outwards, as she searched for her spectacles through the flat. By the time she found them—on the ledge above the bathing place in the bathroom, of all places: what did she want with her spectacles in *there*?—she had lost the newspaper. When she found it, it was spotted all over with grease for she had left it beside the stove on which the fish was frying. This reminded her to see to the fish before it was overdone. "You don't want charred fish for your lunch, do you?" she shouted back when he called. He sat back then, in his tall-backed cane chair, folded his hands over his stomach and knew that if he were to open his mouth now, even a slit, it would be to let out a scream of abuse. So he kept it tightly shut.

When she had finally come to the end of that round of bumbling activity, moving from stove to bucket, shelf to table, cupboard to kitchen, she came out on the balcony again, triumphantly carrying with her the newspaper as well as the spectacles. "So," she said, "are you ready to listen to the news now?"

"Now," he said, parting his lips with the sound of tearing paper, "I'm ready."

But Otima Basu never heard such sounds, such ironies or distresses. Quite pleased with all she had accomplished, and at having half an hour in which to sit down comfortably, she settled herself on top of a cane stool like a large soft cushion of white cotton, oiled hair and gold bangles. Humming a little air from the last Hindi film she had seen, she opened out the newspaper on her soft, doughy lap and began to hum out the headlines. In spite of himself, Amul Basu leaned forward, strained his eyes to catch an interesting headline for he simply couldn't believe this was all the papers had to offer.

" 'Rice smugglers caught' " she read out, but immediately ran along a train of thought of her own. "What can they expect? Everyone knows there is enough rice in the land, it's the hoarders and black-marketeers who keep it from us, naturally people will break the law and take to smuggling . . ."

"What else? What else?" Mr Basu snapped at her. "Nothing else in the papers?"

"Ah—ah—hmm," she muttered as her eyes roved up and down the columns, looking very round and glassy behind the steel-rimmed spectacles. " 'Blue bull menace in Delhi airport can be solved by narcotic drug—' "

"Blue bulls? Blue bulls?" snorted Mr Basu, almost tipping out of his chair. "How do you mean, 'blue bulls'? What's a blue bull? You can't be reading right."

"I am reading right," she protested. "Think I can't read? Did my B.A., helped two children through school and college, and you think I can't read? Blue bulls it says here, blue bulls it is."

"Can't be," he grumbled, but retreated into his chair from her unexpectedly spirited defense. "Must be a printing mistake. There are bulls, buffaloes, bullocks, and *bul-buls*, but whoever heared of a blue bull? Nilgai, do they mean? But that creature is nearly extinct. How can there be any at the airport? It's all rot, somebody's fantasy—"

"All right, I'll stop reading, if you'd rather. I have enough to do in the kitchen, you know," she threatened him, but he pressed his lips together and, with a little

stab of his hand, beckoned her to pick up the papers and
continue.

"Ah—ah—hmm. What pictures are on this week, I
wonder?" she continued, partly because that was a subject of consuming interest to her, and partly because she
thought it a safe subject to move onto. "*Teri Meri Kis-
met*—'the heartwarming saga of an unhappy wife.' No, no,
no. *Do Dost*—winner of three Filmfare awards—ahh . . ."

"Please, please, Otima, the news," Mr Basu reminded
her.

"Nothing to interest you," she said but tore herself
away from the entertainments column for his sake.
" 'Anti-arthritis drug'—not your problem. 'Betel leaves
cause cancer.' Hmph. I know at least a hundred people
who chew betel leaves and are as fit—"

"All right. All right. What else?"

"What news are you interested in then?" She flared
up, but immediately subsided and browsed on, comfortably scratching the sole of her foot as she did so.
" 'Floods in Assam.' 'Drought in Maharashtra.' When is
there not? 'Two hundred cholera deaths.' 'A woman and
child have a miraculous escape when their house col-
lapses.' 'Husband held for murder of wife.' "See?" she
cried excitedly. "Once more. How often does this happen? 'Husband and mother-in-law have been arrested on
charge of pouring kerosene on Kantibai's clothes and setting her on fire while she slept.' Yes, that is how they
always do it. Why? Probably the dowry didn't satisfy
them, they must have hoped to get one more . . ."

He groaned and sank back in his chair. He knew there
was no stopping her now. Except for stories of grotesque
births like those of two-headed children or five-legged
calves, there was nothing she loved as dearly as tales of
murder and atrocity, and short of his having a stroke or
the fish-seller arriving at the door, nothing could distract
her now. He even heaved himself out of his chair and
shuffled off to the other end of the balcony to feed the
parrot in its cage a green chili or two without her so
much as noticing his departure. But when she had read
to the end of that fascinating item, she ran into another
that she read out in a voice like a law-maker's, and he
heard it without wishing to: "Electricity will be switched

off as urgent repairs to power lines must be made, in Darya Ganj and Kashmere Gate area, from 8 p.m. to 6 a.m. on the twenty-first of May.' My God, that is today."

"Today? Tonight? No electricity?" he echoed, letting the green chili fall to the floor of the cage where other offered and refused chillies lay in a rotting heap. "How will I sleep then?" he gasped fearfully, "without a fan? In this heat?" and already his diaphragm seemed to cave in, his chest to rise and fall as he panted for breath. Clutching his throat, he groped his way back to the cane chair. "Otima, Otima, I can't breathe," he moaned.

She put the papers away and rose with a sigh of irritation and anxiety, the kind a sickly child arouses in its tired mother. She herself, at fifty-six, had not a wrinkle on her oiled face, scarcely a gray hair on her head. As smooth as butter, as round as a cake, life might still have been delectable to her if it had not been for the asthma that afflicted her husband and made him seem, at sixty-one, almost decrepit.

"I'll bring you your inhaler. Don't get worried, just don't get worried," she told him and bustled off to find his inhaler and cortisone. When she held them out to him, he lowered his head into the inhaler like a dying man at the one straw left. He grasped it with frantic hands, almost clawing her. She shook her head, watching him. "Why do you let yourself get so upset?" she asked, cursing herself for having read out that particular piece of news to him. "It won't be so bad. Many people in the city sleep without electric fans—most do. We'll manage—"

"*You'll* manage," he spat at her, "but I?"

There was no soothing him now. She knew how rapidly he would advance from imagined breathlessness into the first frightening stage of a full-blown attack of asthma. His chest was already heaving, he imagined there was no oxygen left for him to breathe, that his lungs had collapsed and could not take in any air. He stared up at the strings of washing that hung from end to end of the balcony, the overflow of furniture that cluttered it, the listless parrot in its cage, the view of all the other crowded, washing-hung balconies up and down the length of the road, and felt there was no oxygen left in the air.

"Stay out here on the balcony, it's a little cooler than inside," his wife said calmly and left him to go about her work. But she did it absently. Normally she would have relished bargaining with the fish-seller who came to the door with a beckti, some whiskered black river fish and a little squirming hill of pale pink prawns in his flat basket. But today she made her purchases and paid him off rather quickly—she was in a hurry to return to the balcony. "All right?" she asked, looking down at her husband sunk into a heap on his chair, shaking with the effort to suck in air. His lips tightened and whitened in silent reply. She sighed and went away to sort out spices in the kitchen, to pour them out of large containers into small containers, to fill those that were empty and empty those that were full, giving everything that came her way a little loving polish with the end of her sari for it was something she loved to do, but she did not stay very long. She worried about her husband. Foolish and unreasonable as he seemed to her in his sickness, she could not quite leave him to his agony, whether real or imagined. When the postman brought them a letter from their son in Bhilai, she read out to him the boy's report on his work in the steel mills. The father said nothing but seemed calmer and she was able, after that, to make him eat a little rice and fish *jhol*, very lightly prepared, just as the doctor prescribed. "Lie down now," she said, sucking at a fish bone as she removed the dishes from the table. "It's too hot out on the balcony. Take some rest."

"Rest?" he snapped at her, but shuffled off into the bedroom and allowed her to make up his bed with all the pillows and bolsters that kept him in an almost sitting position on the flat wooden bed. He shifted and groaned as she heaped up a bolster here, flattened a cushion there, and said he could not possibly sleep, but she thought he did for she kept an eye on him while she leafed through a heap of film and women's magazines on her side of the bed, and thought his eyes were closed genuinely in sleep and that his breathing was almost as regular as the slow circling of the electric fan above them. The fan needed oiling, it made a disturbing clicking sound with every revolution, but who was there to climb up to it and do the oiling and cleaning? Not so easy to get these things done when one's husband is old and ill, she thought. She yawned. She rolled over.

When she brought him his afternoon tea, she asked "Had a good sleep?" which annoyed him. "Never slept at all," he snapped, taking the cup from her hands and spilling some tea. "How can one sleep if one can't breathe?" he growled, and she turned away with a little smile at his stubbornness. But later that evening he was genuinely ill, choked, in a panic at his inability to breathe as well as at the prospect of a hot night without a fan. "What will I do?" he kept moaning in between violent struggles for air that shook his body and left it limp. "What will I do?"

"I'll tell you," she suddenly answered, and wiped the perspiration from her face in relief. "I'll have your bed taken up on the terrace. I can call Bulu from next door to do it—you can sleep out in the open air tonight, eh? That'll be nice, won't it? That will do you good." She brightened both at the thought of a night spent in the open air on the terrace, just as they had done when they were younger and climbing up and down stairs was nothing to them, and at the thought of having an excuse to visit the neighbors and having a little chat while getting them to come and carry up a string bed for them. Of course old Basu made a protest and a great fuss and coughed and spat and shook and said he could not possibly move in this condition, or be moved by anyone, but she insisted and, ignoring him, went out to make the arrangements.

Basu had not been on the terrace for years. While his wife and Bulu led him up the stairs, hauling him up and propping him upright by their shoulders as though he were some lifeless bag containing something fragile and valuable, he tried to think when he had last attempted or achieved what now seemed a tortuous struggle up the steep concrete steps to the warped green door at the top.

They had given up sleeping there on summer nights long ago, not so much on account of old age or weak knees, really, but because of their perpetual quarrels with the neighbors on the next terrace, separated from theirs by only a broken wooden trellis. Noisy, inconsider-

ate people, addicted to the radio turned on full blast. At
times the man had been drunk and troubled and abused
his wife who gave as good as she got. It had been intolerable. Otima had urged her husband, night after night, to
protest. When he did, they had almost killed him. At
least they would have had they managed to cross over to
the Basus' terrace which they were physically prevented
from doing by their sons and daughters. The next night
they had been even more offensive. Finally the Basus
had been forced to give in and retreat down the stairs to
sleep in their closed, airless room under the relentlessly
ticking ceiling fan. At least it was private there. After
the first few restless nights they wondered how they had
ever put up with the public sleeping outdoors and its
disturbances—its "nuisance," as Otima called it in English, thinking it an effective word.

That had not—he groaned aloud as they led him up
over the last step to the green door—been the last visit
he had paid to the rooftop. As Bulu kicked open the
door—half-witted he may be, but he was burly too, and
good-natured, like so many half-wits—and the city sky
revealed itself, in its dirt-swept grays and mauves, on the
same level with them, Basu recalled how, not so many
years ago, he had taken his daughter Charu's son by the
hand to show him the pigeon roosts on so many of the
Darya Ganj rooftops, and pointed out to him a flock of
collector's pigeons like so many silk and ivory fans flirt-
ing in the sky. The boy had watched in silence, holding
onto his grandfather's thumb with tense delight. The
memory of it silenced his groans as they lowered him
onto the bed they had earlier carried up and spread with
his many pillows and bolsters. He sat there, getting back
his breath, and thinking of Nikhil. When would he see
Nikhil again? What would he not give to have that child
hold his thumb again and go for a walk with him!

Punctually at eight o'clock the electricity was switched
off, immediately sucking up Darya Ganj into a box of
shadows, so that the distant glow of Cannaught Place,
still lit up, was emphasized. The horizon was illuminated
as by a fire, roasted red. The traffic made long stripes
of light up and down the streets below them. Lying back,
Basu saw the dome of the sky as absolutely impenetrable,

shrouded with summer dust, and it seemed to him as airless as the room below. Nikhil, Nikhil, he wept, as though the child might have helped.

Nor could he find any ease, any comfort on that unaccustomed string bed (the wooden pallet in their room was of course too heavy to carry up, even for Bulu). He complained that his heavy body sank into it as into a hammock, that the strings cut into him, that he could not turn on that wobbling net in which he was caught like some dying fish, gasping for air. It was no cooler than it had been indoors, he complained—there was not the slightest breeze, and the dust was stifling.

Otima soon lost the lightheartedness that had come to her with this unaccustomed change of scene. She tired of dragging around the pillows and piling up the bolsters, helping him into a sitting position and then lowering him into a horizontal one, bringing him his medicines, fanning him with a palm leaf and eventually of his groans and sobs as well. Finally she gave up and collapsed onto her own string bed, lying there exhausted and sleepless, too distracted by the sound of traffic to sleep. All through the night her husband moaned and gasped for air. Toward dawn it was so bad that she had to get up and massage his chest. When done long and patiently enough, it seemed to relieve him.

"Now lie down for a while. I'll go and get some iced water for your head," she said, lowering him onto the bed, and went tiredly down the stairs like some bundle of damp washing slowly falling. Her eyes drooped, heavy bags held the tiredness under them.

To her surprise, there was a light on in their flat. Then she heard the ticking of the fan. She had forgotten to turn it off when they went up to the terrace and it seemed the electricity had been switched on again, earlier than they had expected. The relief of it brought her energy back in a bound. She bustled up the stairs. I'll bring him down—he'll get some hours of sleep after all, she told herself.

"It's all right," she called out as she went up to the terrace again. "The electricity is on again. Come, I'll help you down—you'll get some sleep in your own bed after all."

"Leave me alone," he replied, quite gently.

"Why? Why?" she cried. "I'll help you. You can get into your own bed, you'll be quite comfortable—"

"Leave me alone," he said again in that still voice. "It is cool now."

It was. Morning had stirred up some breeze off the sluggish river Jumna beneath the city walls, and it was carried over the rooftops of the stifled city, pale and fresh and delicate. It brought with it the morning light, as delicate and sweet as the breeze itself, a pure pallor unlike the livid glow of artificial lights. This lifted higher and higher into the dome of the sky, diluting the darkness there till it, too, grew pale and gradually shades of blue and mauve tinted it lightly.

The old man lay flat and still, gazing up, his mouth hanging open as if to let it pour into him, as cool and fresh as water.

Then, with a swirl and flutter of feathers, a flock of pigeons hurtled upwards and spread out against the dome of the sky—opalescent, sunlit, like small pearls. They caught the light as they rose, turned brighter till they turned at last into crystals, into prisms of light. Then they disappeared into the soft, deep blue of the morning.

Mahasweta Devi
(b. 1926)

Born in Dacca (now Bangladesh) into a middle-class Bengali family, Mahasweta Devi studied at Visva-Bharati and Calcutta University, and earned an M.A. in English at Shantiniketan, a famous experimental university. In 1964 she began teaching at an Indian college for working-class women, Bijaygarh College in Jadavpur, working as a creative writer and journalist as well. During recent decades she has lived among and studied the rural tribal and outcaste communities of West Bengal. In her realistic Bengali fiction, she frequently depicts the oppression of these tribal peoples and untouchables by powerful, high-caste landlords, moneylenders, and corrupt government officials. She has written of the source of her inspiration:

> I have always believed that the real history is made by ordinary people. I constantly come across the re-appearance, in various forms, of folklore, ballads, myths and legends, carried by ordinary people across generations. . . . The reason and the inspiration for my writing are those people who are exploited and used, and yet do not accept defeat. For me, the endless source of ingredients for writing is in these amazingly noble, suffering human beings. Why should I look for my raw material elsewhere, once I have started knowing them? Sometimes it seems to me that my writing is really their doing.

Among more than a dozen Bengali novels, Devi has published *Hajar Churashir Ma* [*No. 1084's Mother*] (1975), which depicts the revolt of a coalition of peasants, aided by idealistic students, against landlords and government representatives who were defrauding them in West Bengal, *Aranyer Adhikar* [*The Occupation of the Forest*] (1977), a historical novel about an insurrection of 1899 for which the author won the Sahitya Academy Award in 1979, and *Chotti Munda evam Tar Tir* [*Chotti Munda and His Arrow*] 1980. Some of her short stories which have been collected in *Agnigarbha* [*Womb of Fire*] (1978) have been translated into English. Six of them appear in *Of Women, Outcastes, Peasants, and Rebels: A Selection of Bengali Short Stories*, edited and translated by Kalpana Bardhan (University of California Press, 1990) and some appear in *Truth Tales: Contemporary Writing by Indian Women* published by Kali for Women in Delhi in 1986. Devi also edits *Bortika*, a magazine in which she publishes nonfiction descriptions of the lives of the poor Bengali laborers.

DHOWLI

1

The bus starts from Ranchi city in early afternoon and reaches Tahad around eight in the evening. The bus stop is in front of the grocery shop, also the only tea shop, both run by Parashnath, next to the post office. The *shop-cum-teastall*, the post office, and the bus stop form the downtown for the cluster of villages. The passengers get off here and walk the rest of their way home. This is where the unpaved wide road ends; so also ends the outside world with which Tahad is connected by this once-a-day rickety bus run by the Rohatgi company. The Punjabi company runs a brisk fleet of forty buses connecting the business centers in Bihar, twenty going up the highways and twenty coming down along the three routes connecting Ranchi with Patna, Hazaribagh, and

Ramgarh. For dirt-poor, remote places like Tahad or Palani, they have a few dilapidated buses running off and on. On the three market days each week, the bus is filled by tribal villagers out to buy and sell. On other days, the bus is almost empty and runs irregularly to cut the company's loss. During the months of monsoon the bus does not come up the unpaved road, and the villages then remain cut off from the outside world.

This year, the rains seemed to be coming early, at the very start of June.

Dhowli was waiting at the bus stop, standing very still, her back to the shop, facing away from the shop's light, the only light there. Parashnath closed his shop when it seemed to him that the bus was not likely to come. He asked Dhowli if she should not be going home now. Dhowli neither answered nor looked at him. She just kept standing. Old Parashnath muttered, worried, as he left for his home at the back of the shop. His wife was sitting there alone, smoking and thinking. Parashnath told her about the girl waiting again for the bus so late in the evening.

"She'll be finished if she keeps up this way."

"If the landlord comes to know what she's been doing . . ."

"That'll be her end. How long has it been since the Misra boy left?"

"Nearly four months now."

"What does she think? An untouchable, Dusad girl can make a Brahman give her home and food?"

"God only knows. But she's not going to be able to hold off for long."

"What makes you think so?"

"The contractor, and the gang of coolies."

"Yes. She doesn't have much of a chance. Such a young girl! Going back and forth alone in the dark night. What for? Isn't she afraid?"

"The wolf was out last night."

Dhowli had also heard that the wolf was out, but she forgot about it. The unbearable pain just under her chest made her forget everything else. The pain would stay there and then move down her body, as it was now.

Dhowli did not know what to do; she could not think of anything.

Dhowli walked back home in the dark. To the shack dimly lit by the smoky oil lamp; their bed on the bamboo bunk; three goats tethered under the bunk. Her mother, lying in the bunk, saw her come in but said nothing. Dhowli tilted the water pot to see if there was any water. She drank some, closed the door, blew out the lamp, and lay down beside her mother. Tears silently flowed from her eyes, tears of hopeless pain. Her mother listened to her crying; she knew why the tears flowed. Later in the night, she said, "We're going to be driven out of the village. You're young. What'll happen to me? Where shall I go?"

"You'll stay here."

"And you? You'll leave?"

"If I have to."

"Where will you go?"

"To death's door."

"It's not so easy! At nineteen, there are obstacles to death's door."

"Not for me."

"Have you been to Sanichari?"

"No!" Dhowli shouted, "I'll not get rid of the baby."

"Will you then go to the Misra house? Tell them that, because their son is the father, they should help to bring up the child carrying their blood?"

"Who is going to believe me? It would have been different if he were here now, if he came back."

"How? He would have looked after you?"

"He promised to."

"They always say such things. You're not the first Dusad girl who has been used by the Misra menfolk. Have they left untouched any young girl of the Dusads, the Dhobis, the Ganjus of the village?"

"He's not like the others."

"No! He knows very well what is expected of a Brahman's son in this situation. He knows what to do, but he's not doing it."

"He's in love with me."

"In love with you? Is that why he has stayed away in

Dhanbad for four months, not even coming to visit his own folks?"

"He doesn't come because he's afraid of his parents."

"You're thinking of love. Here I lost my job of tending their goats. The wolf got one of the kids. They accused me of stealing it."

"What has that got to do with me?"

"They did it to punish you, to show that they're annoyed."

"Throw me out, then."

"I will. Go to sleep now."

"How can you say you'll throw me out? Who do you have but me?"

At this point, mother and daughter started arguing, as they did almost every night these days. This time they were interrupted by the watchman's voice from outside. "Dhowli's mother! All day we hear you shout. Do we have to hear you shout in the night, too? There are other Dusads in the neighborhood. They all know that days are for shouting and nights for sleeping. You're the only one who doesn't respect this simple rule."

"Shut up, and go away. I'll be quiet now."

"What's the problem anyway? Is some coolie trying to get in?"

"It's your home that the coolies try to get in."

"Ram! Ram! Don't even say such a thing!"

The watchman walked away. Mother muttered what was on her mind, "I know the custom here. Everybody is waiting, watching to see if the Misra boy supports you after the baby is born. If he doesn't, they'll come to eat pieces off you."

"It's all your fault. Why did you bring me back to you when my husband died? Why didn't you leave me there, to whatever was to happen?"

"Did they want to keep you? Didn't you insist on coming with me?"

"Because his elder brother would have taken my virtue there."

"And the Misra boy has not here!"

The sarcasm felt like a stab. Dhowli said nothing. Her eyelids were dry inside from crying. She pulled the dry lids down over her tired eyes.

But she could not fall asleep. She had not been able to sleep since the day the Misra boy left, taking the early morning bus, running away like a thief. She knew that she could fall asleep forever with the poison for killing maize insects. But she could not die before seeing that betrayer once more face to face, eye to eye.

Betrayer? No. He left Tahad because his parents made him. They came down so hard on their dearly loved youngest boy; Hanuman Misra of Burudiha threatened them. He wouldn't have left Dhowli unless he was really scared, he who cried like a baby to Dhowli just talking about the possibility that he might be sent away. It still hurt to remember how he wept.

Her mother wanted her to get the medicine from Sanichari to remove the "thorn" from her womb. How could she think of it as a thorn, when it came from their love? It was not like the children of Jhalo, the Ganju wife, and Kundan, the elder Misra son; it was not one of those products of greed and ruthless power.

Dhowli used to sweep their yard. She never lifted her eyes at the young Brahman she knew was always gazing at her. At noon, while tending the goats in the forest, Dhowli was once bathing in the stream when a small leafy branch fell beside her. She looked up and saw the Misra boy. He had followed her. He did not laugh; he did not leer at her; he did nothing she could be ashamed of. He only asked her why she never even looked at him when he was going out of his mind for her.

"Please, *deota*,* don't say such things!"

"What deota! Don't you know that I'm really your slave?"

"I don't want to hear such things."

Dhowli was afraid and turned to leave. Then he said, "You'll have to hear the truth some time, even if you don't want to now."

The young Misra left her with those words, words that still make the breeze waft in her mind, the leaves rustle, and the stream murmur. She stood there after he left. She lingered on, feeling something like a terrible fear

---

*Lord, deity.

beating in her chest. Fear of the unthinkable. The young Misra was so fair, his hair softly curled, and his face so lovely. Anyone could tell from his looks that he was of noble birth. And what was Dhowli? Only a Dusad girl, a widow, with a life of deprivation as far back as she could remember.

When her father died and there was no other man in the family, Kundan took away the lease of land from her mother. Her mother went to them and promised to pay the rent, whatever rent they wanted; she would have the land tilled by her Dusad kinsmen, for, if they wouldn't lease her the land, the two of them would starve to death. Kundan refused. Dhowli's mother then fell at the feet of Kundan's mother, "Please save me and my daughter from starving."

Kundan's mother pleaded with her son, "As long as her husband was alive, he tilled that land and gave us free labor whenever we wanted. Now that he is dead, we can't let her starve."

"Nothing I can do. I've already leased that plot to Jhuman Dusad."

"Let them tend the goats then and clean our garden and yards. We'll give them some money and millet."

She depended on their pity for the gruel at the end of the day. And a son of theirs had just said those words to her. Why? Dhowli knew that her timid eyes, her slender waist, and her budding breasts were her enemies, only to bring her trouble and ruin her. So, she had always kept herself covered as well as she could with her cheap, short sari, and she never looked up when working in their yard, not even at the loads of fruit ripening on the trees. She picked up only the guavas and the custard apples that birds and bats had partly eaten and dropped underneath. Even those she showed to Kundan's mother for permission before bringing them home.

That day, after she came back from the forest, Dhowli scrubbed their brass plate till it gleamed like gold. When her mother was away, she looked at her face in it. A widow was not supposed to see her face in the mirror any more, nor wear the shellac bangles, the vermillion between the brows, the nickel anklets. She saw that her face was beautiful, but a beautiful face was useless for a widow because she could never marry again. She would never even be invited to sing the song "Sita is on her way to her in-laws' place" at another girl's wedding, nor to paint with colored paste flowers, leaves, and birds on the doors and the walls of any celebrating house. Someone like her had just heard the landlord's young son proclaim love, that he was a slave to her. Fear nestled under her chest like some terrible discomfort.

Dhowli told her mother, "You'll sweep the gardens of the Misras, and I would only tend the goats."

"Why?"

"Because, you know, Ma, how the leaves fly when you try to sweep them into a pile. I can't cope with the wind scattering them about."

"Did anyone say anything to you?"

"Who can say what to me, Ma?"

"Don't go far into the forest with the goats. A wolf or a hyena is about."

"Don't worry, Ma. Am I that careless?"

She thought a lot, while tending the goats alone in the woods. She thought about everything she could remember from her childhood—going to the fair, perched on her father's shoulders; spending the day looking at all the shops with their expensive things, and then coming home happy with a paisa worth of sesame candy. Of her marital home, all she remembered were the two rooms, the days of work at the farm of the moneylender to whom they were indebted, and her mother-in-law making the gruel at the end of the day, for the men to eat first before the women ate what was left over.

About her wedding she could not recall much because she must have been very small at the time. She was sent to live with her husband when her body blossomed. Her father had to take a large loan from the Misras for her wedding and sending off, and he had to pay back the loan with his labor until he died. She remembered nothing nice about her husband. He used to beat her. He died of a fever. After he died, her mother-in-law asked her to stay on,

"You have to work at your mother's place too in order to eat. Do the same here."

Dhowli knew that much: she could spend the rest of her life there, working all day, clad in the widow's borderless sari, coarse and short, working every day from sunrise to sunset either on the creditor's threshing floor or as some farmer's laborer or leveling the layer of brick pieces with a mallet making some road or other, and then falling asleep by the side of her mother-in-law after eating whatever there was to eat. But then her husband's elder brother came there and started eyeing her. Her mother-in-law then turned against her and Dhowli left. Her only regret was that she had to leave before she could watch the *nautanki* one more time.* The nautanki performers used to come to the village, hired by the moneylender.

After she returned to Tahad, she did not let herself near any Dusad boy. What good could come of it? The same routine of backbreaking work, with kids in your lap, kids following you around, no food, nothing. Dhowli had no desire for that kind of life, the only kind of life for a Dusad girl.

It was so much better to be alone, alone in the woods, with time to think one's own thoughts. She tended the goats, and once in a while she lay down on the end of her sari spread on the forest floor. She was never afraid of the wolf or the hyena. They fear people just as people fear them. The forest felt so peaceful that the constant discomfort and fear she had after hearing the Misra boy speak so strangely to her was slowly going away. She was at peace again.

Then one evening, when coming back from the fair at Jhujhar, she somehow lost the group of women she came with. She knew that the procurers came to the village fairs to catch just such stray girls. So she was walking back as fast as she could. The Misra boy caught up with her.

"Didn't you hear me calling?"

"Why did you call?"

"Don't you know why?"

"No. Please don't say such things to me. I'm a poor Dusad widow, and you are the landlord. Please don't make fun of me."

Nautanki is a form of vaudeville, with wild and earthy songs and dances, common in north Indian villages.

"But I'm in love with you."

"No, deota. Don't mistake it for love. You are a young Brahman man. You'll marry a bride proper for you. Please stop this."

"But it's you I love. Don't you know what love is?"

"No, I don't. I know that there can be bastards between the landlord and a Ganju or Dusad girl. That happens all the time. But not love."

"But I can't think of anyone but you."

"Please don't play your games with a helpless poor girl."

"I'm not playing games."

"You'll leave after you tire of the game, and what will become of me? Am I to be like Jhalo? No, deota, not that."

"What if I don't let you go?"

"What good is my saying anything? I'll have to accept it. You landlord people, you take whatever pleases you. If you want to take my honor, take it then. Let me be through with it."

"No, no. Don't say that, Dhowli. Forgive me." The Misra boy ran away from her. She came home, totally amazed by his behavior.

Soon after that, when she heard that the Misra boy was not well, that he seemed to have lost interest in life, she was moved and worried. She knew that the Misra boy could have had her any time he wanted. All the Misra men do that, and there is not a thing that the Dhowlis of the world can do to stop it. But why such strange behavior?

She felt overwhelmed. Then the women at the well surrounded her, "Fate is now all smiles on the poor widow!"

"How can fate ever smile on a widow?"

"The landlord's young son is going out of his mind for you!"

"A pack of lies!"

"Everybody knows it's true. The word is around."

"Don't bother me with gossip."

Dhowli left with the water, resolutely denying it, but she was agitated, and she went to the woods with the goats. What would she do now? The whole village was talking about something that had never happened before. Why did the boy lose his mind like that? Now nobody was going to leave her alone.

She avoided going anywhere near the Misra estate. She heard from her mother that the boy was still unwell and they had to call a doctor from Valatod. She wondered if her mother knew what the women at the well knew. She suggested that they go away from the village, to Valatod maybe, and work at road construction, to which her mother just said, "I'm not out of my mind."

Then one day she heard that the Misra boy had recovered, that they were looking for a beautiful bride for him. They hadn't looked particularly for beauty in Kundan's bride; but for this one they were after beauty.

Dhowli had felt relieved, but she had also felt a twinge of pain and simultaneously a joy of victory at the thought that a mere Dusad girl drove a Brahman's son so out of his mind.

Relieved and peaceful again, she went to the woods and had a cooling dip in the stream. Afterward, she dried half of the sari she was wearing by spreading it on a sun-heated stone, and then wrapped it around her upper body. She decided that she would buy another sari next time her mother got paid for their work. It always made her mother angry to see her in a half-wet sari: "Are you a widow or a marketplace whore, that you're showing your body?"

Suddenly, the Misra boy appeared there.

"I don't want to marry a girl of their choice. It's you I want, Dhowli," he told her in earnest.

The forest in the early afternoon is primitive, gentle, and comforting. The Misra boy's voice was imploring, his eyes full of pain and despair. Dhowli was unguarded in mind and body. She gave in.

For two months since that day, she lived as if in a strange dream. The forest was their meeting place, and the time the early afternoon. Both lost caution and sense, one nineteen and the other twenty-three. Every day, Dhowli worried about what was going to happen next.

"You're going to be married off soon."

"With you."

"Don't joke with me, deota."

"I'm not joking. I don't believe in caste. And Tahad is not the only place in the world to live. Besides, our marriage will be all right by the government rules."

"Don't say such things. If you talk defiant, what will Misraji order? They will then drive me away from the village."

"It's not going to be so easy. There are government laws against it."

"The laws are not for people like us."

"You don't know anything."

In the solitude of the forest, the Misra boy was dauntless, telling her of his plans, and his words seemed to mingle with all the myths associated with the old forest, taking on an enchanting and dreamlike quality. The days thus went by. But not for very long. Dhowli found out that she was pregnant. Strangely, the Misra boy was happy about that. He said, "I'm illiterate, just like you. I don't want anything to do with managing all this farmland and orchard and the estate. We'll go to Valatod, and then from there to Dhanbad, and on to Patna. We'll start a shop there and live from it."

But the day Hanuman Misra came to Tahad to settle the matter, the Misra boy could say none of those things to him. Kundan fretted and said that he was going to kill both mother and daughter and dispose of their bodies overnight.

"No, don't do that," Misraji said. "Clean the inside of the house, and the outside will clean itself."

"I want to kill them."

"That's because you're stupid."

"That bitch of her mother said that the wolf took one of the goats. How did she get three goats in her shack? Didn't she have two before?"

"The idiot talks about goats! Your wife has got more sense. I can talk with her, not you. Kill them, but not directly. Starve them. Take away the job. What your silly brother got himself into has affected the prestige of all of us. We must restore our position first. What does it matter if you have one goat less? Listen to me, the first thing you should do now is move him away from here."

The young Misra said that he would not leave the village.

"If you don't, your dead body will. You've brought shame to our family by your stupidity."

The Misra boy in desperation appealed to his mother, "Ma, please! Dhowli is carrying my baby."

"Nothing unusual about it, my boy," she consoled him. "Men of this family have had children by Dusad and Ganju girls. Kundan has three by Jhalo. It's only the heat of your age, my boy."

"What'll happen to Dhowli then?"

"She'll be punished for daring to do what she did. She'll pay. She and her mother will starve to death."

"But it's not her fault, Mother."

"The fault is always the woman's. She caused trouble in a Brahman landlord's home. That equals a crime."

"Mother, you love me, don't you?"

"You're my youngest child."

"Then touch me and swear. I'll listen to you if you'll see that she doesn't starve. Promise."

"I promise," she said hesitantly.

"Also promise me that nobody humiliates her or throws her out."

"I'll try."

"If you don't keep these words, then you know, Mother, that I can be stubborn. I may not be able to stand up to the big Misra. But if you don't keep the promises, then I'll never come to this village, never marry."

"No, no. I'll feed the Dusad girl; I'll look after her."

Dhowli was aware of what was going on, what was in store for her now. She never even thought of protesting. This was not the first time that a Dusad girl had been used by the Brahman landlord's son. According to the village society, all the blame goes to Dhowli. But, because of the love aspect of this case, she was now an outcaste to her own people, in her own community. She had not encouraged any boy of her own caste. That was no fault. If the Misra boy had taken her by force, then she would not have been faulted either; the Dusad community would not have abandoned her for that. There are quite a few children by Brahman men growing up among the Dusads. Her crime, something nobody was prepared to forgive, was that she gave herself to him of her own accord, out of love. All the Dusad-Ganju boys, the coolies, and the labor contractors were now watching how things would settle. If the Misras would support her and the child with a regular supply of corn or money or a job, then they would leave her alone because they did not want to annoy the Misras if they wanted to live in their domain. If not, then they would turn her, a widow with no one but an old mother and a baby, into a prostitute for all of them to use.

Dhowli knew what was going through every mind, and she was numb with fear and sorrow. The woods looked horrible to her, the trees looked like ghoulish guards, and even the rocks seemed to be watching her. She waited for him by the stream. Days passed, but he failed to appear there. When Dhowli was about to give up, he came. Dhowli read her death sentence in his grim face. She cried without a word, her face on his chest. He cried too, his face buried in her hair, her hair smelling of the soap and the scented oil he had given her. He had given her two saris too, but Dhowli never wore them because their printed material was forbidden for a widow.

The Misra boy was filled with hopelessness. All he could say was, "Dhowli, why were you born a Dusad?"

"Spare me the endearments! I can't stand them anymore."

"Listen to me. Don't cry yet."

"Don't I have to cry the rest of my life?"

"I have to leave the village now. I agreed to their conditions for now."

"Why did you tell me those words of love?"

"I'm still telling you."

"Why, master? Your Dhowli is dead now. Don't make fun of a corpse."

"Don't be silly. Listen to me." He made Dhowli sit on a rock. He held her face in his hands and lifted it to his. Then he said to her, "I must stay away for a month, and I'll do so quietly. But I told them that I won't be forced into a marriage, and they agreed not to try."

"They will forget that soon."

"No. Listen, I'll be back as soon as the month is over. I'm not sure where they'll send me or what I'll do in this one month. But I'll manage something for us. I'm not educated, and I don't want a salaried job. And I'm not going to ask my brother for a share of the farmland and orchards. I'll start a shop, and I'll use this time to do it. I need some time away from them to do it, you see?"

"What am I to do?"

"You will stay right in the village."

"What shall we live on? Your brother accused my mother of stealing and sacked her."

"My mother has promised me that she'll supply you with food, and here . . . ," he took out five ten-rupee notes, put them in one end of Dhowli's sari, tied a knot around it, and tucked it in her waist. "Try to stay calm for one month."

Misrilal took leave of her.

Dhowli came back from the forest and told her mother. The two of them put the money in a little can and buried it under their mud floor.

Two days after he had left, Dhowli's mother went to the Misra matriarch and silently stood before her. Silently she got up, brought a kilo of millet and poured it in the outstretched sari of Dhowli's mother, conspicuously avoiding her touch while doing it. Glumly she asked her to come back after three days. After three days, the quantity of grain was reduced to half a kilo. When she next returned after the specified three days, the lady grimly informed her that after the last time she was there, they couldn't find a brass bowl.

"No, lady. Not me . . ."

"My elder son has asked me not to let you inside the house any more. Next time you should stand at the gate and call someone."

Dhowli's mother had to swallow the accusation because it came from a Brahman lady. Next time she was told at the gate that the lady was away, gone to Burudiha to see Hanuman Misra.

Dhowli's mother came home boiling with anger and beat up Dhowli. Dhowli took the beating quietly. When her mother stopped beating, she brought the cleaver and asked her to use it instead because her old hands tired and ached easily and as it was sharpened recently, she would not have to bother to beat her again. Mother and daughter then held each other and cried. When they were through crying, her mother asked her to go to Sanichari

and get some medicine to get rid of the thorn in her
womb.

"I can't do that."

"Listen to me. He is not going to come back for you.
He was just in a rebellious mood toward the family. He
may have good intentions; maybe he wasn't lying when
he promised to come back. But he won't be able to do
it."

"Then I'd rather poison myself."

Mother sat down, pondering a few minutes what her
daughter had just said; then, sighing, she got up, as if
she had just remembered something. "I'm going to the
forest contractor; he once asked if I could cook for him."

"Do you want me to go?"

"No. I'll go. I'm past the age to worry about gossip.
Even if he doesn't pay money, he'll give me some food.
I'll bring it home."

"Go then, before the job is gone."

"And you remember to tend the goats."

This arrangement kept them going a little longer.
Dhowli's mother did not find the cook's job, but she was
taken as the cook's helper, and she brought home the
bread or rice she managed to get.

Their own folks watched how mother and daughter
managed to live—what they did and what they didn't
do. The coolies working under the forest contractor also
watched them. They had cash from their daily wages for
lugging lumber. They had refrained from falling on her
so far only because they were not sure if she was going
to become the favored woman of Kundan's little brother.
They had not given up, though, and watched the goings
on. They did not mind the wait; the contract for cutting
logs and splitting lumber was to continue for a while,
and she was worth waiting for. As a matter of fact, her
attraction increased in their minds with the scandal of a
Brahman boy falling in love with her.

One month was long over. It was four months now. It
had become a ritual with Dhowli to go to the bus stop,
stand silently waiting for the bus to come up, and return
home disappointed. On this night Dhowli thought of the
whole thing, all over again, and then she placed her hand
on her abdomen. She felt the baby move a little. Misrilal

had said, "If it is a boy, we'll name him Murari." But
Misrilal and his words of love now felt like a receding
illusion, a fading dream.

2

In late autumn Dhowli gives birth to a son. Sanichari
delivers the baby. She cuts the umbilical cord with care
and remarks that the baby is so fair because it has
Dhowli's complexion. Dhowli's mother had asked Sanichari earlier to make sure she would be infertile after
this baby. Sanichari gives her the medicine, telling her
that it will make her feel better soon.

Afterward she sits down to talk with Dhowli's mother,
who is worried that the medicine is going to kill her or
make her a permanent invalid. Sanichari assures her with
the account of her success with the medicine in the case
of Kundan's wife.

"What are you going to do now?"

"Whatever god has willed for us."

"The Misra boy is going to be married soon."

"Quiet. Don't let Dhowli hear of it now."

"What will you do after that?"

"Whatever is in store for us will happen."

"Pebbles will start falling at your door at night."

"I know."

"After getting him married, they're going to make the
couple live in Dhanbad. They've set up a cycle store
there for him."

"I told Dhowli this was going to happen."

"As I've already told you, if the landlord doesn't un-
dertake to support her and the baby, I'll try and get the
forest overseer for her."

"We'll think about that later."

Because of Sanichari's Manthara-like cunning, and because she is indispensable for her knowledge of medicinal
herbs and roots, not even the Misras dare to ignore her
or snub her. Seeing Dhowli give birth, delivering her
baby, has touched something in Sanichari's heart. She
starts building support in Dhowli's favor. When she visits
the Misra mother to treat her rheumatic pain, Sanichari
tells her that she just delivered Dhowli's baby boy.

"So what?" says the lady.

"His face is exactly like your boy's."

"Nobody tells me such a lie."

"Don't be silly. Everybody knows that your boy was in love with Dhowli. Your men sow their seeds in our women. It is common, but how often does it become such a problem that Hanuman Misra himself has to come to solve it?"

"Because you raised the matter, let me ask you for something . . ."

"What is it?"

"Can you remove them from the village?"

"Remove them where?"

"I don't care where. The problem is that the girl my boy is going to be married to is not exactly a little girl, and the family has a lot of prestige. If they come to know of this, it will make them very annoyed."

"If you pay enough, they'll leave the village."

"How much?"

"A thousand rupees."

"Let me talk to my elder son."

"You have ruined your reputation in the village by failing to look after them and feed them. Your husband and your elder son made Ganju women pregnant, but they never failed to support them afterward. You have always been generous. How come you turned away from your usual *Bhagwati* role this time?"

"It's because Dhowli's mother stole the brass jug . . ."

"Stop giving false excuses."

The Misra matriarch has to let Sanichari get away with telling her so many unpleasant words so bluntly only because she is her secret supplier of the medicine for holding onto her old husband, who is addicted to a certain washerwoman. She cuts short the exchange and asks Sanichari's advice about what could be done now.

"Do something. You can help her if you want to."

"Let me talk to my elder son."

Her elder son, Kundan, dismisses her worries. He is not going to let that troublesome girl manipulate them—a baby today, and customers at her home tomorrow. He is going to fix it all. His brother will get married in Dhanbad and stay there. The matriarch is reassured by her manly son, and she promptly forgets the nagging worry.

But the patriarch Hanuman Misra absolutely refuses to solve the problem that way. "The boy will come here with the new bride, as is the custom, and later on they will go together to Dhanbad. Why can't he come to his home, his own village? For fear of a Dusad girl? What can she do?"

Dhowli, like everybody else, hears about the verdict. She stays home with the baby in her lap, trying to think about what they are going to live on. Mother's odd jobs are getting more scarce, uncertain, and now she depends on her with the baby. They could sell the goats one at a time, but how long would that feed them? What would they do after that?

Misrilal. Just recalling his name makes her mind go limp even now. All those caresses, those sweet words of love were lies? They could not be. There are fantastic associations with the woods and the spring. The ferocious constable Makkhan Singh once saw a fairy bathing in the stream on a moonlit night; he really saw it because he lost his mind from that night. A Ganju girl named Jhulni was in love with her husband's younger brother, and when chastised by the Panchayat, the two of them went into the woods and ate poisonous seeds to die together. Dhowli knew Jhulni and the boy. These were true events—they happened—and yet sound like mythical stories. Their love was true too, and yet it feels so unreal now! In that same forest, beside that stream, a Brahman youth once called a Dusad girl his little bird, his one and only bride-for-ever. Didn't they once lie on the carpet of fallen red flowers and become one body and soul? Once when the Dusad girl got a thorn in her foot, didn't the Brahman youth gently pick it out and kiss the spot of blood under her foot? It is now hard to believe that these things ever happened. They now seem like made up stories. All that seems real is the baby sleeping in her lap and the constant worry about food.

Misrilal has not kept the promise he made her. He can't. There's nothing that Dhowli can say or do about it. What now? When he comes back to the village after his wedding, will he be moved to pity on seeing his boy?

Will he give a bit of land to help his child live? The
Misra men have done that many times. But Dhowli's
mind says, "No, he won't." What will she do then? Will
she end up opening her door at night when the pebbles
strike? For a few coins from one, some corn or a sari
from another? Is that how she must live?

Dhowli's mind says, "No! Never that way!"

Tomorrow, how is she going to go to the well to fetch
water? All the girls will be talking about the wedding and
the preparations for the groom's party. When a Brahman
landlord groom's party comes back after the wedding,
even the Dusad girls sing and dance, from a little distance
though; and they collect sweets and coins and chickpea
flour. Is she going to join them in singing for the reward?

Sanichari, on her way back from the Misra house, after
giving the boys' mother a piece of her mind, stops to talk
to the fellows in the Dusad neighborhood and tries to
put some sense in their heads.

"The poor girl is ruined and unjustly abandoned by
the Brahman boy, and even you, her own folks, turn
your backs on her. Have you thought about how she is
to live?"

"Nobody ruined Dhowli. She fell in love with him.
And don't expect us to forget that she turned down the
boys from her own caste. So we don't feel involved with
her problems; we don't care whether things go well or
bad for her. Let her do what she can, however she man-
ages it."

"What choices do you think she has now?"

"Let's see if her Brahman lover supports her and looks
after her . . ."

Misrilal does nothing at all. He arrives, all decorated,
at the head of the groom's party back from his wedding.
Only in Dhowli's home is no lamp lit that evening. All
the Dusads, Ganjus, Dhobis, and Tolis get sweets, country liquor, chickpea flour, even new clothes. All agree
that such lavish gift giving has never happened at any
other wedding in the area.

Dhowli waits by the side of the spring next day. She
waits all evening. Misrilal does not come. Coming back

from there, Dhowli stops at Sanichari's place and breaks down. Sanichari informs her that Misrilal was angry when he heard that she and her mother had refused the help his mother offered. "Is that what he told you?"

"Yes."

"Then go and ask him to come and see me. Otherwise, I'm going there with the baby to see his bride, even though I know his brother will kill me for it."

Misrilal does come to see her. He has no words; his eyes are confused. Dhowli reads in his face the power her presence still has on his mind. It makes her happy in a way that also makes her suddenly bold enough to speak up.

"Did you tell Sanichari that we refused your mother's handouts?"

"That's what my mother told me."

"I spit on her lies. Your mother gave us two kilos of millet in all, over a period of ten days. After that she called my mother a thief and turned her away."

"I didn't know that."

"Why did you destroy me like this?"

"I loved . . ."

"I spit on your love. If you had raped me, then I would have received a tenth of an acre as compensation. You are not a man. Your brother is. He gave Jhalo babies, but he also gave her a home and a farm of her own. And you? What have you done?"

"What I've done I was forced to do. I did not do it of my own wish."

"So you follow others' wishes in marrying, in starting your shop, and you follow your own wish only when it comes to destroying the poor and helpless. Do you know that because of you even my own people are now against me?"

"I'll give you . . ."

"What? Money? Make sure it's enough to bring up your son."

"I'll send you regularly from my income from the store."

"But your words are all lies, worthless lies."

"For now . . ."

"How much?"

He brings out a hundred rupees. Dhowli takes it, ties
it in a knot in her sari, and goes on, "With a hundred
rupees these days one can't live for long even in Tahad.
Because you've ruined me anyway, I'll go to Dhanbad
and drop your boy on your lap if I don't get a regular
supply."

"I have to accept whatever you say."

"You ruined my life, turned it to ashes, and you can't
even hear the hard truth? Is it being rich that makes one
so tender-skinned?"

Dhowli comes back, still raging inside. She asks her
mother to go to Valatod and make arrangements for her
to stay with her aunt there. Her mother is struck by
her anger, her belligerence. "If I must sell my body, I'll
do it there, not here."

"Why? Does it bring more money there?"

"How should I know?"

On the next day Misrilal leaves with his new wife.
When they set into the bus and look at the villagers gath-
ered at the bus stop, his brother-in-law points to Dhowli,
"Who's that girl?"

"Which one?"

"The one with a baby in her arms."

"Just a Dusad girl."

"I've never seen such a beautiful Dusad girl."

"Maybe. I never noticed her before."

3

It turns out that Dhowli's aunt in Valatod does not
want her. The sum of a hundred rupees that Misrilal gave
her is now down to nine. He never sent any message or
any more money, although later on other stories came
up about the money, that he once sent twenty rupees
through the bus driver who kept it himself, and so on.
Meanwhile, one of the three goats of Dhowli's mother is
stolen, and eventually they have to sell the other two for
very little, as is always the case when the seller is so hard
pressed.

Dhowli senses that the village, the Misra family, the
gang of contract coolies are all watching her with increasing interest, closing in on her. They have been watching

her boy grow up on gruel and her old mother spend all day in the forest looking for roots and tubers. They have also seen Sanichari going to their hut once in a while, with roasted corn bundled in the fold of her sari. From this they conclude that the Misra boy has finally washed his hands of Dhowli.

Then one night, a well-aimed clod of earth strikes her door. Dhowli shouts, "Whoever you are, you should know that I keep a knife beside me." Someone outside whistles and walks away.

The tap-tap continues; little clods are thrown at her door in the night. Dhowli keeps silent. If it persists, she shouts, "Go home to your mother and to your sister."

Her mother mutters something about how long she would be able to fend them off.

"As long as I can."

"You may have the strength to keep going, but I don't."

"I don't have any more strength either, Ma."

"What are you going to do then?"

"Shall we go to the city and try to live by begging?"

"You think men will see you as a beggar? They'll be after your body."

"I don't have the looks and the body anymore, mother."

"Then why do the clods keep falling at our door every night?"

"It's because they know how desperate I am with the baby."

"I can't take it any more. If it weren't for you and your baby, I would have moved in with Sanichari long ago."

"I'm going to find some job tomorrow. I'll earn by weeding the fields."

"There are many others weeding fields all day long. How much does it bring them?"

"I'll try for some other work then."

Dhowli goes in the morning to Parasshnath's shop and begs him to give her some job, maybe sweeping his shop, to keep her from starving.

Parashnath offers her some millet but says that he

would not hire her because he cannot afford to incur the wrath of the older Misra.

Dhowli takes the millet from him and sits under the tree to think how many days they can live on it, even if she makes a thin gruel. Kundan Misra is out to kill her, starve her, as punishment for turning his brother's head.

Dhowli's mother does not say anything about the pathetic amount of millet that she brought home, but when offered the gruel, she puts down her bowl untouched and says, "Why don't you and your boy eat this. I'll go away and find something on my own."

"You don't want it?"

"If you can't find something to keep alive, better kill yourself."

"You're right. I'll kill myself."

Next day she goes to the stream, thinking all the way of drowning herself. Once she is dead, then her own kinspeople will at least look after her mother. And the baby? As long as her mother is able to live, she will try to bring up the baby.

But she does not meet her death. On the way, a man in a printed *lungi* and shirt catches up with her. He is a coolie supervisor and a coolie himself. He grabs her hand, and asks, "Where is your knife?"

Dhowli looks at his eyes. She feels very little fear and says firmly, "Let go of my hand." The man lets go of her hand.

"Are you the one who throws clods at my door in the night?"

The man says yes and gestures to indicate why.

Dhowli thinks for a minute. Then she says, "All right. I'll open the door. But you must bring money and corn with you. I am not selling on credit."

Dhowli comes back home and asks her mother to take the baby to Sanichari's place to sleep from that night on. To her question, she simply informs her that she is going to open the door when the lump of earth strikes. Seeing that her mother is about to cry, Dhowli impatiently, sternly asks her not to raise a row and to come back home before sunrise.

Then she takes out one of the two printed saris that Misrilal gave her. She borrows some oil from Sanichari to oil her hair; she takes a bath and combs her hair into a plait. She is not sure if there is anything else involved in preparing for the customer of one's body.

When a pebble hits the door, she opens it. The man has brought corn, lentils, salt, and one rupee. Dhowli pays him back, with her body, to the very last penny. As the man takes leave, she reminds him that she will let him in as long as he brings the price. When he asks her not to let anybody else in, she says that whoever will pay can come; her only rule is that she will not sell on credit.

Many are willing to pay; she opens the door to many. Dhowli and her mother start having two full meals a day and wearing saris that are not old rags. After the customer leaves, Dhowli sleeps well, better than she has for a long time. She never knew it would be so easy to sell one's body, without any emotion, for corn and millet and salt. If she had known, they could have had full meals much earlier; the baby could have been better fed and cared for. It now seems to her that she has been very stupid in the past.

Kundan has been watching Dhowli carrying on. He knows that by figuring out the means of survival, Dhowli has defeated his revenge, outwitted his plan to kill them indirectly. The Dusad girl's nonchalance bothers Kundan; her new self-assured attractiveness gnaws at his mind. One day, seeing her draw water from the well with the other women, he asks Sanichari if they are going to drink the water touched by Dhowli. It turns out to be a wrong move, given Sanichari's well-known candor and forthrightness.

"That's none of your business, master. And why should we mind the water she touches? Our people now accept what she has to do."

"Why?"

"Why not? What wrong has she done?"

"She has become a prostitute."

"Your brother forced her to become a prostitute. How would your brother's son have lived if she did not? Everybody seems to be happy now, including your friend and business partner the contractor. His coolies no longer have to stray very far for the fun."

"Better watch what you say when you talk to me."

"I don't have to. Your mother and your wife would have been nowhere but for Sanichari here."

Kundan may make wrong moves, but he knows when to retreat. Every family in the village, rich or poor, needs Sanichari. Nobody can do without her help with the medicinal herbs.

Kundan then takes a trip to Dhanbad to work on his brother.

"Better give her money or land. It's your cowardice that now brings the business of selling flesh to the village, right under our nose."

Misrilal's face becomes ashen. "What do you mean?"

Kundan is wild with joy at having hit the spot. His brother is still in love with the whore, and he has managed to hit him right there. What a coward! No pride in his superiority as a Brahman. A man is not a man unless he behaves like one. In his place, Kundan would not have abandoned his favored kept woman at the order of Hanuman Misra. Kundan must prod his unmanly brother into becoming a man. He must be taught how to keep the untouchables under foot, sometimes acting kindly but always forcefully like a man. Otherwise, it is too large an empire for Kundan to control all by himself—so much farm land and orchards, so many illegitimate children and so many fertile untouchable women, so huge a moneylending business. Kundan must bring his soft, defaulting brother up to manhood, cure his weakness, so that he can help Kundan with the job. He goes for the kill.

"Don't you know? I mean the Dusad girl you fell in love with. I spit on it! She became the mother of a son by making a Brahman fall for her. And now the entrance that was once used by a lion is being used by the pigs and the sewer rats."

"I don't believe you. She can't do it."

"She is doing it. She is making us Brahmans the laughingstock."

"No!"

"Yes. I say yes a hundred times. You're not a man! Just a scared worm! You couldn't stand up to Hanumanji and tell him that you wanted her as your kept woman.

I've kept Jhalo. Didn't Hanumanji forbid me to give her a place to live? Did I obey? I spit on your love. Lovelorn for a Dusad girl! A man takes what he wants and keeps things ordered to his wish, everything from his *paijars** to the Panchayat. You're no man. You made people spit at the Brahmans."

"I won't believe it until I see it with my own eyes. If it's false . . ."

Kundan smiles a sly victorious smile and says, "Then you'll kill me? Good! Didn't I get you the license for a gun?"

Soon after that, Misrilal comes to Tahad, tormented by anger and the venom his brother injected in him. Because Dhowli no longer goes to the bus stop, she does not know that he has come.

As soon as the evening sets in, he throws a pebble at her door. It is a changed Dhowli who opens the door— she is wearing a red sari and green bangles, and her oiled hair is in a plait down her back.

She turns pale at first but recovers almost immediately and invites him coldly, "Does the landlord want to come in?"

Misrilal enters without a word. He sees the new lantern, the bed of clean *shataranji*** and pillows on the bunk, the sack of millet, and the can of oil under the bunk.

"You've become a *randi*?"

"Yes, I have."

"Why?"

"Because you ran away after having your fun, and your brother took away our food. How else can I live? How can I bring up your son?"

"Why didn't you kill yourself?"

"At first I wanted to do that. Then I thought, why should I die? You'll marry, run your shop, go to the cinema with your wife, and I'll be the one to die? Why?"

"I'll kill you then."

"Go ahead."

*Sandals.
**Flatweave cotton rug.

"No Brahman's son is to live on the filthy handouts of the untouchables! How dare you! I'll kill you."

"You can't because you're not a man."

"Don't say that, Dhowli. My brother said that. But don't you say I'm not a man. I'll show you that I'm a man and a Brahman."

Within a few days, Misrilal with the help of Kundan and Hanumanji calls the Panchayat. Without asking anyone in the Panchayat, Hanumanji orders that Dhowli must leave the village; she cannot be allowed to do business in the village. She has to go to Ranchi and get herself registered as a prostitute there. If she does not, her hut will be set on fire to kill her along with her mother and her child. As long as the Brahmans live in the village, as long as Shiva and Narain are worshiped in their homes, such impudent sinning is not going to be tolerated in the village.

When Dhowli protests, "Why didn't the Brahman help me with money to bring up his son," Hanuman Misra shouts, "Shut up, whore!" and throws his sandal at her. Misrilal joins in, "Now at last you know that I am a man and a Brahman."

The Dusads, the Ganjus, and the Dhobis at the meeting do not raise any objection. They only ask how Dhowli is going to be able to go to Ranchi. Kundan answers that his contractor is going to take her there. She has to leave the next morning, no later.

Early in the following morning Dhowli, a bundle in her hand, boards the bus with the contractor. She is not crying. Her mother, with the baby in her arms, cries standing beside the bus. The baby holds out his hands to Dhowli. She tells her mother to keep some *gur* for him for the night, to put a bit of it in his mouth if he cries.

Dhowli's mother now sobs aloud. "It would have been less terrible if you stayed with your husband's brother."

A faint smile, perhaps of pity, appears on Dhowli's lips, hearing her mother say that. In that case, she would have been a whore individually, only in her private life. Now she is going to be a whore by occupation. She is going to be one of many whores, a member of a part of society. Isn't the society more powerful than the individual? Those who run the society, the very powerful—by making her a public whore—have made her a part of the society. Her mother is not going to understand this. So she smiles and says, "Don't forget to keep some gur by the bed, mother. And keep the lamp lit, so he will not be scared in the dark."

Even the driver of the bus of the Rohatgi company cannot bear to look at Dhowli. He sounds the horn and starts the bus. Dhowli does not look back to see her mother and her child for fear that it will also make her see the brass trident atop the temple of the Misras.

Kundan's contractor cannot look at her when asking her to make herself comfortable because Ranchi is a long way from there.

The bus starts speeding, and her village recedes.

The sun rises, and Dhowli watches the sky, blue as in other days, and the trees, as green as ever. She feels hurt, wounded by nature's indifference to her plight. Tears finally run from her eyes with the pain of this new injury. She never expected that the sky and the greens would be so impervious on the day of turning Dhowli into a public whore. Nothing in nature seems to be at all moved by the monstrosity of what is done to her. Has nature then accepted the disgracing of the Dhowlis as a matter of course? Has nature too gotten used to the Dhowlis being branded as whores and forced to leave home? Or is it that even the earth and the sky and the trees, the nature that was not made by the Misras, have now become their private property?

Translated by Kalpana Bardham

Ruth Prawer Jhabvala
(b. 1927)

Born in Cologne, Germany, to Polish-Jewish parents,
Ruth Prawer Jhabvala emigrated to England in 1939.
After earning an M.A. at Queen Mary College of London University, she married C.S.H. Jhabvala, an Indian
architect, in 1951, and moved with him to Delhi. An
insider by virtue of her decades of living in India yet an
outsider by virtue of her Western youth and education,
she frequently depicts characters torn between their
desire for modern Western comfort and the spiritual
consolation of Hinduism and traditional Indian family relationships and cultural values. Pearl K. Bell has noted:

> Jhabvala writes from within the extended Indian-fam-
> ily structure, an affectionately satiric observer of the
> conflict between traditional passivity and Westernized
> ambition within individuals battered by the indifferent
> tides of change in present-day Indian life.

In analyzing one of Jhabvala's recurring subjects, the experience of Westerners in India, S. M. Mollinger has observed that the novelist "uses India as a catalyst, as an
outrageous force that elicits unexpected, frequently frightening, reactions from its visitors." Among her many honors, Jhabvala has been awarded a Booker Prize, a Neil
Gunn International Fellowship, a Guggenheim Fellowship, and a MacArthur Foundation Award. A prolific
novelist and story writer, she has also had a successful
career as a screenwriter, often in collaboration with James
Ivory of Merchant-Ivory Productions. With Ivory, she
wrote *The Guru*, *Shakespeare Wallah*, *The Europeans*
(based on the Henry James novel), and *A Room with a
View* (based on the E. M. Forster novel). Among her

best-known novels are *Amrita* (Norton, 1956), *The Nature of Passion* (Norton, 1957), *Esmond in India* (1958), *A Backward Place* (Norton, 1965), *Heat and Dust* (Harper & Row, 1976), *In Search of Love and Beauty* (Morrow, 1983; repr. Penguin, 1985), and *Poet and Dancer* (Doubleday, 1993). Her stories are collected in six volumes: *Like Birds, Like Fishes* (Norton, 1964); *A Stronger Climate* (Norton, 1969); *An Experience of India* (Norton, 1972); *How I Became a Holy Mother and Other Stories* (Harper & Row, 1976); *Out of India* (Morrow, 1986); and *East into Upper East: Plain Tales from New York and New Delhi* (Counterpoint, 1998).

THE INTERVIEW

I am always very careful of my appearance, so you could not say that I spent much more time than usual over myself that morning. It is true, I trimmed and oiled my moustache, but then I often do that; I always like it to look very neat, like Raj Kapoor's, the film star's. But I knew my sister-in-law and my wife were watching me. My sister-in-law was smiling, and she had one hand on her hip; my wife only looked anxious. I knew she was anxious. All night she had been whispering to me. She had whispered, "Get this job and take me away to live somewhere alone only you and I and our children." I had answered, "Yes," because I wanted to go to sleep. I don't know where and why she had taken this notion that we should go and live alone.

When I had finished combing my hair, I sat on the floor and my sister-in-law brought me my food on a tray. It may sound strange that my sister-in-law should serve me, and not my wife, but it is so in our house. It used to be my mother who brought me my food, even after I was married; she would never allow my wife to do this for me, though my wife wanted to very much. Then, when my mother got so old, my sister-in-law began to serve me. I know that my wife feels deeply hurt by this, but she doesn't dare to say anything. My mother doesn't notice many things anymore, otherwise she certainly would not allow my sister-in-law to bring me my food; she has always been very jealous of this privilege herself, though she never cared who served my brother. Now she has become so old that she can hardly see anything, and most of the time she sits in the corner by the family trunks and folds and strokes her pieces of cloth. For years now she has been collecting pieces of cloth. Some of them are very old and dirty, but she doesn't care, she loves them all equally. Nobody is allowed to touch them. Once there was a great quarrel, because my wife had taken one of them to make a dress for our child. My mother shouted at her—it was terrible to hear her: but then, she has never liked my wife—and my wife was very much afraid and cried and tried to excuse herself. I hit her across the face, not very hard and not because I wanted to, but only to satisfy my mother. The old woman kept quiet then and went back to folding and stroking her pieces of cloth.

All the time I was eating, I could feel my sister-in-law looking at me and smiling. It made me uncomfortable. I thought she might be smiling because she knew I wouldn't get the job for which I had to go and be interviewed. I also knew I wouldn't get it, but I didn't like her to smile like that. It was as if she were saying, "You see, you will always have to be dependent on us." It is clearly my brother's duty to keep me and my family until I can get work and contribute my own earnings to the family household. There is no need for her to smile about it. But it is true that I am more dependent on her now than on anyone else. Since my mother has got so old, my sister-in-law has become more and more the most important person in the house, so that she even keeps the keys and the household stores. At first I didn't like this. As long as my mother managed the household, I was sure of getting many extra tidbits. But now I find that my sister-in-law is also very kind to me—much more kind than she is to her husband. It is not for him that she saves the tidbits, nor for her children, but for me; and when she gives them to me, she never says anything and I never say anything, but she smiles and then I feel confused and rather embarrassed. My wife has noticed what she does for me.

I have found that women are usually kind to me. I think they realize that I am a rather sensitive person and that therefore I must be treated very gently. My mother has always treated me very gently. I am her youngest child, and I am fifteen years younger than my brother who is next to me (she did have several children in between us, but they all died). Right from the time when I was a tiny baby, she understood that I needed greater care and tenderness than other children. She always made me sleep close beside her in the night, and in the day I usually sat with her and my grandmother and my widowed aunt, who were also very fond of me. When I got bigger, my father sometimes wanted to take me to help in his stall (he had a little grocer's stall, where he sold lentils and rice and cheap cigarettes and colored drinks in bottles) but my mother and grandmother and aunt never liked to let me go. Once he did take me with him, and he made me pour some lentils out of paper bags into a tin. I rather liked pouring the lentils—they made such a nice noise as they landed in the tin—but suddenly my mother came and was very angry with my father for making me do this work. She took me home at once, and when she told my grandmother and aunt what had happened, they stroked me and kissed me and then they gave me a hot fritter to eat. The fact is, right from childhood I have been a person who needs a lot of peace and rest, and my food too has to be rather more delicate than that of other people. I have often tried to explain this to my wife, but as she is not very intelligent, she doesn't seem to understand.

Now my wife was watching me while I ate. She was squatting on the floor, washing our youngest baby; the baby's head was in her lap, and all one could see of it was the back of its legs and its naked bottom. My wife did not watch me as openly as my sister-in-law did; only from time to time she raised her eyes to me, I could feel it, and they were very worried and troubled. She too was thinking about the job for which I was going to be interviewed, but she was anxious that I should get it.

"We will go and live somewhere alone," she had said. Why did she say it? When she knows that it is not possible and never will be.

And even if it were possible, I would not like it. I can't live away from my mother; and I don't think I would like to live away from my sister-in-law. I often look at her and it makes me happy. Even though she is not young anymore, she is still beautiful. She is tall, with big hips and big breasts and eyes that flash; she often gets angry, and when she is angry, she is the most beautiful of all. Then her eyes are like fire and she shows all her teeth, which are very strong and white, and her head is proud with the black hair flying loose. My wife is not beautiful at all. I was very disappointed in her when they first married me to her. Now I have got used to her and I even like her, because she is so good and quiet and never troubles me at all. I don't think anybody else in our house likes her. My sister-in-law always calls her "that beauty," but she does not mean it; and she makes her do all the most difficult household tasks, and often she shouts at her and even beats her. This is not right; my wife has never done anything to her—on the contrary, she always treats her with respect. But I cannot interfere in their quarrels.

Then I was ready to go, though I didn't want to go. I knew only too well what would happen at the interview. My mother blessed me, and my sister-in-law looked at me over her shoulder and her great eyes flashed with laughter. I didn't look at my wife, who still sat squatting on the floor, but I knew she was pleading with me to get the job like she had pleaded in the night. As I walked down the stairs, the daughter of the carpenter, who lives in one of the rooms on the lower floor, came out of her door and she walked up the stairs as I walked down, and she passed very close beside me, with her eyes lowered but her arm just touching my sleeve. She always waits for me to come out and then she passes me on the stairs. We have never spoken together. She is a very young girl, her breasts are only just forming; her blouse has short sleeves and her arms are beautiful, long and slender. I think soon she is to be married, I have heard my sister-in-law say so. My sister-in-law laughed when she told me, she said, "It is high time" and then she said something coarse. Perhaps she has noticed that the girl waits for me to pass on the stairs.

No, I did not want to go to the interview. I had been to so many during the last few months, and always the same things happened. I know I have to work, in order to earn money and give it to my mother or my sister-in-law for the household, but there is no pleasure for me in the work. Last time I had work, it was in an insurance office and all day they made me sit at a desk and write figures. What pleasure could there be for me in that? I am a very thoughtful person, and I like always to sit and think my own thoughts; but while I thought my own thoughts in the office, I sometimes made mistakes over the figures and then my superiors were very angry with me. I was always afraid of their anger, and I begged their forgiveness and admitted that I was much at fault. When they forgave me, I was no longer afraid and I continued doing my work and thinking my thoughts. But the last time they would not forgive me again, though I begged and begged and cried what a faulty, bad man I was and what good men they were, and how they were my mother and my father and how I looked only to them for my life and the lives of my children. But when they still said I must go, I saw that the work there was really finished and I stopped crying. I went into the washroom and combed my hair and folded my soap in my towel, and then I took my money from the accountant without a word and I left the office with my eyes lowered. But I was no longer afraid, because what is finished is finished, and my brother still had work and probably one day I would get another job.

Ever since then my brother has been trying to get me into government service. He himself is a clerk in government service and enjoys many advantages: every five years he gets an increase of ten rupees in his salary and he has ten days sick leave in the year and when he retires he will get a pension. It would be good for me also to have such a job; but it is difficult to get, because first there is an interview at which important people sit at a desk and ask many questions. I am afraid of them, and I cannot understand properly what they are saying, so I

answer what I think they want me to answer. But it
seems that my answers are not after all the right ones,
because up till now they have not given me a job.

On my way to this interview, I thought how much nicer
it would be to go to the cinema instead. If I had had ten
annas, perhaps I would have gone; it was just time for
the morning show. The young clerks and the students
would be collecting in a queue outside the cinema now.
They would be standing and not talking much, holding
their ten annas and waiting for the box office to open. I
enjoy these morning shows, perhaps because the people
who come to them are all young men like myself, all
silent and rather sad. I am often sad; it would even be
right to say that I am sad most of the time. But when
the film begins, I am happy. I love to see the beautiful
women, dressed in golden clothes with heavy earrings
and necklaces and bracelets covering their arms, and
their handsome lovers who are all the things I would like
to be. And when they sing their love songs, so full of
deep feelings, the tears sometimes come into my eyes;
but not because I am sad, no, on the contrary, because
I am so happy. After the film is over, I never go home
straightaway, but I walk around the streets and think
about how wonderful life could be.

When I arrived at the place where the interview was,
I had to walk down many corridors and ask directions
from many peons before I could find the right room. The
peons were all rude to me, because they knew what I
had come for. They lounged on benches outside the offices, and when I asked them, they looked me up and
down before answering, and sometimes they made jokes
about me with one another. I was very polite to them,
for even though they were only peons, they had uniforms
and jobs and belonged here, and they knew the right
way whereas I did not. At last I came to the room where
I had to wait. Many others were already sitting there, on
chairs that were drawn up all around the room against
the wall. No one was talking. I also sat on a chair, and
after a while an official came in with a list and he asked
if anyone else had come. I got up and he asked my name,
and then he looked down the list and made a tick with

a pencil. He said to me very sternly, "Why are you late?" I begged pardon and told him the bus in which I had come had had an accident. He said, "When you are called for interview, you have to be here exactly on time, otherwise your name is crossed off the list." I begged pardon again and asked him very humbly please not to cross me off this time. I knew that all the others were listening, though none of them looked at us. He was very stern with me and even scornful, but in the end he said, "Wait here, and when your name is called, you must go in at once."

I did not count the number of people waiting in the room, but there were many. Perhaps there was one job free, perhaps two or three. I knew that all the others were very worried and anxious to get the job, so I became worried and anxious too. The walls of the room were painted green halfway up and white above that and were quite bare. There was a fan turning from the ceiling, but it was not turning fast enough to give much breeze. Behind the big door the interview was going on; one by one we would all be called in behind this closed door.

I began to worry desperately. It always happens like this. When I come to an interview, I don't want the job at all, but when I see all the others waiting and worrying, I want it terribly. Yet at the same time I know that I don't want it. It would only be the same thing over again: writing figures and making mistakes and then being afraid when they found out. And there would be a superior officer to whom I would have to be very deferential, and every time I saw him or heard his voice I would begin to be afraid that he had found out something against me. For weeks and months I would sit and write figures, getting wearier of it and wearier, so that more and more I would be thinking my own thoughts. Then the mistakes would come, and my superior officer would be angry and I afraid.

My brother never makes mistakes. For years he has been sitting in the same office, writing figures and being deferential to his superior officer; he concentrates very hard on his work, and so he doesn't make mistakes. But all the same he is afraid; that is why he concentrates so hard—because he is afraid that he will make a mistake and they will be angry with him and take away his job. He is afraid of this all the time. And he is right: what would become of us all if he also lost his job? It is not the same with me. I think I am afraid to lose my job only because that is a thing of which one is expected to be afraid. When I have actually lost it, I am really relieved. But I am very different from my brother; even in appearance I am very different. It is true, he is fifteen years older than I am, but even when he was my age, he never looked like I do. My appearance has always attracted others, and up to the time I was married, my mother used to stroke my hair and my face and say many tender things to me. Once, when I was walking on my way to school through the bazaar, a man called to me, very softly, and when I came he gave me a ripe mango, and then he took me into a dark passage that led to a disused mosque, and he touched me under my clothes and he said, "You are so nice, so nice." He was very kind to me. I love wearing fine clothes, very thin white muslin kurtas that have been freshly washed and starched and are embroidered at the shoulders. Sometimes I also use scent, a fine khas smell; my hair oil also smells of khas. Some years ago, when the carpenter's daughter was still a small child and did not yet wait for me on the stairs, there was a girl living in the tailor's shop opposite our house and she used to follow me when I went out. But it is my brother who is married to a beautiful wife, and my wife is not beautiful at all. He is not happy with his wife; when she talks to him, she talks in a hard scornful way; and it is not for him that she saves the best food, but for me, even though I have not brought money home for many months.

The big closed door opened and the man who had been in there for interview came out. We all looked at him, but he walked out in a great hurry, with a preoccupied expression on his face; probably he was going over in his mind all that had been said at the interview. I could feel the anxiety in the other men getting stronger, so mine got stronger too. The official with the list came and we all looked at him. He read out another name and the man whose name was called jumped up from his chair; he did not notice that his dhoti had got caught on a nail in the chair and he wondered why he could not go farther. When he realized what had happened, he tried to disentangle himself, but his fingers shook so much that he could not get the dhoti off the nail. The official watched him and said, "Hurry, now, do you think the gentlemen will wait for you for as long as you please?" Then the man also dropped the umbrella he was carrying and now he was trying both to disentangle the dhoti and to pick up the umbrella. When he could not get the dhoti loose, he became so desperate that he tore at the cloth and ripped it free. It was a pity to see the dhoti torn because it was a new one, which he was probably wearing for the first time and had put on specially for the interview. He clasped his umbrella to his chest and walked in a great hurry to the interviewing room, with his dhoti hanging about his legs and his face swollen with embarrassment and confusion.

We all sat and waited. The fan, which seemed to be a very old one, made a creaking noise. One man kept cracking his finger joints—*tik*, we heard, *tik* (it made my own finger joints long to be cracked too). All the rest of us kept very still. From time to time the official with the list came in, he walked around the room very slowly, tapping his list, and then we all looked down at our feet and the man who had been cracking his finger joints stopped doing it. A faint and muffled sound of voices came from behind the closed door. Sometimes a voice was raised, but even then I could not make out what was being said, though I strained very hard.

The last time I had an interview, it was very unpleasant for me. One of the people who was interviewing took a dislike to me and shouted at me very loudly. He was a large fat man and he wore an English suit; his teeth were quite yellow, and when he became angry and shouted, he showed them all, and even though I was very upset, I couldn't help looking at them and wondering how they had become so yellow. I don't know why he was angry. He shouted: "Good God, man, can't you understand what's said to you?" It was true, I could not understand, but I had been trying so hard to answer well. What more did he expect of me? Probably there was something in my appearance that he did not like. It happens that way sometimes—they take a dislike to you, and then of course there is nothing you can do.

When I thought of the man with the yellow teeth, I became more anxious than ever. I need great calm in my life. Whenever anything worries me too much, I have to cast the thought of it off immediately, otherwise there is a danger that I may become very ill. All my limbs were itching so that it was difficult for me to sit still, and I could feel blood rushing into my brain. It was this room that was doing me so much harm: all the other men waiting, anxious and silent, and the noise from the fan and the official with the list walking around, tapping his list or striking it against his thigh, and the big closed door behind which the interview was going on. I felt great need to get up and go away. I didn't *want* the job. I wasn't even thinking about it anymore—I was thinking only about how to avoid having to sit here and wait.

Now the door opened again and the man with the torn new dhoti came out. He was biting his lip and scratching the back of his neck, and he too walked straight out without looking at us at all. The big door was left slightly open for a moment, and I could see a man's arm in a white shirtsleeve and part of the back of his head. His shirt was very white and of good material, and his ears stood away from his head so that one could see how his spectacles fitted into the backs of his ears. I realized at once that this man would be my enemy and that he would make things very difficult for me and perhaps even shout at me. Then I knew it was no use for me to stay there. The official with the list came back and great panic seized me that he would read out my name. I got up quickly, murmuring, "Please excuse me—bathroom," and went out. The official with the list called after me "Hey mister, where are you going?" so I lowered my head and walked faster. I would have started to run, but that might have caused suspicion, so I just walked as fast as I could, down the long corridors and right out of the building. There at last I was able to stop and take a deep breath, and I felt much better.

*   *   *

I stood still for only a little while, then I moved on, though not in any particular direction. There were many clerks and peons moving around in the street, hurrying from one office building to another and carrying files and papers. Everyone seemed to have something to do. I was glad when I had moved out of this block and on to the open space where people like myself, who had nothing to do, sat under the trees or in any other patch of shade they could find. But I couldn't sit there; it was too close to the office blocks, and any moment someone might come and say to me, "Why did you go away?" So I walked farther. I was feeling quite light-hearted; it was such a relief for me not to have to be interviewed.

I came to a row of eating stalls, and I sat down on a wooden bench outside one of them, which was called the Paris Hotel, and asked for tea. I felt badly in need of tea, and since I intended to walk part of the way home, I was in a position to pay for it. There were two Sikhs sitting at the end of my bench who were eating with great appetite, dipping their hands very rapidly into brass bowls. In between eating they exchanged remarks with the proprietor of the Paris Hotel, who sat high up inside his stall, stirring in a big brass pot in which he was cooking the day's food. He was chewing a betel leaf, and from time to time he spat out the red betel juice far over the cooking pot and on to the ground between the wooden benches and tables.

I sat quietly at my end of the bench and drank my tea. The food smelled very good, and it made me realize that I was hungry. I decided that if I walked all the way home, I could afford a little cake (I am very fond of sweet things). The cake was not new, but it had a beautiful piece of bright-green peel inside it. On reaching home I would lie down at once to sleep and not wake up again till tomorrow morning. That way no one would be able to ask me any questions. I would not look at my wife at all, so I would be able to avoid her eyes. I would not look at my sister-in-law either; but she would be smiling, that I knew already—leaning against the wall with her hand on her hip, looking at me and smiling. She would know that I had run away, but she would not say anything.

Let her know! What does it matter? It is true I have no job and no immediate prospect of getting one. It is true that I am dependent on my brother. Everybody knows that. There is no shame in it: there are many people without jobs. And she has been so kind to me up till now, there is no reason why she should not continue to be kind to me. Though I know she is not by nature a kind woman; she speaks mostly with a very harsh tongue and her actions also are harsh. Only to me she has been kind.

The Sikhs at the end of the bench had finished eating. They licked their fingers and belched deeply, the way one does after a good meal. They started to laugh and joke with the proprietor. I sat quiet and alone at my end of the bench. Of course they did not laugh and joke with me. They knew that I was superior to them, for whereas they work with their hands, I am a lettered man who does not have to sweat for a living but sits on a chair in an office and writes figures and can speak in English. My brother is very proud of his superiority, and he has great contempt for carpenters and mechanics and such people who work with their hands. I am also proud of being a lettered man, but when I listened to the Sikhs laughing and joking, the thought came to me that perhaps their life was happier than mine. It was a thought that had come to me before. There is the carpenter who lives downstairs in our house, the one whose daughter waits for me on the stairs, and though he is poor, there is always great eating in his house and many people come and I hear them laughing and singing and even dancing. The carpenter is a big strong man and he always looks happy, never anxious and sick with worry the way my brother does. He doesn't wear shoes and clean white clothes like my brother and I do, nor does he speak any English, but all the same he is happy. Even though his work is inferior, I don't think he gets as weary of it as I do of mine, and he has no superior officer to make him afraid.

Then I thought again about my sister-in-law and I thought that if I were kind to her, she would continue to be kind to me. I became quite excited when I thought of being kind to her. I would know then how her big breasts felt under the blouse, how warm they were and how soft. And I would know about the inside of her mouth with the big strong teeth. Her tongue and palate are very pink, like the pink satin blouse she wears on festive occasions, and I had often wondered whether they felt as soft as the blouse too. Her eyes would be shut and perhaps there would be tears on the lashes; and she would be making warm animal sounds and her big body too would be warm like an animal's. I became very excited when I thought of it; but when the excitement had passed, I was sad. Because then I thought of my wife, who is thin and not beautiful and there is no excitement in her body. But she does whatever I want and always tries to please me. I remembered her whispering to me in the night, "Take me away, let us go and live somewhere alone, only you and I and our children." That can never be, and so always she will have to be unhappy.

I was very sad when I thought of her being unhappy; because it is not only she who is unhappy but I also and many others. Everywhere there is unhappiness. I thought of the man whose new dhoti had been torn and who would now have to go home and sew it carefully so that the tear would not be seen. I thought of all the other men sitting and waiting to be interviewed, all but one or two of whom would not get the job for which they had come to be interviewed, and so again they would have to go to another interview and another and another, to sit and wait and be anxious. And my brother who has a job, but is frightened that he will lose it; and my mother so old that she can only sit on the floor and stroke her pieces of cloth; and my sister-in-law who does not care for her husband; and the carpenter's daughter who is to be married and perhaps she also will not be happy. Yet life could be so different. When I go to the cinema and hear the beautiful songs they sing, I know how different it could be; and also sometimes when I sit alone and think my thoughts, then I have a feeling that everything could be so beautiful. But now my tea was finished and also my cake, and I wished I had not bought them, because it was a long way to walk home and I was tired.

R[asipuram] K[rishnaswami] Narayan
(b. 1906)

Born in Madras, India, into a Hindu Brahmin family, R. K. Narayan was sent to live with his grandmother and uncle at the age of two because of his mother's health problems and his father's numerous transfers to different schools as a headmaster employed by the government. Narayan spoke and studied Tamil (one of the South Indian languages) at home where his grandmother taught him about music, religion, and Indian mythology and literature. Simultaneously, at the Lutheran mission school where he was the only Brahmin enrolled in his class, he studied English and the Christian *Bible*. He was able to rejoin his father when the latter was appointed headmaster of Maharaja's Collegiate High School in Mysore, and he earned an undergraduate degree at Maharaja's College (now the University of Mysore) in 1930. Supported by his family, he began to write, setting his novels and stories in Malgudi, a fictional city in South India. He has chronicled the life of Malgudi in extraordinary detail in fourteen novels and numerous stories published over more than five decades. His Malgudi characters range from people at the highest level of the Hindu religion to the middle-class Brahmin caste to which Narayan himself belongs, to the merchants, teachers, shopkeepers, clerks, herdsmen, civil servants, laborers and beggars, whom he observes with compassion and understanding as well as with a wry sense of the comedy of daily life in India. During a BBC interview with Narayan, William Walsh observed, "Whatever happens in India happens in Malgudi, and whatever happens in Malgudi happens everywhere." Narayan has been awarded the National Prize of the Indian Literary Academy, the Sahitya Akademi Award for the novel *The Guide*, the Padma Bhushan, the National Association of Independent Schools Award, an honorary doctorate in literature at the University of Leeds, and an English-Speaking Union Book Award for *My Days: A Memoir*. Among his best-known novels are *Swami and Friends: A Novel of Malgudi* (Hamish Hamilton, 1935; repr. Fawcett, 1970), *The Dark Room* (Macmillan, 1938), *The English Teacher* (Eyre & Spottiswoode, 1945; repr. as *Grateful to Life and Death*, Michigan State College Press, 1953), *The Financial Expert: A Novel* (Methuen, 1952; repr. Michigan State College Press, 1953), *The Guide* (Viking, 1958), *The Man-Eater of Malgudi* (Viking, 1961), *The Vendor of Sweets* (Viking, 1967), *The Painter of Signs* (Viking, 1976), *A Tiger for Malgudi* (Viking, 1983), and *The World of Nagaraj* (Viking, 1990). Among his story collections are *Malgudi Days* (Indian Thought Publications, 1941; repr. Viking, 1982), *An Astrologer's Day and Other Stories* (Eyre & Spottiswoode, 1947), *Lawley Road: Thirty-Two Short Stories* (Indian Thought Publications, 1956), *Gods, Demons and Others* (Viking, 1965), *A Horse and Two Goats* (Viking, 1970), and *Under the Banyan Tree and Other Stories* (Viking, 1985).

A HORSE AND TWO GOATS

Of the seven hundred thousand villages dotting the map of India, in which the majority of India's five hundred million live, flourish, and die, Kritam was probably the tiniest, indicated on the district survey map by a microscopic dot, the map being meant more for the revenue offical out to collect tax than for the guidance of the motorist, who in any case could not hope to reach it since it sprawled far from the highway at the end of a rough track furrowed up by the iron-hooped wheels of bullock carts. But its size did not prevent its giving itself the grandiose name Kritam, which meant in Tamil "coronet" or "crown" on the brow of this subcontinent. The village consisted of fewer than thirty houses, only one of them built with brick and cement. Painted a brilliant yellow and blue all over with gorgeous carvings of gods and gargoyles on its balustrade, it was known as the Big House. The other houses, distributed in four streets, were generally of bamboo thatch, straw, mud, and other unspecified material. Muni's was the last house in the fourth street, beyond which stretched the fields. In his prosperous days, Muni had owned a flock of forty sheep and goats and sallied forth every morning driving the flock to the highway a couple of miles away. There he would sit on the pedestal of a clay statue of a horse while his cattle grazed around. He carried a crook at the end of a bamboo pole and snapped foliage from the avenue trees to feed his flock; he also gathered faggots and dry sticks, bundled them, and carried them home for fuel at sunset.

His wife lit the domestic fire at dawn, boiled water in a mud pot, threw into it a handful of millet flour, added salt, and gave him his first nourishment for the day. When he started out, she would put in his hand a packed lunch, once again the same millet cooked into a little ball, which he could swallow with a raw onion at midday. She was old, but he was older and needed all the attention she could give him in order to be kept alive.

His fortunes had declined gradually, unnoticed. From a flock of forty which he drove into a pen at night, his stock had now come down to two goats, which were not worth the rent of a half rupee a month the Big House charged for the use of the pen in their backyard. And so the two goats were tethered to the trunk of a drumstick tree which grew in front of his hut and from which occasionally Muni could shake down drumsticks. This morning he got six. He carried them in with a sense of triumph. Although no one could say precisely who owned the tree, it was his because he lived in its shadow.

She said, "If you were content with the drumstick leaves alone, I could boil and salt some for you."

"Oh, I am tired of eating those leaves. I have a craving to chew the drumstick out of sauce, I tell you."

"You have only four teeth in your jaw, but your craving is for big things. All right, get the stuff for the sauce, and I will prepare it for you. After all, next year you may not be alive to ask for anything. But first get me all the stuff, including a measure of rice or millet, and I will satisfy your unholy craving. Our store is empty today. Dhall, chili, curry leaves, mustard, coriander, gingelley oil, and one large potato. Go out and get all this." He repeated the list after her in order not to miss any item and walked off to the shop in the third street.

He sat on an upturned packing case below the platform of the shop. The shopman paid no attention to him. Muni kept clearing his throat, coughing, and sneezing until the shopman could not stand it any more and demanded, "What ails you? You will fly off that seat into the gutter if you sneeze so hard, young man." Muni laughed inordinately, in order to please the shopman, at being called "young man." The shopman softened and said, "You have enough of the imp inside to keep a second wife busy, but for the fact the old lady is still alive." Muni laughed appropriately again at this joke. It completely won the shopman over; he liked his sense of humor to be appreciated. Muni engaged his attention in local gossip for a few minutes, which always ended with a reference to the postman's wife, who had eloped to the city some months before.

The shopman felt most pleased to hear the worst of the postman, who had cheated him. Being an itinerant postman, he returned home to Kritam only once in ten days and every time managed to slip away again without passing the shop in the third street. By thus humoring the shopman, Muni could always ask for one or two items of food, promising repayment later. Some days the shopman was in a good mood and gave in, and sometimes he would lose his temper suddenly and bark at Muni for daring to ask for credit. This was such a day, and Muni could not progress beyond two items listed as essential components. The shopman was also displaying a remarkable memory for old facts and figures and took out an oblong ledger to support his observations. Muni felt impelled to rise and flee. But his self-respect kept him in his seat and made him listen to the worst things about himself. The shopman concluded, "If you could find five rupees and a quarter, you will have paid off an ancient debt and then could apply for admission to swarga. How much have you got now?"

"I will pay you everything on the first of the next month."

"As always, and whom do you expect to rob by then?"

Muni felt caught and mumbled, "My daughter has sent word that she will be sending me money."

"Have you a daughter?" sneered the shopman. "And she is sending you money! For what purpose, may I know?"

"Birthday, fiftieth birthday," said Muni quietly.

"Birthday! How old are you?"

Muni repeated weakly, not being sure of it himself. "Fifty." He always calculated his age from the time of the great famine when he stood as high as the parapet around the village well, but who could calculate such things accurately nowadays with so many famines occurring? The shopman felt encouraged when other customers stood around to watch and comment. Muni thought helplessly, My poverty is exposed to everybody. But what can I do?

"More likely you are seventy," said the shopman. "You also forget that you mentioned a birthday five weeks ago when you wanted castor oil for your holy bath."

"Bath! Who can dream of a bath when you have to scratch the tank-bed for a bowl of water? We would all be parched and dead but for the Big House, where they let us take a pot of water from their well." After saying this Muni unobtrusively rose and moved off.

He told his wife, "That scoundrel would not give me anything. So go out and sell the drumsticks for what they are worth."

He flung himself down in a corner to recoup from the fatigue of his visit to the shop. His wife said, "You are getting no sauce today, nor anything else. I can't find anything to give you to eat. Fast till the evening, it'll do you good. Take the goats and be gone now," she cried

and added, "Don't come back before the sun is down."
He knew that if he obeyed her she would somehow conjure up some food for him in the evening. Only he must
be careful not to argue and irritate her. Her temper was
undependable in the morning but improved by evening
time. She was sure to go out and work—grind corn in
the Big House, sweep or scrub somewhere, and earn
enough to buy foodstuff and keep a dinner ready for him
in the evening.

Unleashing the goats from the drumstick tree, Muni
started out, driving them ahead and uttering weird cries
from time to time in order to urge them on. He passed
through the village with his head bowed in thought. He
did not want to look at anyone or be accosted. A couple
of cronies lounging in the temple corridor hailed him,
but he ignored their call. They had known him in the
days of affluence when he lorded over a flock of fleecy
sheep, not the miserable gawky goats that he had today.
Of course he also used to have a few goats for those who
fancied them, but real wealth lay in sheep; they bred fast
and people came and bought the fleece in the shearing
season; and then that famous butcher from the town
came over on the weekly market days bringing him betel
leaves, tobacco, and often enough some bhang, which
they smoked in a hut in the coconut grove, undisturbed
by wives and well-wishers. After a smoke one felt light
and elated and inclined to forgive everyone including that
brother-in-law of his who had once tried to set fire to his
home. But all this seemed like the memories of a previous birth. Some pestilence afflicted his cattle (he could
of course guess who had laid his animals under a curse),
and even the friendly butcher would not touch one at
half the price . . . and now here he was left with the two
scraggy creatures. He wished someone would rid him of
their company, too. The shopman had said that he was
seventy. At seventy, one only waited to be summoned
by God. When he was dead what would his wife do?
They had lived in each other's company since they were
children. He was told on their day of wedding that he
was ten years old and she was eight. During the wedding
ceremony they had had to recite their respective ages
and names. He had thrashed her only a few times in their

career, and later she had the upper hand. Progeny, none. Perhaps a large progeny would have brought him the blessing of the gods. Fertility brought merit. People with fourteen sons were always so prosperous and at peace with the world and themselves. He recollected the thrill he had felt when he mentioned a daughter to that shopman; although it was not believed, what if he did not have a daughter?—his cousin in the next village had many daughters, and any one of them was as good as his; he was fond of them all and would buy them sweets if he could afford it. Still, everyone in the village whispered behind their backs that Muni and his wife were a barren couple. He avoided looking at anyone; they all professed to be so high up, and everyone else in the village had more money than he. "I am the poorest fellow in our caste and no wonder that they spurn me, but I won't look at them either," and so he passed on with his eyes downcast along the edge of the street, and people left him also very much alone, commenting only to the extent, "Ah, there he goes with his two goats; if he slits their throats, he may have more peace of mind." "What has he to worry about anyway? They live on nothing and have none to worry about." Thus people commented when he passed through the village. Only on the outskirts did he lift his head and look up. He urged and bullied the goats until they meandered along to the foot of the horse statue on the edge of the village. He sat on its pedestal for the rest of the day. The advantage of this was that he could watch the highway and see the lorries and buses pass through to the hills, and it gave him a sense of belonging to a larger world. The pedestal of the statue was broad enough for him to move around as the sun travelled up and westward; or he could also crouch under the belly of the horse, for shade.

The horse was nearly life-size, molded out of clay, baked, burnt, and brightly colored, and reared its head proudly, prancing its forelegs in the air and flourishing its tail in a loop; beside the horse stood a warrior with scythe-like mustachios, bulging eyes, and aquiline nose. The old image-makers believed in indicating a man of strength by bulging out his eyes and sharpening his moustache tips, and also decorated the man's chest with beads which looked today like blobs of mud through the ravages of sun and wind and rain (when it came), but Muni would insist that he had known the beads to sparkle like the nine gems at one time in his life. The horse itself was said to have been as white as a dhobi-washed sheet, and had had on its back a cover of pure brocade of red and black lace, matching the multicolored sash around the waist of the warrior. But none in the village remembered the splendor as no one noticed its existence. Even Muni, who spent all his waking hours at its foot, never bothered to look up. It was untouched even by the young vandals of the village who gashed tree trunks with knives and tried to topple off milestones and inscribed lewd designs on all walls. This statue had been closer to the population of the village at one time, when this spot bordered the village; but when the highway was laid through (or perhaps when the tank and wells dried up completely here) the village moved a couple of miles inland.

Muni sat at the foot of the statue, watching his two goats graze in the arid soil among the cactus and lantana bushes. He looked at the sun; it was tilted westward no doubt, but it was not the time yet to go back home; if he went too early his wife would have no food for him. Also he must give her time to cool off her temper and feel sympathetic, and then she would scrounge and manage to get some food. He watched the mountain road for a time signal. When the green bus appeared around the bend he could leave, and his wife would feel pleased that he had let the goats feed long enough.

He noticed now a new sort of vehicle coming down at full speed. It looked like both a motor car and a bus. He used to be intrigued by the novelty of such spectacles, but of late work was going on at the source of the river on the mountain and an assortment of people and traffic went past him, and he took it all casually and described to his wife, later in the day, everything he saw. Today, while he observed the yellow vehicle coming down, he was wondering how to describe it later to his wife, when it sputtered and stopped in front of him. A red-faced foreigner, who had been driving it, got down and went round it, stooping, looking, and poking under the vehicle; then he straightened himself up, looked at the dash-

board, stared in Muni's direction, and approached him.
"Excuse me, is there a gas station nearby, or do I have
to wait until another car comes—" He suddenly looked
up at the clay horse and cried, "Marvellous," without
completing his sentence. Muni felt he should get up and
run away, and cursed his age. He could not readily put
his limbs into action; some years ago he could outrun a
cheetah, as happened once when he went to the forest
to cut fuel and it was then that two of his sheep were
mauled—a sign that bad times were coming. Though he
tried, he could not easily extricate himself from his seat,
and then there was also the problem of the goats. He
could not leave them behind.

The red-faced man wore khaki clothes—evidently a policeman or a soldier. Muni said to himself, He will chase
or shoot if I start running. Some dogs chase only those
who run—O Siva, protect me. I don't know why this
man should be after me. Meanwhile the foreigner cried,
"Marvellous!" again, nodding his head. He paced around
the statue with his eyes fixed on it. Muni sat frozen for
a while, and then fidgeted and tried to edge away. Now
the other man suddenly pressed his palms together in a
salute, smiled, and said, "Namaste! How do you do?"

At which Muni spoke the only English expressions he
had learnt, "Yes, no." Having exhausted his English vo-
cabulary, he started in Tamil: "My name is Muni. These
two goats are mine, and no one can gainsay it—though
our village is full of slanderers these days who will not
hesitate to say that what belongs to a man doesn't belong
to him." He rolled his eyes and shuddered at the thought
of evil-minded men and women peopling his village.

The foreigner faithfully looked in the direction indicated by Muni's fingers, gazed for a while at the two
goats and the rocks, and with a puzzled expression took
out his silver cigarette case and lit a cigarette. Suddenly
remembering the courtesies of the season, he asked "Do
you smoke?" Muni answered "Yes, no." Whereupon the
red-faced man took a cigarette and gave it to Muni, who
received it with surprise, having had no offer of a smoke
from anyone for years now. Those days when he smoked
bhang were gone with his sheep and the large-hearted
butcher. Nowadays he was not able to find even matches,

let alone bhang. (His wife went across and borrowed a
fire at dawn from a neighbor.) He had always wanted to
smoke a cigarette; only once did the shopman give him
one on credit, and he remembered how good it had
tasted. The other flicked the lighter open and offered a
light to Muni. Muni felt so confused about how to act
that he blew on it and put it out. The other, puzzled but
undaunted, flourished his lighter, presented it again, and
lit Muni's cigarette. Muni drew a deep puff and started
coughing; it was racking, no doubt, but extremely pleasant. When his cough subsided he wiped his eyes and took
stock of the situation, understanding that the other man
was not an Inquisitor of any kind. Yet, in order to make
sure, he remained wary. No need to run away from a
man who gave him such a potent smoke. His head was
reeling from the effect of one of those strong American
cigarettes made with roasted tobacco. The man said, "I
come from New York," took out a wallet from his hip
pocket, and presented his card.

Muni shrank away from the card. Perhaps he was trying to present a warrant and arrest him. Beware of khaki,
one part of his mind warned. Take all the cigarettes or
bhang or whatever is offered, but don't get caught. Beware of khaki. He wished he weren't seventy as the shopman had said. At seventy one didn't run, but surrendered
to whatever came. He could only ward off trouble by
talk. So he went on, all in the chaste Tamil for which
Kritam was famous. (Even the worst detractors could not
deny that the famous poetess Avaiyar was born in this
area, although no one could say whether it was in Kritam
or Kuppam, the adjoining village.) Out of this heritage
the Tamil language gushed through Muni in an unim-
peded flow. He said, "Before God, sir, Bhagwan, who
sees everything, I tell you, sir, that we know nothing of
the case. If the murder was committed, whoever did it
will not escape. Bhagwan is all-seeing. Don't ask me
about it. I know nothing." A body had been found mutilated and thrown under a tamarind tree at the border
between Kritam and Kuppam a few weeks before, giving
rise to much gossip and speculation. Muni added an explanation. "Anything is possible there. People over there

will stop at nothing." The foreigner nodded his head and listened courteously though he understood nothing.

"I am sure you know when this horse was made," said the red man and smiled ingratiatingly.

Muni reacted to the relaxed atmosphere by smiling himself, and pleaded, "Please go away, sir, I know nothing. I promise we will hold him for you if we see any bad character around, and we will bury him up to his neck in a coconut pit if he tries to escape; but our village has always had a clean record. Must definitely be the other village."

Now the red man implored, "Please, please, I will speak slowly, please try to understand me. Can't you understand even a simple word of English? Everyone in this country seems to know English. I have gotten along with English everywhere in this country, but you don't speak it. Have you any religious or spiritual scruples against English speech?"

Muni made some indistinct sounds in his throat and shook his head. Encouraged, the other went on to explain at length, uttering each syllable with care and deliberation. Presently he sidled over and took a seat beside the old man, explaining, "You see, last August, we probably had the hottest summer in history, and I was working in shirt-sleeves in my office on the fortieth floor of the Empire State Building. We had a power failure one day, you know, and there I was stuck for four hours, no elevator, no air conditioning. All the way in the train I kept thinking, and the minute I reached home in Connecticut, I told my wife, Ruth, 'We will visit India this winter, it's time to look at other civilizations.' Next day she called the travel agent first thing and told him to fix it, and so here I am. Ruth came with me but is staying back at Srinagar, and I am the one doing the rounds and joining her later."

Muni looked reflective at the end of this long oration and said, rather feebly, "Yes, no," as a concession to the other's language, and went on in Tamil, "When I was this high"—he indicated a foot high—"I had heard my uncle say . . ."

No one can tell what he was planning to say, as the

other interrupted him at this stage to ask, "Boy, what is the secret of your teeth? How old are you?"

The old man forgot what he had started to say and remarked, "Sometimes we too lose our cattle. Jackals or cheetahs may sometimes carry them off, but sometimes it is just theft from over in the next village, and then we will know who has done it. Our priest at the temple can see in the camphor flame the face of the thief, and when he is caught . . ." He gestured with his hands a perfect mincing of meat.

The American watched his hands intently and said, "I know what you mean. Chop something? Maybe I am holding you up and you want to chop wood? Where is your axe? Hand it to me and show me what to chop. I do enjoy it, you know, just a hobby. We get a lot of driftwood along the backwater near my house, and on Sundays I do nothing but chop wood for the fireplace. I really feel different when I watch the fire in the fireplace, although it may take all the sections of the Sunday *New York Times* to get a fire started." And he smiled at this reference.

Muni felt totally confused but decided the best thing would be to make an attempt to get away from this place. He tried to edge out, saying, "Must go home," and turned to go. The other seized his shoulder and said desperately, "Is there no one, absolutely no one here, to translate for me?" He looked up and down the road, which was deserted in this hot afternoon; a sudden gust of wind churned up the dust and dead leaves on the roadside into a ghostly column and propelled it toward the mountain road. The stranger almost pinioned Muni's back to the statue and asked, "Isn't this statue yours? Why don't you sell it to me?"

The old man now understood the reference to the horse, thought for a second, and said in his own language, "I was an urchin this high when I heard my grandfather explain this horse and warrior, and my grandfather himself was this high when he heard his grandfather, whose grandfather . . ."

The other man interrupted him. "I don't want to seem to have stopped here for nothing. I will offer you a good price for this," he said, indicating the horse. He had concluded without the least doubt that Muni owned this mud horse. Perhaps he guessed by the way he sat on its pedestal, like other souvenir sellers in this country presiding over their wares.

Muni followed the man's eyes and pointing fingers and dimly understood the subject matter and, feeling relieved that the theme of the mutilated body had been abandoned at least for the time being, said again, enthusiastically, "I was this high when my grandfather told me about this horse and the warrior, and my grandfather was this high when he himself . . ." and he was getting into a deeper bog of reminiscence each time he tried to indicate the antiquity of the statue.

The Tamil that Muni spoke was stimulating even as pure sound, and the foreigner listened with fascination. "I wish I had my tape-recorder here," he said, assuming the pleasantest expression. "Your language sounds wonderful. I get a kick out of every word you utter, here"— he indicated his ears—"but you don't have to waste your breath in sales talk. I appreciate the article. You don't have to explain its points."

"I never went to a school, in those days only Brahmin went to schools, but we had to go out and work in the fields morning till night, from sowing to harvest time . . . and when Pongal came and we had cut the harvest, my father allowed me to go out and play with others at the tank, and so I don't know the Parangi language you speak, even little fellows in your country probably speak the Parangi language, but here only learned men and officers know it. We had a postman in our village who could speak to you boldly in your language, but his wife ran away with someone and he does not speak to anyone at all nowadays. Who would if a wife did what she did? Women must be watched; otherwise they will sell themselves and the home." And he laughed at his own quip.

The foreigner laughed heartily, took out another cigarette, and offered it to Muni, who now smoked with ease, deciding to stay on if the fellow was going to be so good as to keep up his cigarette supply. The American now stood up on the pedestal in the attitude of a demonstrative lecturer and said, running his finger along some of the carved decorations around the horse's neck, speaking slowly and uttering his words syllable by syllable, "I could give a sales talk for this better than anyone else. . . . This is a marvelous combination of yellow and indigo, though faded now. . . . How do you people of this country achieve these flaming colors?"

Muni, now assured that the subject was still the horse and not the dead body, said, "This is our guardian, it means death to our adversaries. At the end of Kali Yuga, this world and all other worlds will be destroyed, and the Redeemer will come in the shape of a horse called Kalki; this horse will come to life and gallop and trample down all bad men." As he spoke of bad men the figures of his shopman and his brother-in-law assumed concrete forms in his mind, and he revelled for a moment in the predicament of the fellow under the horse's hoof: served him right for trying to set fire to his home. . . .

While he was brooding on this pleasant vision, the foreigner utilized the pause to say, "I assure you that this will have the best home in the U.S.A. I'll push away the bookcase, you know I love books and am a member of five book clubs, and the choice and bonus volumes mount up to a pile really in our living room, as high as this horse itself. But they'll have to go. Ruth may disapprove, but I will convince her. The TV may have to be shifted, too. We can't have everything in the living room. Ruth will probably say what about when we have a party? I'm going to keep him right in the middle of the room. I don't see how that can interfere with the party—we'll stand around him and have our drinks."

Muni continued his description of the end of the world. "Our pundit discoursed at the temple once how the oceans are going to close over the earth in a huge wave and swallow us—this horse will grow bigger than the biggest wave and carry on its back only the good people and kick into the floods the evil ones—plenty of them about—" he said reflectively. "Do you know when it is going to happen?" he asked.

The foreigner now understood by the tone of the other that a question was being asked and said, "How am I transporting it? I can push the seat back and make room in the rear. That van can take in an elephant"—waving precisely at the back of the seat.

Muni was still hovering on visions of avatars and said again, "I never missed our pundit's discourses at the temple in those days during every bright half of the month, although he'd go on all night, and he told us that Vishnu is the highest god. Whenever evil men trouble us, he comes down to save us. He has come many times. The first time he incarnated as a great fish, and lifted the scriptures on his back when the flood and sea waves . . ."

"I am not a millionaire, but a modest businessman. My trade is coffee."

Amidst all this wilderness of obscure sound Muni caught the word "coffee" and said, "If you want to drink 'kapi,' drive further up, in the next town, they have Friday market and there they open 'kapi-otels'—so I learn from passersby. Don't think I wander about. I go nowhere and look for nothing." His thoughts went back to the avatars. "The first avatar was in the shape of a little fish in a bowl of water, but every hour it grew bigger and bigger and became in the end a huge whale which the seas could not contain, and on the back of the whale the holy books were supported, saved, and carried." Once he had launched on the first avatar, it was inevitable that he should go on to the next, a wild boar on whose tusk the earth was lifted when a vicious conqueror of the earth carried it off and hid it at the bottom of the sea. After describing this avatar Muni concluded, "God will always save us whenever we are troubled by evil beings. When we were young we staged at full moon the story of the avatars. That's how I know the stories; we played them all night until the sun rose, and sometimes the European collector would come to watch, bringing his own chair. I had a good voice and so they always taught me songs and gave me the women's roles. I was always Goddess Lakshmi, and they dressed me in a brocade sari, loaned from the Big House . . ."

The foreigner said, "I repeat I am not a millionaire. Ours is a modest business; after all, we can't afford to buy more than sixty minutes of TV time in a month, which works out to two minutes a day, that's all, although in the course of time we'll maybe sponsor a one-hour show regularly if our sales graph continues to go up . . ."

Muni was intoxicated by the memory of his theatrical days and was about to explain how he had painted his face and worn a wig and diamond earrings when the visitor, feeling that he had spent too much time already, said, "Tell me, will you accept a hundred rupees or not for the horse? I'd love to take the whiskered soldier also but no space for him this year. I'll have to cancel my air ticket and take a boat home, I suppose. Ruth can go by air if she likes, but I will go with the horse and keep him in my cabin all the way if necessary." And he smiled at the picture of himself voyaging across the seas hugging this horse. He added, "I will have to pad it with straw so that it doesn't break . . ."

"When we played *Ramayana*, they dressed me as Sita," added Muni. "A teacher came and taught us the songs for the drama and we gave him fifty rupees. He incarnated himself as Rama, and he alone could destroy Ravana, the demon with ten heads who shook all the worlds; do you know the story of *Ramayana*?"

"I have my station wagon as you see. I can push the seat back and take the horse in if you will just lend me a hand with it."

"Do you know *Mahabharata*? Krishna was the eighth avatar of Vishnu, incarnated to help the Five Brothers regain their kingdom. When Krishna was a baby he danced on the thousand-hooded giant serpent and trampled it to death; and then he suckled the breasts of the demoness and left them flat as a disc, though when she came to him her bosoms were large, like mounds of earth on the banks of a dug-up canal." He indicated two mounds with his hands.

The stranger was completely mystified by the gesture. For the first time he said, "I really wonder what you are saying because your answer is crucial. We have come to the point when we should be ready to talk business."

"When the tenth avatar comes, do you know where you and I will be?" asked the old man.

"Lend me a hand and I can lift off the horse from its pedestal after picking out the cement at the joints. We can do anything if we have a basis of understanding."

At this stage the mutual mystification was complete, and there was no need even to carry on a guessing game at the meaning of words. The old man chattered away in a spirit of balancing off the credits and debits of conversational exchange, and said in order to be on the credit sale, "Oh, honorable one, I hope God has blessed you with numerous progeny. I say this because you seem to be a good man, willing to stay beside an old man and talk to him, while all day I have none to talk to except when somebody stops by to ask for a piece of tobacco. But I seldom have it, tobacco is not what it used to be at one time, and I have given up chewing. I cannot afford it nowadays." Noting the other's interest in his speech, Muni felt encouraged to ask, "How many children have you?" with appropriate gestures with his hands.

Realizing that a question was being asked, the red man replied, "I said a hundred," which encouraged Muni to go into details. "How many of your children are boys and how many girls? Where are they? Is your daughter married? Is it difficult to find a son-in-law in your country also?"

In answer to these questions the red man dashed his hand into his pocket and brought forth his wallet in order to take immediate advantage of the bearish trend in the market. He flourished a hundred-rupee currency note and said, "Well, this is what I meant."

The old man now realized that some financial element was entering their talk. He peered closely at the currency note, the like of which he had never seen in his life; he knew the five and ten by their colors although always in other people's hands, while his own earning at any time was in coppers and nickels. What was this man flourishing the note for? Perhaps asking for change. He laughed to himself at the notion of anyone coming to him for changing a thousand- or ten-thousand-rupee note. He said with a grin, "Ask our village headman, who is also a moneylender; he can change even a lakh of rupees in gold sovereigns if you prefer it that way; he thinks nobody knows, but dig the floor of his puja room and your head will reel at the sight of the hoard. The man disguises himself in rags just to mislead the public. Talk to the headman yourself because he goes mad at the sight of me. Someone took away his pumpkins with the creeper and he, for some reason, thinks it was me and my goats

. . . that's why I never let my goats be seen anywhere near the farms." His eyes travelled to his goats nosing about, attempting to wrest nutrition from minute greenery peeping out of rock and dry earth.

The foreigner followed his look and decided that it would be a sound policy to show an interest in the old man's pets. He went up casually to them and stroked their backs with every show of courteous attention. Now the truth dawned on the old man. His dream of a lifetime was about to be realized. He understood that the red man was actually making an offer for the goats. He had reared them up in the hope of selling them some day and, with the capital, opening a small shop on this very spot. Sitting here, watching toward the hills, he had often dreamt how he would put up a thatched roof here, spread a gunny sack out on the ground, and display on it fried nuts, colored sweets, and green coconut for the thirsty and famished wayfarers on the highway, which was sometimes very busy. The animals were not prize ones for a cattle show, but he had spent his occasional savings to provide them some fancy diet now and then, and they did not look too bad. While he was reflecting thus, the red man shook his hand and left on his palm one hundred rupees in tens now, suddenly realizing that this was what the old man was asking. "It is all for you or you may share it if you have a partner."

The old man pointed at the station wagon and asked, "Are you carrying them off in that?"

"Yes, of course," said the other, understanding the transportation part of it.

The old man said, "This will be their first ride in a motor car. Carry them off after I get out of sight, otherwise they will never follow you, but only me even if I am travelling on the path to Yama Loka." He laughed at his own joke, brought his palms together in a salute, turned around and went off, and was soon out of sight beyond a clump of thicket.

The red man looked at the goats grazing peacefully. Perched on the pedestal of the horse, as the westerly sun touched off the ancient faded colors of the statue with a fresh splendor, he ruminated, "He must be gone to fetch some help, I suppose!" and settled down to wait. When a truck came downhill, he stopped it and got the help of a couple of men to detach the horse from its pedestal and place it in his station wagon. He gave them five rupees each, and for a further payment they siphoned off gas from the truck, and helped him to start his engine.

Muni hurried homeward with the cash securely tucked away at his waist in his dhoti. He shut the street door and stole up softly to his wife as she squatted before the lit oven wondering if by a miracle food would drop from the sky. Muni displayed his fortune for the day. She snatched the notes from him, counted them by the glow of the fire, and cried, "One hundred rupees! How did you come by it? Have you been stealing?"

"I have sold our goats to a red-faced man. He was absolutely crazy to have them, gave me all this money and carried them off in his motor car!"

Hardly had these words left his lips when they heard bleating outside. She opened the door and saw the two goats at her door. "Here they are!" she said. "What's the meaning of all this?"

He muttered a great curse and seized one of the goats by its ears and shouted, "Where is that man? Don't you know you are his? Why did you come back?" The goat only wriggled in his grip. He asked the same question of the other, too. The goat shook itself off. His wife glared at him and declared, "If you have thieved, the police will come tonight and break your bones. Don't involve me. I will go away to my parents. . . ."

Khushwant Singh
(b. 1915)

Born in Hadali in the Punjab (now part of Pakistan), Khushwant Singh received a B.A. at Government College in Lahore, India, in 1934 and became a barrister-at-law in England after study at London's Inner Temple and King's College, where he earned an LL.B. in 1938. A noted novelist, short-story writer, editor, and journalist, he practiced law at Lahore's High Court in the 1940s, served as a press attaché to Canada, as a public relations officer in England as well as working for UNESCO in Paris in the 1950s. His two-volume *History of the Sikhs* (Princeton University Press, 1962) was commissioned jointly by the Rockefeller Foundation and Muslim University in Aligarh. He has been a visiting lecturer at Oxford University, the University of Rochester, Princeton University, and Swarthmore College. From 1969–1979 he was the editor of the *Illustrated Weekly of India* published in Bombay, and from 1980–1983 he was editor of the *Hindustan Times*, published in New Delhi where he now makes his home. A member of Parliament's upper house from 1980–1986, in recent years he has become chief literary adviser to Penguin Books, India. His best-known work in the West, the novel *Train to Pakistan* (Chatto & Windus, 1956; repr. Grove, 1961), depicts a pair of lovers from different religious backgrounds, one a Muslim, the other a Sikh, caught up in the 1947 partition of Pakistan from India. In discussing the novel, critic Vasant Anant Shahane (in *Kushwant Singh*) has commented that it is characterized by "its stark realism, its absolute fidelity to the truth of life, its trenchant exposition of one of the most moving, even tragic, events of contemporary Indian history. . . ." Among his other works of fiction are the novels *I Shall Not Hear the Nightingale* (Grove, 1959),

Delhi (Penguin Books, India, 1989); his story collections include *The Mark of Vishnu and Other Stories* (Saturn Press, 1950), *The Voice of God and Other Stories* (Jaico Publishing House, 1957), *A Bride for the Sahib and Other Stories* (Hind Pocket Books, 1967), and *Black Jasmine* (Jaico Publishing House, 1971). In 1984 he returned the Padma Bhushan Award, which he had received from the president of India a decade earlier in protest against the government's sending of armed troops into the Golden Temple at Amritsar.

THE WOG

"What can I do for you gentlemen?"

Mr. Sen asked the question without looking up. He pushed the cleaner through the stem of his pipe and twirled it round. As he blew through it, his eye fell on the rose and marigold garlands in the hands of his callers. So they knew that he had been married that morning! He had tried to keep it as quiet as possible. But as he had learned so often before, it was impossible to keep anything a secret for too long in his nosy, native land.

He screwed on the bowl to the stem and blew through the pipe again. Through his lowered eyes, he saw his visitors shuffling their feet and nudging each other. He unwrapped his plastic tobacco pouch and began filling his pipe. After an uneasy minute of subdued whispers, one of the men cleared his throat.

"Well, Mr. Bannerjee, what is your problem?" asked Mr. Sen in a flat monotone.

"Saar," began the Superintendent of the clerical staff, "whee came to wheesh your good shelph long liphe and happinesh." He beckoned to the Chaprasis: "Garland the Shahib."

The Chaprasis stepped in front with the garlands held

aloft. The Sahib stopped them with a wave of his pipe. "*Mez par*—on the table," he commanded in his gentle but firm voice. The Chaprasis' hands came down slowly; their fawning smiles changed to stupid grins. They put the garlands on the table and stepped behind the semicircle of clerks.

"If that is all," said Mr. Sen standing up, "we can get back to our work. I thank you gentlemen for your good wishes." He bowed slightly to indicate that they should leave. "Bannerjee, will you look in later to discuss the redistribution of work while I am away?"

"Shuttenly Saar."

The men joined the palms of their hands, murmured their "*namastes*" and filed out.

Sen joined his hands across the waistcoat and watched the smoke from his pipe rise in a lazy spiral toward the ceiling. A new chapter in his life had begun. That's how Hindus described marriage—the third of the four stages of life according to the Vedas. It was alarming, he reflected, how his thought processes slipped into clichés and how Hinduism extended its tentacles in practically every sphere of life. His father had not been a particularly orthodox Hindu and had sent him to an Anglo-Indian School where the boys had changed his name from Santosh to Sunny. Thereafter he had gone to Balliel. He had entered the Administrative Service before the Independent Indian Government with its newfangled nationalist ideas had made Hindi and a vernacular language compulsory. His inability to speak an Indian language hadn't proved a handicap. As a matter of fact, it impressed most Indians. Although his accent and mannerisms made him somewhat of an outsider, it was more than compensated by the fact that it also put him outside the vicious circle of envy and back-biting in which all the others indulged. They sought his company because he was an ub-Indian Indian, because he was a brown British gentleman, because he was what the English contemptuously described as a Wog—a westernized oriental gentleman.

Sen's main contact with his country was his mother. Like an orthodox Hindu widow she shaved her head, only wore a plain white sari and went in bare feet. He

was her only child so they both did the best they could
for each other. She ran his home. He occasionally ate
rice, curried fish and sticky over-sweetened confections
she made on special occasions. Other times she had the
bearer cook him the lamb chops and the shepherd pies
he liked better. She had converted one of the rooms to
a temple where she burned incense and tinkled bells to
a diminutive image of the black-faced, red-tongued goddess, Kali. But she never insisted on his joining her in
worship. Although he detested Indian movies, he made
it a point to take her to one every month. She, at her
end, did not object to his taking his evening Scotch and
soda or smoking in her presence. She never questioned
him about his movements. They got on extremely well
till she started talking about his getting married. At first
he had laughed it off. She became insistent and started
to nag him. She wanted to see him properly settled. She
wanted to fondle a grandson just once before she died,
she said with tears in her eyes. At last he gave in. He
did not have strong views on marriage or on whom he
would marry. Since he had come back to settle in India,
he could not do worse than marry one of his coun-
trywomen. "All right Ma, you find me a wife. I'll marry
anyone you want me to marry," he said one day.

His mother did not bring up the subject again for many
days. She wrote to her brother living at Dehra Doon, in
the Himalayan foothills, to come down to Delhi. The
two drafted an advertisement for the matrimonial columns and asked for insertions in two successive Sunday
editions of the Hindustan Times. It read: "Wanted a fair
good looking virgin of a high class respectable family for
an Oxford educated Bengali youth of 25 drawing over
Rs. 1,000 p.m. in first class gazetted Government Service. Applicant should be conversant with H. H. affairs.
C and D no bar. Correspond with horoscope. P.O. Box
No. 4200."

The first insertion brought over fifty letters from parents who enclosed not only the horoscopes of their
daughters but their photographs as well to prove that
they were fair and therefore good looking. A fortnight
later the applications were sorted out and Sunny's
mother and uncle triumphantly laid out nearly a hundred

photographs on the large dining table. Their virginity and capacity to deal with household affairs had, of necessity, to be taken on trust. But despite the professed indifference to the C and D, the applicants selected for consideration were of the same caste as the Sens and whose fathers had made offers of substantial dowries. Now it was for Sunny to choose.

This was the first time that Sunny had heard of the matrimonial advertisement. He was very angry and acutely embarrassed as some anxious parents had travelled up all the way from Calcutta, bribed the clerks concerned at the newspaper office and called on him at the office. He told his mother firmly that if it did not stop, he would call off the whole thing. But as he had given his word, he would accept anyone chosen for him. His mother and uncle quickly settled the matter by selecting a girl whose father promised the largest dowry and gave a substantial portion of it as earnest money at the betrothal ceremony. The parties took the horoscopes of the affianced couple to a Pandit who consulted the stars and, having had his palm crossed with silver, pronounced the pair ideally suited to each other and the dates that suited the parties to be most auspicious. That was as much as Sunny Sen could take. He told them quite bluntly that he would be married at the Registry or not at all. His mother and uncle sensed his mounting irritation and gave in. The bride's parents made a nominal protest: the cost of a wedding on the traditional pattern which included feasting the bridegroom's party and relations, giving of presents and paying the priests could run into thousands of rupees. The registrar's fee was only Rs .5/-. That was how Srijut Santosh Sen came to marry Kumari Kalyani, the eldest of Srijut Profulla and Srimati Protima Das's five daughters. Mr. Das was, like his son-in-law, a first class gazetted Government servant.

The honeymoon also created difficulties. His mother blushed as if he had said something improper. The Dases were outraged at the suggestion that their daughter should go away for a fortnight unaccompanied by a younger sister. But they resigned their daughter to her fate. Her husband had been brought up as a Sahib and she must follow his ways.

Sen's thoughts were interrupted by his colleague Santa Singh bursting into the room. The Sikh was like the rest of his race, loud and aggressive: "Brother, you think you can run away without giving us a party?" He yelled as he came, "We insist on having a feast to welcome our sister-in-law."

Sen stood up quickly and put his hand across the table to keep the Sikh at an arm's length. Santa Singh ignored the proferred hand, came round the table and enveloped his friend in his arms. He planted his wet and hirsute kisses on the Sahib's cheeks. "Congratulations, brother, when are we to meet our sister-in-law?"

"Soon, very soon," replied Sen extricating himself from the Sikh's embrace and wiping his cheeks. And before the words were out of his mouth, he knew he had blundered: "As soon as we get back from our honeymoon."

"Honeymoon!" exclaimed Santa Singh with a leer; he took Sen's hands in his and squeezed them amorously. "I hope you've had yourself massaged with chameleon oil; puts more punch into things. You should also add crushed almonds in your milk. Above all, don't overdo it. Not more than . . . ." There was no stopping the Sikh from giving unsolicited advice on how to approach an inexperienced virgin and the proper use of aphrodisiacs. Sen kept smiling politely without making comment. When he had enough, he interrupted the Sikh's soliloquy by extending his hand. "It was very kind of you to have dropped in. We will call on you and Mrs. Singh as soon as we are back in Delhi."

Santa Singh took Sen's hand without any enthusiasm. "Goodbye. Have a nice time," he blurted and went out. Sen sat down with a sigh of relief. He knew he had not been rude. He had behaved with absolute rectitude— exactly like an English gentleman.

A minute later the Chaprasi raised the thick curtains to let in Mr. Swami, the Director of the Department. Sen again extended his hand across the table to keep the visitor at arm's length: the native's desire to make physical contact galled him. "Good morning, Sir."

The Director touched Sen's hand with his without answering the greeting. His mouth was full of betel saliva.

He raised his face to hold it from dribbling out and bawled out to the Chaprasi: "Hey, spitoon *lao*."

The Chaprasi ran in with the vessel which Sen had ordered to be removed from his room and held it under the Director's chin. Mr. Swami spat out the bloody phlegm in the spitoon. Sen opened his table drawer and pretended he was looking for his match box. The Director sat down and lit his *bidi*. "Eh, you Sen, you are a dark harse. By God, a pitch black harse, if I may say so." Mr. Swami fancied his knowledge of English idiom. "So quietly you go and get yourself hitched. My steno says 'Sir, we should celebrate holiday to celebrate Sahib's marriage!' I say, 'What marriage, man?' 'Sir, Mr. Sen got married this morning.' 'By God,' I said, 'I must get the truth, the whole truth and nothing but the truth right from the harse's mouth—the dark harse's mouth." The Director stretched his hand across the table. "Clever guy you eh?" he said with a smirk. Sen touched his boss's hand with the tip of his fingers. "Thank you, Sir."

"What for thank you? And you come to the office on the day you get married. Heavens won't fall if you stay away a few days. I as your boss order you to go back home to your wife. I will put in a demi-official memo. What do you say?"

The Director was pleased with himself and extended his hand. Sen acknowledged his boss's wit by taking his hand. "Thank you, Sir. I think I will go home."

"My God, you are a Sahib! I hope your wife is not a Mem Sahib. That would be too much of a joke."

The Director left but his betel-stained smirk lingered on like the smile of the Cheshire Cat and his last remark began to go round and round in Sen's head with an insistent rhythmic beat. "I hope your wife isn't a Mem Sahib, not a Mem Sahib, not a Mem Sahib. I hope your wife is not a Mem Sahib."

Would his wife be a Mem Sahib, he mused as he drove back home for lunch. It was not very likely. She claimed to be an M.A. in English literature. But he had met so many of his countrymen with long strings of firsts who could barely speak the English language correctly. To start with, there was the Director himself with his "okey dokes" and "by gums" who, like other South Indians, pronounced eight as yate, an egg as a yugg, and who always stumbled on words beginning with an 'M.' He smiled to himself as he recalled the Director instructing his private secretary to get Mr. M. M. Amir, Member of Parliament, on the phone. "I want Yum Yum Yumeer Yumpee." The Bengalis had their own execrable accent: they added an airy 'h' whenever they could after a 'b' or a 'W' or an 's.' A virgin sounded like some exotic tropical plant, "the Vharjeen," "will" as a wheel, and the simple simple as a "shimple."

There was much crying at the farewell and the bride continued to sniffle for a long time afterwards in the car. She had drawn her sari over her forehead down to her eyes and covered the rest of her face with a silk handkerchief into which she blew her nose. When Sen lit his pipe, she firmly clamped the handkerchief on her nostrils. "Does the smoke bother you?" was the first sentence he spoke to his wife. She replied by a vigorous shake of the head.

They stopped at a mango orchard by the roadside to have lunch. His mother had made two separate packets with their names in Bengali pinned on them. The one marked "Sunny" had roasted chicken and cheese sandwiches. The other contained boiled rice and pickles in a small brass cup with curried lentils. His wife poured the lentils on the rice and began to eat with her fingers.

They ate without speaking to each other. Within a few minutes they had an audience of anxious passersby and children from a neighboring village. Some sat on their haunches; others just stood gaping at the couple or commenting on their being newly married. Sen knew how to deal with the rustic. "Are you people hungry?" he asked sarcastically.

The men turned away sheepishly; but the urchins did not budge. "Bugger off, you dirty bastards," roared Sen raising his hand as if to strike. The children ran away to a safe distance and began to yell back at Sen, mimicking his English. "Buggeroff, Buggeroff," they cried. "*Arey* he is a Sahib, a big Sahib."

Sen ignored them and spoke politely to his wife. "Pardon the language," he said with a smile. "Would you like to sample one of my sandwiches? I don't know whether you eat meat; take the lettuce and cheese; it is fresh cheddar."

Mrs. Sen took the sandwich with her curry-stained fingers. She tore a strip off the toast as if it were a *Chappati*, scooped up a mixture of rice, curry and cheddar and put it in her mouth. She took one bite and stopped munching. Through her thick glasses she stared at her husband as if he had given her poison. She turned pale and being unable to control herself any further, spat out the food in her mouth. She turned her face the other way and brought up the rice and curry.

"I am dreadfully sorry," stammered Sen. "The cheddar upset you. I should have known."

Mrs. Sen wiped her mouth with the end of her sari and asked for water. She rinsed her mouth and splashed it on her face. The lunch was ruined. "We better be on our way," said Sen, standing up. "That is if you feel better."

She tied up her brass cup in a duster and followed him to the car. They were on the road again. She fished out a silver box from her handbag and took out a couple of betel leaves. She smeared one with lime and catechu paste, put in cardamom and sliced betel nuts, rolled it up and held it out for her husband.

"I'm afraid I don't touch the stuff," he said apologetically. "I'll stick to my pipe if you don't mind." Mrs. Sen did not mind. She slipped the leaf in her own mouth and began to chew contentedly.

They got to the rest-house in good time. The rest-house bearer took in the luggage and spread the bedding rolls. He asked Mrs. Sen what they would like for dinner. She referred him to her husband. "Just anything for me," he replied, "omelette or anything. Ask the Mem Sahib what she would like for herself. I will take a short walk before dinner."

"Don't go too far Sahib," continued the bearer. "This is wild country. There is a footpath down to the river which the Sahibs who come to fish take. It is quite safe."

Sen went into the bedroom to ask his wife if she would like to come out for a walk. She was unpacking her things. He changed his mind. "I'll go for a short stroll

toward the river. Get the bearer to put out the Scotch
and soda in the verandah; there's a bottle in my suitcase.
We'll have a drink before dinner.''

His wife nodded her head.

The well-beaten fishermen's footpath snaked its way
through a dense foliage of *sal* and flame of the forest,
ending abruptly on the pebbly bank of the river. The
Ganges was a magnificent sight; a broad and swift-
moving current of clear, icy-blue water sparkling in the
bright sun. It must have been from places like where
he stood, he thought, that the sages of olden times had
pronounced the Ganges the holiest of all the rivers in the
world. He felt a sense of kinship with his Aryan ancestors, who worshipped the beautiful in nature, sang hymns
to the rising sun, raised goblets of fermented soma juice
to the full moon and who ate beef and were lusty with
full-bosomed and large-hipped women. Much water had
flowed down the Ganges since then and Hinduism was
now like the river itself at its lower reaches—as at Calcutta where he was born. At Calcutta it was a sluggish
expanse of slime and sludge carrying the excrement of
millions of pilgrims who polluted it at Hardwar, Benares,
Allahabad, Patna and other "holy" cities on its banks,
and who fouled its water by strewing charred corpses for
the fish and the turtles to eat. It had become the Hinduism of the Cow-protectors, prohibitionists—and chewers
of betel leaves. That must be it, he thought cheerfully.
His was the pristine Hinduism of the stream that sparkled
before him; that of the majority, of the river after it had
been sullied by centuries of narrow prejudices. He
walked over the pebbled bank, took up a palmful of the
icy-cold water and splashed it on his face.

The shadows of the jungle lengthened across the
stream and the cicadas began to call. Sen turned back
and quickly retraced his steps to the bungalow. The sun
was setting. It was time for a sundowner.

Tumblers and soda were laid out on the table in the
verandah. The bearer heard his footsteps and came with
a bunch of keys in his open hand. "I did not like to open
the Sahib's trunk," he explained. "Please take out the
whiskey."

"Why didn't you ask the Mem Sahib to take it out?"

The bearer looked down at his feet. "She said she could not touch a bottle of alcohol. She gave me the keys but I don't like to meddle with the Sahib's luggage. If things are misplaced . . ."

"That's all right. Open my suitcase. The bottles of whiskey and brandy are right on the top. And serve the dinner as soon as the Mem Sahib is ready."

It was no point asking his wife to sit with him. He poured himself a large Scotch and lit his pipe. Once more his thoughts turned to the strange course his life had taken. If he had married one of the English girls he had met in his University days how different things would have been. They would have kissed a hundred times between the wedding and the wedding night; they would have walked hand in hand through the forest and made love beside the river; they would have lain in each other's arms and sipped their Scotch. They would have nibbled at knick-knacks in between bouts of love; and they would have made love till the early hours of the morning. The whiskey warmed his blood and quickened his imagination. He was back in England. The gathering bloom and the dark, tropical forest, accentuated the feeling of loneliness. He felt an utter stranger in his own country. He did not hear the bearer announcing that dinner had been served. Now his wife came out and asked in her quaint Bengali accent, "Do you want to shit outside?"

"What?" he asked gruffly, waking up from his reverie.

"Do you want to shit inshide or outshide. The deener ees on the table."

"Oh, I'll be right in. You go ahead. I'll join you in a second," Good lord! What would his English friends have said if she had invited them in this manner! The invitation to defecate was Mrs. Sen's first communication with her husband.

A strong sweet smell of coconut oil and roses assailed Sen's nostrils as he entered the dining room. His wife had washed and oiled her hair; it hung in loose snaky coils below her waist. The parting was daubed with bright vermillion powder to indicate her status as a married woman. He had no doubt that she had smeared her body with the attar of roses as her mother had probably instructed. She sat patiently at the table; being a Hindu woman, she could not very well start eating before her husband.

"Sorry to keep you waiting. You should have started. Your dinner must be cold."

She simply wagged her head.

They began to eat; he, his omelette and buttered slice of bread with his fork and knife. She, her rice and lentil curry mushed in between her fingers and palm of her right hand. Sen cleared his throat many times to start a conversation. But each time the vacant and bewildered look behind the thick lenses of his wife's glasses made him feel that words would fail to convey their meaning. If his friends knew they would certainly have a big laugh. "Oh Sunny Sen! How could he start talking to his wife? He hadn't been properly introduced. Don't you know he is an Englishman?"

The dinner was eaten in silence. Kalyani Sen emitted a soft belch and took out her betel-leaf case. She rolled a leaf, paused for a split-second and put it in her mouth. Sunny had promised himself the luxury of expensive Havana cigars over his honeymoon. He took one out of its phallic metal case, punctured its bottom with a gold clipper and lit it. The aromatic smoke soon filled the dining room. This time his wife did not draw the fold of her sari across her face; she simply clasped her hands in front of her mouth and discreetly blocked her nostrils with the back of her hands.

They sat in silence facing each other across the table; she chewing her leaf—almost like a cow chewing the cud, thought Sen. He, lost in the smoke of his long Cuban cigar. It was oppressive—and the barrier between them, impassable. Sen glanced at his watch and stood up. "News," he exclaimed loudly. "Mustn't miss the news." He went into the bedroom to fetch his transistor radio set.

Two beds had been laid side by side with no space between them; the pillows almost hugged each other. The sheets had been sprinkled with the earthy perfume of *khas* fibre and looked as if they also awaited the consummation of the marriage performed earlier in the day. How, thought Sen, could she think of this sort of thing when (they hadn't even been introduced! No, hell) barely a civil word had passed between them? He quickly took out his radio set and hurried back to the dining room.

He tuned in to Delhi. While he listened in to the news, the bearer cleared the table and left salaaming "Good night, Sir." Mrs. Sen got up, collected her betel-leaf case and disappeared into the bedroom.

The fifteen minutes of news was followed by a commentary on sports. Sen had never bothered to listen in to it. He was glad he did because the commentary was followed by the announcement of a change in the program. A concert of vocal Hindustani music by Ustad Badey Ghulam Ali Khan had been put off to relay a performance by the Czech Philharmonic Orchestra from New Delhi. Ghulam Ali Khan was the biggest name in Indian music and even the Anglicized natives had to pretend that they admired the cacophony of gargling sounds he produced from the pit of his stomach. Members of the diplomatic corps were known to sit through four hours of the maestro's performances lest they offend their Indian hosts or be found less cultured than staffs of rival embassies. The Czech Philharmonic had come to India for the first time and the wogs who ran Delhi's European Music Society had got away with it. Pity, thought Sen, he wasn't in town; he could have invited the right people for dinner (tails, of course!) followed by the concert. How would his wife have fitted in a party of this sort?

The sound of applause came over the air, followed by an announcement that the opening piece was a selection from Smetana's The Bartered Bride. Sen was transported back to the glorious evening at Covent Garden and the Festival Hall. Smetana was followed by Bartok. The only thing that broke the enchantment was the applause between the movements. How could one expect the poor, benighted natives to know that the end of a movement was not the end of the symphony!

There was an interval of ten minutes. The last piece was Sen's favorite—Dvorak's Symphony No. 5 in E minor. He poured himself a liquor brandy (V.S.O.P.), drew a chair and stretched his legs on it. He had never heard Dvorak as well performed even in Europe. A Cuban cigar, an excellent Cognac and the world's greatest music, what more could one ask for! He gently decapitated the cigar of its ashy ahead, lay back in the armchair and closed his eyes in complete rapture. By the final movement he was fast asleep with the cigar slowly burning itself out between his lips.

Neither the applause, at the end of the concert, nor the silence and the cackling of the radio woke Sen from his slumber. When the cigar got too hot, he opened his mouth and let it drop on his lap. It slowly burned through his trouser and then singed the hair on his under-belly. He woke with a start and threw the butt on the ground.

Although the cigar had only burned a tiny hole near a fly button, the room was full of the smell of burning cloth. That was a narrow escape, thought Sen. He switched off the transistor and glanced at his watch. It was well after midnight. He blew out the oil lamp and went to the bedroom.

An oil lamp still burned on the table. His wife had fallen asleep—obviously after having waited for him. She had not changed nor taken off her jewelry. She had put mascara in her eyes. Her tears had washed some of it on to her cheeks and the pillow had a smudge of soot.

Sen changed into his pajamas and slipped into his bed. He stared at his wife's gently heaving bosom and her open mouth. How could he? In any case, he didn't have the slightest desire. He turned the knob on the lamp. The yellow flame turned to a blue fluting on the edge of the wick, spluttered twice, then gave up the struggle and plunged the room into a black solitude.

The bearer came in with the tea-tray and woke him up. "Sahib, it is after nine. Mem Sahib has been up for the last four or five hours. She has had her bath, said her prayer and has been waiting for you to get up to have her *chota hazri*."

Sen rubbed his eyes. The sun was streaming through the verandah into the room. His wife had made a swiss roll of her bedding and put it away on the top of her steel trunk. "I'll have my tea in the verandah," he replied getting up. He went into the bedroom, splashed cold water on his face and went out.

"Sorry to keep you waiting; I seem to do it all the time. You should really never wait for me." He stretched himself and yawned. "I am always . . . what on earth."

His wife had got up and while his face was still lifted toward the ceiling, bent down to touch his feet. He was her husband, lord and master. He looked down in alarm. She looked up, tears streamed down both her cheeks. "I am unworthy," she said half-questioning and half-stating her fears. And before he could reply, she drew the flap of her sari across her eyes and fled inside.

"What the hell is all this?" muttered Sen and collapsed into an armchair. He knew precisely what she meant. He sat a long while scratching his head with his eyes fixed in a hypnotic stare on the sunlit lawn. He had no desire to go in and make up to his wife.

The bearer came, looked accusingly at the untouched tray of tea and announced that breakfast was on the table. Sen got up reluctantly. She would obviously not have anything to eat unless he cajoled her. And he was damned if he was going to do it. Again he was wrong. She was at the table. He avoided looking at her.

"Tea?" he questioned and filled her cup and then his own. Once again they ate their different foods in their different ways without saying a word to each other. And as soon as the meal was over, she went to her betel leaves and he to his pipe. She retired to her bedroom. He took his transistor and returned to the verandah to listen in to the morning news.

The arrival of the postman at noon put the idea in his head. It was only a copy of the office memorandum sanctioning him leave for a fortnight. He walked in waving the yellow envelope bearing the legend—"On India Government Service Only."

"I am afraid we have to return at once. It's an urgent letter from the Minister. He has to answer some questions in Parliament dealing with our department. I'll get the bearer to help you pack while I give the car a check up. Bearer, bearer," he yelled as he walked out.

Half an hour later they were on the road to Delhi; a little before sunset, Sen drove into his portico. The son and mother embraced each other and only broke apart when the bride knelt down to touch her mother-in-law's feet. "God bless you my child," said the older woman touching the girl on the shoulder, "but what . . ."

Her son pulled out the yellow envelope from his

pocket and waved it triumphantly. "An urgent summons from the Minister. These chaps don't respect anyone's private life. I simply had to come."

"Of course," replied his mother, wiping off a tear. She turned to her daughter-in-law. "Your parents will be delighted to know you are back. Why don't you ring them up?" A few minutes later Mrs. Sen's parents drove up in a taxi. There were more tears at the reunion, more explanations about the letter from the Minister. There was also relief. Now that the bride had spent a night with her husband and consummated the marriage, she could return to her parental home for a few days.

Sen spent the next morning going round the local bookshops and coffee houses. The weekend followed. On Sunday morning, when his mother was at prayer, he rang up the Director at his home to explain his return and ask for permission to resume work. "My mother has been keeping indifferent health and I did not want to leave her alone for too long." He knew this line of approach would win both sympathy and approval. The Director expressed concern and spoke warmly of a Hindu son's sacred duty toward his widowed mother. "And we must celebrate your wedding and meet your wife . . . as soon as your mother is better."

"Yes, Sir. As soon as she is up to the mark, we will invite you over."

The mother being "a bit under the weather" and "not quite up to the mark" became Sen's explanation for cancelling his leave and not having a party. It even silenced Santa Singh who had planned a lot of ribaldry at Sen's expense.

Days went by—and then weeks. Kalyani came over with her mother a couple of times to fetch her things. She came when her husband was in the office and only met her mother-in-law. It was conveyed to Sunny Sen that, under the circumstances, it was for the husband to go and fetch his wife from her home. Sen put off doing so for some time—and then had to go away on a tour of inspection to Southern India. It was a fortnight after his return that his parents-in-law learned that he was back in town. The relations between the two families became very strained. Nothing was said directly but talk about the Sens being dowry seekers and Sen's mother being a difficult woman started going round. Then Sunny got a letter from his father-in-law. It was polite but distinctly cold. From the contents it was obvious that it had been drafted and written on the advice of a lawyer with a carbon copy made for use if necessary. It referred to the advertisement in the matrimonial columns and the negotiations preceding the marriage, the money given on betrothal and in the dowry, the wedding and its consummation in the forest rest house on the Ganges. Sen was asked to state his intentions.

For the first time, Sen realized how serious the situation had become. He turned to his mother. A new bond was forged between the mother and son. "It is a matter of great shame," she said firmly. "We must not let this business go too far. You must fetch her. I will go away to my brother at Dehra Doon for a few days."

"No, Ma, I will not have anyone making insinuations against you," he replied, and pleaded, "In any case you must not leave me."

"No one has made any insinuations and I am not leaving you. This will always be my home; where else can I live except with my own flesh and blood. But you must get your wife. Let her take over the running of the house and become its mistress as is her right. Then I will come back and live without worrying my head with servants and cooking and shopping."

Sen flopped back in his chair like one exhausted. His mother came over behind him and took his head between her hands. "Don't let it worry you too much. I will write to my brother to come over to fetch me. He will go to your father-in-law's and bring over your wife. Before we leave, I will show her everything, give her the keys and tell the servants to take orders from her. When you come back from the office you will find everything running smoothly." She kissed her son's hair. "And do be nice to her, she is only a child. You know how much I am looking forward to having a grandson to fondle in my lap!"

Sen found the whole thing very distasteful. He felt angry with himself for allowing things to come to such a pass. And he felt angrier with his wife for humiliating his

mother and driving her out of her home. He would have
nothing to do with her unless she accepted his mother.
He instructed his cook-bearer about the arrangements of
the bedrooms. If the new mistress asked any questions,
he was to say that those were his master's orders.

On Monday morning, when the bearer brought him
his morning tea, he told him not to expect him for lunch
and to tell his wife not to wait for him for dinner as he
might be working late in the office. He had breakfast
with his mother and uncle. He promised to write to his
mother everyday to tell her how things were going. "You
must try and understand her point of view," admonished
his mother. "She has been brought up in a different
world. But love and patience conquers all."

Sen was the last to leave his office. He drove straight
to the Gymkhana Club. For an hour he sat by the bathing
pool, drinking ice-cold lager and watching the bathers.
There were European women from the diplomatic corps
with their children; there were pretty Punjabi girls in
their pony tails and bikinis; there were swarthy young
college students showing off their Tarzan-like torsos as
they leapt from the diving board. This surely was where
he belonged—where the east and the west met in a sort
of minestrone soup of human limbs of many pigments,
black, brown, pink and white. Why couldn't he have
married one of these girls, taught her proper English instead of Americanized chi-chi which they thought was
smart talk.

The bathers went home. Sen got up with a sigh and
went to the bar. He was greeted by several old friends.
"Hi, Sunny, you old bastard. What's this one hears about
you?"

Sunny smiled. "I don't have to proclaim everything I
do from the house tops, do I?"

"Like hell you do. You stand drinks all round or we'll
de-bag you and throw you out in front of all the women."
Three of them advanced towards him.

"Lay off chaps. Bearer give these B.F.'s what they
want. What's the poison?"

They sat on the high stools and downed their drinks
with "Cheers," "Here's mud in your eye," and "Bottoms
up."

"Where's your wife?" asked one. "Don't tell me you are going to keep her in the seclusion of the *purdah* like a native!"

"No ruddy fears," answered Sen. "She's gone to her mother's. Would you chaps like another?"

One round followed another till it was time for the bar to close. One of the men invited him home for dinner. Sen accepted without a murmur.

It was almost 1 A.M. when Sen drove back into his house. He was well fortified with Scotch to gloss over any awkwardness. He switched on the light in the hall and saw trunks piled up against the wall. His wife had obviously come back. There was no light in her bedroom. She must have gone to sleep many hours earlier. He switched off the half-light, tiptoed to his bedroom, switched on the table-lamp, went back and bolted the door from the inside. A few minutes later, he was fast asleep.

The bearer's persistent knocking woke him up. His head rocked as he got up to unfasten the bolt. What would the bearer think of the Sahib bolting his door against his wife? He couldn't care less. The throbbing in his head demanded all his attention.

"Shall I take tea for the Mem Sahib?" he asked.

"She does not have bed-tea," replied Sen. "Isn't she up yet?"

"I don't know Sahib; she has also bolted her door from the inside."

Sen felt uneasy. He swallowed a couple of aspirins and gulped down a cup of strong tea. He lay back on his pillow to let the aspirins take effect. His imagination began to run away with him. She couldn't. No, of course not! Must have waited for him till midnight, was scared of being alone and must have bolted the doors and was sleeping late. But he had been nasty to her and she might be over-sensitive. He decided to rid himself of the thought. He got up and knocked at the door. There was no response. He went to the bathroom and then tried her door again. There was no sound from the inside. He went to the window and pressed it with both his hands. The two sides flew apart and crashed against the wall.

Even that noise did not waken her. He peered in and caught the gleam of her glasses on her nose.

With a loud cry Sen ran back into the house and called for the bearer. The master and servant put their shoulders to the door and battered against it. The bolt gave way and they burst in the room. The woman on the bed didn't stir. A white fluid trickled from her gaping mouth to the pillow. Her eyes stared fixedly through the thick glasses. Sen put his hand on her forehead. It was the first time he had touched his wife. And she was dead.

On the table beside her bed was an empty tumbler and two envelopes. One bore her mother's name in Bengali; the other was for him. A haunted smile came on his lips as he read the English address:

> "To
>
> Mr. S. Sen, Esq."

SELECTED INDIAN ANTHOLOGIES

Alter, Stephen and Wimal Dissanayake, eds. *The Penguin Book of Modern Indian Short Stories*. Delhi: Penguin Books, India, 1990.

Bardham, Kalpana, trans. and ed. *Of Women, Outcastes, Peasants, and Rebels: A Selection of Bengali Short Stories*. Berkeley: University of California Press, 1990.

Ezekiel, Nissim and Meenakshi Mukherjee, eds. *Another India: An Anthology of Contemporary Indian Fiction and Poetry*, Delhi: Penguin Books, India, 1990.

Jose, F. Sionil, ed. *Asian Pen Anthology*. New York: Taplinger Publishing Company, 1966.

Kali for Women, ed. *Truth Tales: Contemporary Writing by Indian Women*. Delhi: Kali for Women, 1986; New York: The Feminist Press, 1990.

Natwar-Singh, K., ed. *Tales from Modern India*. New York: The Macmillan Company, 1966.

Roadarmel, Gordon C., trans. and ed. *A Death in Delhi: Modern Hindi Short Stories*. Berkeley: University of California Press, 1972.

Saksena, Manmohan, ed. *Indian Short Stories*. London and New York: Oxford University Press, 1951.

Subramanyam, Ka Naa, ed. *Tamil Short Stories*: New Delhi: Author's Guild of India Cooperative Society, 1978.

JAPANESE
STORIES

Kōbō Abe
(1924–1993)

Born in Tokyo, Kōbō Abe spent his childhood in the Manchurian city of Mukden, which was occupied by an invading Japanese army from 1931 to 1945. Alienated from his own militaristic and nationalistic homeland, he changed his name from Kimfusa to the more Chinese-sounding Kōbō, and rejoiced when he learned that Japan was about to be defeated. In 1948, he received a medical degree from Tokyo University, but decided not to follow in his father's footsteps and practice medicine; instead, he pursued a literary career. A novelist and playwright, Abe typically blends detailed realism with grotesque fantasy. His work, often compared to that of Franz Kafka, Eugène Ionesco, and Samuel Beckett, utilizes elements of the detective and science fiction genres and depicts themes of rootlessness, alienation, and the fragility of human identity. During a Japanese television interview, Abe asserted that

> Except for writers, who have always been cursed in Japan with vision and therefore estrangement, the modern, mass-media-consuming Japanese works blindly and is successful at suffering. The new, westernized society of self can only exist by devouring the old.

His best-known novel, *The Woman in the Dunes,* was made into an internationally successful film directed by Teshigahara Hiroshi. Awarded a special jury prize at the 1964 Cannes Film Festival, the work depicts the experience of a man imprisoned in a house at the bottom of a remote sand pit because the primitive people who live there have selected him to replace the dead husband of the household. The prisoner's work is to shovel the sifting sand each day, thus helping to ensure the survival of this peculiar community. A prolific writer, Abe was the recipient of the Post-War Literature Prize, the Akutagawa Prize, and of two awards for drama: the Kishida and Kanizaki Prizes. Among Abe's novels (published by Knopf) are *The Woman in the Dunes* (1964), *The Face of Another* (1966), *The Ruined Map* (1969), *Inter Ice Age Four* (1970), *The Box Man* (1975), *Secret Rendezvous* (1979), *The Ark Sakura* (1988), and *The Kangaroo Notebook* (Knopf, 1996). Among his plays are *Friends*, based on the story "Intruders" (Grove, 1969), and *The Man Who Turned into a Stick* (Tokyo University Press, 1975). Some of his stories are collected in *Beyond the Curve* (Kodansha International, 1991).

THE MAGIC CHALK

Next door to the toilet of an apartment building on the edge of the city, in a room soggy with roof leaks and cooking vapors, lived a poor artist named Argon.

The small room, nine feet square, appeared to be larger than it was because it contained nothing but a single chair set against the wall. His desk, shelves, paint box, even his easel had been sold for bread. Now only the chair and Argon were left. But how long would these two remain?

Dinnertime drew near. "How sensitive my nose has become!" Argon thought. He was able to distinguish the colors and proximity of the complex aromas entering his room. Frying pork at the butcher's along the streetcar line: yellow ocher. A southerly wind drifting by the front of the fruit stand: emerald green. Wafting from the bakery: stimulating chrome yellow. And the fish the housewife below was broiling, probably mackerel: sad cerulean blue.

The fact is, Argon hadn't eaten anything all day. With a pale face, a wrinkled brow, an Adam's apple that rose and fell, a hunched back, a sunken abdomen, and trembling knees, Argon thrust both hands into his pockets and yawned three times in succession.

His fingers found a stick in his pocket.

"Hey, what's this? Red chalk. Don't remember it being there."

Playing with the chalk between his fingers, he produced another large yawn.

"Aah, I need something to eat."

Without realizing it, Argon began scribbling on the wall with the chalk. First, an apple. One that looked big enough to be a meal in itself. He drew a paring knife beside it so that he could eat it right away. Next, swallowing hard as baking smells curled through the hallway and window to permeate his room, he drew bread. Jam-filled bread the size of a baseball glove. Butter-filled rolls. A loaf as large as a person's head. He envisioned glossy browned spots on the bread. Delicious-looking cracks, dough bursting through the surface, the intoxicating aroma of yeast. Beside the bread, then, a stick of butter as large as a brick. He thought of drawing some coffee. Freshly brewed, steaming coffee. In a large, jug-like cup. On a saucer, three matchbox-size sugar cubes.

"Damn it!" He ground his teeth and buried his face in his hands. "I've got to eat!"

Gradually his consciousness sank into darkness. Beyond the windowpane was a bread and pastry jungle, a mountain of canned goods, a sea of milk, a beach of sugar, a beef and cheese orchard—he scampered about until, fatigued, he fell asleep.

A heavy thud on the floor and the sound of smashing crockery woke him up. The sun had already set. Pitch black. Bewildered, he glanced toward the noise and gasped. A broken cup. The spilled liquid, still steaming, was definitely coffee, and near it were the apple, bread, butter, sugar, spoon, knife, and (luckily unbroken) the saucer. The pictures he had chalked on the wall had vanished.

"How could it . . . ?"

Suddenly every vein in his body was wide awake and pounding. Argon stealthily crept closer.

"No, no, it can't be. But look, it's real. Nothing fake about the smothering aroma of this coffee. And here, the bread is smooth to the touch. Be bold, taste it. Argon, don't you believe it's real even now? Yes, it's real. I believe it. But frightening. To believe it is frightening. And yet, it's real. It's edible!"

The apple tasted like an apple (a "snow" apple). The bread tasted like bread (American flour). The butter tasted like butter (same contents as the label on the wrapper—not margarine). The sugar tasted like sugar (sweet). Ah, they all tasted like the real thing. The knife gleamed, reflecting his face.

By the time he came to his senses, Argon had somehow finished eating and heaved a sigh of relief. But when he recalled why he had sighed like this, he immediately became confused again. He took the chalk in his fingers and stared at it intently. No matter how much he scrutinized it, he couldn't understand what he didn't understand. He decided to make sure by trying it once more. If he succeeded a second time, then he would have to concede that it had actually happened. He thought he would try to draw something different, but in his haste just drew another familiar-looking apple. As soon as he finished drawing, it fell easily from the wall. So this is real after all. A repeatable fact.

Joy suddenly turned his body rigid. The tips of his nerves broke through his skin and stretched out toward the universe, rustling like fallen leaves. Then, abruptly, the tension eased, and, sitting down on the floor, he burst out laughing like a panting goldfish.

"The laws of the universe have changed. My fate has changed, misfortune has taken its leave. Ah, the age of fulfillment, a world of desires realized . . . God, I'm sleepy. Well, then, I'll draw a bed. This chalk has become as precious as life itself, but a bed is something you always need after eating your fill, and it never really wears out, so no need to be miserly about it. Ah, for the first time in my life I'll sleep like a lamb."

One eye soon fell asleep, but the other lay awake.

After today's contentment he was uneasy about what tomorrow might bring. However, the other eye, too, finally closed in sleep. With eyes working out of sync he dreamed mottled dreams throughout the night.

Well, this worrisome tomorrow dawned in the following manner.

He dreamed that he was being chased by a ferocious beast and fell off a bridge. He had fallen off the bed . . . No. When he awoke, there was no bed anywhere. As usual, there was nothing but that one chair. Then what had happened last night? Argon timidly looked around the wall, tilting his head.

There, in red chalk, were drawings of a cup (it was broken!), a spoon, a knife, apple peel, and a butter wrapper. Below these was a bed—a picture of the bed off which he was supposed to have fallen.

Among all of last night's drawings, only those he could not eat had once again become pictures and returned to the wall. Suddenly he felt pain in his hip and shoulder. Pain in precisely the place he should feel it if he had indeed fallen out of bed. He gingerly touched the sketch of the bed where the sheets had been rumpled by sleep and felt a slight warmth, clearly distinguishable from the coldness of the rest of the drawing.

He brushed his finger along the blade of the knife picture. It was certainly nothing more than chalk; there was no resistance, and it disappeared leaving only a smear. As a test he decided to draw a new apple. It neither turned into a real apple and fell nor even peeled off like a piece of unglued paper, but rather vanished beneath his chafed palm into the surface of the wall.

His happiness had been merely a single night's dream. It was all over, back to what it was before anything had happened. Or was it really? No, his misery had returned fivefold. His hunger pangs attacked him fivefold. It seemed that all he had eaten had been restored in his stomach to the original substances of wall and chalk powder.

When he had gulped from his cupped hands a pint or so of water from the communal sink, he set out toward the lonely city, still enveloped in the mist of early dawn. Leaning over an open drain that ran from the kitchen of a restaurant about a hundred yards ahead, he thrust his hands into the viscous, tarlike sewage and pulled something out. It was a basket made of wire netting. He washed it in a small brook nearby. What was left in it seemed edible, and he was particularly heartened that half of it looked like rice. An old man in his apartment building had told him recently that by placing the basket in the drain one could obtain enough food for a meal a day. Just about a month ago the man had found the means to afford bean curd lees, so he had ceded the restaurant drain to the artist.

Recalling last night's feast, this was indeed muddy, unsavory fare. But it wasn't magic. What actually helped fill his stomach was precious and so could not be rejected. Even if its nastiness made him aware of every swallow, he must eat it. Shit. This was the real thing.

Just before noon he entered the city and dropped in on a friend who was employed at a bank. The friend smiled wryly and asked, "My turn today?"

Stiff and expressionless, Argon nodded. As always, he received half of his friend's lunch, bowed deeply and left.

For the rest of the day, Argon thought.

He held the chalk lightly in his hand, leaned back in the chair, and as he sat absorbed in his daydreams about magic, anticipation began to crystallize around that urgent longing. Finally, evening once again drew near. His hope that at sunset the magic might take effect had changed into near confidence.

Somewhere a noisy radio announced that it was five o'clock. He stood up and on the wall drew bread and butter, a can of sardines, and coffee, not forgetting to add a table underneath so as to prevent anything from falling and breaking as had occurred the previous night. Then he waited.

Before long darkness began to crawl quietly up the wall from the corners of the room. In order to verify the course of the magic, he turned on the light. He had already confirmed last night that electric light did it no harm.

The sun had set. The drawings on the wall began to fade, as if his vision had blurred. It seemed as if a mist was caught between the wall and his eyes. The pictures grew increasingly faint, and the mist grew dense. And soon, just as he had anticipated, the mist had settled into solid shapes—success! The contents of the pictures suddenly appeared as real objects.

The steamy coffee was tempting, the bread freshly baked and still warm.

"Oh! Forgot a can opener."

He held his left hand underneath to catch it before it fell, and, as he drew, the outlines took on material form. His drawing had literally come to life.

All of a sudden, he stumbled over something. Last night's bed "existed" again. Moreover, the knife handle (he had erased the blade with his finger), the butter wrapper, and the broken cup lay fallen on the floor.

After filling his empty stomach, Argon lay down on the bed.

"Well, what shall it be next? It's clear now that the magic doesn't work in daylight. Tomorrow I'll have to suffer all over again. There must be a simple way out of this. Ah, yes! a brilliant plan—I'll cover up the window and shut myself in darkness."

He would need some money to carry out the project. To keep out the sun required some objects that would not lose their substance when exposed to sunlight. But drawing money is a bit difficult. He racked his brains, then drew a purse full of money . . . The idea was a success, for when he opened up the purse he found more than enough bills stuffed inside.

This money, like the counterfeit coins that badgers made from tree leaves in the fairy tale, would disappear in the light of day, but it would leave no trace behind, and that was a great relief. He was cautious nonetheless and deliberately proceeded toward a distant town. Two heavy blankets, five sheets of black woolen cloth, a piece of felt, a box of nails, and four pieces of squared lumber. In addition, one volume of a cookbook collection that caught his eye in a secondhand bookstore along the way. With the remaining money he bought a cup of coffee, not in the least superior to the coffee he had drawn on the wall. He was (why?) proud of himself. Lastly, he bought a newspaper.

He nailed the door shut, then attached two layers of

cloth and a blanket. With the rest of the material, he covered the window, and he blocked the edges with the wood. A feeling of security, and at the same time a sense of being attacked by eternity, weighed upon him. Argon's mind grew distant, and, lying down on the bed, he soon fell asleep.

Sleep neither diminished nor neutralized his happiness in the slightest. When he awoke, the steel springs throughout his body were coiled and ready to leap, full of life. A new day, a new time . . . tomorrow wrapped in a mist of glittering gold dust, and the day after tomorrow, and more and more overflowing armfuls of tomorrows were waiting expectantly. Argon smiled, overcome with joy. Now, at this very moment, everything, without any hindrance whatsoever, was waiting eagerly among myriad possibilities to be created by his own hand. It was a brilliant moment. But what, in the depths of his heart, was this faintly aching sorrow? It might have been the sorrow that God had felt just before Creation. Beside the muscles of his smile, smaller muscles twitched slightly.

Argon drew a large wall clock. With a trembling hand he set the clock precisely at twelve, determining at that moment the start of a new destiny.

He thought the room was a bit stuffy, so he drew a window on the wall facing the hallway. Hm, what's wrong? The window didn't materialize. Perplexed for a moment, he then realized that the window could not acquire any substance because it did not have an outside; it was not equipped with all the conditions necessary to make it a window.

"Well, then, shall I draw an outside? What kind of view would be nice? Shall it be the Alps or the Bay of Naples? A quiet pastoral scene wouldn't be bad. Then again, a primeval Siberian forest might be interesting." All the beautiful landscapes he had seen on postcards and in travel guides flickered before him. But he had to choose one from among them all, and he couldn't make up his mind. "Well, let's attend to pleasure first," he decided. He drew some whiskey and cheese and, as he nibbled, slowly thought about it.

The more he thought, the less he understood.

"This isn't going to be easy. It could involve work on

a larger scale than anything I—or anyone—has ever tried to design. In fact, now that I think about it, it wouldn't do simply to draw a few streams and orchards, mountains and seas, and other things pleasing to the eye. Suppose I drew a mountain; it would no longer be just a mountain. What would be beyond it? A city? A sea? A desert? What kind of people would be living there? What kind of animals? Unconsciously I would be deciding those things. No, making this window a window is serious business. It involves the creation of a world. Defining a world with just a few lines. Would it be right to leave that to chance? No, the scene outside can't be casually drawn. I must produce the kind of picture that no human hand has yet achieved."

Argon sank into deep contemplation.

The first week passed in discontent as he pondered a design for a world of infinitude. Canvases once again lined his room, and the smell of turpentine hung in the air. Dozens of rough sketches accumulated in a pile. The more he thought, however, the more extensive the problem became, until finally he felt it was all too much for him. He thought he might boldly leave it up to chance, but in that case his efforts to create a new world would come to nothing. And if he merely captured accurately the inevitability of partial reality, the contradictions inherent in that reality would pull him back into the past, perhaps trapping him again in starvation. Besides, the chalk had a limited life-span. He had to capture the world.

The second week flew by in inebriation and gluttony.

The third week passed in a despair resembling insanity. Once again his canvases lay covered with dust, and the smell of oils had faded.

In the fourth week Argon finally made up his mind, a result of nearly total desperation. He just couldn't wait any longer. In order to evade the responsibility of creating with his own hand an outside for the window, he decided to take a great risk that would leave everything to chance.

"I'll draw a door on the wall. The outside will be decided by whatever is beyond the door. Even if it ends in failure, even if it turns out to be the same apartment

scene as before, it'll be far better than being tormented
by this responsibility. I don't care what happens, better
to escape."

Argon put on a jacket for the first time in a long while.
It was a ceremony in honor of the establishment of the
world, so one couldn't say he was being extravagant.
With a stiff hand he lowered the chalk of destiny. A
picture of the door. He was breathing hard. No wonder.
Wasn't the sight beyond the door the greatest mystery a
man could contemplate? Perhaps death was awaiting him
as his reward.

He grasped the knob. He took a step back and opened
the door.

Dynamite pierced his eyes, exploding. After a while
he opened them fearfully to an awesome wasteland glar-
ing in the noonday sun. As far as he could see, with the
exception of the horizon, there was not a single shadow.
To the extent that he could peer into the dark sky, not
a single cloud. A hot dry wind blew past, stirring up a
dust storm.

"Aah . . . It's just as though the horizon line in one
of my designs had become the landscape itself. Aah . . ."

The chalk hadn't resolved anything after all. He still
had to create it all from the beginning. He had to fill
this desolate land with mountains, water, clouds, trees,
plants, birds, beasts, fish. He had to draw the world all
over again. Discouraged, Argon collapsed onto the bed.
One after another, tears fell unceasingly.

Something rustled in his pocket. It was the newspaper
he had bought on that first day and forgotten about. The
headline on the first page read, "Invasion Across 38th
Parallel!" On the second page, an even larger space devoted to a photograph of Miss Nippon. Underneath, in
small print, "Riot at N Ward Employment Security Office," and "Large-scale Dismissals at U Factory."

Argon stared at the half-naked Miss Nippon. What intense longing. What a body. Flesh of glass.

"This is what I forgot. Nothing else matters. It's time
to begin everything from Adam and Eve. That's it—Eve!
I'll draw Eve!"

Half an hour later Eve was standing before him, stark
naked. Startled, she looked around her.

"Oh! Who are you? What's happened? Golly, I'm naked!"

"I am Adam. You are Eve." Argon blushed bashfully.

"I'm Eve, you say? Ah, no wonder I'm naked. But why are you wearing clothes? Adam, in Western dress— now that's weird."

Suddenly her tone changed.

"You're lying! I'm not Eve. I'm Miss Nippon."

"You're Eve. You really are Eve."

"You expect me to believe this is Adam—in those clothes—in a dump like this? Come on, give me back *my* clothes. What am I doing here anyway? I'm due to make a special modeling appearance at a photo contest."

"Oh, no. You don't understand. You're Eve, I mean it."

"Give me a break, will you? Okay, where's the apple? And I suppose this is the Garden of Eden? Ha, don't make me laugh. Now give me my clothes."

"Well, at least listen to what I have to say. Sit down over there. Then I'll explain everything. By the way, can I offer you something to eat?"

"Yes, go ahead. But hurry up and give me my clothes, okay? My body's valuable."

"What would you like? Choose anything you want from this cookbook."

"Oh, great! Really? The place is filthy, but you must be pretty well fixed. I've changed my mind. Maybe you really are Adam after all. What do you do for a living? Burglar?"

"No, I'm Adam. Also an artist, and a world planner."

"I don't understand."

"Neither do I. That's why I'm depressed."

Watching Argon draw the food with swift strokes as he spoke, Eve shouted, "Hey, great, that's great. This *is* Eden, isn't it? Wow. Yeah, okay, I'll be Eve. I don't mind being Eve. We're going to get rich—right?"

"Eve, please listen to me."

In a sad voice, Argon told her his whole story, adding finally, "So you see, with your cooperation we must design this world. Money's irrelevant. We have to start everything from scratch."

Miss Nippon was dumbfounded.

"Money's irrelevant, you say? I don't understand. I don't get it. I absolutely do not understand."

"If you're going to talk like that, well, why don't you open this door and take a look outside."

She glanced through the door Argon had left half open.

"My God! How awful!"

She slammed the door shut and glared at him.

"But how about *this* door," she said, pointing to his real, blanketed door. "Different, I'll bet."

"No, don't. That one's no good. It will just wipe out this world, the food, desk, bed, and even you. *You* are the new Eve. And we must become the father and mother of our world."

"Oh no. No babies. I'm all for birth control. I mean, they're such a bother. And besides, I won't disappear."

"You will disappear."

"I won't. I know myself best. I'm me. All this talk about disappearing—you're really weird."

"My dear Eve, you don't know. If we don't re-create the world, then sooner or later we're faced with starvation."

"What? Calling me 'dear' now, are you? You've got a nerve. And you say I'm going to starve. Don't be ridiculous. My body's valuable."

"No, your body's the same as my chalk. If we don't acquire a world of our own, your existence will just be a fiction. The same as nothing at all."

"Okay, that's enough of this junk. Come on, give me back my clothes. I'm leaving. No two ways about it, my being here is weird. I shouldn't be here. You're a magician or something. Well, hurry up. My manager's probably fed up with waiting. If you want me to drop in and be your Eve every now and then, I don't mind. As long as you use your chalk to give me what I want."

"Don't be a fool! You can't do that."

The abrupt, violent tone of Argon's voice startled her, and she looked into his face. They both stared at each other for a moment in silence. Whatever was in her thoughts, she then said calmly, "All right, I'll stay. But, in exchange, will you grant me one wish?"

"What is it? If you stay with me, I'll listen to anything you have to say."

"I want half of your chalk."

"That's unreasonable. After all, dear, you don't know how to draw. What good would it do you?"

"I do know how to draw. I may not look like it, but I used to be a designer. I insist on equal rights."

He tilted his head for an instant, then straightening up again, said decisively, "All right, I believe you."

He carefully broke the chalk in half and gave one piece to Eve. As soon as she received it, she turned to the wall and began drawing.

It was a pistol.

"Stop it! What are you going to do with that thing?"

"Death, I'm going to make death. We need some divisions. They're very important in making a world."

"No, that'll be the end. Stop it. It's the most unnecessary thing of all."

But it was too late. Eve was clutching a small pistol in her hand. She raised it and aimed directly at his chest.

"Move and I'll shoot. Hands up. You're stupid, Adam. Don't you know that a promise is the beginning of a lie? It's you who made me lie."

"What? *Now* what are you drawing?"

"A hammer. To smash the door down."

"You can't!"

"Move and I'll shoot!"

The moment he leaped the pistol rang out. Argon held his chest as his knees buckled and he collapsed to the floor. Oddly, there was no blood.

"Stupid Adam."

Eve laughed. Then, raising the hammer, she struck the door. The light streamed in. It wasn't very bright, but it was real. Light from the sun. Eve was suddenly absorbed, like mist. The desk, the bed, the French meal, all disappeared. All but Argon, the cookbook which had landed on the floor, and the chair were transformed back into pictures on the wall.

Argon stood up unsteadily. His chest wound had healed. But something stronger than death was summoning him, compelling him—the wall. The wall was calling him. His body, which had eaten drawings from the wall continuously for four weeks, had been almost entirely transformed by them. Resistance was impossible now. Argon staggered toward the wall and was drawn in on top of Eve.

The sound of the gunshot and the door being smashed were heard by others in the building. By the time they ran in, Argon had been completely absorbed into the wall and had become a picture. The people saw nothing but the chair, the cookbook, and the scribblings on the wall. Staring at Argon lying on top of Eve, someone remarked, "Starved for a woman, wasn't he."

"Doesn't it look just like him, though?" said another.

"What was he doing, destroying the door like that? And look at this, the wall's covered with scribbles. Huh. He won't get away with it. Where in the world did he disappear to? Calls himself a painter!"

The man grumbling to himself was the apartment manager.

After everyone left, there came a murmuring from the wall.

"It isn't chalk that will remake the world . . ."

A single drop welled out of the wall. It fell from just below the eye of the pictorial Argon.

Translated by Alison Kibrick

Sawako Ariyoshi
(1931–1984)

A graduate of Tokyo Women's College, Sawako Ariyoshi, who was born in Wakayama, Japan, spent part of her childhood in Java. A prolific novelist, she dramatized significant issues in her fiction such as the suffering of the elderly, the effects of pollution on the environment, and the effects of social and political change on Japanese domestic life and values, especially upon the lives of women. A *New York Times* reviewer described her as "A subtle and deft writer whose sense of form and character make her book [*The Twilight Years*] linger in the mind long after the story has ended." That novel, published in Japan in 1972 (Kodansha International, 1984), depicts the life of a working woman who is caring for her elderly, dying father-in-law. Among Ariyoshi's other novels is *The River Ki*, an insightful portrait of the lives of three rural women, a mother, daughter, and granddaughter, published in Japan in 1959 (Kodansha International, 1979). Brian Weiss in *Best Sellers*, commented that "the story is rich in details of Japanese domestic life" and added: "The characters are affectionately depicted in bold strokes. . . ." *The Doctor's Wife*, a historical novel published in Japan in 1966 (Kodansha International, 1978), dramatizes the roles of nineteenth-century Japanese women as it chronicles the experience of a pioneer doctor with breast cancer surgery. It is based on the life of Hanaoka Seishū, the Japanese physician who developed and used anesthesia in 1805, decades before its introduction in surgery in the West. Several of Ariyoshi's short works such as "The Village of Eguchi," "Jiuta," and "The Ink Stick" have been translated and published in *Japan Quarterly*, and several of her novels have been adapted for the theater or filmed. Recipient of a Rockefeller Foundation Fellowship in 1959, Ariyoshi had received numerous Japanese literary awards and was at the height of her career when she died quietly in her sleep.

THE TOMOSHIBI

It was almost incredible that a small, quiet bar like The Tomoshibi should exist in the Ginza. Although it was located on an alley branching off a back street of Higashi Ginza, a noisy place where bars stood side by side in a row, it was still part of the Ginza. To the right, there was a large coffee shop, and to the left there was a well-known men's clothing store. The three shops across the street—a restaurant, a coffee shop, and an accessories store—were famous, and so, this one corner overflowed, with a true Ginza-like atmosphere, almost as if it were on the main street itself.

However, The Tomoshibi was inconspicuous in all respects. It was only natural that it wasn't noticeable during the day, since the bar opened at five in the afternoon; but in any case, since the frontage was narrow—only about six feet wide—it was overwhelmed by the imposing appearance of the neighboring stores on both sides. It didn't seem likely that there would be such a bar in a place like this.

There was a small lantern placed outside, above the door, and on this "The Tomoshibi" was written in quaint lettering. In the evening, even when it became both in name and in reality a *tomoshibi*, it did not shine very boldly.

When the night grew late and all the neighbors had closed shop, the street became silent. Even people looking for a place to drink would go right past it, not noticing that the street even had a bar.

The fact was, then, that the patrons of The Tomoshibi were an exceedingly limited group of regular customers. However, The Tomoshibi hadn't many of what one usually think of as "regular customers," the type of people who gather together out of affection for the proprietress and barmaids.

There were few customers who came to The Tomoshibi every night; neither were there many stray customers who wandered in. Nevertheless, the bar was always filled to capacity, and although the popularity of the proprietress, who was called "Mama-san," might have helped a little, the patrons and the barmaids all knew the exact reason why.

It is true that the bar was small. In a space of about ninety square feet, there was a cramped restroom, a large refrigerator, a tiny counter behind which Mama-san and one barmaid could stand, and just enough chairs and tables for the other barmaid to entertain customers. Even with only the three of them, when none of the customers had showed up yet, a dry wind did not blow in the bar. Thus anyone who casually entered The Tomoshibi alone would be enveloped by a warm atmosphere, and immediately feel at home.

Here, no one felt like chasing away the blues by noisily badmouthing their superiors while under the influence; nor were there any customers who told vulgar jokes to first get into a state of mind sufficiently disillusioned to bring on a quick drunk.

"Hello there!" Mama-san greeted a customer who hadn't come for several months. Speaking as if he had come the day before yesterday, the customer asked, "It's been a while since I've seen the girl who used to work here—what's happened to her?"

"She got married," Mama-san replied quietly.

"Hmm, got married, huh?" The customer spoke as if he were surprised and impressed, and he looked around the bar once again.

"I see. . . . I guess if she were from this bar, a barmaid could really get married decently." As if he were quite convinced, he sipped his whiskey-on-the-rocks and sighed.

Mama-san and a barmaid known as Shizu-chan, who

were seated quietly on chairs away from the counter, exchanged furtive smiles.

The girl, Eiko, who had been helping Mama-san behind the counter, had committed suicide about three weeks ago.

Any girl who decides to come to work in a bar has her own complex reasons. And, while she works, her life usually becomes even more complicated. Although she had found employment in a quiet bar like this, Eiko probably suffered from more hardships than the average person. It had looked as if she was confiding everything to Mama-san, and had been seeking her advice. Yet there was probably something she had not been able to confide, and maybe that had become unbearable. One night, she took some pills and died. Since she was a quiet girl, perfectly suited for The Tomoshibi, there had not been anything out of the ordinary in her conduct, and even the worldly-wise Mama-san had not noticed anything.

Since it was a whole day before the suicide was discovered, nothing could be done. There was no will, and her humble one-room apartment was left neatly in order. There was a savings passbook left for her younger brother, her only blood relative, but it certainly did not contain an extraordinary sum of money. That a young, nameless barmaid had died one night was such a small happening that it wouldn't even be mentioned in an obscure corner of a newspaper.

That is why Mama-san did not want to do anything that would cast a shadow on the memories of the customers who remembered Eiko.

"Is that so? She got married? Hmmm. . . ." The customer, perhaps because the alcohol had begun to take its effect, re-articulated his initial surprise, but Mama-san only commented gently, "Quite so, she got married."

"What kind of guy was he? Was he a customer here?"

"There's no use in being jealous. It's already too late." When Mama-san laughed in her sweet voice, the customer also gave a forced laugh, and at that point they ended the conversation.

"Another drink, please."

"Coming! Coming! Isn't it cold today?"

Although there were peanuts and smoked squid on the narrow counter, with the second glass of whiskey Mama-san provided some fresh cucumber with a dash of lemon, free of charge. The customer picked up a slice with his fingers, and while eating with a crunching sound, asked, "Did you choose all those paintings by yourself?" He was examining the inside of the bar again.

"Yes, but they're all reproductions!"

Several framed pictures, none of them any larger than fifteen square inches, were hung on the wall. Among these, two were Chagalls, one was a Miró, one was an oil painting by Takayama Uichi, and one was a wood-block print by Minami Keiko.

Those by Takayama and the Minami were originals, and those by Chagall and Miró were lithographs, but Mama-san always said that they were replicas and didn't care to elaborate further.

Mama-san had bought them only because they were pictures that she had liked, and not because they were the works of famous artists. But if some customers didn't like the pictures, that was that, no matter what she said.

A picture in which lovers embraced on the roof of a small house in the moonlight. And a sweet, dream-like picture of a young girl singing, enveloped by a bird of fire. Next to the two Chagalls hung a surrealistic picture, with bright colors like a child's scribbles. It was the Miró. This was Mama-san's greatest pride, for she had thrown caution to the winds and bought it, although it was extremely expensive. Yet since the customers who came to the bar could barely appreciate the Chagalls, the Miró seemed even more incomprehensible to them.

However, when one looked at all of them, including the Takayama painting of greenery and butterflies, and the Minami woodblock print of autumn leaves and fish, even the Miró became part of a coherent whole which created a fairy tale-like, innocent, and happy atmosphere throughout the bar. Perhaps it was because of this atmosphere that customers were convinced that barmaids from this bar could become brides after all.

"Last night I had such a beautiful dream."

All of a sudden, Shizu-chan started to speak. Since it was a small bar, whatever anyone said could be overheard by everyone else, so there was no need to turn their heads. The good thing about this bar was the fact that both Mama-san and Shizu-chan had beautiful voices. Some customers said flatly that it was better just to listen to their voices when they started to speak, rather than to look at their faces.

"What kind of dream?" Mama-san responded in a leisurely tone.

"In my dream, I met a boy whom I had been extremely fond of when I was small."

"How incriminating!"

Because Shizu-chan had started to tell her story in such a passionate manner, one of the customers tried to tease her, but Mama-san waited patiently for her next words.

"This boy was the village headman's son. Since we were the children of tenant farmers, in spite of being in the same class at school, we didn't dare go near him. Even so, all the girls liked the young master. When he came close, I could hardly breathe!"

"It must have been your first love!"

"Yes, I guess it was. But it's been over ten years since I left the village. I've never had such a dream in all these years, so I wonder why I should have one now. Last night's dream just came out of the blue. It really surprised me!"

"Was the young master a child? Or had he grown up?"

"I'm not too sure. I'm not even sure whether I was a child or whether I was like I am now. . . ."

"Isn't that nice!"

"In any case, it was incredibly beautiful. There were birds of fire flying around us."

The Chagall painting had apparently made its way into Shizu-chan's dream. Yet while she was talking, she seemed to enter a dreamy state of mind once again. Even after she had finished talking, she remained staring into space as if entranced.

"I'll go home after one more drink. I think I'll go to sleep early tonight and dream of my first love, too."

Customers would be engulfed by the mood of the bar before they knew it. Shizu-chan was skillful at telling her life story in this fragmentary way, under the pretense of relating, for example, a story about her dreams. Since she differed from the many barmaids who allure customers by going over their sad life stories in great detail, from childhood to more recent hardships, there were quite a number of customers who came to the bar wanting to talk to her.

"And so, Shizu-chan, you haven't returned home ever since you came out to Tokyo?"

"No, even though my father and mother are there, and they've been asking me to come home soon."

"Don't you like the countryside?"

"That's not the point. There are many reasons why I have to stay in Tokyo."

"Is some man giving you a hard time, then?"

"No man would ever give me a hard time!"

Although she was replying seriously, it still sounded so funny that the customers would unexpectedly burst out laughing. It was probably because of Shizu-chan's natural virtue that nobody would think of teasing her by saying, "Would you like me to give you a hard time?"

Only Mama-san knew that Shizu-chan's parents had died when she was still a child, and that she was having a rough time of it at her aunt's, into whose family she had been adopted. When Shizu-chan said her parents were awaiting her return, only Mama-san sensed the truth behind the lie.

In the back streets of the Ginza, drunken men would usually spend their time speaking loudly and amorously of women, and drunken women would speak similarly of men. Yet in this bar, even if conversations of that type did get started, they never lasted very long. Strangely enough, though, conversations about pet dogs or cats would continue on and on endlessly.

There was a Siamese cat at The Tomoshibi. It was Mama-san's pet, and every day she carried it with her to work. It had a light gray, slender body, and its legs and the tip of its tail were dark sepia. Since it had a straight, shapely nose, Mama-san believed that it was a beautiful cat.

"Don't be ridiculous! Don't you know that the flatter a cat's nose is, the more attractive it's supposed to be?"

"Impossible! Cats or human beings, it's the same. The higher the nose is, the better."

"You're wrong!"

"Well then, please look carefully. Use your aesthetic sense to judge this. Here. . . ."

Mama-san picked up her beloved cat and thrust it out in front of the customer's nose.

"I still think it's funny. . . ."

If the customer should persist in this manner, things would get serious. In high spirits, Mama-san would refill the glass of whiskey and say, "Here, pull yourself together with this, and look carefully once again. Here Chika, Chika, make a nice face. . . ."

One might wonder whether the customer or Mama-san would be the first to give in, but it was always the cat in question who, hating to stay still, got bored with trying to outstare the customer, yawned out loud, scratched Mama-san's hand, and jumped down. The area on top of the window above the heater was Chika's seat, and once she retreated there, she would not come out, no matter how one called or invited her.

"Mama-san, don't you like dogs!"

"I like them, but you can't keep a dog in a bar."

"I really like dogs. Even when I get home late after drinking, I always wake up at seven in the morning, since I have to take Hachirō out for a walk."

"Is his name Hachirō? How cute!"

"Is it an Akita?" Shizu-chan interrupted.

"How did you know?" the customer asked in surprise.

"Oh, it's just a lucky guess. I thought a name like Hachirō might be quite appropriate for an Akita."

With this boost to his spirits, the customer drew out a billfold from the inside pocket of his suit and, produced a photograph from it.

He was a customer who perfectly matched the proprietress and barmaids. The snapshot was of his dog.

"See, look, isn't he a handsome one?"

His eyes and mouth were certainly those of an Akita, but the line between the ears and the neck was rather questionable. Yet even so, Mama-san was charmed by the eyes and mouth and said, "How adorable! He looks like a fine, lively dog."

Her manner of praise was clever, but young Shizu-chan, who was peering over from the side, was too honest.

"Hmm, is this really an Akita?" she questioned in a loud voice.

"It's an Akita, all right. This dog's father, you know, has quite a pedigree."

"What about the mother?"

"Well, you see. . . ." he said regretfully, drinking up the remaining whiskey. "It's a case of 'a woman of humble birth marrying into royalty.' "

In other words, Hachirō was a mutt. However, if lineage were to be determined patrilineally, as in the imperial family, then without doubt he would be a descendant of the noble Akita breed.

Being quick with her wits, Mama-san said, "They were quite gallant parents, weren't they?" and saved the customer from his predicament.

With this, the customer regained his balance. Ordering a double-on-the-rocks, he began to speak in great detail of how Hachirō was such a fine dog that he didn't bring disgrace to his father's name.

Birds of a feather flock together, and that night as many as four dog-lovers had gathered there. Since each of them had to introduce the pedigree, name, personality, and distinguishing features of his pet, The Tomoshibi didn't close until quite late.

"Since it's late, Shizu-chan, I'll take you home," Mama-san said to Shizu-chan, who was waiting with her collar pulled up. Mama-san locked the door and stopped a taxi.

"Please take us first to Higashi Nakano, then Shibuya." No matter how tiring a night she might have had, her manner of speaking was always kind.

As the car drove along through the night streets, Shizu-chan started to giggle about something she remembered.

"What is it?"

"Oh, I was just thinking of the dog contest we had."

"Wasn't it funny—everyone thought his own was the best."

"But they were all mongrels!"

"That's why we didn't get into a fight."

Mama-san was smiling serenely, the purebred Siamese cat fast asleep on her lap. It was a conceited cat with a picky appetite. None of the customers who boasted about their half-breed dogs dared to show their antipathy toward Chika, because she was protected by Mama-san's goodness.

"You know, Shizu-chan . . ."

"Yes?"

"If these late nights continue, we'll surely need a replacement for Eiko."

"I think so, too."

"Unless we find someone who will take turns with you working late, you'll get too tired. Do you know of anyone who would be good?"

"Well, I don't have too many friends, so . . ."

After a while, Mama-san, looking out of the window, murmured, "What a fool Eiko was to die!"

Almost ready to cry herself, Shizu-chan said hurriedly to the taxi driver, "Oh, please stop here. That corner will be fine. Yes, right here."

Although Mama-san had taken her home on several occasions in the past, Shizu-chan would always get off by the main road and avoid being taken by car to the front of her house. Since there must have been some reason, Mama-san didn't insist on accompanying her any farther. She would quietly see Shizu-chan off, turning around in the taxi which had started to move, and would watch her figure disappear into the darkness. Small dirty houses stood clustered, side by side.

"Position for barmaid. A young person, with or without experience. The Tomoshibi."

Mama-san wrote this with a brush on a small piece of paper. For three days her routine was to put up the sign at night when leaving, and take it down before eight in the evening when the customers came. Three or four applicants came knocking at the door, despite the fact that it was such a tiny advertisement and for such an inconspicuous bar.

During the hours before her customers came, Mama-san held "interviews" in the bar, and when there were customers, in the coffee shop next door.

One girl was so young she seemed like a firm plum still attached to a branch. It appeared that she had come to the accessories store across the street and read the advertisement by chance. Her family was apparently well-off, and she had been casually thinking that she wanted to work. Mama-san shuddered at her naive boldness.

"When you discuss this matter with your parents, please make sure that you tell them I said this is not the sort of place you should be coming to."

"Oh, then there's no use in discussing it with them. Am I unqualified?"

In the eyes that asked, "Am I unqualified?" shone fearless, youthful, as yet unblemished pride. Hoping that this child would be able to grow up just as she was, Mama-san gently smiled and nodded.

"Yes, you're unqualified."

"Oh, shucks!"

Since she stuck her tongue out and left without seeming too disappointed, Mama-san felt greatly relieved.

On another occasion, a sickly, tired woman came by.

"Why did you quit the other bar?"

"The proprietress scolded me too often. About not being lively and boisterous. She complained a lot, but how could I help it? After all, that's my nature!"

"That's true."

"But I have my own good customers. That's why the proprietress didn't want to let me go, but I don't like working under someone I have personality conflicts with."

Realizing quite clearly that she wouldn't get along with her either, Mama-san smiled and stood up.

"As you can see, our bar is rather small, isn't it? We don't need any more customers than we already have. If fate so ordains, I'll see you again."

It seemed as if the many layers of grime from the woman's harsh daily life were smeared across her coarse skin. Wishing she had the confidence to try and wash away this person's unhappiness at The Tomoshibi, Mama-san was sad that she couldn't hire her.

However, even if Mama-san invited this person to

come and work at the bar, sooner or later she would leave of her own accord.

Mama-san had always hired the type of barmaids who would stay only at The Tomoshibi.

"Good evening!" a voice called cheerfully.

A figure dressed in bright colors entered the door, and the bar became crowded at once. It was the madam of one of the five largest bars in the Ginza.

"My, I haven't seen you for such a long time!"

Mama-san, in her usual manner, invited her in warmly. Mama-san's smile never changed according to whom she was talking. Some ten years ago, Madam and Mama-san had worked in the same bar. They both became independent in the same Ginza area around the same time. However, Madam had been quite a businesswoman. Therefore, after moving from place to place, her bar and her name had become so noted that any person who dealt with the Ginza could not have failed to hear of them.

"This bar hasn't changed at all!"

"I guess it's been two years since you last came."

"How I envy you! I suppose if you don't have to make alterations in the interior of your bar for two whole years, you don't have to spend much money. As for my place, since the customers are so demanding, we frequently have to change the wall hangings and the paintings. . . ."

It was probably because Madam had some good qualities that her constant complaining about her financial situation, as well as her total envy of this small bar, were not intolerably offensive. Drinkers are very honest with themselves, so unless the proprietress is somewhat good-natured, customers won't be attracted to the bar.

"I have something to talk with you about," Madam said suddenly in a low voice, pulling Mama-san out to the coffee shop next door.

"Don't you have an opening at your place?"

"Well, I am looking for someone right now, but there aren't very many people who would come to work at a bar like ours."

Madam took Mama-san's modesty seriously, and after firmly nodding, leaned forward.

"I know of a nice girl. . . . Will you take a look at her?"

"But isn't she one of the girls at your place?"

"That's true, but she won't last there. She's just too nice. I don't know what to do, because whenever a customer teases her even a little bit, she starts to cry. I tell her over and over again that unless you strike back when you're teased you can't survive in the Ginza, but it's completely useless. The girls at my place are always being offered positions at rival bars whenever I'm not paying close attention, except for that one. She's fairly popular with the customers, but she still has an inferiority complex. Touch upon that complex and she gets depressed. I just haven't any idea what to do!"

"What kind of inferiority complex?" Mama-san attempted to pursue the matter further, but Madam waved her hands dramatically and ignored the question.

"Well, in any case I'll tell her to stop by and see you after work, so take a look at her. She's the perfect girl for your place. It would be easy for me to fire her, but she's such a nice girl that I don't have the heart to kick her out. Do it for me, all right?"

Madam pulled out a one-thousand yen bill and picked up the check from the table in one swift move. Having finished her business, she hastily paid for the coffee and left.

Forced to accept the proposition, Mama-san returned to the bar. She didn't feel so badly after she remembered that Madam always behaved in the same way.

Since the two bars belonged to such different categories, they were not in competition with each other, and even if Madam tried to pass off a secondhand article that was of no use at her place, Mama-san would not be offended. On the contrary, she rather enjoyed going over in her mind what Madam had said, "She's such a nice girl that she can't work at my bar." That she was such a nice girl she was not even appropriate for the very best bar in the Ginza district certainly pleased Mama-san.

Therefore, when the night grew late and Momoko appeared—quietly opening the door and inquiring, "May I come in?"—Mama-san said almost by reflex, "Oh, I've heard all about you. Everything's all set. Please start working here from five tomorrow evening."

Shizu-chan seemed to take in Momoki's round face and lovely lips immediately, as well as the fact that her dark blue overcoat was very becoming.

Just before leaving for home, Shizu-chan asked nonchalantly, "Is the person who came by a little while ago working with us from tomorrow?" But Mama-san, who was busy getting ready to close up and go home, answered without going into great detail, "Yes, I'll introduce her to you tomorrow."

Mama-san was rather noisily occupied in the restroom.

"Shizu-chan."

"Yes?"

"It's quite late, so you can go home first."

"Are you sure it's all right?"

Shizu-chan wondered what Mama-san could be up to, but anxious to head for home just as soon as she could, she left straight away.

The next day, having been delayed by collecting bills, Shizu-chan arrived at the bar a little later than usual and found Mama-san cleaning here and there inside the bar with the new girl.

"Good morning!"

"Oh, good morning! This is Shizu-chan, and this is Momoko-chan."

Mama-san introduced them in an intimate manner, as if she were bringing together two of her children. Momoko bowed humbly, and Shizu-chan felt slightly embarrassed. Deep inside, she had received quite a shock.

Dimly aware of the fact that Madam, who was an old friend of Mama-san, had spoken to Mama-san about this matter, Shizu-chan had been worried about what kind of person was going to come. Yet unlike last night's impression of her, the minute she looked at Shizu-chan today, Shizu-chan was taken aback.

She's cross-eyed, Shizu-chan realized at once. To use a Japanese expression, her eyes were "London-Paris"— her right eye was focused on London, while her left eye looked toward Paris. Furthermore, one of her eyes was a bit too close to the other. Besides these, there were no other faults in her appearance.

When Momoko went to the restroom, and there were still no customers, Shizu-chan found her chance to speak. "Mama-san," she began.

Mama-san, in a low, yet sharp voice, said firmly, "Shizu-chan, the subject of her eyes is taboo." Since Shizu-chan was also a nice girl, she accepted this immediately. Something deep within moved her to tears.

Perhaps because there was one more person in the bar than before, thus making it more lively, many customers turned up that night. The regular customers quickly took notice of Momoko. But since, unlike Eiko, she stood further behind the counter than Mama-san and was occupied with diligently opening and closing the refrigerator door, they couldn't talk to her very much.

Very few customers came to this bar simply for the barmaids, however, so no one was very dissatisfied with her behavior. The Tomoshibi remained completely the same as it had been. The customers quietly sipped their drinks, and when once in a while they did say something, Mama-san would take up the conversation, with Shizu-chan in her carefree and easygoing manner joining in.

One customer did find something different from before. This man, who had been chugging his beer, returned from the restroom with a strange expression on his face and asked, "What happened to the mirror?"

"Oh, someone broke it," answered Mama-san.

"You must have had some rough customers!"

"We can get a new mirror, but it might be broken again. Besides, we really ought to be able to put up with the inconvenience."

Probably only Shizu-chan noticed that Mama-san, upon realizing the source of Momoko's inferiority complex, had taken her in only after removing the mirror from the restroom.

"Anyway, our customers aren't the type that have to feel guilty when they look at their drunken faces in the mirror," Mama-san said in her mellow voice.

"Right! That's right!"

This cheered the customers; there was no chance of them being put out by it. Although the type of customer who got drunk and became boisterous rarely came to The Tomoshibi, there were, among the regular customers, some young men who liked to sing quiet songs. However, once they started to get tipsy, they demanded that Mama-san and the girls sing, too. Mama-san would say, "No, I can't because I'm tone-deaf," and escape, refusing to sing under any circumstances. If one flattered Shizu-chan, though, telling her that she was good, she would sing a number of songs in her melodious voice. Since she made every popular song come out like an elementary school tune, her specialty had become nursery songs. Everyone was impressed by her specialty. Her singing was popular probably because it was most appropriate for the atmosphere of the bar. She could certainly not have been called very talented.

"Mama-san, wasn't Eiko-chan pretty good, too? Wasn't she?" With his eyes half closed as if trying to remember, a customer asked, "Didn't she go away to get married? Is she happy?"

"Yes, yes, she's very happy."

"Shizu-chan began to sing:

> When she was fifteen Nanny got married
> Letters from home
> No longer came.

"In this present age, what do you think we lack the most and need the most?"

In one corner of the room there were customers discussing serious topics while drinking their whiskey.

"Hmmm, let's see, . . . how about dreams? As far as I'm concerned, right now that's what I lack the most and need the most."

"Well, I agree, but I don't call them 'dreams.' "

"Then what are they?"

"Fairy tales."

"Hmm, fairy tales. I guess you're right."

While that conversation was going on, Shizu-chan was singing away in front of customers in another corner.

"Well, what do you think about being able to listen to nursery rhymes in a Ginza bar?"

"Now I'm beginning to understand why you said you wanted to come here."

Sometimes a dreadfully tone-deaf person in high spirits would sing along with Shizu-chan.

After four or five days, Momoko was in a state of total astonishment. She wondered if this, too, could possibly be a bar.

Some types of people aren't affected by hardships; Momoko was the type who wasn't affected by past experiences. Even though this was the fourth time she had found herself employed in a bar, she possessed naive qualities which made it seem as if she had only worked in a bar for the first time yesterday. Shizu-chan began to act as if she were Momoko's elder sister all the time, and on occasions when Mama-san wasn't present, she would ask, "Well, do you think you'll be able to handle working here?" and peer into Momoko's face.

"Yes, I look forward to coming to work. And also, it almost seems like this isn't a bar, but some other kind of place."

"Well, if it's not a bar, what is it?"

"A kindergarten!"

Shizu-chan almost fell out of her chair, laughing. Before very long, Mama-san returned and Shizu-chan presented her with this masterpiece. Mama-san was reminded of the fact that the Chagalls and the Miró, all hanging on the wall, were also childlike. Even the small, low chair in the corner was appropriate for a kindergarten, she thought.

Around Christmas and at the end of the year, The Tomoshibi was not affected by irregular waves of customers. Just as there were never times when the bar was full and customers couldn't come in, so there was never a day when there were absolutely no customers. Momoko was most grateful for the fact that she wasn't compelled to wear a fancy kimono just because it was Christmas or New Year's.

Mama-san casually wore lovely, unobtrusive things, but she did not force her pleasure in clothes on other people.

"Happy New Year!"

"We value your patronage and hope to see you again this year."

Early in the new year, one customer dashed in as soon

as they opened the bar crying "Happy New Year!"
Mama-san politely repeated her New Year's greetings,
and without waiting for any prompting from him, asked,
"Well?"

"They were born!"

"Well, that is an auspicious event indeed! How many
of them?"

As usual, they were discussing dogs.

"Six. . . . I went out of my way to make sure that only
purebreds got to her, but I failed again. Half of them
are spotted. Even their faces are quite different from
their mother's."

"That's probably the aftereffects of a previous mate."

"I've heard that's so . . . once you've made a mistake,
you can't breed purebreds."

"But aren't the puppies cute?"

"Cute things are cute, even if they're mutts. There are
too many of them, but I can't bring myself to give them
away. My son also says that they're his children and loves
them very much. It's a nice feeling."

As they spoke, another person who shared their interest wandered in, and leaning forward, commented,
"Even though you may think they're mongrels, sometimes it happens that while you're rearing them, they
become purebreds, just like one of their parents."

"Isn't that a miracle!"

"A miracle, indeed! In my experience, this is where
the owner's character plays a great part!"

"I see. . . ."

"Yes, it's really true. Was it in Aesop that the ugly
duckling became a white swan?"

"Wasn't that Hans Christian Andersen?"

"Whichever! In any case, things like that happen."

"So then, will you try to raise all six of them? A miracle might happen to at least one."

For a while after that, miracles were the topic of conversation. After those customers had gone their merry
ways, and before the next wave of customers arrived,
Momoko said, "Mama-san, miracles really do happen,
don't they?" She started to speak very seriously.

When Shizu-chan asked "Have you ever seen one?"

Momoko nodded in assent, saying, "My eyes are getting better!"

Momoko continued in front of her two listeners who were holding their breath.

"From when I was small, I was always teased about my eyes. As I got older, it was even harder to bear, and I was always crying. Since I could make better money in a bar than at other jobs, I was able to help my family, but the customers always mentioned my eyes. It was really painful."

Looking up suddenly, Momoko's eyes lost the correct balance between right and left, and one side inclined outwards.

"Ever since I came to this bar, nobody has commented on my eyes. In the beginning, I thought that you were purposely avoiding the subject. But even the customers didn't say anything. When I came to think of it, nobody seemed to even notice my eyes. On New Year's Day, I went to the mirror and was almost too scared to look—until then, I had always disliked large mirrors and had used a compact to do my makeup. Then, well, miraculously, my eyes were cured! I don't know why they got better, but I think that miracles do happen after all."

Mama-san, who had been listening attentively to Momoko's story, said, "Really? How wonderful!" She spoke with great feeling, placing her hand on Momoko's shoulder. Shizu-chan looked as if she were going to cry if she spoke, so she quickly turned her back to Momoko and said in a deliberately dry tone, "How wonderful!"

To the two of them, it did not seem as if the miracle Momoko had spoken about had taken place, but if that was what Momoko believed, then a miracle had definitely occurred.

"Hello there!"

Once again familiar customers were coming through the door.

"Welcome! Happy New Year!" Momoko greeted them cheerfully.

Translated by Keiko Nakamura

Yasunari Kawabata
(1899–1972)

Born in Osaka, Yasunari Kawabata lived with his grandfather until he was fourteen. His parents had died before
he reached the age of three, and his maternal grandmother with whom he had been sent to live died shortly
thereafter as did his only sister. Upon his grandfather's
death, Kawabata roomed in an Osaka middle-school dor-
mitory and later attended Tokyo's First Higher School
and Imperial University from which he was graduated in
1924. Critics often conjecture that the numerous family
deaths he experienced at such a young age made him
particularly conscious of the loneliness and transience of
human life, themes that often occur in his work. In response to those who labeled him a nihilist, he asserted:
"I have never written a story that has decadence or nihil-
ism for its main theme. What seems so is in truth a kind
of longing for vitality." The first Japanese author to receive the Nobel Prize for Literature, in 1968, "for his
narrative mastery, which with great sensibility expresses
the essence of the Japanese mind," he was the recipient
of numerous honors, including West Germany's Goethe
Medal, France's Order des Arts et Lettres, the Prix du
Meilleur Livre Etranger, a cultural medal from the Japanese government, and the Akutagawa Prize. His early
reputation in the 1920s and 1930s was established by the
publication of numerous short vignettes, which he called
"palm-of-the-hand stories." A novelist, short-story
writer, playwright, and critic, his major novels were completed after World War II. The novel *Snow Country*,
which began as a series of stories in the 1930s, and
achieved its final form in 1947, and the novel *Thousand
Cranes* were published in a single volume (Knopf, 1969),
whereas several earlier, short works have been collected

in *The Izu Dancer and Others*, text in English and Japanese (Harashobo, 1964), and in *The House of Sleeping Beauties and Other Stories* (Ballantine, 1969). Among Kawabata's other novels are *The Sound of the Mountain* (Knopf, 1970), *The Master of Go* (Knopf, 1972), *The Lake* (Kodansha International, 1974), *Beauty and Sadness* (Random House, 1975), and *The Old Capital* (North Point Press, 1987). In 1972, Kawabata committed suicide by gas at his home in Zushi, Japan. Some believed that his action was connected to the ritual suicide, in 1970, of his friend and protégé Yukio Mishima.

THE MOON ON
THE WATER

It occurred to Kyōko one day to let her husband, in bed upstairs, see her vegetable garden by reflecting it in her hand mirror. To one who had been so long confined, this opened a new life. The hand mirror was part of a set in Kyōko's trousseau. The mirror stand was not very big. It was made of mulberry wood, as was the frame of the mirror itself. It was the hand mirror that still reminded her of the bashfulness of her early married years when, as she was looking into it at the reflection of her back hair in the stand mirror, her sleeve would slip and expose her elbow.

When she came from the bath, her husband seemed to enjoy reflecting the nape of her neck from all angles in the hand mirror. Taking the mirror from her, he would say: "How clumsy you are! Here, let me hold it." Maybe he found something new in the mirror. It was not that Kyōko was clumsy, but that she became nervous at being looked at from behind.

Not enough time had passed for the color of the mulberry-wood frame to change. It lay in a drawer. War came, followed by flight from the city and her husband's becoming seriously ill; by the time it first occurred to Kyōko to have her husband see the garden through the mirror, its surface had become cloudy and the rim had been smeared with face powder and dirt. Since it still reflected well enough, Kyōko did not worry about this cloudiness—indeed she scarcely noticed it. Her husband, however, would not let the mirror go from his bedside and polished it and its frame in his idleness with the peculiar nervousness of an invalid. Kyōko sometimes imagined that tuberculosis germs had found their way into the imperceptible cracks in the frame. After she had combed her husband's hair with a little camellia oil, he sometimes ran the palm of his hand through his hair and then rubbed the mirror. The wood of the mirror stand remained dull, but that of the mirror grew lustrous.

When Kyōko married again, she took the same mirror stand with her. The hand mirror, however, had been burned in the coffin of her dead husband. A hand mirror with a carved design had now taken its place. She never told her second husband about this.

According to custom, the hands of her dead husband had been clasped and his fingers crossed, so that it was impossible to make them hold the hand mirror after he had been put into the coffin. She laid the mirror on his chest.

"Your chest hurt you so. Even this must be heavy."

Kyōko moved the mirror down to his stomach. Because she thought of the important role that the mirror had played in their marital life, Kyōko had first laid it on his chest. She wanted to keep this little act as much as possible from the eyes even of her husband's family. She had piled white chrysanthemums on the mirror. No one had noticed it. When the ashes were being gathered after the cremation, people noticed the glass which had been melted into a shapeless mass, partly sooty and partly yellowish. Someone said: "It's glass. What is it, I wonder?" She had in fact placed a still smaller mirror on the hand mirror. It was the sort of mirror usually carried in a toilet case, a long, narrow, double-faced mirror. Kyōko had dreamed of using it on her honeymoon trip.

The war had made it impossible for them to go on a honeymoon. During her husband's lifetime she never was able to use it on a trip.

With her second husband, however, she went on a honeymoon. Since her leather toilet case was now very musty, she bought a new one—with a mirror in it too.

On the very first day of their trip, her husband touched Kyōko and said: "You are like a little girl. Poor thing!" His tone was not in the least sarcastic. Rather it suggested unexpected joy. Possibly it was good for him that Kyōko was like a little girl. At this remark, Kyōko was assailed by an intense sorrow. Her eyes filled with tears and she shrank away. He might have taken that to be girlish too.

Kyōko did not know whether she had wept for her own sake or for the sake of her dead husband. Nor was it possible to know. The moment this idea came to her, she felt very sorry for her second husband and thought she had to be coquettish.

"Am I so different?" No sooner had she spoken than she felt very awkward, and shyness came over her.

He looked satisfied and said: "You never had a child . . ."

His remark pierced her heart. Before a male force other than her former husband Kyōko felt humiliated. She was being made sport of.

"But it was like looking after a child all the time."

This was all she said by way of protest. It was as if her first husband, who had died after a long illness, had been a child inside her. But if he was to die in any case, what good had her continence done?

"I've only seen Mori from the train window." Her second husband drew her to him as he mentioned the name of her hometown. "From its name* it sounds like a pretty town in the woods. How long did you live there?"

"Until I graduated from high school. Then I was drafted to work in a munitions factory in Sanjō."

"Is Sanjō near, then? I've heard a great deal about Sanjō beauties. I see why you're so beautiful."

"No, I'm not." Kyōko brought her hand to her throat.

---

* *Mori* means "grove."

"Your hands are beautiful, and I thought your body should be beautiful too."

"Oh no."

Finding her hands in the way, Kyōko quietly drew them back.

"I'm sure I'd have married you even if you had had a child. I could have adopted the child and looked after it. A girl would have been better," he whispered in Kyōko's ear. Maybe it was because he had a boy, but his remark seemed odd even as an expression of love. Possibly he had planned the long, ten-day honeymoon so that she would not have to face the stepson quite so soon.

Her husband had a toilet case for traveling, made of what seemed to be good leather. Kyōko's did not compare with it. His was large and strong, but it was not new. Maybe because he often traveled or because he took good care of it, the case had a mellow luster. Kyōko thought of the old case, never used, which she had left to mildew. Only its small mirror had been used by her first husband, and she had sent it with him in death.

The small glass had melted into the hand mirror, so that no one except Kyōko could tell that they had been separate before. Since Kyōko had not said that the curious mass had been mirrors, her relatives had no way of knowing.

Kyōko felt as if the numerous worlds reflected in the two mirrors had vanished in the fire. She felt the same kind of loss when her husband's body was reduced to ashes. It had been with the hand mirror that came with the mirror stand that Kyōko first reflected the vegetable garden. Her husband always kept that mirror beside his pillow. Even the hand mirror seemed to be too heavy for the invalid, and Kyōko, worried about his arms and shoulders, gave him a lighter and smaller one.

It was not only Kyōko's vegetable garden that her husband had observed through the two mirrors. He had seen the sky, clouds, snow, distant mountains, and nearby woods. He had seen the moon. He had seen wild flowers, and birds of passage had made their way through the mirror. Men walked down the road in the mirror and children played in the garden.

Kyōko was amazed at the richness of the world in the

mirror. A mirror which had until then been regarded only as a toilet article, a hand mirror which had served only to show the back of one's neck, had created for the invalid a new life. Kyōko used to sit beside his bed and talk about the world in the mirror. They looked into it together. In the course of time it became impossible for Kyōko to distinguish between the world that she saw directly and the world in the mirror. Two separate worlds came to exist. A new world was created in the mirror and it came to seem like the real world.

"The sky shines silver in the mirror," Kyōko said. Looking up through the window, she added: "When the sky itself is grayish." The sky in the mirror lacked the leaden and heavy quality of the actual sky. It was shining.

"Is it because you are always polishing the mirror?"

Though he was lying down, her husband could see the sky by turning his head.

"Yes, it's a dull gray. But the color of the sky is not necessarily the same to dogs' eyes and sparrows' eyes as it is to human eyes. You can't tell which eyes see the real color."

"What we see in the mirror—is that what the mirror eye sees?"

Kyōko wanted to call it the eye of their love. The trees in the mirror were a fresher green than real trees, and the lilies a purer white.

"This is the print of your thumb, Kyōko. Your right thumb."

He pointed to the edge of the mirror. Kyōko was somehow startled. She breathed on the mirror and erased the fingerprint.

"That's all right, Kyōko. Your fingerprint stayed on the mirror when you first showed me the vegetable garden."

"I didn't notice it."

"You may not have noticed it. Thanks to this mirror, I've memorized the prints of your thumbs and index fingers. Only an invalid could memorize his wife's fingerprints."

Her husband had done almost nothing but lie in bed since their marriage. He had not gone to war. Toward the end of the war he had been drafted, but he fell ill after several days of labor at an airfield and came home at the end of the war. Since he was unable to walk, Kyōko went with his elder brother to meet him. After her husband had been drafted, she stayed with her parents. They had left the city to avoid the bombings. Their household goods had long since been sent away. As the house where their married life began had been burned down, they had rented a room in the home of a friend of Kyōko's. From there her husband commuted to his office. A month in their honeymoon house and two months at the house of a friend—that was all the time Kyōko spent with her husband before he fell ill.

It was then decided that her husband should rent a small house in the mountains and convalesce there. Other families had been in the house, also fugitives from the city, but they had gone back to Tokyo after the war ended. Kyōko took over their vegetable garden. It was only some six yards square, a clearing in the weeds. They could easily have bought vegetables, but Kyōko worked in the garden. She became interested in vegetables grown by her own hand. It was not that she wanted to stay away from her sick husband, but such things as sewing and knitting made her gloomy. Even though she thought of him always, she had brighter hopes when she was out in the garden. There she could indulge her love for her husband. As for reading, it was all she could do to read aloud at his bedside. Then Kyōko thought that by working in the garden she might regain that part of herself which it seemed she was losing in the fatigue of the long nursing.

It was in the middle of September that they moved to the mountains. The summer visitors had almost all gone and a long spell of early autumn rains came, chilly and damp.

One afternoon the sun came out to the clear song of a bird. When she went into the garden, she found the green vegetables shining. She was enraptured by the rosy clouds on the mountain tops. Startled by her husband's voice calling her, she hurried upstairs, her hands covered with mud, and found him breathing painfully.

"I called and called. Couldn't you hear me?"

"I'm sorry. I couldn't."

"Stop working in the garden. I'd be dead in no time if I had to keep calling you like that. In the first place, I can't see where you are and what you're doing."

"I was in the garden. But I'll stop."

He was calmer.

"Did you hear the lark?"

That was all he had wanted to tell her. The lark sang in the nearby woods again. The woods were clear against the evening glow. Thus Kyōko learned to know the song of the lark.

"A bell will help you, won't it? How about having something you can throw until I get a bell for you?"

"Shall I throw a cup from here? That would be fun."

It was settled that Kyōko might continue her gardening; but it was after spring had come to end the long, harsh mountain winter that Kyōko thought of showing him the garden in the mirror.

The single mirror gave him inexhaustible joy, as if a lost world of fresh green had come back. It was impossible for him to see the worms she picked from the vegetables. She had to come upstairs to show him. "I can see the earthworms from here, though," he used to say as he watched her digging in the earth.

When the sun was shining into the house, Kyōko sometimes noticed a light and, looking up, discovered that her husband was reflecting the sun in the mirror. He insisted that Kyōko remake the dark-blue kimono he had used during his student days into pantaloons for herself. He seemed to enjoy the sight of Kyōko in the mirror as she worked in the garden, wearing the dark blue with its white splashes.

Kyōko worked in the garden half-conscious and half-unconscious of the fact that she was being seen. Her heart warmed to see how different her feelings were now from the very early days of her marriage. Then she had blushed even at showing her elbow when she held the smaller glass behind her head. It was, however, only when she remarried that she started making up as she pleased, released from the long years of nursing and the mourning that had followed. She saw that she was be-

coming remarkably beautiful. It now seemed that her
husband had really meant it when he said that her body
was beautiful.

Kyōko was no longer ashamed of her reflection in the
mirror—after she had had a bath, for instance. She had
discovered her own beauty. But she had not lost that
unique feeling that her former husband had planted in
her toward the beauty in the mirror. She did not doubt
the beauty she saw in the mirror. Quite the reverse: she
could not doubt the reality of that other world. But between her skin as she saw it and her skin as reflected in
the mirror she could not find the difference that she had
found between that leaden sky and the silver sky in the
mirror. It may not have been only the difference in distance. Maybe the longing of her first husband confined
to his bed had acted upon her. But then, there was now
no way of knowing how beautiful she had looked to him
in the mirror as she worked in the garden. Even before
his death, Kyōko herself had not been able to tell.

Kyōko thought of, indeed longed for, the image of
herself working in the garden, seen through the mirror
in her husband's hand, and for the white of the lilies, the
crowd of village children playing in the field, and the
morning sun rising above the far-off snowy mountains—
for that separate world she had shared with him. For
the sake of her present husband, Kyōko suppressed this
feeling, which seemed about to become an almost physical yearning, and tried to take it for something like a
distant view of the celestial world.

One morning in May, Kyōko heard the singing of wild
birds over the radio. It was a broadcast from a mountain
near the heights where she had stayed with her first husband until his death. As had become her custom, after
seeing her present husband off to work, Kyōko took the
hand mirror from the drawer of the stand and reflected
the clear sky. Then she gazed at her face in the mirror.
She was astonished by a new discovery. She could not
see her own face unless she reflected it in the mirror.
One could not see one's own face. One felt one's own
face, wondering if the face in the mirror was one's actual
face. Kyōko was lost in thought for some time. Why

had God created man's face so that he might not see it himself?

"Suppose you could see your own face, would you lose your mind? Would you become incapable of acting?"

Most probably man had evolved in such a way that he could not see his own face. Maybe dragonflies and praying mantises could see their own faces.

But then perhaps one's own face was for others to see. Did it not resemble love? As she was putting the hand mirror back in the drawer, Kyōko could not even now help noticing the odd combination of carved design and mulberry. Since the former mirror had burned with her first husband, the mirror stand might well be compared to a widow. But the hand mirror had had its advantages and disadvantages. Her husband was constantly seeing his face in it. Perhaps it was more like seeing death itself. If his death was a psychological suicide by means of a mirror, then Kyōko was the psychological murderer. Kyōko had once thought of the disadvantages of the mirror, and tried to take it from him. But he would not let her.

"Do you intend to have me see nothing? As long as I live, I want to keep loving something I can see," her husband said. He would have sacrificed his life to keep the world in the mirror. After heavy rains they would gaze at the moon through the mirror, the reflection of the moon from the pool in the garden. A moon which could hardly be called even the reflection of a reflection still lingered in Kyōko's heart.

"A sound love dwells only in a sound person." When her second husband said this, Kyōko nodded shyly, but she could not entirely agree with him. When her first husband died, Kyōko wondered what good her continence had done; but soon the continence became a poignant memory of love, a memory of days brimming with love, and her regrets quite disappeared. Probably her second husband regarded woman's love too lightly. "Why did you leave your wife, when you are such a tender-hearted man?" Kyōko would ask him. He never answered. Kyōko had married him because the elder brother of her dead husband had insisted. After four months as friends they were married. He was fifteen years older.

When she became pregnant, Kyōko was so terrified that her very face changed.

"I'm afraid. I'm afraid." She clung to her husband. She suffered intensely from morning sickness and she even became deranged. She crawled into the garden barefooted and gathered pine needles. She had her stepson carry two lunch boxes to school, both boxes filled with rice. She sat staring blankly into the mirror, thinking that she saw straight through it. She rose in the middle of night, sat on the bed, and looked into her husband's sleeping face. Assailed by terror at the knowledge that man's life is a trifle, she found herself loosening the sash of her night robe. She made as if to strangle him. The next moment she was sobbing hysterically. Her husband awoke and retied her sash gently. She shivered in the summer night.

"Trust the child in you, Kyōko." Her husband rocked her in his arms.

The doctor suggested that she be hospitalized. Kyōko resisted, but was finally persuaded.

"I will go to the hospital. Please let me go first to visit my family for a few days."

Some time later her husband took her to her parents' home. The next day Kyōko slipped out of the house and went to the heights where she had lived with her first husband. It was early in September, ten days earlier than when she had moved there with him. Kyōko felt like vomiting. She was dizzy in the train and obsessed by an impulse to jump off. As the train passed the station on the heights, the crisp air brought her relief. She regained control of herself, as if the devil possessing her had gone. She stopped, bewildered, and looked at the mountains surrounding the high plateau. The outline of the blue mountains where the color was now growing darker was vivid against the sky, and she felt in them a living world. Wiping her eyes, moist with warm tears, she walked toward the house where he and she had lived. From the woods which had loomed against the rosy evening glow that day there came again the song of a lark. Someone was living in the house and a white lace curtain hung at the window upstairs. Not going too near, she gazed at the house.

"What if the child should look like you?" Startled at her own words, she turned back, warm and at peace.

Translated by George Saitō

Yukio Mishima
(Kimitake Hiraoka)
(1925–1970)

Born Kimitake Hiraoka, Yukio Mishima is the Japanese author most widely known in the West. He was born in Tokyo, the son of a government official. As a child, Mishima was sent to live with and care for his paternal grandmother, an elderly and debilitated woman whose numerous illnesses probably resulted from venereal disease transmitted by her husband, a corrupt island governor. A sickly child himself, Mishima was diagnosed as tubercular in his youth, an illness that precluded his serving in the Japanese army during World War II. He studied law at Tokyo University and was pressured by his father into taking a bureaucratic job in the Ministry of Finance. The extraordinary success of his autobiographical novel *Confessions of a Mask*, in 1949, enabled him to resign from the Ministry after one year to devote himself to a full-time career as a writer. Among the subjects that permeate his fiction are the exploration of death, especially suicide, homosexual relationships, the rejection of modern life as sterile and meaningless, and an idealized Japanese past. A well-known celebrity in Japan, Mishima acted in and directed motion pictures, playing the leading role in *Yukoku* a film he wrote and directed that was based on his short story "Patriotism." In 1976, an American film with Kris Kristofferson and Sarah Miles was based on Mishima's *The Sailor Who Fell from Grace with the Sea*. The author himself is the subject of a well-known 1985 film by Paul Schrader, which is titled *Mishima*. A political activist, Mishima formed the Shield Society, a private army consisting of eighty-three university men who believed that Japan should reject Westernization and return to the ancient samurai tradition. In 1970, he committed seppuku, the ritual samurai suicide he had planned in detail for a number of years. Among Mishima's best-known novels (all published by Knopf unless otherwise noted) are: *Confessions of a Mask* (New Directions, 1958), *The Sound of Waves* (1956), *The Temple of the Golden Pavilion* (1959), *After the Banquet* (1963), *The Sailor Who Fell from Grace with the Sea* (1965), *Thirst for Love* (1969), and the tetralogy published as *The Sea of Fertility: A Cycle of Four Novels*, consisting of *Spring Snow* (1972), *Runaway Horses* (1973), *The Temple of Dawn* (1973), and *The Decay of the Angel* (1974). A number of his stories are collected in *Death in Midsummer* (New Directions, 1966) and *Acts of Worship* (Kodansha International, 1990); some of his plays are collected in *Five Modern No Plays* (1959).

ACT OF WORSHIP

1

When first commanded by Professor Fujimiya to accompany him on a pilgrimage to the Kumano shrines, Tsuneko was thoroughly startled.

It was meant, apparently, as a way of thanking her for looking after his personal needs for the past ten years. A widow of forty-five with no one of her own, she had first come to him for private tuition in writing Japanese verse; then, finding that the old woman who kept house for him had just, most inconveniently, died, she had begun to look after him herself. In all those ten years, though, there had not been the least hint of anything erotic between them.

She had never been beautiful, and lacked all feminine appeal. Utterly undistinguished by nature, self-effacing in everything, she was constitutionally incapable of making demands on other people. Even her marriage to a man who had died after two years had been no love match, but one imposed on her by relatives. It was odd that such a woman should have taken to writing poetry, but it was precisely this personality of hers, it seemed, together with her lack of any special gifts, that had made the Professor decide to take her into his house.

Even so, a more basic reason behind the move was Tsuneko's own need to look up to someone; and for this there was no worthier object than Professor Fujimiya.

The Professor, who held the chair of Japanese literature at Seimei University, was a Doctor of Letters and himself well known as a poet. His studies of the "Kokin mysteries," a secret literary tradition based on the *Kokinshu* anthology of verse, were noted for elucidating the process—a subtle fusion of aristocratic and popular culture—whereby the debased tradition of the courtly literature of the Heian period, while increasingly lapsing into empty form, became involved with popular religious beliefs and grew increasingly mystic in character until finally, in the Tokugawa period, it produced a peculiar cult in which Shinto, Buddhist, and Confucian theories were oddly mingled. During the past ten years these studies had been succeeded by others involving another secret tradition derived from the *Tale of Genji*. The result was that the Professor's lectures on Heian literature tended to stray from their proper path and to acquire the medieval flavor of these traditions.

Alongside the devotion to scientific proof and methodicalness that characterized his work, it was the mystic that held the greatest fascination for him: he was, above all, a poet. His approach to the celebrated *Mystery of the Three Birds,* a key work in one of the traditions, was a case in point. He took as his subject the three birds of the title, *inaosedori, momochidori,* and *yobukodori*—which are of course imaginary birds not to be found in any zoo, mystic symbols of the three great principles of the universe—and drew a parallel with the flowers in Zeami's *Kadensho.* His ideas were embodied in his own *Flowers and Birds,* a work whose prose-poem beauty had given it a wide readership.

Around him had gathered a swarm of followers to whom he was a god; each of them eyed the others jealously lest a rival should usurp his favor, and it was no easy matter for him to observe a proper fairness among them.

All this might suggest that the Professor, at both the social and individual levels, cut a rather dazzling figure. Yet to those who associated with him personally no one could have been more solitary and outlandish.

He was, for one thing, unprepossessing in the extreme. A childhood injury had left him with a walleye and an accompanying sense of inferiority that accounted in part for the gloom and inwardness of his personality. There were times, it's true, when he would joke with those close to him—would demonstrate, even, the hectic liveliness of a sickly child at play—yet nothing succeeded in obliterating the air of introspection, or in transcending the suggestion of excessive self-awareness, like wings unsuitably large for the body, in a man who was thoroughly acquainted with his own disposition and accepted the limitations it imposed.

The Professor had a peculiar soprano voice which in moments of great intensity would acquire an almost metallic ring. Even those in closest attendance on him could never tell when he might fly into a rage. From time to time, during one of his lectures, a student would be ordered without explanation to leave the room. The reason, on closer inquiry, might prove to be that the student in question had been wearing a bright red sweater that day, or that he'd been scratching his head with a pencil and scattering dandruff.

Yet even now, at the age of sixty, the Professor retained a gentler, weaker, and more childlike side to his character. Conscious of it, he was always afraid that it might lose him the respect of others, and was correspondingly insistent that his students should observe the proprieties. Even so, students from other faculties who had no interest whatever in his academic achievements had dubbed him "Dr. Weirdo."

The spectacle of the Professor crossing the cheerful modern campus of Seimei University with a bunch of his disciples in tow was so eye-catching that it had become one of the famous local sights. Wearing glasses tinted a pale mauve, clad in a badly fitting, old-fashioned suit, he walked with the feeble sway of a willow tree in the wind. His shoulders sloped steeply and his trousers were baggy, ill contrasting with hair that was dyed black and slicked down to an unnatural neatness. The students who walked behind him bearing his briefcase wore, as was only to be expected of such a resolutely anachronistic crew, the black uniforms with stiff white collars that everyone else at the university shunned; it gave them the air of a suite of ill-omened ravens. As in the sickroom of someone gravely ill, they were not permitted to speak in loud or over-lively voices. Such conversation as took place was carried out in whispers, so that people watching from a distance would remark with amusement: "There goes the funeral again!"

Not that levity was entirely absent. For instance, as they passed close to some students playing American football, one of the Professor's followers might say,

"Miyazaka composed a piece of doggerel the other day, sir:

> See, the Merikens
> At their muddy *kemari*—
> The days are drawing out,"

to which the Professor would reply in fine good humor:

"I won't have that! It's not so much the quality of the verse I object to, but he should pay me a royalty for use of the phrase. I refuse to comment on the poem till he's done so!"

This would be one of the master's and disciples' happier moments. "Muddy *kemari*" was a phrase the Professor had invented in a recent verse satirizing football— *kemari* being the slow, dignified game played at the ancient imperial court—and the point of the joke was that the student had misappropriated his new coinage. This kind of humor had a subtly fawning air reminiscent of puppies playing with one eye on their watchful parent. But no one, in practice, qualified as a student of the Professor's unless he found such things genuinely funny.

At times like this a light murmur of laughter, like rising dust in spring, would float up from the flock of ravens; the Professor himself rarely laughed out loud. Then, almost immediately, the mirth would die down again. To a distant observer, the impression would be of some weird ritual game in which a gloomily reverent group bound by secret rites had momentarily compromised the rules governing the expression of the emotions, thereby tightening still further the bonds, so incomprehensible to others, that held it together.

Occasionally, the sorrow and loneliness that lay so heavy in the Professor's heart would find an outlet in his poetry, but at normal times they were only to be glimpsed faintly—through glass, as it were, as one glimpses strange fish lurking behind rocks in an aquarium. There was no indication of what it was that confined the Professor within his personal grief; nor did those who pressed the question maintain any lasting acquaintance with him. Now and again, he would favor the innermost circle of his followers with a disquisition on "the canker, melancholy," that afflicted him:

"According to Robert Burton's classic theory, there are four types of humor in the human body—blood, phlegm, choler, and melancholy. The last-named, a cold, thick, black acidic fluid, is produced by the spleen, and its function (according to Burton) is to regulate the blood and bile, as well as to give nourishment to the bones. Among the things cited as causes of melancholia are the influence of spirits, demons, and the heavenly bodies. Where foodstuffs are concerned, beef in particular is said to encourage melancholy—and, as you may have observed, I am fond of beef. According to Burton, moreover, the scholar's is by its nature the most unstable of occupations; whoever seeks to become an outstanding scholar and to master the whole range of knowledge is destined eventually to lose health, wealth—life itself. He is, accordingly, particularly prone to melancholia. In short, it would be remarkable, fulfilling all the conditions as I do, if I were *not* possessed by the canker of melancholy."

His listeners, knowing that he only said such things

when he was in a good humor, would be perplexed as to whether they should take this seriously or not.

Another of the Professor's prominent qualities was a tendency to jealousy. Though a confirmed friend of youth, he had once overheard a favorite student, one of those permitted to attend the special seminars that he held at his own house, relating in a loud voice how he had made a hit with the proprietress of a certain bar, and had promptly excommunicated the boy in question on the grounds of unsuitable conduct. He always insisted that these special study meetings at his own residence should be wrapped in an aura of youthful purity, an aura akin to that enveloping the sanctuary of a Shinto shrine and as such suited to these sessions aimed at evoking the divine spirit of poesy. The smell of hair oil, the odor of unwashed linen, were taboo; his one desire on such occasions was that the cavernous gloom of his best room should be filled with the breath of youth, light and fresh as the fragrance of newly planed cedar wood, and with the shining eyes and young voices of innocent enthusiasm.

Inexpert in attack yet doughty in strategic withdrawal, the Professor had, even in wartime, proved beyond reproach in preserving the integrity of learning. It was one reason for the fanatic following he attracted in the postwar years.

The sorrow already mentioned pervaded not just his verse but his studies, the expression on his face, his clothing—indeed, everything about him. Walking alone, he went with downcast eyes; if he chanced to find a puppy, say, that had strayed onto the campus, he would squat down and stay there for a while, stroking its head. Even a strange, dirty, sore-infested puppy would make him stop, though he was too fastidious to consider keeping one at home. The impression he gave at such times was of wanting to see his solitude reaffirmed, framed like a picture, of deliberately seeking opportunities to act out the loneliness again for his own benefit. As he painted this picture of droll self-pity, the Professor's unnaturally black hair would gleam provocatively in the spring sunlight, and the shadows of the silk trees in the campus would flow down over his sloping shoulders—till suddenly the dog, sensing something wrong, would wrinkle its nose, draw in its tail, and withdraw hastily with a growl. Clasped in the hand with which the Professor had been stroking it lay one of the cotton pads soaked in alcohol that he always carried on his person. All but dripping with pure alcohol, the pads were prepared for him every morning without fail by Tsuneko: white, flossy wads packed in a shining silver container and yielding at the lighest touch a damp, volatile chill like that of melting frost. . . .

This, then, was the man and scholar in attending whom Tsuneko had spent ten years of her life.

The Fujimiya residence where the Professor, a perennial bachelor, lived his celibate life had its own strict and fastidious routine. The territories in which a woman was and was not permitted to set foot were clearly demarcated. The foods the Professor liked were: beef; a certain kind of snapper; persimmons; and such vegetables as field peas, brussels sprouts, and broccoli.

His only recreation was the Kabuki, which he would attend either in the company of his followers or with former disciples, at the invitation of the latter. Tsuneko had never once received a command to accompany him. Occasionally, he would give her half a day off with a suggestion that she "go and see a moving picture," but he never even mentioned going to the theater.

There was no television in the house, only an ancient radio with poor reception.

The Fujimiya residence was an old, purely traditional structure standing in its own garden, one of those that had survived the war in Masago-cho, in the Hongo district of Tokyo. Although the Professor disliked Western-style rooms—not a single chair was allowed in the house—at mealtimes he preferred, exceptionally, Western food. The kitchen, where he never went himself and into which even the students were not allowed, had become Tsuneko's solitary citadel. It never occurred to him, on the other hand, to modernize its facilities, which consisted solely of two old-fashioned gas rings. It was Tsuneko's skill alone that, on occasion, produced under such conditions a meal for a dozen or more people, and that made both ends meet every month; nor did a single complaint about recent rises in prices ever reach the Professor's ears.

Every morning and evening without fail he took a bath, but, despite Tsuneko's years of service, no traditional intimacies such as washing his back for him were permitted. Even to approach the Professor during his ablutions was strictly forbidden; once she had laid out a change of clothes in the anteroom and informed him that all was ready, it was safer for her to retreat to as great a distance as possible. On one occasion during the early days of her employment, she had been summoned by a clap of hands from the bathroom and had made the mistake of responding almost instantaneously—"Did you call, sir?"—from outside the frosted glass door beyond which the Professor's dim form moved. She had been roundly scolded for her pains. For a woman servant to appear too soon after such a summons was, in the Professor's eyes, improper.

The Fujimiya residence afforded plenty of retreats where a person could, if he or she so wished, get out of the way, but rooms that contained books in any number were out of bounds to women. It was forbidden to clean such rooms, much less lay hands on the books themselves without permission.

Books had spread like mold, eating their way through each of the ten rooms in turn. Overflowing from the study, they encroached on the next room, converting it into a kind of lightless dungeon, then spread along the corridors, making it impossible to pass without edging sideways. The tidying and dusting of the books, too, was permitted only to members of his inner circle, who vied with each other for the privilege. Nor was anyone really qualified for membership until, as a result of frequently performing such tasks, he was instantly able, on being given the title of a volume published in, say, 1897, to remember on what shelf it was kept.

The students and other disciples who frequented the house were forbidden to talk to Tsuneko in too friendly a manner. Ever since the occasion when a student, seeing her so hard worked, had been moved to offer a helping hand, thus incurring the Professor's displeasure, Tsuneko had had the sense not to make herself conspicuous in any way, or to speak more than was strictly necessary.

The one thing in life that Tsuneko had to look forward to was the poetry meeting held regularly every month. On that day alone, she was allowed to take her place at the foot of the table, was treated as one of the Professor's followers, and received an exhaustive criticism of her own efforts at writing verse. On ordinary days, there was little to do in the house, and she welcomed the solitude as a chance to devote herself to improving her slow-developing skills as a poet.

This, too, was one reason why Tsuneko looked up to the Professor as though he were a god, or the sun itself. At times other than the poetry meeting, he would never say a word to her about poetry. It was precisely because this was the kind of master she had always served that the star of the poetry meetings shone with a special brilliance in her eyes.

So routine had the feeling of reverence become in the Fujimiya household that it was difficult to believe that such emotions could count for so little in the world at large. As a scholar of Japanese literature of no ordinary accomplishment, as a poet who wrote both modern verse and traditional *tanka*, the Professor, in Tsuneko's eyes, occupied a middle ground between heaven and earth. Sometimes, even, she saw herself as a shrine maiden in a sort of secret religious community centering around his person.

That the Professor and Tsuneko lived alone together was a matter of common knowledge; various rumors had gone the rounds concerning them, and some of the women who attended the poetry meetings had gone so far as to cast insulting glances in her direction. She became correspondingly reticent in her behavior, eschewing all makeup and striving after an ever greater sobriety of dress, thinking nothing of making herself look, in the process, ten years older than her age.

A glance at the mirror made it quite obvious that her looks were not of a kind to find favor with men.

The face was entirely devoid of sexual appeal. None of its features would ever stir a man to amorous thoughts. The nose was undistinguished to a fault, the eyes were too narrow, the teeth tended to protrude, the cheeks were hollow and the ears poorly fleshed, while her figure as a whole lacked any sort of fullness. For the Professor to be coupled in rumor with a woman like herself would do infinite harm to his reputation, let alone her own. In dress and behavior therefore she must, she decided, maintain the style of—at best—a maidservant, a style as ill matched as possible to the Professor's standing.

At the same time, since the latter disliked any suggestion of slovenliness, she must avoid any laxness in her appearance. She should be simple and modest, and contrive thereby to make it all the clearer to others that she was not attractive.

All this trouble she took out of a sincere desire in everything to serve the Professor, who on his side accepted the service without giving the sincerity a second thought. Yet never for a moment did it occur to her to hold this against him.

Fortunately, as the years went by and she passed the forty mark without losing any of her deferential manner toward him, the rumors finally began to dwindle. She was beginning to look more and more elderly—to resemble, even, the frankly old woman whose place she had taken ten years earlier.

The Professor's daily routine was as follows.

Invariably he awoke at six, without having to be roused. Before this, therefore, it was necessary to clean out the rooms without making any noise, and to get the bath hot.

On rising, he didn't show himself immediately but went straight to the bathroom via the library. After gargling and washing, he had a leisurely soak in the bath, set razor to his barely perceptible beard, carefully dyed his hair, and got dressed. The existence of a poem in which he likened himself satirically to Saito Sanemori, the aging warrior who dyed his hair black lest he be thought too old for battle, suggested that on one score at least he was sensitive to public scrutiny.

In the meantime, Tsuneko would have prepared the breakfast and laid out the morning papers.

Next, the Professor would proceed to the domestic shrine, where he paid his respects in correct Shinto style, then sat himself at the breakfast table and bade Tsuneko, with whom this was the first encounter, good morning. Very occasionally, without smiling, he would make some obscure remark such as "I had a good dream last night. Something pleasant may be going to happen today," but for the most part he was silent. Except when he was traveling, and irrespective of the season, this same pattern was followed every morning. He was said to have been sickly in his youth, but for the past ten years he had had no illness at all to speak of.

In this way, Tsuneko lived totally hidden in his shadow, effacing her own personality, given solely to reverence and service. During the early years, there had been relatives who urged her to remarry. By now, however, tired of her stubbornness, they had ceased even to make hints. In taking Tsuneko into his household the Professor had, undeniably, shown a remarkably good eye for character.

Even so, several times a year, Tsuneko would sense a doubt sprouting in her mind like a mushroom, and would stamp it out in alarm.

It would happen on days when she was left alone to look after the spacious house.

On these occasions, she would often, quite suddenly, be inspired to write poetry. Where the urge came from she had no idea: strangely enough, she found she was able to write verse without feeling either joy or sorrow. Yet her habitual turns of phrase—which persisted however often the Professor tried to correct them—were in practice excessively influenced by the master's own poetry, or rather by the sadness that pervaded it.

"These aren't your own feelings," the Professor had once declared with severe sarcasm in front of the others. "You're simply borrowing the container of someone else's sorrow and putting yourself into it. It's like going to someone else's house to take a bath."

And she honestly felt it was so herself; but then, if there was anyone on earth who could make her feel *real* sadness, it was the Professor—and he refused to do so. She could only believe that her mentor, while himself vulnerable to the flux of unspecified emotions, was deliberately avoiding imparting either joy or grief to her.

The fact remained, however, that she was often visited
by an urge to write verse; it was what gave meaning to
her life. Which meant, surely, that the inspiration must
come from within herself. Yet however consciously she
delved, she failed to find any corresponding emotion
deep inside her. Once, with the idea that it might reveal
the world of her subconscious, she'd even tried writing a
few poems in an avant-garde style, and had been roundly
rebuked for it.

She would be standing, perhaps, facing the garden in
the rainy season, looking at the clump of reeds planted
in the foreground, darkened now with the threat of showers, with the distant rumbling of a train and the roar of
cars reaching her ears across the gloom of the day. It
was at times like this that the desire to write occurred;
but always something in her own mind, something about
the opening line, got in the way. Should it be, say, "The
dead one . . ."? No—that gave the inappropriate impression that she was still bothered by her husband's death,
which in fact had long ceased to mean anything to her.
"The distant one . . ."? That was equally unsuitable, in
that it suggested longing for an absent lover, which was
nonsense. The words in short didn't flow naturally, but
came filtered through a kind of weir.

This sadness that strayed into her mind at the sight of
objects in the natural scene must, she felt sure, be an
unconscious imitation of the haze of grief hanging over
the Professor's verse. Even if there were no actual desire
to imitate, it still seemed to her that anything in the way
of sorrow must spring from the same abundant source.

It was at this point that she would start to wonder.
After living under the same roof for a full ten years, and
however the Professor might seek to avoid her in everyday life, she had inevitably developed her own way of
viewing things, and come to feel that she knew him better
than anyone else. Thus she had personal knowledge of
the fact that almost nothing had disturbed the even tenor
of his life during those ten years. To some people, a life
of such placid monotony—a life, too, free of any particular economic stringency and with a generous supply of
adulation—would be a source of envy.

It hardly seemed possible that the grief he distilled

from this peaceful life was due solely to a lack of confidence in his own appearance—to his walleye. The world contained any number of men who were uglier than he, with neither ability nor learning, who nevertheless enjoyed perfectly ordinary domestic lives. Why had he, unlike everyone else, clung so obstinately to solitude—deliberately encouraged sorrow—rejected life with such daunting oversensitivity?

At this point in her speculations, she had a strong feeling that if only she could grasp the secret whereby he spun such sophisticated sadness from such a prosaic life, she herself would be able to write poetry worthy of comparison with his. What could the secret be? Suspicion suddenly reared its head, and with a quickening pulse she found her mind straying involuntarily to the most forbidden thoughts. . . .

2

The circumstances described above will doubtless suggest the degree of Tsuneko's surprise when commanded to accompany the Professor on his pilgrimage to the Kumano shrines.

Though the Professor was himself a native of the Kumano district, he had never been back to the village where he was born. There were doubtless reasons to account for this but Tsuneko had never probed into them, and remained none the wiser. On the one occasion when someone claiming to be a relative had visited Tokyo and come calling, the Professor, with almost frightening indifference, had sent the man packing without even showing his face.

Nevertheless, though he always obstinately avoided visiting his birthplace, he had in fact made several trips to Kumano. And now, once more, he had expressed a desire to go: to take advantage of the summer vacation to make a long-deferred pilgrimage to the Three Shrines of Kumano. Moreover this time, it seemed, it was to be a purely private trip, with no lectures or meetings whatever to tie him down.

One advantage of being a scholar was that there was no shortage of young associates willing to look after the house in his absence. So arrangements were made for three of them to stay there, and Tsuneko asked a local caterer to send in meals for them.

The first question that bothered her was what to wear on the journey and what clothes to take with her. The Professor told her, rather irritably, to please herself. So, with no one else to consult, she racked her brains and finally decided to take out some of her savings and have just one new summer kimono made.

Concerning the books she was to bring, however, the Professor was quite specific.

"You'll never be any good at lyric poetry," he said, "so why not use this opportunity to try your hand at descriptive verse? And don't go trying to imitate the modern realistic school. I suggest you study the collected poems of Eifuku Mon'in."

Eifuku Mon'in, of course, was the celebrated poet of the Kamakura period, consort of Fushimi, the ninety-second emperor. A member of the Kyogoku school of verse and as such well represented in the imperial anthology known as the *Gyokuyoshu*, she is noted for descriptive works that display her skill at what Kyogoku Tamekane called "imparting a special fragrance to words." The poem that reads:

> The sun declines
> Behind the eaves,
> The shadows shift
> And fade, linger a while
> On flowers below

was one of which Tsuneko was particularly fond. She hadn't been interested much in the poet to begin with, but under the Professor's influence had come to appreciate the subtle emotion, subtler than that of the average lyric poem, that often lurked in the latter half of what was, in theory, a purely descriptive piece like this.

A volume of Eifuku Mon'in's verse, then. . . . As for clothes, she decided in the end to take her whole store of summer kimonos, since she was likely to sweat. She even took two of her own light cotton kimonos for use inside the hotel, as the Professor was bound to disapprove if she wore the vulgar kind supplied by the management. With one thing or another, her bag swelled steadily.

The Professor, on the other hand, being used to travel, was taking the same battered suitcase as usual, his only extra provisions consisting of an adequate stock of absorbent cotton and a pocket warmer in case he suffered one of his occasional bouts of stomach pain. Ashamed of the size of her own bag, Tsuneko did her best to reduce its contents, but without success.

The three aides who were to look after the house came to stay the night before they left. Saké was served at dinner on the Professor's orders, and the conversation, so far as she could tell, roved in animated fashion over academic topics, travel, and the theater. If only their mentor had been rather more lively, the young men might well have indulged in mild banter on the subject of "second honeymoons." But this, of course, was impossible in the Fujimiya residence; though when even the send-off at Tokyo Station the following morning failed to produce any such jokes, Tsuneko almost began to find it rather unnatural.

The heat that summer was particularly fierce, and by the time the train pulled out at 7:45 the platform was already sweltering.

The send-off party consisted of two of the people who were to look after the house and four students who had got wind of the Professor's departure. Tsuneko, who hitherto had always said goodbye to her master at his front door, shrank from the unaccustomed spotlight of the occasion. In theory, she should have been overwhelmed with joy and a sense of honor, but in fact she felt a twinge of uneasiness: a hint, even, of irrational fear that this journey might be a final gesture preceding her own dismissal.

When a student offered to take her bag, she stubbornly refused, fearing a reprimand, until a "Why not? The young have got energy to spare" from the Professor finally encouraged her to part with it and have it lifted onto the luggage rack for her. In the harsh sunlight that reached to the middle of the platform, the people who'd come to see them off mopped at the dripping sweat. As

Assistant Professor Nozoe—who was over thirty and the most senior of the Professor's entourage—said goodbye to Tsuneko, he took it upon himself to add in an aside: "I hope you'll look after him. He gets particularly difficult when he's traveling."

At first, Tsuneko was struck by his thoughtfulness, but on reflection decided that he'd got things the wrong way around. Such parting advice wouldn't have been out of place coming from a wife, but there was no reason why she, who had been attending to the Professor's personal needs for a full ten years, should take it from *him*.

They were all, she suspected, secretly uneasy at the idea of leaving their mentor entirely in her charge, if only for a matter of two or three days. Far from complimenting her on her good fortune, they gave the impression of silently reproaching the Professor for this sudden vagary. It was, after all, a sensational event. . . .

She wished the train would hurry up and leave.

Looking at them out there on the platform, she felt that all of them, personal protégés and ordinary students alike, had something vaguely anachronistic in their manner and appearance that made them conspicuous. Soberly dressed in white short-sleeved shirts and black trousers, they all, down to the youngest student, carried fans in imitation of their patron. The very air with which they swung the fans from cords on their wrists was, precisely, the Professor's. Even Tsuneko, who didn't get out much, knew that today's youngsters didn't carry fans.

At last the train started moving. Although the car they were in had air conditioning, the Professor didn't remove his jacket: he never did so, even in summer.

For a minute or two he sat with his eyes closed, then suddenly opened them as though startled and took the silver container out of his pocket.

The Professor had beautiful hands, as dry and chaste as handmade paper, but the number of dark spots had become increasingly noticeable recently, and constant wiping with alcohol had macerated the fingertips so that they suggested a drowned corpse. It was with such hands that he now took a piece of cotton soaked in alcohol and used it to wipe religiously the armrests, the window ledge, and everywhere else that he might come in contact with. As soon as one piece began to turn black he discarded it, so the container was soon empty.

"I'll make some more," said Tsuneko, intending to replenish it. But the hand she stretched out to get a new supply from the Professor's suitcase on the luggage rack was, quite suddenly, brushed aside in one of the stern, apparently pointless gestures of rejection that she'd observed in him from time to time. She had the impression that, through the relentlessly pervasive aura of alcohol, he had darted a particularly unkind glance at her. The look in his eyes went well with the smell.

The Professor's bad eye was on the left; the eyeball moved even though it couldn't see, so that strangers had the illusion of being looked at with that eye. After ten years in attendance, however, Tsuneko could tell immediately, through the violet spectacles, which way the healthy eye on the right was moving.

To be looked at so coldly after a decade of such personal service was disconcerting: it suggested, somehow, that he regretted bringing her with him almost as soon as they had set out. But Tsuneko was past being shocked. If anything, she was gratified by the suggestion of a spoiled child behaving in the way most natural to it.

She was so busy making swabs with the cotton and alcohol her companion had himself extracted from his bag that they were out of Tokyo before she could pay any attention to the morning scenery she had been looking forward to viewing from the train window. Her task finally finished, she held out the silver container, and waited for him to say something.

"Did you bring the Eifuku Mon'in collection?" he asked eventually, in his high soprano.

"Yes, I did," she replied, taking it from a carrier bag and showing it to him.

"I suggest you pay careful attention to the scenery. I have a feeling this trip will show you what it is you lack. It's partly my own fault, I'm sure, for keeping you shut up in the house all the time, but your recent poems have made me feel that it's time I tried to expand your vision. And you, on your side, must open up your mind, without resistance, to landscapes and nature in general, and remodel your verse without bothering too much about what you've done so far. I don't mean, of course, that you should write a lot of poetry while we're away. You don't need to write. The important thing is to fertilize your poetic sensibility."

"I see. . . . That's very kind of you."

Even as he delivered this homily in his high-pitched voice, the Professor's eyes were surveying Tsuneko restlessly, as though warning her that if he found the slightest trace of grubbiness on the neck of her kimono she would pay for it. Tsuneko, however, was deeply moved by this, the first kindly personal advice she'd had from him as a teacher. Overcome by the idea of his taking so much trouble, she barely managed to get out a "So kind, to bother with someone so hopeless," then was obliged to produce a handkerchief in a hurry and clap it to the brimming tears.

She knew that crying would annoy him, but the tears refused to stop. Yet even as she cried, she was privately reaffirming her determination, before the journey was over, to get at the secret behind his poetic gifts. If only she could put her finger on it, she might actually do something (though the Professor himself might not be too pleased about it) to return the kindness he had shown her.

The Professor took out a book, and from that point until somewhere around Atami devoted himself to reading as though he'd forgotten her very existence.

Kumano could have been reached easily enough by night train, but the Professor, who disliked overnight travel, had chosen to go by day, thanks to which the journey threatened to prove quite a strain. Beyond Nagoya, there wasn't even any air conditioning.

Arriving in Nagoya at noon, they ate lunch in a hotel opposite the station, then after a short rest boarded a diesel-engined semi-express on the Nishi-Kansai line. Even after they were on the train, the memory of the strained atmosphere over lunch lingered, making Tsuneko view with misgiving the prospect of other similar lunches during their trip.

The dining room on the top floor of the hotel, its windows filled entirely by a view of cloudy sky, had been all but deserted. The white tablecloths, even the white

napkins, had taken on the gray tinge of the clouds beyond the great glass panes, and Tsuneko felt awkward,
not because of any ignorance of Western table manners,
but because it didn't feel right to be sitting down opposite
the Professor in a formal way like this.

The meal also brought sharply home to her a mistake
in her calculations: the more soberly she dressed and the
older she tried to appear, the greater in fact was the
danger of being mistaken for his wife. As it was, she
would have done better to get herself up in a flashier
style less appropriate to the circumstances. If only she'd
been the type that could wear Western clothes, she could
have put on a two-piece suit or something, thus increasing the chances of being taken as his secretary.

The miscalculation, however, was strictly on Tsuneko's
side; there was nothing to suggest any such error on the
part of the Professor, who had not criticized her appearance when they set out and was still behaving quite
agreeably even now. Trying to fathom the workings of
his mind, she felt lost again in a fog of incomprehension.
Could he perhaps—though it was scarcely imaginable—
be deliberately hoping that they would be mistaken for
man and wife?

For lunch, the Professor had had cold meat, while Tsuneko had had white fish cooked *à la meunière*. When the
coffee came, she held out the silver sugar bowl for him
to help himself from first, and as he took it their fingertips came into brief contact. She apologized immediately,
but a suspicion plagued her that he had seen the contact
as premeditated on her part. It continued to plague her
in the maddening heat on the train, so that every time
the steady waving of the Professor's fan suddenly stopped
her heart seemed to stop with it. She had never reacted
in this way before. Perhaps the sense of responsibility
she'd felt ever since the train had left Tokyo Station had
made her oversensitive? The incident, for which there
was no way of apologizing naturally, continued to weigh
on her till, combining with the heat, it made it impossible
for her to enjoy the scenery outside.

She recalled the sensation as the Professor's fingers
had momentarily touched her own. There was nothing
really unusual about what had happened; much the same

thing must have occurred often enough back at home, at breakfast, on ordinary days. The incident in the hotel, however, had taken place in a large, deserted dining room, before the eyes of several loitering waiters, and the sensation had impressed itself on her with corresponding keenness. It had been—it occurred to her now—like touching the damp petals of a large white magnolia flower, with the cloying scent of a bloom just past its prime.

3

On the first night of the trip, Tsuneko had all kinds of shocking dreams; it must have been tiredness from the long train journey, for she normally prided herself on her ability to sleep soundly. In one particular vision, Professor Fujimiya appeared and chased her in such disgusting form that slumber fled and continued to elude her for some time.

She was in her room in a hot-spring inn in Kii Katsuura, a small room (separate, of course, from the Professor's) built out over the sea so that one could hear the sound of the water furtively lapping the shore below. Listening to it in the darkness, she had a feeling that small animals, smacking their chops and jostling each other, were crawling up the wooden supports beneath the building. But, frightened and trembling though she was, she must have gone off to sleep again, for she was still in bed long after her usual hour on the following morning.

She was woken by the ringing of the telephone. It was the Professor, to say that he was already up. Her clock said half past six, and the room was full of morning sunlight. Leaping hastily out of bed, she washed, rapidly dressed herself, and went to the Professor in his room.

"Good morning to you." The greeting was casual; but just at that moment she caught sight of what seemed to be the edge of something in a purple crepe wrapping cloth, clumsily concealed beneath the table. She must have been too quick getting ready, and have unintentionally surprised him in the act of looking over some private documents. If so, it was hardly her own fault, but she disliked the suggestion of snooping; she considered withdrawing again, but felt it would look too self-conscious, and gave up the idea.

"It seems you slept well," said the Professor—who had already dyed his hair and shaved—in a benign soprano. His voice in the early morning had a special flutelike clarity, almost like the warbling of a bird.

"Yes, thank you. I'm very sorry. I overslept."

"Never mind. It's a good thing to lie in occasionally. But you ought to be a little more considerate. It doesn't do to get flurried and rush to my room in a panic. It's hardly as though I'd had a stroke and needed you to hurry as much as that. In a case like this, you should say you're sorry quietly, over the telephone, tell me in a normal fashion how many minutes you'll take, then get ready in a leisurely way and come along at the time you said. That's the proper way for a woman to behave."

"Yes, of course. I'm really very sorry."

"There's no need to apologize. Just be more careful in future. There's a passage in *Advice for Actors* that says, 'to seek to take everything upon oneself, ignoring the others concerned, is referred to disparagingly as "going it alone." ' It's a useful warning for anyone, not just the actor. After all, service to others must always be calculated to fit the particular situation."

"Yes, of course. I'll try to be more careful. It was stupid of me."

To be grumbled at in this way did not, oddly enough, annoy Tsuneko. On the contrary, it gave her the illusion of being somehow small and cute, as though she'd turned into a meek little girl again. And the suggestion that their situation was special, unlike the way things were done in ordinary society, heightened the sense of satisfaction still further. For example, it was often said that young girls working in department stores nowadays would quit if they were told off, however mildly. For her, though, provided she kept her pride and her confidence in the idea that she was indispensable, to be scolded was if anything a pleasure. . . .

Even as she entertained these thoughts, Tsuneko was not entirely free of a desire to peer into the forbidden depths of the Professor's mind. Was his severity a form of fatherly affection, or was it simply objective criticism? If her behavior really bothered him so much, why didn't he get rid of her, instead of going out of his way to bring her with him on this journey?

"I've asked them to get us a boat," said the Professor after a while.

Tsuneko took the cue to go out on the veranda and gaze at the scenery. The sea was already dazzling in the midsummer light, but this was a landlocked bay, and not a single wave was to be seen in the vicinity. On the near side of Nakanoshima island, which lay directly ahead, rows of pearl cultivation rafts floated on the water, while to the left, at the northern extremity of the bay, lay a harbor from which the constant thud of ships' engines was audible. The hills on the opposite side of the bay were wrapped in an almost unnaturally dark green; a cable car ran up to their summit, about two hundred and fifty feet above sea level, and she could see where the green had been stripped away around the observation platform, revealing the red earth.

The bay opened to the south. On the horizon beyond, clouds in clusters lay emulating islands, and far out toward it the sea, shadowed by the clouds above, was like a pallid face.

Tsuneko had the sense not to gush about lovely scenery and the like, yet she was, after all, a poet in her own small way, and here, faced with this morning seascape, she felt the long years in the dark dwelling in Hongo suddenly dwindling to the merest speck of soot, and took a deep breath as though to draw in for future reference as much as possible of the view before her eyes.

At this point a maid brought in the small tables bearing their breakfasts.

"Oh—I'll see to things for the Professor," said Tsuneko so that the maid, who was supposed to serve them rice and tea toward the end, wouldn't hover over them during the meal. She'd deliberately emphasized the "Professor" to make their relationship quite clear; she was afraid this would seem officious again, but fortunately the Professor made no comment.

After breakfast and before the boat left, however, they

did have a spot of bother. The management sent along someone with several square decorated cards of the kind on which distinguished guests are expected to write something to commemorate their visit. This made the Professor rather cross, and Tsuneko was obliged to go to the manager and explain, apologetically, that he had no time for that sort of thing.

The Professor had hired a small sightseeing boat for their own exclusive use. They left the harbor, crossing waters that were green and soupy in the shadow of the islands, and set off around the coast to the west. The voice of the hotel clerk, who had joined them on board as their guide, reached them only fitfully, bawling above the sound of the engine, so that Tsuneko could hardly tell which was which of the oddly shaped rocks he was identifying.

There was a "Lion Rock," with several pine trees growing on it that were supposed to represent the mane, and a "Camel Rock" with two humps. Dotted here and there in the open sea where the waves were noticeably higher than in the bay, the rocky islets had a smugness about them that Tsuneko personally found rather tiresome. Uninhabited, they sat there for inspection, though with half their forms hidden underwater, silently content to be given labels that were appropriate or not according to how you looked at them; most so-called beauty spots, she supposed, were the same. They reminded her of her own past: even the term "married couple," it occurred to her now, had been a pretense no more grounded in actuality than the lion and the camel. Compared with such relationships, her life with the Professor was a reality that no name could ever hope to define: not some half-submerged rock, not something just squatting there to be stared at. . . .

Taking in a view of a cape beyond which, they were told, lay a stretch of deep water where whales were often caught, the vessel turned back to the east and, reaching the entrance to the bay, passed through an awe-inspiring cave that pierced a particularly large and magnificent rock known as "the Crane."

The Professor, who was holding on tightly to the side

of the boat, was clearly enjoying his trip, in the way a child would do.

He was fond of danger provided it was on a limited scale, not too serious, and incurred in a spirit of play. To him, she suspected, even the soft slaps that the thrusting waves dealt the underside of the boat as it went through the cave felt like small, personal gestures of revenge for a long and somber life of study. It must have been gratifying to feel these little counter-shocks disturbing—stirring into a flurry—the dark, still waters that had gathered in his mind after endless brooding on the more stable shore.

With these thoughts, Tsuneko kept her eyes resolutely on the seascape, refraining from addressing the Professor until finally an increasing number of fantastically shaped rocks to the east, clustered around a distant promontory and wrapped in the haze hanging over the sea, happened to suggest to her the legendary home of the Taoist Immortals and, breaking her silence at last, she said:

"I wonder where we're going."

It had suddenly seemed to her as if the boat, with the Professor and herself on board, was bearing them toward some utopian land—was approaching, after long adversity and suffering, a world in which ugliness no longer had any part. Where appearances were concerned, she had always been sensitive to the Professor's and her own shortcomings. They would never be taken for a handsome pair: to link them erotically in the mind was to make imagination look the other way. In bringing her along, the Professor had almost certainly been aware of this. And just as certainly he had had it borne home on him again and again, in the course of his sixty years, that in a love affair the plaudits of the onlookers are almost as important as the sincere feelings of the principals. Being twice as sensitive as other men, and a lover of beauty into the bargain, he probably felt that the times he spent alone with Tsuneko, seated at the very stern of life, were the only times when he could relax: relax in the knowledge that, having no part in beauty, he was in no danger of doing it any injury.

It was thus, sitting far astern, that the pair of them were sailing toward the promised land. . . .

Though it was unlikely that he had followed Tsuneko's train of thought quite as far as this, the Professor was not one to let her brief question as to where they were going pass lightly. A more conventional man might have answered with a "Where? I imagine we'll just do the sights, then go back to where we started." Instead, a slight irritation flashed somewhere behind his violet spectacles, as though he feared entanglement in some tiresome vagary of the female psyche. Being quite used to such wariness, and quite prepared to respect it, Tsuneko hastened to explain the reason for her question:

"I mean—it was just that the scenery over there reminded me somehow of the Land of the Immortals, and I had a feeling that the boat was taking us straight in that direction."

"Why, yes, of course. 'Land of the Immortals'—how very apt. The way the mist hangs over everything suggests exactly that. And in fact, of course, Kumano always has been closely associated with the Taoist Immortals. Admittedly, the only home of theirs I know of that's actually in the sea is Horai. . . ."

Which wasn't exactly a warm response, but Tsuneko, of course, had only herself to blame.

Just at that moment, the hotel clerk pointed toward the shore and shouted:

"Look, over there! D'you see the vertical white line to the left of Mt. Myoho? That's the Nachi Falls. They say this is the only spot in the whole of Japan where you can view a waterfall from the sea like this. So you'd better take a good look."

Sure enough, on the dark green right-hand slope of Mt. Myoho there was a place where the bare earth of the mountain was visible and, set against it, what looked like a pillar of white, unpainted wood. Tsuneko looked hard, and it almost seemed that the single white line was quivering slightly and climbing jerkily upward, though it might have been that the haze over the sea created a distorted mirage of motion.

A thrill passed through her.

If it was indeed the Nachi Falls, what they were doing was like stealing a forbidden look at some deity from a distant vantage point. By rights, of course, one ought to stand gazing up in awe at the waterfall from the edge of its basin; but the deity of the fall might be so used to stretching up its noble form high above men's heads that for a moment it had grown careless, thus allowing human eyes out at sea this total view of itself, endearingly small in the distance.

This induced in turn the fanciful notion that they had caught a forbidden glimpse of a goddess bathing. Yes— Tsuneko now decided—the deity of the waterfall was, quite definitely, a nymph.

Whether the Professor would go along with such fancies she wasn't sure; feeling it inappropriate to disclose them just now, she decided to make a poem out of them sometime later and submit it for his approval.

"Well, then, shall we get back to the inn?" he said. "We can go out and pay our respects to the waterfall later. I never get tired of seeing the Nachi Falls. A visit there always leaves me feeling spiritually purified."

He was gripping the side of the boat uneasily as he spoke, holding himself slightly clear of the incessantly rocking seat in the stern—though this time, perhaps because he trusted in the disinfecting properties of sea breezes, he had brought none of his cotton swabs on board.

Tsuneko herself felt glad at this evidence that the Professor was enjoying the journey; for it was clear, even to a bystander, what a strain the work of a great scholar was. On the one hand, the ever-present danger that the discovery of a single piece of long-forgotten material might suddenly upset a whole fabric of theory meant that a structure built up boldly on intuition—providing the intuition kept a sharp eye on the future—was, in principle at least, longer lasting. Yet on the other hand this approach was, in itself, in constant danger of lapsing into either poetry or art. The Professor had spent his whole life walking the fine tightrope between poetic intuition and documentary evidence. There had been times, of course, when the former approach had been correct and others, presumably, when it hadn't; yet it seemed safe to say that it had been right more often than the documentary one. The long, solemn struggle he had waged, unseen, in his study was something beyond Tsuneko's

powers of apprehension. Nevertheless, however clear the
inner vision attained there through the honing and refin-
ing of intellect and intuition, she could still guess at a
fatigue transcending the human will, a fatigue that had
taken its toll both physically and spiritually. It might be
that, when a person strove too hard to apprehend something outside himself, some kind of exchange occurred
eventually between him and the object of his interest,
leaving him subtly altered. Possibly, even, it was an intu-
itive sense of this state of affairs that had led ignorant
students to label the Professor "Dr. Weirdo."

All in all, Tsuneko told herself, it was a very good
thing that a man like this should get away from it all; and
it was understandable too that he should have chosen—
lest fresh and overstimulating impressions tire him—a
place that he had visited before. And she began to feel
that rather than drag him back spiritually to the confines
of his study by being oversensitive to his moods, it might
be better for her to make mindless conversation designed
to take the tension out of him.

However well meant, when a woman like Tsuneko
conceives a plan of this sort, it is bound to seem artificial
and clumsy in the realization. In the car after they left
the hotel on the way to Nachi, she rejoiced aloud over
the fact that the car was air-conditioned:

"How thoughtful of them," she said. "Why—even in
Tokyo you don't get air-conditioned taxis! In the old
days, I suppose, people visited the waterfall partly because it was so cool there, but nowadays you can actually
get cool on the way. It makes you feel a bit spoiled,
doesn't it? And there was I in Tokyo, every time you
went on a trip, worrying about how tiring it must be for
you, when in fact it seems quite comfortable. . . ."

This, and more of the same, was designed of course to
draw the Professor out, to make him take pity on her
ignorance and facile conjectures, and talk to her of the
hardships of travel undertaken in the cause of
scholarship.

But he was not one to react in any such commonplace
way just because he happened to be away from home.
Gently, he allowed his eyes to close. Tsuneko worried

for a moment in case he felt ill, but it seemed this wasn't
so.

The eyes, closed behind the pale mauve lenses, were
surrounded by a mass of wrinkles, so that it was difficult
to make out where the line of the eyelids stopped and
the wrinkles started. His ability to shut out the outside
world at a moment's notice reminded her of certain kinds
of insect. At the same time, it meant that she had a rare
opportunity to scrutinize him from close to. In doing so,
it occurred to her that she was inspecting his face thoroughly for the first time in ten years; until now, she'd
done no more than cast timid glances up at it from lowered eyes.

The sunlight flickering through the car window showed
where flecks of undissolved black dye had left dark
smudges at the hairline. Seeing them, she felt it wouldn't
have happened if only he had left things to her; it came
of his insisting on doing things alone, using his one good
eye. Seen close up, his looks weren't really so terrible;
the unprepossessing appearance for which he was famous
was due mainly to the bad proportions of his body as a
whole and the incongruity of his voice. In fact, the small
and gently curving mouth had a boyish freshness surprising in a man of sixty. If only he would stop being stubborn and let a woman look after what he wore, there
was no telling what a dapper new Professor might be
made of him. . . .

At this point in her speculations a sixth sense born of
long years' experience made her swiftly avert her gaze
and assume an unconcerned expression, so that when the
Professor opened his eyes he seemed totally unaware that
until a moment before he had been under such intense
scrutiny.

The Nachi Falls had been one of the nation's holy sites
throughout the two thousand years since the emperor
Jimmu had first accorded it divine status and worshiped
it as Oanamuchi-no-kami (another name for Okuninushi-
no-kami). There had been eighty-three imperial visits,
beginning with that of the retired emperor Uda, and the
emperor Kazan had done a thousand days' personal penance beneath the fall.

The spot, moreover, had been celebrated as a center

of ascetic practices ever since En-no-gyoja had first thought to stand beneath its cold waters as a form of spiritual discipline. The waterfall had been dubbed Hiro Gongen—the "Flying Water Bodhisattva"—and the building that stood by it was still known officially as the "Flying Water Shrine."

"One doesn't really need to know anything about it in advance in order to appreciate it," said the Professor without lifting his head from the back of his seat, speaking in the monotonous, lethargic tone he used for his lectures. "But to approach it with the benefit of some knowledge should add to its interest.

"I think you had better know something at least about the origins of popular worship at the Three Shrines of Kumano.

"As one might expect of a site dedicated originally to Okuninushi-no-kami, the Kumano shrines seem to have been closely linked with the Izumo people, and despite the remoteness of their location they were already well known in the time of the *Chronicles of Japan*. The prevalence of densely wooded, gloomy mountains inspired the idea that the spot gave access to the land of the dead. In later ages, these ancient associations with the nether world came to overlap with a belief in the Pure Land of Kannon, thus giving rise to the peculiar form of faith associated with Kumano.

"The three shrines were originally independent of each other, but over the years all kinds of beliefs became amalgamated into one, and their histories and the gods they enshrined were unified, leading eventually to their being venerated as a trinity.

"Rites of national significance were performed here as early as the Nara period, and Buddhist ceremonies were often held in front of the Shinto gods. A reference in the *Kegon Sutra* to Fudaraku, the Pure Land of Kannon, as being 'on a mountain lying to the south' led people to suppose that it was somewhere on a southern coast. Thus it came to be identified with the coastal region that included the Nachi Falls, and people began to worship there in the hope of attaining prosperity and happiness."

So the coast as they had seen it earlier from the boat, with the Nachi Falls behind it, had been a prospect of the Pure Land itself! What strange chance of fate was it—wondered Tsuneko—that she should have seen the paradise of Kannon on the very first morning of this curious journey?

"The identification of native Shinto gods with the divinities of Buddhism thus gave rise to the idea that the waterfall was a manifestation of the Bodhisattva Kannon. Subsequently, however, in the late Heian period, the popular belief that the deity represented in the main shrine's Shojoden was in fact the Buddha Amida got the better of the view of Nachi as the Pure Land of Kannon; and the contemporary preoccupation with rebirth in the Pure Land of Amida, fostered by a growing belief that the age of the Buddhist Law was in decline, created a fashion at the shrines for the rigorous ascetic practices of which the three years' penance done by the cloistered emperor Kazan was just one example.

"In time, administration of the three shrines passed into the hands of the Buddhist priesthood; a type of itinerant ascetic called *yamabushi* appeared, and there emerged the cult known as Shugendo, which combined service to the Shinto gods with ascetic Buddhist observances in remote mountain settings. . . ."

The Professor's lecture seemed likely to go on for some time, but she was retaining, as she listened, only those parts that promised to be useful in her verse.

It was puzzling that, though undoubtedly brought up here in Kumano, he was just as undoubtedly determined to avoid his birthplace. Perhaps the reason lay in what she had just heard—in the region's associations with eternal night, in its suggestions of a land of the dead, a gloomy netherworld of dark green shadow, which had made him long for yet fear it at the same time and had brought him here again on this journey. His own personal qualities, certainly, were quite appropriate to someone born in such a haunted region. But wasn't it possible too that, for all his resistance to the living world, he had left behind in the deep green Pure Land of this district something of beauty, something that, albeit anxiously, he was hoping to make his own again? . . .

Tsuneko was still toying with these thoughts when the car drew up in front of the gateway of the Nachi sanctuary. They got out of the air-conditioned vehicle, shrinking from the blast of heat that struck their faces, and set off down the stone steps leading to the adjacent sub-shrine, where the sunlight pouring through the trees lay copiously like hot snow.

By now the Nachi Falls was directly before them. The single sacred staff of gold erected on a rock shone brilliantly as it caught the distant spray; its gilded form, set bravely in opposition to the waterfall, appeared and disappeared in the smoke from a mass of burning incense sticks.

Catching sight of the Professor, the shrine's chief priest came up and greeted him with obvious respect, then showed them to a spot close to the pool formed at its base, where ordinary visitors were not allowed because of the danger of falling rocks. The great black lock on the red-lacquered gate was rusty and refused to open at first; once they were inside, the path led perilously over rocks till it came to the pool's edge.

Settling herself with difficulty on a flattish stone, where the fine spray fell pleasantly on her face, Tsuneko raised her eyes to the waterfall, so close now that it seemed to pour onto her breast.

It was no longer a nymph; it was a huge, fierce-looking male god.

Ceaselessly, the torrent slid its white foam over a rock-face that was like a polished metal mirror. High above its crest a summer cloud showed its dazzling brow, and a single, withered cryptomeria thrust its sharp needle into the blue sky's eye. Halfway down, the foam, striking the rock, shattered in all directions, so that as she gazed she felt that the wall of rock itself was crumbling, bulging forward, and coming down on top of her; if she bent her head and looked sideways, she could almost fancy that the places where water and rock collided were spurting countless springs in unison. The lower halves of rockface and water stood almost completely apart, so that one could clearly see the shadow of the fall rushing down the mirror-surface of the stone.

The torrent gathered breezes about it. On the nearby hillside, trees, grass, and bamboo thicket waved in the constant wind, shining with a dangerous-looking sharpness where they had caught the spray. With a rim of sunlight around their foliage, the restless trees had a wild and desperate air that was uniquely beautiful. "Like madwomen in the Noh," thought Tsuneko.

Before she realized it her ears had got so used to the roaring all around her that she was quite oblivious to it. Only when she stared, absorbed, into the still, deep green waters of the basin did the sound, perversely, revive in her ears. The profound sluggishness of the pool's surface was broken only by sharp-edged ripples like a pond in heavy rain.

"This is the first time I've seen such a splendid waterfall," she said, and bowed her head slightly in gratitude for having been brought to see it.

"For you, everything is the first time," the Professor answered in a tinkling voice, without turning from his position standing directly facing the cascade.

The voice had never sounded to her so mysterious, or so spitefully disparaging.

Could he be taunting her as being, spiritually at least, a total innocent, even though he knew that she'd been married? Surely it was excessively unkind to imply that someone was an innocent at forty-five? She might be an attendant at the Fujimiya shrine, but why should he mock the very purity that he himself insisted on?

"Shall we go?" she found herself saying, getting up to match the suggestion. As she did so, her foot slipped on the mossy rock; she started to fall, and at that instant, with the unexpected swiftness of a young man, the Professor thrust out a hand to help her. For less than a moment Tsuneko hesitated, uncertain whether to take the pale, antiseptic hand held out to her.

The hand floated in the roar of the waterfall, a divine apparition threatening abduction to lands unknown. A large magnolia flower loomed before her eyes, its petals elegantly freckled and sweet-smelling. . . . But her body was in danger of losing its balance and falling on the slippery rock. Finally she submitted, yielding to the enticement, aware that it was illusion even to consider it as such, yet in a state of pleasant giddiness that bordered on a swoon.

Unfortunately, the Professor's strength was not up to

the burden. When she took hold of him, he started to fall in turn. If they had both staggered and collapsed onto the rocks, they might have been seriously injured. But an instant sense of the Professor's importance made Tsuneko brace her legs, and with great difficulty she just managed to keep him up.

As they straightened up, they were both panting and flushed in the face. The Professor's spectacles were in danger of slipping off, and she hastily set them to rights for him; it was a gesture that at ordinary times he would surely have repulsed, but now he merely said "Thank you" in a voice suffused with embarrassment. He couldn't have made Tsuneko happier.

4

It was an odd summer morning: one on which, without conscious design, all kinds of bonds were loosened and many taboos lifted. Probably the Professor himself was not particularly aware of having lifted them, but had simply felt like letting things take their own course for once.

To pay one's respects at the Nachi Grand Shrine, repository of the divine spirit of the Nachi Falls, it was necessary to climb, in the full heat of the summer sun, a flight of more than four hundred stone steps. Since the climb was grueling enough to make one sweat profusely even in spring and autumn, only a handful of people ever thought of taking it on at the height of summer and at this time of day. Young people nowadays must have weak legs, Tsuneko reflected, for she noticed boys and girls who were ready to give up after the first few dozen steps; she looked at them quizzically, only to find herself in trouble once they were past the first resting place on the way.

The Professor climbed in silence, ignoring the resting places with their promise of refreshments, rejecting Tsuneko's helping hand. It was a mystery where such stamina had been lurking in him. He let Tsuneko carry the jacket of his suit, but refused to buy a walking stick, pressing on through the reflected heat with not enough breeze even to belly out his unfashionably wide-cut trousers, lifting himself doggedly from one step to the next,

his steeply sloping shoulders bent forward, his gait swaying as ever. The back of his shirt was already soaked
with sweat, but he wouldn't allow himself to use his fan
or do anything more than mop the sweat dripping from
his forehead with the handkerchief clasped in his hand.
His profile as he flogged himself on, head bent, eyes
fixed on the bleached surface of the steps, bore noble
suggestions of a life spent in the solitary pursuit of knowledge and at the same time, typically, suggested a desire
to let people see the suffering inherent in his solitude. It
was a painful sight that left, like the salt left after seawa-
ter has evaporated, a trace of the sublime.

Watching him, Tsuneko could not bring herself to
complain on her own behalf. Her heart felt as though it
was thrusting up into her throat, her knees hurt with the
unaccustomed exercise, her calves were painful, and her
legs grew more and more unsteady, as though she were
walking on clouds. Worst of all was the infernal heat.
Her head swam, she seemed likely to faint from fatigue—
and yet, as time went by, something pure seemed to well
up out of the depths of the fatigue, like fresh water
springing from sandy soil. Perhaps, it occurred to her, it
was only at moments like this—only after this kind of
hardship—that one achieved with any real sense of conviction a vision of the Pure Land of Kumano of which
the Professor had spoken in the car. It was a land of
mysterious shadow, sheltered by the cool green cover of
trees, a land where there was no sweat, where one's chest
never hurt. . . .

And there, perhaps—the idea came into her mind, and
promptly became a stick for her to cling to, giving her
the courage to go on climbing—there, perhaps, it was
fated that the Professor and she should cast off restraint
and come together in all their purity. For ten years, although the hope had never once been consciously acknowledged, she had dreamed of mutual respect exalted
into no ordinary love, but a sublime love that dwelt in
the shade of old cedars deep in the mountains. It would
not be the commonplace love of ordinary men and
women; nor would it be the mutual vaunting of good
looks that sometimes passed for love. The Professor and
she would come to each other as two transparent pillars

of light, in some spot where they could look down with
scorn on the people on earth below. And perhaps that
spot lay at the top of these very steps up which she was
now toiling.

Deaf to the singing of the cicadas all about, blind to
the green of the cedars crowding both sides of the steps,
she went on, aware of nothing but the sunlight, a kind
of dizziness in itself, beating down directly on the nape
of her neck, till she reached a stage where she seemed
to be tottering along in a billowing, luminous haze.

But when they reached the precincts of the Nachi
Grand Shrine and she had splashed cold water from the
font on her hair, moistened her throat, and finally relaxed enough to look around her at the scene, it was no
Pure Land she saw but brightly lit reality.

The broad view was bounded by mountains, Eboshi-
ga-take and Hikari-ga-mine to the north and the summits
of Mt. Myoho to the south; skirting the coniferous woods
below, they could see the bus road to Myoho, where
there was a temple enshrining the hair of the dead. A
single break in the hills to the east gave a glimpse of the
sea: present reminder of the sense of awe that the sun,
rising in the gap and wondrously transforming the dark
mountains, must have inspired in men of old. Like an
arrow of rose-colored, life-giving light released with a
sudden twang into the land of the dead, its rays would
effortlessly have pierced the solemn banks of mist that
were always said to lie about the mountains of Kumano,
the haze described in the tenth book of the *Tales of the
Heike* as "the compassionate mists of grace." . . .

Here again Professor Fujimiya was on friendly terms
with the chief priest, and they were shown through a red-
lacquered lattice gateway into the inner garden.

The main deity of this shrine was Fusumi-no-okami
(another name for Izanami-no-omikami) but, as was the
peculiarity of all three Kumano shrines, the most important deities of the other two sites were venerated here as
well. Thus when they entered the courtyard they could
see six buildings—Takimiya, Shojo-den, Naka-no-gozen,
Nishi-no-gozen (the main sanctuary), Wakamiya, and
Hasshinden—standing in a row, the shape of each structure, the very tiles of its roof, giving expression to the

masculine power or feminine grace of the god or goddess enshrined within. The old saying was right when it claimed that "the very mountains defend the faith": Kumano was a special religious realm where gods and Buddhas jostled each other for space.

Beneath the summer sun, the shrine buildings and the rich verdure of cedar-covered hills behind created a brilliant contrast of vermilion and green.

With an amiable "Take your time, won't you," the chief priest went off, leaving them in sole possession of the inner garden with its celebrated old weeping cherry tree and its rock shaped like a raven. In the heat, even the moss had a whitish, fuzzy look. The garden lay hushed: one could almost hear the gods breathing softly as they took their noontide nap.

"Look—," said the Professor, pointing to the six shrine roofs visible beyond a tall wooden fence, "the 'frog's-leg' brackets in the eaves are all different."

But Tsuneko was too struck by something uneasy in the Professor's own manner to look in the direction he indicated. Although he'd wiped off the sweat and neatly donned his jacket so that he looked positively cool, with no sign of the hardships of a while ago, he had somehow acquired a vaguely harassed expression. His gaze, too, roved restlessly around the roots of the trees nearby. About to ask him whether he had dropped something, Tsuneko checked herself abruptly.

For just at this point, he set her heart beating fast by carefully drawing from his pocket the object in a purple wrapping cloth that she had glimpsed that morning. Apparently unconcerned that she was watching, he proceeded to untie the cloth, revealing a lining of dazzling white silk on which lay three decorative combs made of boxwood, every detail down to the delicate carving of Chinese bellflowers plainly visible in the fierce sunlight.

The sheer elegance of these objects produced a strong reaction in Tsuneko, who simultaneously had caught sight of three Chinese characters inscribed in red with a writing brush, one on each of the combs.

One was a character that could be read *ko* or *ka*.

One, though she wasn't certain, looked like *yo*.

One was probably *ko*.

A single glance was not enough to be quite sure, but it was a safe guess that, taken together, they made up a woman's name: Kayoko. Moreover, the three vermilion characters, written in what looked suspiciously like the Professor's hand, had such an extreme feminine grace that they imprinted themselves as unmistakably on her mind as if she had caught a brief glimpse of some dignified lady in the nude. Though they were done in the square, formal style, each stroke was executed with a delicacy and loving care that told of the intense feeling with which the Professor had wielded the brush. Almost certainly the woman of the mysterious red characters had been lurking in her soft bed of white-lined cloth ever since the start of their trip. Tsuneko couldn't help resenting the fact that all through the journey so far the Professor had been concealing from her this, the only woman's name with which he'd been personally associated during the past ten years. Quite suddenly, the Pure Land she had been busily picturing to herself throughout that long, sweat-drenched climb vanished, leaving her—not in heaven—but in hell; for the first time in her life, Tsuneko was jealous.

Although the episode might seem to have lasted quite a while, in fact the Professor exposed the set of three combs to Tsuneko's eyes for only the briefest of moments before taking out the one inscribed with *ka*, wrapping the others up carefully in the cloth again, and putting them away in his pocket.

"I have to get this buried somewhere, quickly. Find me a good place near the roots of a tree. Somewhere where it'll be easy to dig a hole."

"Yes, of course." Even as she spoke, Tsuneko pitied herself for the way sheer habit made her, despite her own distress, comply instantly with his command. Though her mind resisted, her eyes were already searching the garden.

"I wonder if the foot of that weeping cherry wouldn't be best."

"Yes. A good idea. Particularly in the spring, under the blossom . . ."

And with almost indecent haste he went up to the tree, knelt at its roots, gently removed the fuzz of moss, then began vigorously scraping out the soil underneath with his nails. This was unlike his usual antiseptic self, but perhaps he considered that sacred soil was free of germs.

In an instant, the comb had vanished into the earth, and the graceful red inscription with it. With Tsuneko's help, he neatly replaced the moss to hide any sign of the ground having been disturbed. Then, still on his knees, he joined his hands briefly in prayer—and immediately looked about him to check that no one was coming, an action that somehow suggested less the Professor she was used to than someone guilty of a crime.

Eventually, trying to look casual, he got to his feet and, taking a cleaning pad from another pocket, proceeded to wipe his fingers assiduously, giving another piece to Tsuneko for the same purpose. It was the first time he'd ever shared his pads with her. And as she carefully cleaned the dirt from her nails, with the cool, businesslike smell of the alcohol in her nostrils, she had the feeling that all unwittingly she'd been made an accomplice in this little crime.

5

They spent that night at Shingu. The following day they were to visit the Hayatama Shrine in the morning, then take a car to the Nimasu Shrine, in Motomiya-machi, in the afternoon. With that, their triple pilgrimage to the shrines of Kumano would be accomplished.

But ever since the affair of the combs Tsuneko had taken to dwelling on her own thoughts. She continued to do as the Professor said but, even though they were still on their journey, the new, cheerful self had disappeared, replaced by a Tsuneko in no way different from the one who inhabited the gloomy interior of the residence in Hongo.

Since the shrine visits were scheduled for the morrow, they returned to the inn once they had done the sights of Shingu. There was nothing more to do that day, so Tsuneko took out the collection of Eifuku Mon'in's verse that she had brought with her, with the aim of spending the time till dinner reading. Officially, the Professor too was reading in his own room, though she suspected he was taking a nap.

In her heart, she felt bitter toward him—a feeling sustained by the fact that, despite her obvious depression, he had still made no reference to the combs. It wasn't, of course, the kind of subject she could bring up herself, so, until the Professor broached it from his side, she was left to brood on the riddle alone.

Tsuneko had rarely looked into the mirror even when completely alone in the house in Hongo, but now she did so whenever she had an idle moment by herself. The mirror here, on a cheap red-lacquered stand of the kind often found in such rooms, was quite adequate for inspecting a face with so few pretensions.

Not surprisingly, the book had no portrait of Eifuku Mon'in on it, and there was no way of guessing what she had looked like, but it was doubtful that her face had been anything like her own, with its small eyes, its scraggy cheeks and fleshless earlobes and, worse still, its slightly protruding teeth. No, in every respect—material circumstances, social status, physical appearance—the woman had been utterly different from herself. Why then had the Professor told her to read the poems?

Born the eldest daughter of Saionji Sanekane, the Chief Minister of the day, the poet had gone into service at court at the age of eighteen. She had been appointed a lady-in-waiting, then had gone on to become second consort to the emperor Fushimi. When the emperor abdicated to become a Buddhist monk, she had been given a new name, Eifuku Mon'in. On the death of the retired emperor, she took holy orders, at the age of forty-six, with the Buddhist name of Shinnyogen. Thereafter, while devoting herself to the study of Buddhism, she became the leading female poet of the Kyogoku school of *tanka*, under the patronage of the next emperor, Hanazono. The turbulence of the Kemmu Restoration left her declining years undisturbed, and she finally died at the age of seventy-two.

Hers was a politically difficult period, with the imperial house split into two opposing lines. Her last years in particular saw the rebellion of Ashikaga Takauji, followed by the Kemmu Restoration and the age of the

Northern and Southern Courts. Yet her poetry remained
unaffected by political and social developments, diligently pursuing its task of framing a delicate observation
of nature in a language of great grace and subtle nuance.
She never once forgot the injunction, traditionally as-
cribed to Teika, to compose verse "with compassion and
a sense of the sorrow of existence."

One thing that troubled Tsuneko was the fact that Eifuku Mon'in had taken the tonsure when she was only
one year older than she herself was at present: could the
Professor be hinting that she, too, ought to become a
nun a year from now?

Nor was that all. The period when the poet's work was
at its most exquisitely beautiful, the very epitome of the
style of the *Gyokuyoshu* anthology to which she was such
an important contributor, corresponded precisely with
her forties. In 1313, when the anthology was completed
and presented to the emperor for inspection, she would
have been forty-three. This meant that such highly effective specimens of the *Gyokuyoshu* style of natural description as:

> Chillier still
> The wind, blowing,
> Brings mingled snow
> In this cold twilit sky
> Of spring rain

and:

> Where the hills begin
> The song of birds
> Heralds the dawn;
> First here, then there,
> The blossom takes on color

were composed when she was around the age that Tsuneko was now.

It seemed unlikely even so that, until the death in later
years of the emperor Fushimi, Eifuku Mon'in ever experienced any real emotional pain. Perhaps the idea that
art was born only of suffering was an erroneous modern

assumption? If so, then the Professor might only be trying to tell her, encouragingly, that first-rate poetry could be produced even out of her own emotional doldrums—which would mean, too, that she was badly off the mark in trying to ferret out the secret of his own sadness, stirring up feelings where there was no need for them.

Under any government and in any society, for beautiful scenery to produce beautiful verse surely required that the poet, if a woman, should have beauty and position in the manner of Eifuku Mon'in, or, if a man, some strong, unshakable ideas of his own. And every time the elegance of a particular poem by Eifuku Mon'in impressed her strongly, she would feel her own hopeless lack of qualifications to write such verse, making her want to throw the book, which the Professor had been good enough to lend her, down on the floor. Then, having indeed thrown it down, she would feel she had been horribly disloyal to him—and pick it up again, only to find that just holding it was almost more than she could bear.

All she could see in it was a book crammed with the surface brilliance of a superficial woman—unfeeling, unnecessarily decorative lines devoid of both joy and sadness. What, she wondered, would one of the Professor's male associates do if he felt the same way as she did now? Probably, she decided, he would dash himself against his mentor like an angry wave (though one, of course, that observed the proprieties), and the latter would meet this spiritual upheaval with mildness and tolerance.

Abruptly, she left the room with the book clasped to her breast. Trotting along the corridor, she knelt in the approved fashion before the sliding doors of the Professor's room and called:

"May I come in?"

"Do," came the mild, high-pitched voice from the other side of the doors, a voice that might have been either a man's or a woman's. She went in.

As she'd feared, the Professor was seated at a low table in front of an electric fan, reading a thick volume whose fluttering pages he held down with one finger.

"I've come to return the book you kindly lent me."

"Have you finished it, then?"

"Yes, well . . . no."

"You don't have to give it back till you've finished it. Why don't you keep it till the end of the trip?"

"I see."

She could tell that her equivocal answers were irritating him. Afraid of a scolding, she suddenly bowed low on the tatami:

"Professor—I can't write poetry any more."

"Why?" he asked, with the calm of extreme surprise.

"It's no use. However hard I work at it, I . . . Someone like me . . ."

Before she could finish, the first real tears she had ever shed in the Professor's presence came welling up.

One might almost have thought he had been looking forward to precisely this kind of eventuality, which he could never have borne at normal times, as one of the pleasures of the journey. For an unexpectedly childlike, almost roguish twinkle appeared in the depths of the mauve spectacles, even though his tone was solemn and his face reproving as he said:

"Now listen to me. You mustn't give up halfway. I thought you were the sort of person who almost never got emotional, but the lesson to be learned from Eifuku Mon'in is the importance in art of concealing one's emotions. Even the kind of poetry that is usually considered 'subjective art' is in no way an exception. Modern verse has lost sight of this basic principle. I myself have been corrupted by modern poetry into writing the kind of verse I do, which is why I recommended that collection to you—to keep you from repeating my own mistake. So you mustn't let it have the opposite effect like this.

"Eifuku Mon'in reveals nothing directly in her work, but—" He turned the pages of the book that Tsuneko had put on the table for him, searching for something. "Ah, here we are. Take this poem, for instance, from the thirtieth poetry party in the second year of Kagen:

> The night sky
> Is moonless, raining;
> Near dawn
> A firefly's light
> Glimmers in the eaves.

"It's an exact description, yet it has an indefinable pathos that effectively conveys the personal sadness underlying the outward splendor of her life. Precisely because she was so sensitive and vulnerable, she rigorously trained herself to conceal her emotions, with the result that these descriptive poems, so emotionally restrained, have a subtle power to suggest feeling. Don't you think so?"

Everything he said, of course, was quite correct; it made it impossible for her to bare her own emotions any further. Yet she couldn't help being aware, at the same time, that something in her mind, some kernel of feeling, had become still firmer. In the end, he had said nothing about the source of the combs. When she thought of the purple wrapping, stored away so carefully in the pocket of the very jacket that he, with such an innocent expression, had given her to carry, and which she on her side, because it was *his* jacket, had held away from her so that it shouldn't get sweat on it as she nearly killed herself struggling up four hundred steps under the blazing sun— when she thought of it, she couldn't stop the feeling from turning into pure resentment. . . .

That evening, nevertheless, nothing untoward happened, and the following morning they set out while it was still cool to visit the Hayatama Shrine. The deity of this shrine—the Professor explained—was generally said to be the god Izanagi-no-mikoto, but according to a passage in the *Chronicles of Japan* it was in fact a god formed from Izanagi's saliva. Saliva, he said, was a symbol of the soul, and the divine spirit in question was intimately connected with burial and services for the dead.

This, together with the loving respect the Professor had shown as he buried the comb, would seem to suggest that the original owner of the combs was no longer alive. Tsuneko, who had been preoccupied with these objects ever since the day before, had had a dream the previous night in which Eifuku Mon'in and the lady of the combs were merged in a dim vision of a woman, a woman no longer of this world yet of unparalleled beauty and nobility. With the three boxwood combs in her hair, her pale, mournful face had loomed out of the depths of the Ku-

mano cedar woods, the train of her robe stretching on
and on like the night, trailing far behind her and away
into the dark sky. The precise nature of the garment
wasn't clear, but Tsuneko must have pictured Eifuku
Mon'in wearing something similar. At its neck, fabrics
lay in multiple layers from which the face rose like a wan
moon. Suddenly, she realized that the many layers were
all of white, patterned silk; and at that moment, day
began slowly to dawn and the robe, its color revealed as
the plain purple of mourning, took on a progressively
richer hue.

Of course—the purple wrapping cloth! she thought;
and the dream vanished.

She was to encounter the cloth again that morning in
the inner garden of the Hayatama Shrine. Here, in contrast to the other site, the precincts were appallingly
noisy, the crimson buildings reverberating incessantly
with the din, like that of power saws at a lumber mill,
made by steamers setting off up the Kumano River behind the shrine.

As a result, the Professor's secret undertaking was accomplished, under the cover of noise, more easily than
at Nachi, and the comb with its character *yo*, once taken
from the purple wrapping, was buried among the roots
of a shrub in no time at all.

That left the one inscribed with *ko*.

Folding the remaining comb tenderly in the cloth, the
Professor thrust it deep into the inside pocket of his
jacket, then, again without saying a word and without a
glance at Tsuneko's inquiring expression, turned a weary,
sloping-shouldered back on her and led the way out of
the garden.

6

The interest that Professor Fujimiya took in Eifuku
Mon'in was inspired not by her verse alone, but also by
the fact that the age of the *Gyokuyoshu* was a crucial
one in the history of the "Kokin mysteries."

The authority of the Kokin tradition had originally derived from a political struggle. In the antagonism between the Kyogoku and Nijo schools of poets that

accompanied the splitting of the imperial line into two rival courts, the Nijo school, as a means of demonstrating its own long-established authority at the expense of the newer Kyogoku school, had gradually begun to present the tradition—till then of no particular substance—as something of great profundity. From then on the original rivalry had, as witnessed by the celebrated *Petitions by Two Nobles of the Enkei Era*, degenerated into the naked expression of a hatred and jealousy that concealed in turn an underlying struggle for political power and wealth. These facts of history Tsuneko knew herself from having been allowed a humble place at the Professor's tutorials.

Two members of the Mikohidari family, which claimed descent from the Kokin poet Michinaga—Tameyo of the Nijo school and Tamekane of the Kyogoku school—were at daggers drawn. Angered by the appointment of Tamekane as sole compiler of a projected imperial anthology, Tameyo appealed to the emperor to disqualify his relative, while the latter on his side made a counter appeal. These were the aforementioned *Petitions by Two Nobles*. Despite this, Tamekane hastened to compile the *Gyokuyoshu* on his own. One of the chief poets represented in it was, of course, Eifuku Mon'in. The struggle eventually ended in victory for the Nijo school and the consequent emergence in its definitive form of the Kokin secret tradition. Professor Fujimiya's studies thus naturally centered on this Nijo school—yet personally he was unquestionably sympathetic to the losing side.

There was no telling what, in the first place, might have touched off his interest in such things: a squalid struggle in a bygone court, and a mystic authority forged by main force. One thing certain was that there were also two conflicting elements in his own personality. While sympathizing with the Kyogoku school in its decline, he worked hard to acquire an increasingly mystic stature of his own; and while devoting his life to studies suggesting that most academic and artistic disputes involved the simple pursuit of self-interest, he was himself an artist, the author of a large number of graceful, poignant poems.

Thus, while Tsuneko was deeply impressed by the Professor's persistence in handling objects that emitted the strange radioactivity known as beauty, to the point where he was weirdly transformed by exposure to it, she could only conclude that to do the same was completely beyond her own abilities. Quite possibly, that was what had given him such an unusually solitary, chilly personality—the suspicion that the beauty distilled from the ugly struggles provoked by man's greed appeared, not on the victorious side but more stealthily, amongst those who were defeated or doomed to extinction; whereas he personally, hoping to establish (albeit in provisional form) his own lasting authority, disliked any hint of such extinction.

In this way Tsuneko, growing calmer, found herself able to take another, less urgent look at him. But remembering that she was going to have to face the purple cloth again that afternoon, she didn't feel up to pursuing the subject.

The Nimasu Shrine, the focal point of the three holy sites, is said to have been established as early as the reign of the emperor Sujin, and the god worshiped there is Ketsumiko-no-kami, the same as at the Kumano sub-shrine at Ou, in the province of Izumo.

According to the Professor's account, Nimasu still showed the lingering influence of the shamanism of the Izumo people. In fact, the religious practices of all the Kumano shrines betrayed strong traces of ideas differing from those proper to esoteric Buddhism, which gave them a flavor not found in other Shugendo rites.

There was a bus they could have taken, but to Tsuneko's relief the Professor, who was not mean with money when traveling, said he would hire an air-conditioned car again.

Unfortunately, the drive along the Kumano River followed a rough, stony road on which they repeatedly encountered trucks loaded with timber. Each time, they were enveloped in swirling clouds of dust, so that although the windows were closed with the air conditioning on, it was impossible to enjoy at leisure the view of the river below.

The original shrine had once stood in the middle of the Otonashi River, and had been of great magnificence, but it was destroyed by floods in 1889 and rebuilt two years later on its present site by this river. There were various waterfalls on the far bank, but particularly memorable for Tsuneko was seeing one called Shirami-no-Taki, an offshoot of the Nachi Falls spilling from the rear of the main cascade, which the Professor felt it worth stopping the car to view.

In fact, even though it was refreshing to see the trees and grass round about damp and glossy where everywhere else was white with the dust thrown up by the trucks, it proved to be a perfectly ordinary waterfall. Still, the idea that this was pure, holy water emerging from behind the huge Nachi Falls itself gave the single thread, dropping from the sky as she looked up at it, its own distinction. It occurred to her that, thanks to her companion, she had been allowed to get thoroughly acquainted with every aspect of Nachi: the distant view of it from the sea the day before, then the spray falling on them as they stood by its basin, and today this glimpse of a hidden self, in the background. . . .

Eventually they reached the parting point of the rivers, then followed the Kumano further to the west, over hill and through dale, passing by the Yunomine hot-spring resort, until, just as the wide basin of the Otonashi, a tributary, spread out before them, a graceful shrine building appeared beside the river in a grove of trees.

As she got out of the car, Tsuneko marveled at the beauty of the surrounding hills wrapped in summer sunlight. There were few people about; the clear air was redolent of cedar; and the muddle of the modern world just beyond only conferred a strange plausibility on the traditional belief that this was the paradise of Amida. Even the cry of the cicadas, out of sight in the cedars, had none of its usual shrillness but was still and pervasive, like a fine sheet of bronze foil overlying everything.

Passing beneath the massive, finely proportioned gateway of unpainted wood, they walked slowly along the white gravel of the approach to the shrine, between an avenue of cedars whose foliage grew thick right down to the lowest branches. Seen from the foot of the stone steps leading to the shrine itself, the sky was enclosed in a uniform green, broken only by the touch of a sunbeam on the upper part of a trunk, or a cluster of dun-colored dead needles.

Halfway up the steps, a quotation from the Noh play *Makiginu*, inscribed on a wooden signboard, reminded Tsuneko of the old story.

"It's about a man from the capital who comes here to offer up a thousand rolls of silk, isn't it?" she said.

"That's right. He comes at the command of the emperor, who has had a vision in his sleep. But on the way the man sees some winter-flowering plum blossom, which inspires him to write a poem as an offering to the god Tenjin of Otonoashi. As a result, he's late arriving at the shrine and is seized and bound, but is rescued by the god personally, manifesting himself in the form of a shrine maiden . . ."

"Who extols the virtues of verse. . . ."

"Exactly. Singing the praises of Buddhism in terms of poetry."

As Tsuneko remembered it, the play had included the lines "The Shojoden enshrines / The Buddha Amida," which suggested the dead, and also: "Ply, ply the comb / On the disheveled hair . . . ," but she refrained from mentioning them because she didn't want to give the impression of being preoccupied with death and combs.

By the side of the steps as they climbed, they noticed a moss-covered stone pillar said to have been set up by Izumi Shikibu. Then, as they reached the top and emerged onto the broad, open space before the shrine, they saw the great bronze knobs that had once topped the railings of the bridge over the Otonashi River, casting strong shadows on the earth on either side of the graveled path that lay white and hushed beneath the afternoon sun.

The entrance had its bamboo blind, red and white with black tassels, rolled up to reveal the interior, but the Professor, giving it no more than a glance, made straight for the shrine office, whence a priest took him and Tsuneko into the inner garden.

There are times when things conspire to thwart: the priest here, who never left their side for a moment, was young and an admirer, it seemed, of the Professor's writings. He began talking about *Flowers and Birds* and showed no sign of stopping. The Professor listened civilly and answered suitably, but his inward impatience conveyed itself quite clearly to Tsuneko. He was eager to be rid of the priest, so that he could bury the third comb.

Noticing him becoming increasingly terse, his responses increasingly reluctant, she had a strong sense of how important the task in hand must be to him, and of how long he must have worked to ensure its success. For such a great scholar to be so obsessed with something seemingly so frivolous implied a correspondingly weighty reason. Reluctantly, the thought rose in her mind, romantic and wistful at the same time, of how beautiful the girl Kayoko must have been; and she found herself wanting to help the Professor achieve his dearest wish.

Thus Tsuneko made up her mind that it was time for her to interfere just once more on this journey. Catching the priest's eye, she drew him to one side.

"Perhaps I shouldn't mention it," she said, "but the Professor always says that he likes to pray quietly by himself when he visits a shrine garden. Although I'm supposed to be his companion on this trip, I think perhaps I'll excuse myself for a while. Don't you think that's best?"

No one could ignore such a broad hint: the priest followed Tsuneko out, and as they went she didn't fail to notice the quick look of gratitude that the Professor gave her from behind his mauve spectacles.

Outside, in the shade of the outer building's broad eaves, Tsuneko waited with a pounding heart. Never, she felt, had she looked forward to his return with more emotion. Almost unawares, she had come to hope and pray that the Professor's three combs would be laid successfully to rest, one in each of the three inner gardens of the Kumano shrines. One reason why she could await him now with such freedom from jealousy or grief—with such happiness, even—might have been that the other woman, however beautiful, was almost certainly no longer living, while her own wanderings through this deep green world of the dead had disposed her by now to forgive its inhabitants their trespasses.

Before long, the sight of the Professor emerging from a side gate in the distance, busily wiping his fingers with a cotton pad, informed her that things had gone successfully. In the sunlight, the floss at his fingertips shone pure white like the flowers of the sacred *sakaki* tree. . . .

It was as the Professor—having firmly refused the shrine office's offer to serve him tea—was sitting in a deserted tea shop to one side of the forecourt, sipping a glass of what was described as "Holy Kumano Water," that he told Tsuneko the history of the combs.

She listened with solemn attention, though the Professor himself related the story, not in the self-conscious, hesitating manner one would have expected with such a tale, but with the characteristic flat delivery that he adopted for his lectures on the romances of the Heian period.

It began with an account of why he had always shunned his home village. This was due, apparently, to its associations with the sad story of a certain woman.

Before coming up to college in Tokyo, the Professor had loved and been loved by a girl called Kayoko, but their parents had broken up the relationship. The Professor had gone away to study, and Kayoko had fallen ill and died only shortly afterward. It had been, he explained incidentally, an illness brought about by the sorrow of frustrated love.

So it was out of respect for Kayoko's memory that he had remained single all his life; and throughout everything he had borne in mind a vow he had made to the girl.

Kayoko had expressed a wish that they should go together on a pilgrimage to the three shrines of Kumano. But the idea of their going on a trip alone together was unthinkable, while marriage was impossible because of family opposition. So the young Professor had declared, disguising his true feelings with a joke:

"Right. I'll take you there when I'm sixty!"

And now he had reached sixty, and had come here to visit the shrines of Kumano, bearing the three combs that symbolized Kayoko. . . .

As the narrative drew to a close, Tsuneko was struck by its beauty. At last, she felt, the secrets of the Professor's solitary life and his deep sadness had been explained. Or rather, she felt this for a moment: for almost simultaneously she had a sense that the mystery surrounding the Professor had, in fact, only deepened, that the story was just *too* beautiful to carry real conviction. The strongest proof of this was that suddenly, as though an evil spirit had been exorcised, no trace of lingering jealousy or uneasiness remained. Nor was she surprised to find herself listening to his story in a completely normal frame of mind, absorbed in the narrative as such.

For the first time, the feminine intuition that she had never trusted before came into vigorous play, alerting her to an element of fantasy in the tale. Yes: from first to last, it should be taken as fiction. If so, then the commitment to this fantasy that the Professor had believed in until the age of sixty, and that had been fulfilled with the burial of the three combs, was something quite astonishing—in a way, a fragile and romantic metaphor of his whole life's work.

And yet—Tsuneko's sense of smell, suddenly sharpened by the last two days' journey, was sniffing out something further still—surely it wasn't even a fantasy? Wasn't the real truth that for some extraordinary reason the Professor, without the least faith in this ritual of burying the three combs, much less the fantasy as a whole, had sought to create, toward the close of his lonely life, a legend about himself?

As a legend, it might seem trite and sentimental; but if that was the kind of thing he liked, it couldn't be helped. With a start of conviction Tsuneko realized, inevitably, that she had hit the mark.

She had been chosen to be the witness.

If it weren't so, why should the tale he had told with such sorrow seem so ill-suited to him? Why should his walleye, his soprano voice, his dyed hair, his baggy trousers, everything about him, give the lie so strongly to the story? One rule that life had taught Tsuneko was that the only things that happened to a person were those that were appropriate to him; the rule had applied with great accuracy to herself, and there was no reason why it shouldn't also apply to the Professor.

At this point, she made a firm resolution on one thing: that from the moment of hearing the story until her dying day she would never betray, whether in front of the Pro-

fessor or other people, the least sign of not believing it.
That was the only logical outcome of the years of loyal
service she had given him. At the same time, there arose
in her an overwhelming sense of relief; it was as though
the despair she had felt the previous day as she looked
into the mirror had been cured, leaving no trace of a
shadow. From now on, the Professor and she would live
in her heart as they really were. Like the character in
Makiginu who was tied up as a punishment for his preoccupation with poetry, Tsuneko had been released from
her bonds by the spirit of Kumano.

"This young lady, Kayoko—," she said, breaking the
silence in case, too prolonged, it should seem odd, "she
must have been awfully pretty."

The cold holy water remaining in the glass he held was
clear and still, as though turned to transparent crystal.

"Yes, she was beautiful. More beautiful than any other
woman I've met in my life."

Through his mauve spectacles the Professor directed a
dreamy look at the midday sky; but nothing he said could
hurt Tsuneko any more.

"I'm sure she was—very beautiful. I can almost imagine what she was like from those three combs."

"Lovely as the day. A vision—you should try making
a poem out of it," said the Professor. And Tsuneko,
radiant, replied:

"Yes, I certainly will."

Translated by John Bester

Yūko Tsushima
(b. 1947)

Born in Tokyo, Satoko Tsushima is the daughter of a famous literary father, Shuji Tsushima, who under the name Osamu Dazai had published a considerable number of novels and stories during the 1930s and 1940s. Yūko was, however, only a year old when her father committed suicide. During her childhood she had a close relationship with her elder, mentally retarded brother who died in 1960. She began publishing stories in 1969 during her senior year of college, changing her name from Satoko to Yūko. Although she does not consider herself a "part of the feminist movement," Tsushima often depicts a spirited, unconventional heroine who is no longer restricted by traditional values. A recurring theme in her work is the failure of a woman's family to give her the nurturing and warmth that she needs. Her very contemporary plots, however, often contain numerous allusions to Japanese folklore and traditions. For example, in "The Silent Traders" (awarded the Yasunari Kgwabata Prize in 1983) references to the legendary nomadic mountain men enrich a story about a modern-day relationship. A prolific writer, she was awarded the Tamura Toshiko Prize in 1976, the Izumi Kyoka Prize in 1977, the Women's Literature Prize in 1978, the Noma Prize for New Writers in 1979, and the Yomiuri Literature Prize in 1986. Margaret Drabble has praised Tsushima as "a subtle, surprising, elegant writer who courageously tells unexpected truths about an unfamiliar, yet recognizable, world." Three of Tsushima's works that have been translated into English are *The Shooting Gallery* (Pantheon, 1988), a collection of short stories, *Child of Fortune* (Kodansha International, 1991), a novel about the crisis in the life of a teacher who seems indifferent to the love of her husband and daughter, and *Woman Running in the Mountains* (Pantheon, 1991), a novel about a contemporary, young, Japanese woman who is pregnant and unmarried.

THE SILENT TRADERS

There was a cat in the wood. Not such an odd thing, really: wildcats, pumas, and lions all come from the same family and even a tabby shouldn't be out of place. But the sight was unsettling. What was the creature doing there? When I say "wood," I'm talking about Rikugien, an Edo-period landscape garden in my neighborhood. Perhaps "wood" isn't quite the right word, but the old park's trees—relics of the past amid the city's modern buildings—are so overgrown that the pathways skirting its walls are dark and forbidding even by day. It does give the impression of a wood; there's no other word for it. And the cat, I should explain, didn't look wild. It was just a kitten, two or three months old, white with black patches. It didn't look at all ferocious—in fact it was a dear little thing. There was nothing to fear. And yet I was taken aback, and I tensed as the kitten bristled and glared in my direction.

The kitten was hiding in a thicket beside the pond, where my ten-year-old daughter was the first to spot it. By the time I'd made out the elusive shape and exclaimed "Oh, you're right!" she was off calling at the top of her voice: "There's another! And here's one over here!" My other child, a boy of five, was still hunting for the first kitten, and as his sister went on making one discovery after another he stamped his feet and wailed "Where? Where is it?" His sister beckoned him to bend down and showed him triumphantly where to find the first cat. Several passersby, hearing my daughter's shouts, had also been drawn into the search. There were many strollers in the park that Sunday evening. The cats were everywhere, each concealed in its own clump of bushes. Their eyes followed people's feet on the graveled walk, and at the slightest move toward a hiding place the cat would scamper away. Looking down from an adult's height it was hard enough to detect them at all, let alone keep count, and this gave the impression of great numbers.

I could hear my younger child crying. He had disappeared while my back was turned. As I looked wildly around, my daughter pointed him out with a chuckle: "See where he's got to!" There he was, huddled tearfully in the spot where the first kitten had been. He'd burst in eagerly, but succeeded only in driving away the kitten and trapping himself in the thicket.

"What do you think you're doing? It'll never let *you* catch it." Squatting down, my daughter was calling through the bushes. "Come on out, silly!"

His sister's tone of amusement was no help to the boy at all. He was terrified in his cobwebbed cage of low-hanging branches where no light penetrated.

"That's no use. You go in and fetch him out." I gave her shoulder a push.

"He got himself in," she grumbled, "so why can't he get out?" All the same, she set about searching for an opening. Crouching, I watched the boy through the thick foliage and waited for her to reach him.

"How'd he ever get in there? He's really stuck," she muttered as she circled the bushes uncertainly, but a moment later she'd broken through to him, forcing a way with both hands.

When they rejoined me, they had dead leaves and twigs snagged all over them.

After an attempt of her own to pick one up, my daughter understood that life in the park had made these tiny kittens quicker than ordinary strays and too wary to let anyone pet them. Explaining this to her brother, she looked to me for agreement. "They were born here, weren't they? They belong here, don't they? Then I wonder if their mother's here too?"

The children scanned the surrounding trees once again.

"She may be," I said, "but she'd stay out of sight,

wouldn't she? Only the kittens wander about in the open. Their mother's got more sense. I'll bet she's up that tree or some place like that where nobody can get at her. She's probably watching us right now."

I cast an eye at the treetops as I spoke—and the thought of the unseen mother cat gave me an uncomfortable feeling. Whether these were alley cats that had moved into the park or discarded pets that had survived and bred, they could go on multiplying in the wood—which at night was empty of people—and be perfectly at home.

It is exactly twenty-five years since my mother came to live near Rikugien with her three children, of which I was the youngest at ten. She told us the park's history, and not long after our arrival we went inside to see the garden. In spite of its being on our doorstep we quickly lost interest, however, since the grounds were surrounded by a six-foot brick wall with a single gate on the far side from our house. A Japanese garden was not much fun for children anyway, and we never went again as a family. I was reminded that we lived near a park, though, because of the many birds—the blue magpies, Eastern turtledoves, and tits—that I would see on the rooftops and in trees. And in summer I'd hear the singing of evening cicadas. To a city child like me, evening cicadas and blue magpies were a novelty.

I visited Rikugien with several classmates when we were about to leave elementary school, and someone hit on the idea of making a kind of time capsule. We'd leave it buried for ten years—or was it twenty? I've also forgotten what we wrote on the piece of paper that we stuffed into a small bottle and buried at the foot of a pine on the highest ground in the garden. I expect it's still there as I haven't heard of it since, and now whenever I'm in Rikugien I keep an eye out for the landmark, but I'm only guessing. We were confident of knowing exactly where to look in years to come, and if I can remember that so clearly it's puzzling that I can't recognize the tree. I'm not about to dig any holes to check, however—not with my own children watching. The friends who left this sentimental reminder were soon to part, bound for different schools. Since then, of course, we've ceased to think of one another, and I'm not so sure now that the bottle episode ever happened.

The following February my brother (who was close to my own age) died quite suddenly of pneumonia. Then in April my sister went to college and, not wanting to be left out, I pursued her new interests myself: I listened to jazz, went to movies, and was friendly toward college and high school students of the opposite sex. An older girl introduced me to a boy from senior high and we made up a foursome for an outing to the park—the only time I got all dressed up for Rikugien. I was no beauty, though, nor the popular type, and while the others were having fun I stayed stiff and awkward, and was bored. I would have liked to be as genuinely impressed as they were, viewing the landscape garden for the first time, but I couldn't work up an interest after seeing the trees over the brick wall every day. By that time we'd been in the district for three years, and the name "Rikugien" brought to mind not the tidy, sunlit lawns seen by visitors, but the dark tangles along the walls.

My desire for friends of the opposite sex was short-lived. Boys couldn't provide what I wanted, and what boys wanted had nothing to do with me.

While I was in high school, one day our ancient spitz died. The house remained without a dog for a while, until Mother was finally prompted to replace him when my sister's marriage, soon after her graduation, left just the two of us in an unprotected home. She found someone who let her have a terrier puppy. She bought a brush and comb and began rearing the pup with the best of care, explaining that it came from a clever hunting breed. As it grew, however, it failed to display the expected intelligence and still behaved like a puppy after six months; and besides, it was timid. What it did have was energy as, yapping shrilly, it frisked about the house all day long. It may have been useless but it was a funny little fellow. Its presence made all the difference to me in my intense boredom at home. After my brother's death, my mother (a widow since I was a baby) passed her days as if at a wake. We saw each other only at mealtimes, and then we seldom spoke. In high school a

fondness for the movies was about the worst I could have
been accused of, but Mother had no patience with such
frivolity and would snap angrily at me from time to time.
"I'm leaving home when I turn eighteen," I'd retort. I
meant it, too.

It was at that time that we had the very sociable dog.
I suppose I'd spoiled it as a puppy, for now it was always
wanting to be let in, and when I slid open the glass door
it would bounce like a rubber ball right into my arms
and lick my face and hands ecstatically.

Mother, however, was dissatisfied. She'd had enough
of the barking; it got on her nerves. Then came a day
when the dog went missing. I thought it must have got
out of the yard. Two or three days passed and it didn't
return—it hadn't the wit to find the way home once it
strayed. I wondered if I should contact the pound. Concern finally drove me to break our usual silence and ask
Mother: "About the dog . . ." "Oh, the dog?" she replied. "I threw it over the wall of Rikugien the other
day."

I was shocked—I'd never heard of disposing of a dog
like that. I wasn't able to protest, though. I didn't rush
out to comb the park, either. She could have had it destroyed, yet instead she'd taken it to the foot of the brick
wall, lifted it in her arms, and heaved it over. It wasn't
large, only about a foot long, and thus not too much of
a handful even for Mother.

Finding itself tossed into the wood, the dog wouldn't
have crept quietly into hiding. It must have raced through
the area barking furiously, only to be caught at once by
the caretaker. Would the next stop be the pound? But
there seemed to me just a chance that it hadn't turned
out that way. I could imagine the wood by daylight, more
or less: there'd be a lot of birds and insects, and little
else. The pond would be inhabited by a few carp, turtles,
and catfish. But what transformations took place at
night? As I didn't dare stay beyond closing time to see
for myself, I wondered if anyone could tell of a night
spent in the park till the gates opened in the morning.
There might be goings-on unimaginable by day. Mightn't
a dog entering that world live on, not as a tiny terrier,
but as something else?

I had to be thankful that the dog's fate left that much to the imagination.

From then on I turned my back on Rikugien more firmly than ever. I was afraid of the deep wood, so out of keeping with the city: it was the domain of the dog abandoned by my mother.

In due course I left home, a little later than I'd promised. After a good many more years I moved back to Mother's neighborhood—back to the vicinity of the park—with a little daughter and a baby. Like my own mother, I was one who couldn't give my children the experience of a father. That remained the one thing I regretted.

Living in a cramped apartment, I now appreciated the Rikugien wood for its greenery and open spaces. I began to take the children there occasionally. Several times, too, we released pet turtles or goldfish in the pond. Many nearby families who'd run out of room for aquarium creatures in their overcrowded apartments would slip them into the pond to spend the rest of their lives at liberty.

Rocks rose from the water here and there, and each was studded with turtles sunning themselves. They couldn't have bred naturally in such numbers. They must have been the tiny turtles sold at fairground stalls and pet shops, grown up without a care in the world. More of them lined the water's edge at one's feet. No doubt there were other animals on the increase—goldfish, loaches, and the like. Multistoried apartment buildings were going up around the wood in quick succession, and more living things were brought down from their rooms each year. Cats were one animal I'd overlooked, though. If tipping out turtles was common practice, there was no reason why cats shouldn't be dumped here, and dogs too. No type of pet could be ruled out. But to become established in any numbers they'd have to escape the caretaker's notice and hold their own against the wood's other hardy inhabitants. Thus there'd be a limit to survivors: cats and reptiles, I'd say.

Once I knew about the cat population, I remembered the dog my mother had thrown away, and I also remembered my old fear of the wood. I couldn't help wondering how the cats got along from day to day.

Perhaps they relied on food left behind by visitors—but all of the park's trash baskets were fitted with mesh covers to keep out the crows, whose numbers were also growing. For all their nimbleness, even cats would have trouble picking out the scraps. Lizards and mice were edible enough. But on the other side of the wall lay the city and its garbage. After dark, the cats would go out foraging on the streets.

Then, too, there was the row of apartment towers along one side of the wood, facing the main road. All had balconies that overlooked the park. The climb would be quick work for a cat, and if its favorite food were left outside a door it would soon come back regularly. Something told me there must be people who put out food: there'd be elderly tenants and women living alone. Even children. Children captivated by a secret friendship with a cat.

I don't find anything odd about such a relationship—perhaps because it occurs so often in fairy stories. But to make it worth their while the apartment children would have to receive something from the cat; otherwise they wouldn't keep it up. There are tales of mountain men and villagers who traded a year's haul of linden bark for a gallon and a half of rice in hard cakes. No villager could deal openly with the lone mountain men; so great was their fear of each other, in fact, that they avoided coming face to face. Yet when a bargain was struck, it could not have been done more skillfully. The trading was over in a flash, before either man had time to catch sight of the other or hear his voice. I think everyone wishes privately that bargains could be made like that. Though there would always be the fear of attack, or discovery by one's own side.

Supposing it were my own children: what could they be getting in return? They'd have no use for a year's stock of linden bark. Toys, then, or cakes. I'm sure they want all sorts of things, but not a means of support like linden bark. What, then? Something not readily available to them; something the cat has in abundance and to spare.

The children leave food on the balcony. And in return the cat provides them with a father. How's that for a bargain? Once a year, male cats procreate; in other words, they become fathers. They become fathers ad nauseam. But these fathers don't care how many children they have—they don't even notice that they are fathers. Yet the existence of offspring makes them so. Fathers who don't know their own children. Among humans, it seems there's an understanding that a man only becomes a father when he recognizes the child as his own; but that's a very narrow view. Why do we allow the male to divide children arbitrarily into two kinds, recognized and unrecognized? Wouldn't it be enough for the child to choose a father when necessary from among suitable males? If the children decide that the tom that climbs up to their balcony is their father, it shouldn't cause him any inconvenience. A father looks in on two of his children from the balcony every night. The two human children faithfully leave out food to make it so. He comes late, when they are fast asleep, and they never see him or hear his cries. It's enough that they know in the morning that he's been. In their dreams, the children are hugged to their cat-father's breast.

We'd seen the children's human father six months earlier, and together we'd gone to a transport museum they wanted to visit. This came about only after many appeals from me. If the man who was their father was alive and well on this earth, I wanted the children to know what he looked like. To me, the man was unforgettable: I was once preoccupied with him, obsessed with the desire to be where he was; nothing had changed when I tried having a child, and I'd had the second with him cursing me. To the children, however, especially the younger one, he was a mere shadow in a photograph that never moved or spoke. As the younger child turned three, then four, I couldn't help being aware of that fact. This was the same state that I'd known myself, for my own father had died. If he were dead it couldn't be helped. But as long as he was alive I wanted them to have a memory of their father as a living, breathing person whose eyes moved, whose mouth moved and spoke.

On the day, he was an hour late for our appointment.
The long wait in a coffee shop had made the children
tired and cross, but when they saw the man a shy silence
came over them. "Thanks for coming," I said with a
smile. I couldn't think what to say next. He asked
"Where to?" and stood to leave at once. He walked
alone, while the children and I looked as though it was
all the same to us whether he was there or not. On the
train I still hadn't come up with anything to say. The
children kept their distance from the man and stared nonchalantly out of the window. We got off the train like
that, and again he walked ahead.

The transport museum had an actual bullet train car,
steam locomotives, airplanes, and giant panoramic lay-
outs. I remembered enjoying a class trip there while at
school myself. My children, too, dashed excitedly around
the exhibits without a moment's pause for breath. It was
"Next I want to have a go on that train," "Now I want
to work that model." They must have had a good two
hours of fun. In the meantime we lost sight of the man.
Wherever he'd been, he showed up again when we'd finished our tour and arrived back at the entrance. "What'll
we do?" he asked, and I suggested giving the children a
drink and sitting down somewhere. He nodded and went
ahead to look for a place near the museum. The children
were clinging to me as before. He entered a coffee shop
that had a cake counter and I followed with them. We
sat down, the three of us facing the man. Neither child
showed the slightest inclination to sit beside him. They
had orange drinks.

I was becoming desperate for something to say. And
weren't there one or two things he'd like to ask me?
Such as how the children had been lately. But to bring
that up, unasked, might imply that I wanted him to watch
with me as they grew. I'd only been able to ask for this
meeting because I'd finally stopped feeling that way.
Now it seemed we couldn't even exchange such polite
remarks as "They've grown" or "I'm glad they're well"
without arousing needless suspicions. It wasn't supposed
to be like this, I thought in confusion, unable to say a
word about the children. He was indeed their father, but
not a father who watched over them. As far as he was

concerned the only children he had were the two borne by his wife. Agreeing to see mine was simply a favor on his part, for which I could only be grateful.

If we couldn't discuss the children, there was literally nothing left to say. We didn't have the kind of memories we could reminisce over; I wished I could forget the things we'd done as if it had all been a dream, for it was the pain that we remembered. Inquiring after his family would be no better. His work seemed the safest subject, yet if I didn't want to stay in touch I had to think twice about this, too.

The man and I listened absently as the children entertained themselves.

On the way out the man bought a cake which he handed to the older child, and then he was gone. The children appeared relieved, and with the cake to look forward to they were eager to get home. Neither had held the man's hand or spoken to him. I wanted to tell them that there was still time to run after him and touch some part of his body, but of course they wouldn't have done it.

I don't know when there will be another opportunity for the children to see the man. They may never meet him again, or they may have a chance two or three years from now. I do know that the man and I will probably never be completely indifferent to each other. He's still on my mind in some obscure way. Yet there's no point in confirming this feeling in words. Silence is essential. As long as we maintain silence, and thus avoid trespassing, we leave open the possibility of resuming negotiations at any time.

I believe the system of bartering used by the mountain men and the villagers was called "silent trade." I am coming to understand that there was nothing extraordinary in striking such a silent bargain for survival. People trying to survive—myself, my mother, and my children, for example—can take some comfort in living beside a wood. We tip various things in there and tell ourselves that we haven't thrown them away, we've set them free in another world, and then we picture the unknown woodland to ourselves and shudder with fear or sigh fondly. Meanwhile the creatures multiplying there gaze

stealthily at the human world outside; at least I've yet to
hear of anything attacking from the wood.

Some sort of silent trade is taking place between the
two sides. Perhaps my children really have begun dealings with a cat who lives in the wood.

Translated by Geraldine Harcourt

SELECTED JAPANESE ANTHOLOGIES

Birnbaum, Phyllis, trans. and ed. *Rabbits, Crabs, Etc.: Stories by Japanese Women*. Honolulu: University of Hawaii Press, 1983.

Dunlop, Lane, trans. and ed. *A Late Chrysanthemum: Twenty-one Stories from the Japanese*. San Francisco: North Point Press, 1986.

Gessel, Van C. and Tomone Matsumoto, eds. *The Showa Anthology: Modern Japanese Short Stories*. Vol. 1 (1929–1961) and vol. 2 (1961–1984). Tokyo and New York: Kodansha International Ltd./Harper & Row, 1985.

Hibbett, Howard, ed. *Contemporary Japanese Literature*. Tokyo and Rutland, VT: Charles E. Tuttle Co., 1978.

Keene, Donald, ed. *Modern Japanese Literature From 1868 to the Present Day*. New York: Grove Press, 1956.

Lippit, Noriko and Kyoko Selden, eds. *Stories by Contemporary Japanese Women Writers*. Armonk, NY and London: M. E. Sharpe, 1983.

Lippit, Norika Mizuta and Kyoko Iriye Seldon, trans. and eds. *Japanese Women Writers*. Armonk, NY: M. E. Sharpe, 1991.

Mitsios, Helen, ed. *New Japanese Voices: The Best Contemporary Fiction from Japan*: New York: Atlantic Monthly Press, 1991.

Morris, Ivan. *Modern Japanese Stories*. Tokyo and Rutland, VT: Charles E. Tuttle Co., 1962.

Oe, Kenzaburo, ed. *The Crazy Iris and Other Stories of the Atomic Aftermath*. New York: Grove Press, 1985.

Tanaka, Yuriko, ed. *To Live and To Write: Selections by Japanese Women Writers 1913–1938*. Seattle: The Seal Press, 1987.

Tanaka, Yuriko and Elizabeth Hanson, eds. *This Kind of Woman: Ten Stories by Japanese Women Writers, 1960–1976*. Stanford: Stanford University Press, 1982.

Ueda, Makoto, ed. *The Mother of Dreams and Other Short Stories*. Tokyo and New York: Kodansha International Ltd./Harper & Row, 1986.

LATIN
AMERICAN
STORIES

Isabel Allende
(b. 1942)

Born in Lima, Peru, Isabel Allende lived in Bolivia, Europe, and the Middle East with her mother and diplomat stepfather during her adolescence. She is the niece of Chile's assassinated President Salvador Allende. After August Pinochet's right-wing coup and the murder of her uncle in 1973, Allende, her husband, and children fled from Chile to exile in Caracas, Venezuela. A television journalist, dramatist, columnist for the Venezuelan newspaper *El Nacional*, and author of stories for children, the Chilean writer has described the circumstances that inspired her first novel, *La casa de los espiritus* (1982), translated as *The House of the Spirits* (Knopf, 1985). In 1981, her maternal grandfather, who was almost one hundred years of age and had remained in Chile, discussed his impending death with her on the telephone. Allende recalls her reaction: "I wanted to tell my grandfather that I was never going to forget him, he would never die, just as my grandmother had never died. . . . And I started writing a letter, telling him the same things he had told me when I was a child." She never mailed that letter. Instead, it was transmuted into a work of art. Allende continues:

> That's why at the beginning of the book Alba (the granddaughter of Clara and Esteban) writes to keep alive the memory of her past and to survive her own terror. That's how I felt. I wanted to survive the terrible experience of exile, and I wanted to keep alive the memory of the past—the house that I lost, the people that are dead, those that disappeared, the friends that were scattered all around the world.

A *New York Times* reviewer who characterized the resulting novel as "spectacular" commented that "*The House of the Spirits* with its all-informing genius, and humane sensibility, is a unique achievement, both personal witness and possible allegory of the past, present, and future of Latin America." Her second novel, *Of Love and Shadows* (Knopf, 1987), depicts the lives of two lovers who live in a corrupt and scandal-ridden dictatorship. *Eva Luna* (Knopf, 1988), her third novel, was followed by a collection of short fiction framed by a narrative device. These stories in *The Stories of Eva Luna* (Macmillan, 1991) are purported to be the tales told by Allende's character, Eva, in response to the request: " 'Tell me a story you have never told anyone before. Make it up for me.' " Her most recent novels include *The Infinite Plan* (HarperCollins, 1993), *Aphrodite: A Memoir of the Senses* (HarperFlamingo, 1998), and *Daughter of Fortune* (HarperCollins, 1999).

CLARISA

Clarisa was born before the city had electricity, she lived to see the television coverage of the first astronaut levitating on the moon, and she died of amazement when the Pope came for a visit and was met in the street by homosexuals dressed up as nuns. She had spent her childhood among pots of ferns and corridors lighted by oil lamps. Days went by slowly in those times. Clarisa never adjusted to the fits and starts of today's time; she always seemed to have been captured in the sepia tints of a nineteenth-century portrait. I suppose that once she had had a virginal waist, a graceful bearing, and a profile worthy of a medallion, but by the time I met her she was already a rather bizarre old woman with shoulders rounded into two gentle humps and with white hair coiled around a sebaceous cyst the size of a pigeon egg crowning her noble head. She had a profound, shrewd gaze that could penetrate the most hidden evil and return unscathed. Over the course of a long lifetime she had come to be considered a saint, and after she died many people placed her photograph on the family altar along with other venerable images to ask her aid in minor difficulties, even though her reputation for being a miracle worker is not recognized by the Vatican and undoubtedly never will be. Her miraculous works are unpredictable: she does not heal the blind, like Santa Lucia, or find husbands for spinsters, like St. Anthony, but they say she helps a person through a hangover, or problems with the draft, or a siege of loneliness. Her wonders are humble and improbable, but as necessary as the spectacular marvels worked by cathedral saints.

I met Clarisa when I was an adolescent working as a servant in the house of La Señora, a lady of the night, as Clarisa called women of her occupation. Even then she was distilled almost to pure spirit; I thought at any minute she might rise from the floor and fly out the window. She had the hands of a healer, and people who could not pay a doctor, or were disillusioned with traditional science, waited in line for her to relieve their pain or console them in their bad fortune. My *patrona* used to call her to come lay her hands on her back. In the process, Clarisa would rummage about in La Señora's soul with the hope of turning her life around and leading her along the paths of righteousness—paths my employer was in no hurry to travel, since that direction would have unalterably affected her commercial enterprise. Clarisa would apply the curative warmth of the palms of her hands for ten or fifteen minutes, depending on the intensity of the pain, and then accept a glass of fruit juice as payment for her services. Sitting face to face in the kitchen, the two women would have their chat about human and divine topics, my *patrona* more on the human side and Clarisa more on the divine, never straining tolerance nor abusing good manners. Later, when I found a different job, I lost sight of Clarisa until we met once again some twenty years later and reestablished a friendship that has lasted to this day, overcoming the many obstacles that lay in our way, including death, which has put a slight crimp in the ease of our communications.

Even in the times when age had slowed her former

missionary zeal, Clarisa persevered steadfastly in her good works, sometimes even against the will of the beneficiaries—as in the case of the pimps on Calle República, who had to bear the mortification of the public harangues that good lady delivered in her unwavering determination to redeem them. Clarisa gave everything she owed to the needy. As a rule she had only the clothes on her back, and toward the end of her life it was difficult to find a person any poorer than she. Charity had become a two-way street, and you seldom could tell who was giving and who receiving.

She lived in an old rundown three-story house; some rooms were empty but some she rented as a storehouse for a saloon, so that the rancid stench of cheap liquor always hung in the air. She had never moved from the dwelling she had inherited from her parents because it reminded her of an aristocratic past, and also because for more than forty years her husband had buried himself alive in a room at the back of the patio. He had been a judge in a remote province, an office he had carried out with dignity until the birth of his second child, when disillusion robbed him of the will to accept his fate, and like a mole he had taken refuge in the malodorous cave of his room. He emerged only rarely, a scurrying shadow, and opened the door only to hand out his chamber pot and to collect the food his wife left for him every day. He communicated with her by means of notes written in his perfect calligraphy and by knocks on the door—two for yes and three for no. Through the walls of his room you could hear asthmatic hacking and an occasional longshoreman's curse intended for whom, no one never knew.

"Poor man, I pray that God will soon call him to His side, and he will take his place in the heavenly choir," Clarisa would sigh without a suspicion of irony. The opportune passing of her husband, however, was one grace Divine Providence never granted, for he has survived to the present day. He must be a hundred by now, unless he has already died and the coughs and curses we hear are only echoes from the past.

Clarisa married him because he was the first person to ask her, and also because her parents thought that a judge would be the best possible match. She left the sober comfort of her paternal hearth and reconciled herself to the avarice and vulgarity of her husband with no thought of a better fate. The only time she was ever heard to utter a nostalgic comment about the refinements of her past was in regard to a grand piano that had enchanted her as a girl. That is how we learned of her love for music and much later, when she was an old woman, a group of us who were her friends gave her a modest piano. It had been over sixty years since she had been anywhere near a keyboard, but she sat down on the piano stool and played, by memory and without hesitation, a Chopin nocturne.

A year or so after her marriage to the judge, she gave birth to an albino daughter, who as soon as she began to walk accompanied her mother to church. The tiny creature was so dazzled by the pageantry of the liturgy that she began pulling down drapes to "play bishop," and soon the only game that interested her was imitating the ecclesiastical ritual, chanting in a Latin of her own invention. She was hopelessly retarded; her only words were spoken in an unknown tongue, she drooled incessantly, and she suffered uncontrollable attacks during which she had to be tied like a circus animal to prevent her from chewing the furniture and attacking guests. With puberty, however, she grew more tractable, and helped her mother around the house. The second child was born into the world totally devoid of curiosity and bearing gentle Asian features; the only skill he ever mastered was riding a bicycle, but it was of little benefit to him since his mother never dared let him out of the house. He spent his life pedaling in the patio on a stationary bicycle mounted on a music stand.

Her children's abnormality never affected Clarisa's unalterable optimism. She considered them pure souls immune to evil, and all her relations with them were marked by affection. Her greatest concern was to save them from earthly suffering, and she often asked herself who would look after them when she was gone. The father, in contrast, never spoke of them, and used the pretext of his retarded children to wallow in shame, abandon his career, his friends, even fresh air, and entomb himself in his room, copying newspapers with monklike patience in a series of stenographic notebooks. Meanwhile, his wife spent the last cent of her dowry, and her inheritance, and took on all kinds of jobs to support the family. In her own poverty, she never turned her back to the poverty of others, and even in the most difficult periods of her life she continued her works of mercy.

Clarisa had a boundless understanding of human weaknesses. One night when she was sitting in her room sewing, her white head bent over her work, she heard unusual noises in the house. She got up to see what they might be, but got no farther than the doorway, where she ran into a man who held a knife to her throat and threatened, "Quiet, you whore, or I'll slash your throat."

"This isn't the place you want, son. The ladies of the night are across the street, there where you hear the music."

"Don't try to be funny, this is a robbery."

"What did you say?" Clarisa smiled, incredulous. "And what are you going to steal from me?"

"Sit down in that chair. I'm going to tie you up."

"I won't do it, son. I'm old enough to be your mother. Where's your respect?"

"Sit *down*, I said!"

"And don't shout, you'll frighten my husband, and he's not at all well. By the way, put that knife down, you might hurt someone," said Clarisa.

"Listen, lady, I came here to rob you," the flustered robber muttered.

"Well, there's not going to be any robbery. I will not let you commit a sin. I'll *give* you some money of my own will. You won't be taking it from me, is that clear? I'm giving it to you." She went to her purse and took out all the money for the rest of the week. "That's all I have. We're quite poor, as you see. Come into the kitchen, now, and I'll set the kettle to boil."

The man put away his knife and followed her, money in hand. Clarisa brewed tea for both of them, served the last cookies in the house, and invited him to sit with her in the living room.

"Wherever did you get the notion to rob a poor old woman like me?"

The thief told her he had been watching her for days; he knew that she lived alone and thought there must be something of value in that big old house. It was his first crime, he said; he had four children, he was out of a job, and he could not go home another night with empty hands. Clarisa pointed out that he was taking too great a risk, that he might not only be arrested but was putting his immortal soul in danger—although in truth she doubted that God would punish him with hell, the worst might be a while in purgatory, as long, of course, as he repented and did not do it again. She offered to add him to her list of wards and promised she would not bring charges against him. As they said goodbye, they kissed each other on the cheek. For the next ten years, until Clarisa died, she received a small gift at Christmastime through the mail.

Not all Clarisa's dealings were with the indigent; she also knew people of note, women of breeding, wealthy businessmen, bankers, and public figures, whom she visited seeking aid for the needy, with never a thought for how she might be received. One day she presented herself in the office of Congressman Diego Cienfuegos, known for his incendiary speeches and for being one of the few incorruptible politicians in the nation, which did not prevent his rising to the rank of Minister and earning a place in history books as the intellectual father of an important peace treaty. In those days Clarisa was still young, and rather timid, but she already had the unflagging determination that characterized her old age. She went to the Congressman to ask him to use his influence to procure a new modern refrigerator for the Teresian Sisters. The man stared at her in amazement, questioning why he should aid his ideological enemies.

"Because in their dining room the Little Sisters feed a hundred children a day a free meal, and almost all of them are children of the Communists and evangelicals who vote for you," Clarisa replied mildly.

That was the beginning of a discreet friendship that was to cost the politician many sleepless nights and many donations. With the same irrefutable logic, Clarisa obtained scholarships for young atheists from the Jesuits, used clothing for neighborhood prostitutes from the

League of Catholic Dames, musical instruments for a Hebrew choir from the German Institute, and funds for alcohol rehabilitation programs from viniculturists.

Neither the husband interred in the mausoleum of his room nor the debilitating hours of her daily labors prevented Clarisa's becoming pregnant again. The midwife advised her that in all probability she would give birth to another abnormal child, but Clarisa mollified her with the argument that God maintains a certain equilibrium in the universe, and just as He creates some things twisted, He creates others straight; for every virtue there is a sin, for every joy an affliction, for every evil a good, and on and on, for as the wheel of life turns through the centuries, everything evens out. The pendulum swings back and forth with inexorable precision, she said.

Clarisa passed her pregnancy in leisure, and in the proper time gave birth to her third child. The baby was born at home with the help of the midwife and in the agreeable company of the two inoffensive and smiling retarded children who passed the hours at their games, one spouting gibberish in her bishop's robe and the other pedaling nowhere on his stationary bicycle. With this birth the scales tipped in the direction needed to preserve the harmony of Creation, and a grateful mother offered her breast to a strong boy with wise eyes and firm hands. Fourteen months later Clarisa gave birth to a second son with the same characteristics.

"These two boys will grow up healthy and help me take care of their brother and sister," she said with conviction, faithful to her theory of compensation; and that is how it was, the younger children grew straight as reeds and were gifted with kindness and goodness.

Somehow Clarisa managed to support the four children without any help from her husband and without injuring her family pride by accepting charity for herself. Few were aware of her financial straits. With the same tenacity with which she spent late nights sewing rag dolls and baking wedding cakes to sell, she battled the deterioration of her house when the walls began to sweat a greenish mist. She instilled in the two younger children her principles of good humor and generosity with such splendid results that in the following years they were always beside her caring for their older siblings, until the day the retarded brother and sister accidentally locked themselves in the bathroom and a leaking gas pipe transported them gently to a better world.

When the Pope made his visit, Clarisa was not quite eighty, although it was difficult to calculate her exact age; she had added years out of vanity, simply to hear people say how well preserved she was for the ninety-five years she claimed. She had more than enough spirit, but her body was failing; she could barely totter through the streets, where in any case she lost her way, she had no appetite, and finally was eating only flowers and honey. Her spirit was detaching itself from her body at the same pace her wings germinated, but the preparations for the papal visit rekindled her enthusiasm for the adventures of this earth. She was not content to watch the spectacle on television because she had a deep distrust of that apparatus. She was convinced that even the astronaut on the moon was a sham filmed in some Hollywood studio, the same kind of lies they practiced in those stories where the protagonists love or die and then a week later reappear with the same faces but a new destiny. Clarisa wanted to see the pontiff with her own eyes, not on a screen where some actor was consumed in the Pope's robes. That was how I found myself accompanying her to cheer the Pope as he rode through the streets. After a couple of hours fighting the throngs of faithful and vendors of candles and T-shirts and religious prints and plastic saints, we caught sight of the Holy Father, magnificent in his portable glass cage, a white porpoise in an aquarium. Clarisa fell to her knees, in danger of being crushed by fanatics and the Pope's police escort. Just at the instant when the Pope was but a stone's throw away, a rare spectacle surged from a side street: a group of men in nun's habits, their faces garishly painted, waving posters in favor of abortion, divorce, sodomy, and the right of women to the priesthood. Clarisa dug through her purse with a trembling hand, found her eyeglasses, and set them on her nose to assure herself she was not suffering a hallucination.

She paled. "It's time to go, daughter. I've already seen too much."

She was so undone that to distract her I offered to buy her a hair from the Pope's head, but she did not want it without a guarantee of authenticity. According to a socialist newspaperman, there were enough capillary relics offered for sale to stuff a couple of pillows.

"I'm an old woman, and I no longer understand the world, daughter. We'd best go home."

She was exhausted when she reached the house, with the din of the bells and cheering still ringing in her temples. I went to the kitchen to prepare some soup for the judge and heat water to brew her a cup of camomile tea, in hopes it would have a calming effect. As I waited for the tea, Clarisa, with a melancholy face, put everything in order and served her last plate of food to her husband. She set the tray on the floor and for the first time in more than forty years knocked on his door.

"How many times have I told you not to bother me," the judge protested in a reedy voice.

"I'm sorry, dear, I just wanted to tell you that I'm going to die."

"When?"

"On Friday."

"Very well." The door did not open.

Clarisa called her sons to tell them about her imminent death, and then took to her bed. Her bedroom was a large dark room with pieces of heavy carved mahogany furniture that would never become antiques because somewhere along the way they had broken down. On her dresser sat a crystal urn containing an astoundingly realistic wax Baby Jesus, rosy as an infant fresh from its bath.

"I'd like for you to have the Baby, Eva. I know you'll take care of Him."

"You're not going to die. Don't frighten me this way."

"You need to keep Him in the shade, if the sun strikes Him, He'll melt. He's lasted almost a century, and will last another if you protect Him from the heat."

I combed her meringue hair high on her head, tied it with a ribbon, and then sat down to accompany her through this crisis, not knowing exactly what it was. The moment was totally free of sentimentality, as if in fact she was not dying but suffering from a slight cold.

"We should call a priest now, don't you think, child?"

"But Clarisa, what sins can you have?"

"Life is long, and there's more than enough time for evil, God willing."

"But you'll go straight to heaven—that is, if heaven exists."

"Of course it exists, but it's not certain they'll let me in. They're very strict there," she murmured. And after a long pause, she added, "When I think over my trespasses, there was one that was very grave . . ."

I shivered, terrified that this old woman with the aureole of a saint was going to tell me that she had intentionally dispatched her retarded children to facilitate divine justice, or that she did not believe in God and had devoted herself to doing good in this world only because the scales had assigned her the role of compensating for the evil of others, an evil that was unimportant anyway since everything is part of the same infinite process. But Clarisa confessed nothing so dramatic to me. She turned toward the window and told me, blushing, that she had not fulfilled her conjugal duties.

"What does that mean?" I asked.

"Well, I mean I did not satisfy my husband's carnal desires, you understand?"

"No."

"If you refuse your husband your body, and he falls into the temptation of seeking solace with another woman, you bear that moral responsibility."

"I see. The judge fornicates, and the sin is yours."

"No, no. I think it would be both our sins. . . . I would have to look it up."

"And the husband has the same obligation to his wife?"

"What?"

"I mean, if you had had another man, would your husband share the blame?"

"Wherever did you get an idea like that, child!" She stared at me in disbelief.

"Don't worry, because if your worst sin was that you slighted the judge, I'm sure God will see the joke."

"I don't think God is very amused by such things."

"But Clarisa, to doubt divine perfection *would* be a great sin."

She seemed in such good health that I could not imagine her dying, but I supposed that, unlike us simple mortals, saints have the power to die unafraid and in full control of their faculties. Her reputation was so solid that many claimed to have seen a circle of light around her head and to have heard celestial music in her presence, and so I was not surprised when I undressed her to put on her nightgown to find two inflamed bumps on her shoulders, as if her pair of great angel wings were about to erupt.

The rumor of Clarisa's coming death spread rapidly. Her children and I had to marshal an unending line of people who came to seek her intervention in heaven for various favors, or simply to say goodbye. Many expected that at the last moment a significant miracle would occur, such as, the odor of rancid bottles that pervaded the house would be transformed into the perfume of camelias, or beams of consolation would shine forth from her body. Among the visitors was her friend the robber, who had not mended his ways but instead become a true professional. He sat beside the dying woman's bed and recounted his escapades without a hint of repentance.

"Things are going really well. I rob only upper-class homes now. I steal from the rich, and that's no sin. I've never had to use violence, and I work clean, like a true gentleman," he boasted.

"I will have to pray a long time for you, my son."

"Pray on, Grandmother. It won't do me any harm."

La Señora came, too, distressed to be saying goodbye to her beloved friend, and bringing a flower crown and almond-paste sweets as her contribution to the death vigil. My former patrona did not know me, but I had no trouble recognizing her despite her girth, her wig, and the outrageous plastic shoes printed with gold stars. To offset the thief, she came to tell Clarisa that her advice had fallen upon fertile ground, and that she was now a respectable Christian.

"Tell Saint Peter that, so he'll take my name from his black book" was her plea.

"What a terrible disappointment for all these good

people if instead of going to heaven I end up in the cauldrons of hell," Clarisa said after I was finally able to close the door and let her rest for a while.

"If that happens, no one down here is going to know, Clarisa."

"Thank heavens for that!"

From early dawn on Friday a crowd gathered outside in the street, and only her two sons' vigilance prevented the faithful from carrying off relics, from strips of paper off the walls to articles of the saint's meager wardrobe. Clarisa was failing before our eyes and, for the first time, she showed signs of taking her own death seriously. About ten that morning, a blue automobile with Congressional plates stopped before the house. The chauffeur helped an old man climb from the back seat; the crowds recognized him immediately. It was *don* Diego Cienfuegos, whom decades of public service had made a national hero. Clarisa's sons came out to greet him, and accompanied him in his laborious ascent to the second floor. When Clarisa saw him in the doorway, she became quite animated; the color returned to her cheeks and the shine to her eyes.

"Please, clear everyone out of the room and leave us alone," she whispered in my ear.

Twenty minutes later the door opened and *don* Diego Cienfuegos departed, feet dragging, eyes teary, bowed and crippled, but smiling. Clarisa's sons, who were waiting in the hall, again took his arms to steady him, and seeing them there together I confirmed something that had crossed my mind before. The three men had the same bearing, the same profile, the same deliberate assurance, the same wise eyes and firm hands.

I waited until they were downstairs, and went back to my friend's room. As I arranged her pillows, I saw that she, like her visitor, was weeping with a certain rejoicing.

"*Don* Diego was your grave sin, wasn't he?" I murmured.

"That wasn't a sin, child, just a little boost to help God balance the scales of destiny. You see how well it worked out, because my two weak children had two strong brothers to look after them."

Clarisa died that night, without suffering. Cancer, the doctor diagnosed, when he saw the buds of her wings;

saintless, proclaimed the throngs bearing candles and flowers; astonishment, say I, because I was with her when the Pope came to visit.

Translated by Margaret Sayers Peden

Jorge Luis Borges
(1899–1986)

Among the most influential twentieth-century writers, Jorge Luis Borges was born in Buenos Aires, Argentina, into a household in which both English and Spanish were spoken. As a frail child he was a voracious reader, spending considerable time in his father's extensive library. Stranded in Switzerland in 1914 at the outbreak of World War I, Borges studied at the Collège de Genève where he received his degree in 1918. For almost a decade he was a municipal librarian in Buenos Aires, and subsequently became the director of the National Library of Argentina. A professor of English literature at the University of Buenos Aires beginning in 1956, he was relatively unknown as a poet, novelist, and story writer until 1961 when, together with the Irish playwright Samuel Beckett, he won the International Publishers Prize (Prix Formentor). At the age of sixty-two, with the simultaneous publication in six countries of his collection of short stories *Ficciones: 1935–1944*, he achieved international acclaim. In *Jorge Luis Borges*, Jaime Alazraki asserted: "As with Joyce, Kafka, or Faulkner, the name of Borges has become an accepted concept; his creations have generated a dimension that we designate 'Borgesian.' " Critics agree that Borges, in rejecting complete reliance on traditional realism or naturalism, has molded the shape of modern fiction in both Latin America and the United States. In his introduction to *Labyrinths*, James E. Irby describes the major subjects of "Borgesian" fiction based on the author's own categories:

> Borges once claimed that the basic devices of all fantastic literature are only four in number: the work within the work, the contamination of reality by

dream, the voyage in time, and the double. These are both his essential themes—the problematical nature of the world, of knowledge, of time, of the self—and his essential techniques of construction.

The international influence and recognition of Borges is reflected in even a partial list of his awards and honors, which include an Ingram Merrill Foundation Award, Matarazzo Sobrinho Inter-American Literary Prize; Jerusalem Prize; Alfonso Reyes Prize (Mexico); Gold Medal, French Academy; Order of Merit, German Federal Republic; Icelandic Falcon Cross; Miguel de Cervantes Award (Spain); Balzan Prize (Italy); Legion d'Honneur (France); and an honorary knighthood of the British Empire. Among his collections of stories are *Ficciones: 1935–1944* (Grove Press, 1962), *The Aleph and Other Stories: 1933–1969* (Dutton, 1970), *Dr. Brodie's Report* (Dutton, 1971), *A Universal History of Infamy* (Dutton, 1972), *Chronicles of Bustos Domecq* (Dutton, 1976), *The Book of Sand* (Dutton, 1977), and *Six Problems for Don Isidro*, in collaboration with Adolfo Bioy Casares (Dutton, 1983). Among his collections of poetry are: *Selected Poems: 1923–1967* (Delacorte Press, 1972), *In Praise of Darkness* (Dutton, 1974), and *The Gold of Tigers: Selected Later Poems.* (Dutton, 1977). Three combined volumes of poetry, fiction and nonfiction are: *A Personal Anthology* (Grove Press, 1967), *Labyrinths: Selected Stories and Other Writings* (New Directions, 1962; repr. Modern Library, 1983), and *Borges: A Reader* (Dutton, 1981).

THE BOOK OF SAND

> Thy rope of sands . . .
> *—George Herbert*

The line is made up of an infinite number of points; the plane of an infinite number of lines; the volume of an infinite number of planes; the hypervolume of an infinite number of volumes. . . . No, unquestionably this is not— *more geometrico*—the best way of beginning my story. To claim that it is true is nowadays the convention of every made-up story. Mine, however, *is* true.

I live alone in a fourth-floor apartment on Belgrano Street, in Buenos Aires. Late one evening, a few months back, I heard a knock at my door. I opened it and a stranger stood there. He was a tall man, with nondescript features—or perhaps it was my myopia that made them seem that way. Dressed in gray and carrying a gray suit-case in his hand, he had an unassuming look about him. I saw at once that he was a foreigner. At first, he struck me as old; only later did I realize that I had been misled by his thin blond hair, which was, in a Scandinavian sort of way, almost white. During the course of our conversa-tion, which was not to last an hour, I found out that he came from the Orkneys.

I invited him in, pointing to a chair. He paused awhile before speaking. A kind of gloom emanated from him— as it does now from me.

"I sell Bibles," he said.

Somewhat pedantically, I replied, "In this house are several English Bibles, including the first—John Wiclif's. I also have Cipriano de Valera's, Luther's—which, from a literary viewpoint, is the worst—and a Latin copy of the Vulgate. As you see, it's not exactly Bibles I stand in need of."

After a few moments of silence, he said, "I don't only sell Bibles. I can show you a holy book I came across on the outskirts of Bikaner. It may interest you."

He opened the suitcase and laid the book on a table. It was an octavo volume, bound in cloth. There was no

doubt that it had passed through many hands. Examining
it, I was surprised by its unusual weight. On the spine were
the words "Holy Writ" and, below them, "Bombay."

"Nineteenth century, probably," I remarked.

"I don't know," he said. "I've never found out."

I opened the book at random. The script was strange
to me. The pages, which were worn and typographically
poor, were laid out in double columns, as in a Bible.
The text was closely printed, and it was ordered in versi-
cles. In the upper corners of the pages were Arabic numbers. I noticed that one left-hand page bore the number
(let us say) 40,514 and the facing right-hand page 999. I
turned the leaf; it was numbered with eight digits. It also
bore a small illustration, like the kind used in dictionar-
ies—an anchor drawn with pen and ink, as if by a schoolboy's clumsy hand.

It was at this point that the stranger said, "Look at
the illustration closely. You'll never see it again."

I noted my place and closed the book. At once, I reopened it. Page by page, in vain, I looked for the illustration of the anchor. "It seems to be a version of Scriptures
in some Indian language, is it not?" I said to hide my
dismay.

"No," he replied. Then, as if confiding a secret, he
lowered his voice. "I acquired the book in a town out
on the plain in exchange for a handful of rupees and a
Bible. Its owner did not know how to read. I suspect
that he saw the Book of Books as a talisman. He was of
the lowest caste; nobody but other untouchables could
tread his shadow without contamination. He told me his
book was called the Book of Sand, because neither the
book nor the sand has any beginning or end."

The stranger asked me to find the first page.

I laid my left hand on the cover and, trying to put my
thumb on the flyleaf, I opened the book. It was useless.
Every time I tried, a number of pages came between the
cover and my thumb. It was as if they kept growing from
the book.

"Now find the last page."

Again I failed. In a voice that was not mine, I barely
managed to stammer, "This can't be."

Still speaking in a low voice, the stranger said, "It can't

be, but it *is*. The number of pages in this book is no more or less than infinite. None is the first page, none the last. I don't know why they're numbered in this arbitrary way. Perhaps to suggest that the terms of an infinite series admit any number."

Then, as if he were thinking aloud, he said, "If space is infinite, we may be at any point in space. If time is infinite, we may be at any point in time."

His speculations irritated me. "You are religious, no doubt?" I asked him.

"Yes, I'm a Presbyterian. My conscience is clear. I am reasonably sure of not having cheated the native when I gave him the Word of God in exchange for his devilish book."

I assured him that he had nothing to reproach himself for, and I asked if he were just passing through this part of the world. He replied that he planned to return to his country in a few days. It was then that I learned that he was a Scot from the Orkney Islands. I told him I had a great personal affection for Scotland, through my love of Stevenson and Hume.

"You mean Stevenson and Robbie Burns," he corrected.

While we spoke, I kept exploring the infinite book. With feigned indifference, I asked, "Do you intend to offer this curiosity to the British Museum?"

"No. I'm offering it to you," he said, and he stipulated a rather high sum for the book.

I answered, in all truthfulness, that such a sum was out of my reach, and I began thinking. After a minute or two, I came up with a scheme.

"I propose a swap," I said. "You got this book for a handful of rupees and a copy of the Bible. I'll offer you the amount of my pension check, which I've just collected, and my black-letter Wiclif Bible. I inherited it from my ancestors."

"A black-letter Wiclif!" he murmured.

I went to my bedroom and brought him the money and the book. He turned the leaves and studied the title page with all the fervor of a true bibliophile.

"It's a deal," he said.

It amazed me that he did not haggle. Only later was I to realize that he had entered my house with his mind

made up to sell the book. Without counting the money,
he put it away.

We talked about India, about Orkney, and about the
Norwegian jarls who once ruled it. It was night when the
man left. I have not seen him again, nor do I know his
name.

I thought of keeping the Book of Sand in the space
left on the shelf by the Wiclif, but in the end I decided
to hide it behind the volumes of a broken set of The
Thousand and One Nights. I went to bed and did not
sleep. At three or four in the morning, I turned on the
light. I got down the impossible book and leafed through
its pages. On one of them I saw engraved a mask. The
upper corner of the page carried a number, which I no
longer recall, elevated to the ninth power.

I showed no one my treasure. To the luck of owning
it was added the fear of having it stolen, and then the
misgiving that it might not truly be infinite. These twin
preoccupations intensified my old misanthropy. I had
only a few friends left; I now stopped seeing even them.
A prisoner of the book, I almost never went out anymore. After studying its frayed spine and covers with a
magnifying glass, I rejected the possibility of a contriv-
ance of any sort. The small illustrations, I verified, came
two thousand pages apart. I set about listing them alpha-
betically in a notebook, which I was not long in filling
up. Never once was an illustration repeated. At night, in
the meager intervals my insomnia granted, I dreamed of
the book.

Summer came and went, and I realized that the book
was monstrous. What good did it do me to think that I,
who looked upon the volume with my eyes, who held it
in my hands, was any less monstrous? I felt that the book
was a nightmarish object, an obscene thing that affronted
and tainted reality itself.

I thought of fire, but I feared that the burning of an
infinite book might likewise prove infinite and suffocate
the planet with smoke. Somewhere I recalled reading
that the best place to hide a leaf is in a forest. Before
retirement, I worked on Mexico Street, at the Argentine
National Library, which contains nine hundred thousand
volumes. I knew that to the right of the entrance a curved

staircase leads down into the basement, where books and maps and periodicals are kept. One day I went there and, slipping past a member of the staff and trying not to notice at what height or distance from the door, I lost the Book of Sand on one of the basement's musty shelves.

Translated by Norman Thomas Di Giovanni

Carlos Fuentes
(b. 1928)

Born in Mexico City to a career-diplomat father, Carlos
Fuentes was educated at the National University of Mexico where he received an L.L.B. and in Switzerland
where he was a graduate student at the Institute des
Hautes Etudes Internationales. A prolific Mexican novelist, short-story writer, playwright, and critic, he has
served his country in several political and cultural capac-
ities as well. Beginning as a member of the International
Labor Organization in Geneva, Switzerland, he became
secretary of its Mexican delegation in 1950. Later, in
Mexico City, he served as an administrator at the Ministry of Foreign Affairs, as secretary and assistant director
of the cultural department of the National University of
Mexico, and in 1975 was appointed Mexico's ambassador
to France. He has taught literature and creative writing
at the University of Mexico, University of California
at San Diego, University of Concepcion in Chile, University of Paris, University of Pennsylvania, and Columbia University. Among his honors are a Centro
Mexicano de Escritoires Fellowship, a Woodrow Wil-
son Institute for Scholars Fellowship, and the Romulo
Gallegos Prize for *Terra Nostra*. In discussing his preoccupation with Mexican history during an interview,
Fuentes has commented:

> Pablo Neruda used to say that every Latin American
> writer goes around dragging a heavy body, the body
> of his people, of his past, of his national history. We
> have to assimilate the enormous weight of our past so
> that we will not forget what gives us life. If you forget
> your past, you die.

Among Fuentes' novels that have been translated are *Where the Air Is Clear* (Ivan Obolensky, 1960), *The Good Conscience* (Ivan Obolensky, 1961), *The Death of Artemio Cruz* (Farrar, Straus, 1964), *Aura* (Farrar, Straus, 1965), *A Change of Skin* (Farrar, Straus, 1968), *Holy Place* (Dutton, 1972), *Terra Nostra* (Farrar, Straus, 1976), *Hydra Head* (Farrar, Straus, 1978), *Distant Relations* (Farrar, Straus, 1982), *Old Gringo* (Harper & Row, 1986), *Christopher Unborn* (Farrar, Straus, 1989), *Voluptuario* (St. Martin's Press, 1996), and *Witnesses of Time* (Aperture Foundation, 2000). A number of his short stories are collected in *Burnt Water* (Farrar, Straus, 1980).

THE COST OF LIVING

To Fernando Benítez

Salvador Renteria arose very early. He ran across the roof terrace. He did not light the water heater but simply removed his shorts. The needling drops felt good to him. He rubbed himself with a towel and returned to the room. From the bed Ana asked him whether he wanted any breakfast. Salvador said he'd get a cup of coffee somewhere. The woman had been two weeks in bed and her gingerbread-colored face had grown thin. She asked Salvador whether there was a message from the office, and he placed a cigarette between his lips and said that they wanted her to come in person to sign.

Ana sighed and said: "How do they expect me to do that?"

"I told them you couldn't right now, but you know how they are."

"What did the doctor tell you?"

He threw the unsmoked cigarette through the broken pane in the window and ran his fingers over his mustache and his temples. Ana smiled and leaned back against the tin bedstead. Salvador sat beside her and took her hand and told her not to worry, that soon she would be able to go back to work. They sat in silence, staring at the wooden wardrobe, the large box that held tools and provisions, the electric oven, the washstand, the piles of old newspapers. Salvador kissed his wife's hand and went out of the room to the terrace. He went down the service stairs and then crossed through the patios on the ground floor, smelling the medley of cooking odors from the other rooms in the rooming house. He picked his way among skates and dogs and went out into the street. He entered a store that occupied what had formerly been the garage to the house, and the elderly shopkeeper told him that *Life en Español* hadn't arrived yet, and he continued to move from stand to stand, unlocking padlocks.

He pointed to a stand filled with comic books and said: "Maybe you should take another magazine for your wife. People get bored stuck in bed."

Salvador left. In the street a gang of kids were shooting off cap pistols, and behind them a man was driving some goats from pasture. Salvador ordered a liter of milk from him and told him to take it up to number 12. He stuck his hands in his pockets and walked backward, almost trotting, so as not to miss the bus. He jumped onto the moving bus and searched for thirty centavos in his jacket pocket, then sat down to watch the cypresses, houses, iron grilles, and dusty streets of San Francisco Xocotitla pass by. The bus ran alongside the train tracks and across the bridge at Nonoalco. Steam was rising from the rails. From his wooden seat, Salvador saw the provision-laden trucks coming into the city. At Manuel Gonzalez, an inspector got on to tear the tickets in half, and Salvador got off at the next corner.

He walked to his father's house by way of Vallejo. He crossed the small patch of dry grass and opened the door. Clemencia said hello and Salvador asked whether his old man was up and around yet, and Pedro Rentería stuck his head around the curtain that separated the bedroom from the tiny living room and said: "What an early bird! Wait for me. I just got up."

Salvador ran his hands over the backs of the chairs. Clemencia was dusting the rough pine table and then took a cloth and pottery plates from the glass-front cupboard. She asked how Anita was and adjusted her bosom beneath the flowered robe.

"A little better."

"She must need someone to look after her. If only she didn't act so uppity . . ."

They exchanged glances and then Salvador looked at the walls stained by water that had run down from the roof. He pushed aside the curtain and went into the messy bedroom. His father was cleaning the soap from his face. Salvador put an arm around his father's shoulders and kissed him on the forehead. Pedro pinched his stomach. They looked at each other in the mirror. They looked alike, but the father was more bald and curly-haired, and he asked what Salvador was doing out and about at this hour, and Salvador said he couldn't come later, that Ana was very sick and wasn't going to be able to work all month and that they needed money. Pedro shrugged his shoulders and Salvador said he wasn't going to ask for money.

"What I thought was that you might be able to talk to your boss; he might have something for me. Some kind of work."

"Well, yes, maybe so. Help me with these suspenders."

"It's just . . . well, look, I'm not going to be able to make it this month."

"Don't worry. Something will come along. Let me see if I can think of something."

Pedro belted his pants and picked up the chauffeur's cap from the night table. He embraced Salvador and led him to the table. He sniffed the aroma of the eggs Clemencia set before them in the center of the table.

"Help yourself, Chava, son. I'd sure like to help you. But, you know, Clemencia and I live pretty close to the bone, even if I do get my lunch and supper at the boss's house. If it wasn't for that . . . I was born poor and I'll die poor. Now, you've got to realize that if I begin asking personal favors, Don José being as tough as he is, then I'll have to pay them back somehow, and so long raise. Believe me, Chava, I need to get that two hundred and fifty out of him every payday."

He prepared a mouthful of tortilla and hot sauce and lowered his voice.

"I know how much you respect your mother, and I, well, it goes without saying . . . But this business of keeping two houses going when we could all live together and save one rent . . . Okay, I didn't say a word. But now, tell me, why aren't you living with your in-laws?"

"You know what Doña Concha's like. At me all day about how Ana was born for this and Ana was born for that. You know that's why we moved out."

"So, if you want your independence, you'll have to work your way. Don't worry. I'll think of something."

Clemencia wiped her eyes with the corner of her apron and sat down between father and son.

"Where are the kids?" she asked.

"With Ana's parents," Salvador replied. "They're going to stay there awhile, while she's getting better."

Pedro said he had to take his boss to Acapulco. "If you need anything, come to Clemencia. I've got it! Go see Juan Olmedo. He's an old buddy of mine and he has a fleet of taxis. I'll call him and tell him you're coming."

Salvador kissed his father's hand and left.

Salvador opened the frosted-glass door and entered a reception room in which a secretary and an accountant were sitting in a room with steel furniture, a typewriter, and an adding machine. He told the secretary who he was and she went into Señor Olmedo's private office and then asked him to come in. Olmedo was a very small, thin man; they sat down in leather chairs facing a low, glass-topped table with photographs of banquets and ceremonies beneath the glass. Salvador told Olmedo he needed work to augment his teacher's salary and Olmedo began to leaf through some large black notebooks.

"You're in luck," he said, scratching his sharp-pointed, hair-filled ear. "There's a very good shift here from seven to twelve at night. There are lots of guys after this job, because I protect my men." He slammed the big book shut. "But since you're the son of my old friend Pedrito, well, I'm going to give it to you. You can begin today. If you work hard, you can get up to twenty pesos a day."

For a few seconds, Salvador heard only the *tac-tac-tac*

of the adding machine and the rumble of cars along 20 de Noviembre Avenue. Olmedo said he had to go out and asked Salvador to come with him. They descended in the elevator without speaking, and when they reached the street, Olmedo warned him that he must start the meter every time a passenger stopped to do an errand, because there was always some knothead who would carry his passenger all over Mexico City on one fare. He took him by the elbow and they went into the Department of the Federal District and up the stairs and Olmedo continued, telling him not to let just anyone get in.

"A stop here, a stop there, and the first thing you know you've gone clear from the Villa to Pedregal on a fare of one-fifty. Make them pay each time!"

Olmedo offered some gumdrops to a secretary and asked her to show him into the boss's office. The secretary thanked him for the candy and went into the boss's private office and Olmedo joked with the other employees and invited them to have a few beers on Saturday and a game of dominoes.

Salvador shook hands with Olmedo and thanked him, and Olmedo said: "Is your license in order? I don't want any trouble with Transit. You show up this evening, before seven. Ask for Toribio, he's in charge of dispatch. He'll tell you which car is yours. Remember! None of those one-peso stops; they chew up your doors. And none of that business of several stops on one fare. The minute the passenger steps out of the car, even to spit, you ring it up again. Say hello to your old man."

He looked at the Cathedral clock. It was eleven. He walked awhile along Merced and amused himself looking at the crates filled with tomatoes, oranges, squash. He sat down to smoke in the plaza, near some porters who were drinking beer and looking through the sports pages. After a time he was bored and walked toward San Juan de Letrán. A girl was walking ahead of him. A package fell from her arms and Salvador hurried to pick it up, and the girl smiled at him and thanked him.

Salvador pressed her arm and said: "Shall we have a lemonade?"

"Excuse me, señor, I'm not in the habit . . ."

"I'm sorry. I didn't mean to be fresh."

The girl continued walking ahead of him with short hurried steps. She waggled her hips beneath a white skirt. She looked in the shop windows out of the corner of her eyes. Salvador followed her at a distance. Then she stopped at an ice-cream cart and asked for a strawberry ice and Salvador stepped forward to pay and she smiled and thanked him. They went into a soft-drink stand and sat on a bench and ordered two apple juices. She asked him what he did and he asked her to guess and began to shadowbox and she said he must be a boxer and he laughed and told her he'd trained as a boy in the City Leagues but that actually he was a teacher. She told him she worked in the box office of a movie theater. She moved her arm and turned over the bottle of juice and they both laughed a lot.

They took a bus together. They did not speak. He took her hand and they got off across from Chapultepec Park. Automobiles were moving slowly through the streets in the park. There were many convertibles filled with young people. Many women passed by, dragging, embracing, or propelling children. The children were licking ice-cream sticks and clouds of cotton candy. They listened to the whistles of the balloon salesman and the music of a band in the bandstand. The girl told him she liked to guess the occupations of the people walking in Chapultepec. She laughed and pointed: black jacket or open-necked shirts, leather shoes or sandals, cotton skirt or sequined blouse, striped jersey, patent-leather heels: she said they were a carpenter, an electrician, a clerk, a tax assessor, a teacher, a servant, a huckster. They arrived at the lake and rented a boat. Salvador took off his jacket and rolled up his sleeves. The girl trailed her fingers in the water and closed her eyes. Salvador quietly whistled a few melodies as he rowed. He stopped and touched the girl's knee. She opened her eyes and rearranged her skirt. They returned to the dock and she said she had to go home to eat. They made a date to see each other the next evening at eleven, when the ticket booth closed.

*   *   *

He went into Kilo's and looked for his friends among the linoleum-topped, tubular-legged tables. He saw from a distance the blind man, Macario, and went to sit with him. Macario asked him to put a coin in the jukebox, and after a while Alfredo arrived and they ordered chicken tacos with guacamole, and beer, and listened to the song that was playing: "Ungrateful woman, she went away and left me, must have been for someone more a man than me." They did what they always did: recalled their adolescence and talked about Rosa and Remedios, the prettiest girls in the neighborhood. Macario urged them on. Alfredo said that the young kids today were really tough, carrying knives and all that. Not them. When you looked back on everything, they had really been pretty dumb. He remembered when the gang from the Poly challenged them to a game of soccer just to be able to kick them around and the whole thing ended in a scrap there on the empty lot on Mirto Street, and Macario had shown up with a baseball bat and the guys from Poly were knocked for a loop when they saw how the blind man clobbered them with a baseball bat. Macario said that was when everyone had accepted him as a buddy, and Salvador said that more than anything else it had been because of those faces he made, turning his eyes back in his head and pulling his ears back; it was enough to bust you up laughing. Macario said the one dying of laughter was him, because ever since he'd been ten years old his daddy had told him not to worry, that he'd never have to work, that the soap factory was finally going well, so Macario had devoted himself to cultivating his physique to be able to defend himself. He said that the radio had been his school and he'd gotten his jokes and his imitations from it. Then they recalled their buddy Raimundo and fell silent for a while and ordered more beer and Salvador looked toward the street and said that he and Raimundo always walked home together at night during exam time, and on the way back to their houses Raimundo asked him to explain algebra to him and then they stopped for a moment on the corner of Sullivan and Ramón Guzmán before going their own ways, and Raimundo would say: "You know something? I'm scared to go past this block. Here where our neighborhood

ends. Farther on, I don't know what's going on. You're
my buddy and that's why I'm telling you. I swear, I'm
scared to go past this block."

And Alfredo recalled how when he graduated his family had given him an old car and they had all gone on a
great celebration, making the rounds of the cheap night-
clubs in the city. They had been very drunk and Raimundo said that Alfredo didn't know how to drive and
began to struggle to take the wheel from Alfredo and
the car had almost turned over at a traffic island on the
Reforma and Raimundo said he was going to throw up,
and the door flew open and Raimundo fell to the street
and broke his neck.

They paid their bill and said goodbye.

He taught his three afternoon classes, and when he
finished his fingers were stained with chalk from drawing
the map of the republic on the blackboard. When the
session was over and the children had left, he walked
among the desks and sat down at the last bench. The
single light bulb hung from a long cord. He sat and
looked at the areas of color indicating mountains, tropical watersheds, deserts, and the plateau. He never had
been a good draftsman: Yucatán was too big, Baja California too short. The classroom smelled of sawdust and
leather bookbags. Cristobal, the fifth-grade teacher,
looked in the door and said: "What's new?"

Salvador walked toward the blackboard and erased the
map with a damp rag. Cristobal took out a package of
cigarettes and they smoked, and the floor creaked as they
fitted the pieces of chalk in their box. They sat down to
wait, and after a while the other teachers came in and
then the director, Durán.

The director sat on the lecture platform chair and the
rest of them sat at the desks and the director looked at
them with his black eyes and they all looked at him, the
dark face and the blue shirt and maroon tie. The director
said that no one was dying of hunger and that everyone
was having a hard time and the teachers became angry
and one said that he punched tickets on a bus after teaching two sessions and another said that he worked every
night in a sandwich shop on Santa María la Redonda and
another that he had set up a little shop with his savings

and he had only come for reasons of solidarity. Durán told them they were going to lose their seniority, their pensions, and, if it came to that, their jobs, and asked them not to leave themselves unprotected. Everyone rose and they all left, and Salvador saw that it was already six-thirty and he ran out to the street, cut across through the traffic, and hopped on a bus.

He got off in the Zóacalo and walked to Olmedo's office. Toribio told him that the car he was going to drive would be turned in at seven, and to wait awhile. Salvador closed himself in the dispatch booth and opened a map of the city. He studied it, then folded it and corrected his arithmetic notebooks.

"Which is better? To cruise around the center of the city or a little farther out?" he asked Toribio.

"Well, away from the center you can go faster, but you also burn more gasoline. Remember, *you* pay for the gas."

Salvador laughed. "Maybe I'll pick up a gringo at one of the hotels, a big tipper."

"Here comes your car," Toribio said to him from the booth.

"Are you the new guy?" yelled the flabby driver manning the cab. He wiped the sweat from his forehead with a rag and got out of the car. "Here she is. Ease her into first or sometimes she jams. Close the doors yourself or they'll knock the shit out of 'em. Here she is, she's all yours."

Salvador sat facing the office and placed the notebooks in the door pocket. He passed the rag over the greasy steering wheel. The seat was still warm. He got out and ran the rag over the windshield. He got in again and arranged the mirror to his eye level. He drove off. He raised the flag. His hands were sweating. He took 20 de Noviembre Street. A man immediately stopped him and ordered him to take him to the Cosmos Theater.

The man got out in front of the theater and his friend Cristobal looked into the side window and said: "What a surprise." Salvador asked him what he was doing and Cristobal said he was going to Flores Carranza's printing shop on Ribera de San Cosme and Salvador offered to take him; Cristobal got into the taxi but said that it wasn't to be a free ride for a buddy: he would pay. Salvador laughed and said that's all he needed. They talked about boxing and made a date to go to the Arena Mexico on Friday. Salvador told him about the girl he'd met that morning. Cristobal began talking about the fifth-grade students and they arrived at the printing plant, and Salvador parked and they got out. They entered through a narrow door and continued along a dark corridor. The printing office was in the rear and Señor Flores Carranza greeted them and Cristobal asked whether the broadsides were ready. The printer removed his visor and nodded and showed him the broadsides with red-and-black letters calling for a strike. The employees handed over the four packages. Salvador took two bundles and started ahead while Cristobal was paying the bill.

He walked down the long, dark corridor. In the distance, he heard the noise of automobiles along Ribera de San Cosme. Halfway along the corridor he felt a hand on his shoulder and someone said: "Take it easy, take it easy."

"Sorry," Salvador said. "It's very dark here."

"Dark? It's going to get black."

The man stuck a cigarette between his lips and smiled, but Salvador only said: "Excuse me." But the hand fell again on his shoulder and the fellow said he must be the only teacher who didn't know who *he* was, and Salvador began to get angry and said he was in a hurry and the fellow said: "The S.O.B., you know? That's me!"

Salvador saw that four cigarettes had been lighted at the mouth of the corridor, at the entrance to the building, and he hugged the bundles to his chest and looked behind him and another cigarette glowed before the entrance to the print shop.

"King S.O.B., the biggest fucking sonofabitch of 'em all, that's me. Don't tell me you never heard of *me!*" Salvador's eyes were becoming adjusted to the darkness and he could now see the man's hat and the hand taking one of the bundles.

"That's enough introduction, now. Give me the posters, teacher."

Salvador dislodged the hand and stepped back a few paces. The cigarette from the rear advanced. A humid current filtered down the corridor at the height of his calves. Salvador looked around.

"Let me by."

"Let's have those flyers."

"Those flyers are going with me, buddy."

He felt the burning tip of the cigarette behind him close to his neck. Then he heard Cristobal's cry. He threw one package, and with his free arm smashed at the man's face. He felt the squashed cigarette and its burning point on his fist. And then he saw the red saliva-stained face coming closer. Salvador whirled with his fists closed and he saw the knife and then felt it in his stomach.

The man slowly withdrew the knife and snapped his fingers, and Salvador fell with his mouth open.

Translated by Margaret Sayers Peden

Gabriel García Márquez
(b. 1928)

Among the best-known Latin American writers, Gabriel García Márquez was born in Aracataca, Colombia, the oldest child in a large family. He studied at the Universidad Nacional de Colombia and the Universidad de Cartegena and worked as a journalist and foreign correspondent for the Colombian *El Heraldo, El Espectador*, and Prensa Latina, a news agency, as well as for the Mexican periodicals *La Familia* and *Sucesos*. Although he began publishing fiction with the novella *Leaf Storm* in 1955, not until the publication of *One Hundred Years of Solitude* in 1967 did he achieve international acclaim. That novel, which depicted a hundred years of the history of the doomed Buendia family, was an immediate best-seller which was translated into more than thirty languages. George R. McMurray, in his book *Gabriel García Márquez*, has analyzed the novelist's technique:

> His works are illumined by flashes of irony and the belief that human values are perennial. The amazing totality of his fictional world is also achieved through the contrapuntal juxtaposition of objective reality and poetic fantasy that captures simultaneously the essence of both Latin American and universal man.

Awarded the Nobel Prize for literature in 1982, García Márquez has also received the Colombian Association of Writers and Artists Award, the Premio Literario Esso (Colombia), the Chianciano Award (Italy), the Prix de Meilleur Livre Etranger (France), the Romulo Gallegos Prize (Venezuela), the Books Abroad/Neustadt International Prize for Literature, and the *Los Angeles Times* Book Prize for Fiction in 1988 for *Love in the Time of*

Cholera. The novels of García Márquez in English include *One Hundred Years of Solitude* (Harper & Row, 1970), *The Autumn of the Patriarch* (Harper & Row, 1976), *In Evil Hour* (Harper & Row, 1979), *Chronicle of a Death Foretold* (Knopf, 1983), *Love in the Time of Cholera* (Knopf, 1988; repr. Penguin, 1989), *The General in His Labyrinth* (Knopf, 1990; repr. Penguin, 1991), and *Of Love and Other Demons* (Knopf, 1995). His short fiction is collected in *No One Writes to the Colonel and Other Stories* (Harper & Row, 1968), *Leaf Storm and Other Stories* (Harper & Row, 1972), and *Innocent Eréndira and Other Stories* (Harper & Row, 1978); *Collected Stories* (Harper & Row, 1984) contains the stories of all three earlier volumes. His most recent collection is *Strange Pilgrims: Twelve Stories* (Knopf, 1993).

DEATH CONSTANT BEYOND LOVE

Senator Onésimo Sánchez had six months and eleven days to go before his death when he found the woman of his life. He met her in Rosal del Virrey, an illusory village which by night was the furtive wharf for smugglers' ships, and on the other hand, in broad daylight looked like the most useless inlet on the desert, facing a sea that was arid and without direction and so far from everything no one would have suspected that someone capable of changing the destiny of anyone lived there. Even its name was a kind of joke, because the only rose in that village was being worn by Senator Onésimo Sánchez himself on the same afternoon when he met Laura Farina.

It was an unavoidable stop in the electoral campaign he made every four years. The carnival wagons had arrived in the morning. Then came the trucks with the rented Indians who were carried into the towns in order to enlarge the crowds at public ceremonies. A short time before eleven o'clock, along with the music and rockets and jeeps of the retinue, the ministerial automobile, the color of strawberry soda, arrived. Senator Onésimo Sánchez was placid and weatherless inside the air-conditioned car, but as soon as he opened the door he was shaken by a gust of fire and his shirt of pure silk was soaked in a kind of light-colored soup and he felt many years older and more alone than ever. In real life he had just turned forty-two, had been graduated from Göttingen with honors as a metallurgical engineer, and was an avid reader, although without much reward, of badly translated Latin classics. He was married to a radiant German woman who had given him five children and they were all happy in their home, he the happiest of all until they told him, three months before, that he would be dead forever by next Christmas.

While the preparations for the public rally were being completed, the senator managed to have an hour alone in the house they had set aside for him to rest in. Before he lay down he put in a glass of drinking water the rose he had kept alive all across the desert, lunched on the diet cereals that he took with him so as to avoid the repeated portions of fried goat that were waiting for him during the rest of the day, and he took several analgesic pills before the time prescribed so that he would have the remedy ahead of the pain. Then he put the electric fan close to the hammock and stretched out naked for fifteen minutes in the shadow of the rose, making a great effort at mental distraction so as not to think about death while he dozed. Except for the doctors, no one knew that he had been sentenced to a fixed term, for he had decided to endure his secret all alone, with no change in his life, not because of pride but out of shame.

He felt in full control of his will when he appeared in public again at three in the afternoon, rested and clean, wearing a pair of coarse linen slacks and a floral shirt, and with his soul sustained by the anti-pain pills. Nevertheless, the erosion of death was much more pernicious than he had supposed, for as he went up onto the platform he felt a strange disdain for those who were fighting for the good luck to shake his hand, and he didn't feel sorry as he had at other times for the groups of barefoot Indians who could scarcely bear the hot saltpeter coals of the sterile little square. He silenced the applause with a wave of his hand, almost with rage, and he began to speak without gestures, his eyes fixed on the sea, which was sighing with heat. His measured, deep voice had the quality of calm water, but the speech that had been memorized and ground out so many times had not occurred to him in the nature of telling the truth, but, rather, as the opposite of a fatalistic pronouncement by Marcus Aurelius in the fourth book of his *Meditations*.

"We are here for the purpose of defeating nature," he began, against all his convictions. "We will no longer be foundlings in our own country, orphans of God in a realm of thirst and bad climate, exiles in our own land. We will be different people, ladies and gentlemen, we will be a great and happy people."

There was a pattern to his circus. As he spoke his aides threw clusters of paper birds into the air and the artificial creatures took on life, flew about the platform of planks, and went out to sea. At the same time, other men took some prop trees with felt leaves out of the wagons and planted them in the saltpeter soil behind the crowd. They finished by setting up a cardboard façade with make-believe houses of red brick that had glass windows, and with it they covered the miserable real-life shacks.

The senator prolonged his speech with two quotations in Latin in order to give the farce more time. He promised rain-making machines, portable breeders for table animals, the oils of happiness which would make vegetables grow in the saltpeter and clumps of pansies in the window boxes. When he saw that his fictional world was all set up, he pointed to it. "That's the way it will be for us, ladies and gentlemen," he shouted. "Look! That's the way it will be for us."

The audience turned around. An ocean liner made of painted paper was passing behind the houses and it was taller than the tallest houses in the artificial city. Only the senator himself noticed that since it had been set up and taken down and carried from one place to another the superimposed cardboard town had been eaten away by the terrible climate and that it was almost as poor and dusty as Rosal del Virrey.

For the first time in twelve years, Nelson Farina didn't

go to greet the senator. He listened to the speech from his hammock amidst the remains of his siesta, under the cool bower of a house of unplaned boards which he had built with the same pharmacist's hands with which he had drawn and quartered his first wife. He had escaped from Devil's Island and appeared in Rosal del Virrey on a ship loaded with innocent macaws, with a beautiful and blasphemous black woman he had found in Paramaribo and by whom he had a daughter. The woman died of natural causes a short while later and she didn't suffer the fate of the other, whose pieces had fertilized her own cauliflower patch, but was buried whole and with her Dutch name in the local cemetery. The daughter had inherited her color and her figure along with her father's yellow and astonished eyes, and he had good reason to imagine that he was rearing the most beautiful woman in the world.

Ever since he had met Senator Onésimo Sánchez during his first electoral campaign, Nelson Farina had begged for his help in getting a false identity card which would place him beyond the reach of the law. The senator, in a friendly but firm way, had refused. Nelson Farina never gave up, and for several years, every time he found the chance, he would repeat his request with a different recourse. But this time he stayed in his hammock, condemned to rot alive in that burning den of buccaneers. When he heard the final applause, he lifted his head, and looking over the boards of the fence, he saw the back side of the farce: the props for the buildings, the framework of the trees, the hidden illusionists who were pushing the ocean liner along. He spat without rancor.

"*Merde,*" he said. "*C'est le Blacamán de la politique.*"

After the speech, as was customary, the senator took a walk through the streets of the town in the midst of the music and the rockets and was besieged by the townspeople, who told him their troubles. The senator listened to them good-naturedly and he always found some way to console everybody without having to do them any difficult favors. A woman up on the roof of a house with her six youngest children managed to make herself heard over the uproar and the fireworks.

"I'm not asking for much, Senator," she said. "Just a donkey to haul water from Hanged Man's Well."

The senator noticed the six thin children. "What became of your husband?" he asked.

"He went to find his fortune on the island of Aruba," the woman answered good-humoredly, "and what he found was a foreign woman, the kind that put diamonds on their teeth."

The answer brought on a roar of laughter. ·

"All right," the senator decided, "you'll get your donkey."

A short while later an aide of his brought a good pack donkey to the woman's house and on the rump it had a campaign slogan written in indelible paint so that no one would ever forget that it was a gift from the senator.

Along the short stretch of street he made other, smaller gestures, and he even gave a spoonful of medicine to a sick man who had had his bed brought to the door of his house so he could see him pass. At the last corner, through the boards of the fence, he saw Nelson Farina in his hammock, looking ashen and gloomy, but nonetheless the senator greeted him, with no show of affection.

"Hello, how are you?"

Nelson Farina turned in his hammock and soaked him in the sad amber of his look.

"Moi, vous savez," he said.

His daughter came out into the yard when she heard the greeting. She was wearing a cheap, faded Guajiro Indian robe, her head was decorated with colored bows, and her face was painted as protection against the sun, but even in that state of disrepair it was possible to imagine that there had never been another so beautiful in the whole world. The senator was left breathless. "I'll be damned!" he breathed in surprise. "The Lord does the craziest things!"

That night Nelson Farina dressed his daughter up in her best clothes and sent her to the senator. Two guards armed with rifles who were nodding from the heat in the borrowed house ordered her to wait on the only chair in the vestibule.

The senator was in the next room meeting with the

important people of Rosal del Virrey, whom he had gathered together in order to sing for them the truths he had left out of his speeches. They looked so much like all the ones he always met in all the towns in the desert that even the senator himself was sick and tired of that perpetual nightly session. His shirt was soaked with sweat and he was trying to dry it on his body with the hot breeze from an electric fan that was buzzing like a horse fly in the heavy heat of the room.

"We, of course, can't eat paper birds," he said. "You and I know that the day there are trees and flowers in this heap of goat dung, the day there are shad instead of worms in the water holes, that day neither you nor I will have anything to do here, do I make myself clear?"

No one answered. While he was speaking, the senator had torn a sheet off the calendar and fashioned a paper butterfly out of it with his hands. He tossed it with no particular aim into the air current coming from the fan and the butterfly flew about the room and then went out through the half-open door. The senator went on speaking with a control aided by the complicity of death.

"Therefore," he said, "I don't have to repeat to you what you already know too well: that my reelection is a better piece of business for you than it is for me, because I'm fed up with stagnant water and Indian sweat, while you people, on the other hand, make your living from it."

Laura Farina saw the paper butterfly come out. Only she saw it because the guards in the vestibule had fallen asleep on the steps, hugging their rifles. After a few turns, the large lithographed butterfly unfolded completely, flattened against the wall, and remained stuck there. Laura Farina tried to pull it off with her nails. One of the guards, who woke up with the applause from the next room, noticed her vain attempt.

"It won't come off," he said sleepily. "It's painted on the wall."

Laura Farina sat down again when the men began to come out of the meeting. The senator stood in the doorway of the room with his hand on the latch, and he only noticed Laura Farina when the vestibule was empty.

"What are you doing here?"

"*C'est de la part de mon père,*" she said.

The senator understood. He scrutinized the sleeping guards, then he scrutinized Laura Farina, whose unusual beauty was even more demanding than his pain, and he resolved then that death had made his decision for him.

"Come in," he told her.

Laura Farina was struck dumb standing in the doorway to the room: thousands of bank notes were floating in the air, flapping like the butterfly. But the senator turned off the fan and the bills were left without air and alighted on the objects in the room.

"You see," he said, smiling, "even shit can fly."

Laura Farina sat down on a schoolboy's stool. Her skin was smooth and firm, with the same color and the same solar density as crude oil, her hair was the mane of a young mare, and her huge eyes were brighter than the light. The senator followed the thread of her look and finally found the rose, which had been tarnished by the saltpeter.

"It's a rose," he said.

"Yes," she said with a trace of perplexity. "I learned what they were in Riohacha."

The senator sat down on an army cot, talking about roses as he unbuttoned his shirt. On the side where he imagined his heart to be inside his chest he had a corsair's tattoo of a heart pierced by an arrow. He threw the soaked shirt to the floor and asked Laura Farina to help him off with his boots.

She knelt down facing the cot. The senator continued to scrutinize her, thoughtfully, and while she was untying the laces he wondered which one of them would end up with the bad luck of that encounter.

"You're just a child," he said.

"Don't you believe it," she said. "I'll be nineteen in April."

The senator became interested.

"What day?"

"The eleventh," she said.

The senator felt better. "We're both Aries," he said. And smiling, he added:

"It's the sign of solitude."

Laura Farina wasn't paying attention because she

didn't know what to do with the boots. The senator, for his part, didn't know what to do with Laura Farina, because he wasn't used to sudden love affairs and, besides, he knew that the one at hand had its origins in indignity. Just to have some time to think, he held Laura Farina tightly between his knees, embraced her about the waist, and lay down on his back on the cot. Then he realized that she was naked under her dress, for her body gave off the dark fragrance of an animal of the woods, but her heart was frightened and her skin disturbed by a glacial sweat.

"No one loves us," he sighed.

Laura Farina tried to say something, but there was only enough air for her to breathe. He laid her down beside him to help her, he put out the light and the room was in the shadow of the rose. She abandoned herself to the mercies of her fate. The senator caressed her slowly, seeking her with his hand, barely touching her, but where he expected to find her, he came across something iron that was in the way.

"What have you got there?"

"A padlock," she said.

"What in hell!" the senator said furiously and asked what he knew only too well. "Where's the key?"

Laura Farina gave a breath of relief.

"My papa has it," she answered. "He told me to tell you to send one of your people to get it and to send along with him a written promise that you'll straighten out his situation."

The senator grew tense. "Frog bastard," he murmured indignantly. Then he closed his eyes in order to relax and he met himself in the darkness. *Remember*, he remembered, *that whether it's you or someone else, it won't be long before you'll be dead and it won't be long before your name won't even be left.*

He waited for the shudder to pass.

"Tell me one thing," he asked then. "What have you heard about me?"

"Do you want the honest-to-God truth?"

"The honest-to-God truth."

"Well," Laura Farina ventured, "they say you're worse than the rest because you're different."

The senator didn't get upset. He remained silent for a long time with his eyes closed, and when he opened them again he seemed to have returned from his most hidden instincts.

"Oh, what the hell," he decided. "Tell your son of a bitch of a father that I'll straighten out his situation."

"If you want, I can go get the key myself," Laura Farina said.

The senator held her back.

"Forget about the key," he said, "and sleep awhile with me. It's good to be with someone when you're so alone."

Then she laid his head on her shoulder with her eyes fixed on the rose. The senator held her about the waist, sank his face into woods-animal armpit, and gave in to terror. Six months and eleven days later he would die in that same position, debased and repudiated because of the public scandal with Laura Farina and weeping with rage at dying without her.

Translated by Gregory Rabassa

Luisa Valenzuela
(b. 1938)

Born in Buenos Aires, Luisa Valenzuela is the daughter of the famous Argentine writer Luisa Mercedes Levinson. Valenzuela began early to publish her fiction and by the age of twenty, she had worked with Jorge Luis Borges. She lived in Paris from 1958 to 1961, publishing short stories, writing for the Argentine newspaper *El Mundo*, contributing to *La Nación*'s literary supplement, and writing programs for French radio and television. She received a Fulbright grant in 1969, enabling her to participate in the International Writers' Program at the University of Iowa. Among her other awards are a Guggenheim Foundation Fellowship, a fellowship at the New York Institute for the Humanities, and recognition by the Fondo Nacional de las Artes and the Instituto Nacional de Cinematografia. Valenzuela recalls the way that she turned to art as a reaction to the military dictatorships that came into power in Argentina after Juan Perón's death:

> Buenos Aires belonged then to violence and state terrorism, and I could only sit in cafés and brood. Till I decided a book of stories could be written in a month, at those same café tables, overhearing scraps of scared conversations, seeping in the general paranoia. *Strange Things Happen Here* (1979) was born, and with it a new political awareness. And action.

In 1979, she moved to New York City where she was writer-in-residence at Columbia University as well as at the Center for Inter-American Relations. Describing her, Julio Cortázar has said:

> Luisa Valenzuela is a woman deeply anchored in her
> condition; she is conscious of the still horrible discrimi-
> nations in our continent, yet she is filled with a joy of
> life which enables her to surpass the first stages of
> protest . . . , taking a legitimate place of equality with
> any writer in the world of letters. To read her is to
> enter fully into reality, and to participate in a search
> for a Latin American identity which continues to en-
> rich itself. The books of Luisa Valenzuela are our
> present but they contain much of our future; there is
> real sun, real love, real liberty in each of her pages.

She has published several collections of fiction, including
Clara: Thirteen Short Stories and a Novel (Harcourt Brace
Jovanovich, 1976), *Strange Things Happen Here*, which
contains the novel *He Who Searches* (Harcourt Brace
Jovanovich, 1979), *Other Weapons* (Ediciones del Norte,
1985), *Open Door* (North Point Press, 1988), and *The Cen-
sors: A Bilingual Selection of Stories* (Curbstone, 1992), as
well as the novels *The Lizard's Tail* (Farrar, Straus, 1983),
Bedside Manners (Serpent's Tail, 1995), and *Clara* (Latin
American Literary Review Press, 1999).

PAPITO'S STORY

A thin wall has always separated us. Now the time has
come for the wall to unite us.

I had never paid much attention to him in the elevator, nor when we walked down the long hall leading to
our respective apartments. He was self-absorbed, lugging
along with him all the trivialities of the daily commute
on the train—smoke that steamed up the mirrors of the
entry hall, shouted conversations that stuck in his ears
and made him deaf to my polite chitchat: Pretty day,
isn't it. Or more likely: Looks like rain. Or: This elevator, it gets more rickety every day.

A few times, he answered—Yes, no, indiscriminately. And I shuffled those monosyllables of his and put them where I pleased. I guess I liked the freedom he gave me to organize our little dialogues according to my own logic.

There are things about him I could not appreciate until tonight: his hunched shoulders, that gray face barely translucent, his wrinkled suits, his waning youth. (Yet tonight I should have put my hand through the wall and made him accept our bond once and for all.)

In the end, he was the one to blame for the uproar that woke me up. And I—Julio—thought they were banging and kicking on my door, and that Open-up-you-son-of-a-bitch was addressed to me. What did the police want with me, I asked myself half-asleep, searching all up and down my pajamas for a weapon.

We'll smash the door open, they shouted. Give up. We've got the whole block surrounded.

My door, unscathed. And I knew then that they were one apartment over, and that he, so blank, so forgettable, was now offering me his one moment of glory and rebellion.

I couldn't open my door to see the cops' faces, drugged with loathing. The loathing of those who believe they are right is one step beyond reason, and I'd rather not confront it.

So I remained there, and glued my ear to the wall to offer him my company, and I don't know if I was happy to discover that someone was with him already. The woman's voice had the sharp ring of hysteria:

"Give yourself up. What's going to happen to me? Give up."

And he, so forgettable up to now, now gaining stature:

"No. I won't give up."

"Yes. Give yourself up. They'll knock the door down and kill me. They'll kill us both."

"Fuck them. We'll kill ourselves first. Come on. Kill yourself with me."

"You're crazy, Papito. Don't say that. I was good to you. Be good to me now, Papito."

* * *

I start to cough, my apartment is filling with tear gas. I run to open a window, though I would like to stay with my ear pressed to the wall—stay with you, Papito.

I open the window. It's true, you're surrounded, Papito. Loads of police and an assault vehicle. All for you, and you so alone.

"There's a woman with me. Let her go," Papito shouts, "let her go or I'll shoot. I'm armed."

Bang! shouts the revolver to prove he is armed.

And the cops:

"Let the woman go. Let her come out."

Crash, bang. The woman leaves.

She doesn't say, Bye-bye, Papito, or Good luck, or anything. There's a deafening nothingness in there, chez Papito. Even I can hear it, though it's hard to hear things that make no sound. I hear the nothingness and Papito's breathing isn't part of it, nor is his terror, nothing. Papito's terror must be immeasurable, though its waves don't reach me—how strange—as do those of the gas they are using to drown him.

Give up, they shout, kick, howl with fury. Give up. We'll count to three. Then we'll bust the door down and come in shooting.

To three, I say to myself, not much of a countdown for a man's life. Father, Son, and Holy Ghost, that's three, and what can Papito do with a trinity all to himself that ticks his life away?

One, they shout from outside, thinking themselves magnanimous. Be strong, Papito. And he must be running in circles in an apartment cramped as mine, at every window running into the visible eye of a telescopic sight.

I don't turn on my lights, just in case. I put my cheek against the wall and I am with you, Papito, inside your skin.

Two, they shout at him at me and he answers: Don't try it. If you break in, I'll kill myself.

I almost didn't hear, three. The shot obliterated it and the astonished running feet and the splintering door and the silence.

A suicide right here, Papito. Now what's left for me? Just to sit on the floor with my head on my knees, hopeless, waiting for the smell of powder to vanish and your finger to loosen on the trigger.

So alone, Papito, and with me so nearby.

After all the scrambling, the calm following an irremediable act. I opened my door and poked my nose out, my head, my whole body, and I managed to sneak into the apartment next door without anybody noticing.

Forgettable Papito little-nothing was a rag tossed on the floor. They nudged him a bit with their boots, trussed him on a stretcher, covered him with a dirty blanket, and headed for the morgue.

A puddle of blood remained that had once been Papito. A sublime stain, the color of life.

In that stain, my neighbor was great. He was important. I leaned down and said to him:

"Shout your name to me and don't be afraid. I can get you a good lawyer."

And I got no answer, as usual.

Translated by Christopher Leland

SELECTED LATIN AMERICAN ANTHOLOGIES

Carpentier, Hortense and Janet Brof, eds. *Doors and Mirrors: Fiction and Poetry from Spanish America*. New York: Viking Press, 1972.

Caistor, Nick, ed. *The Faber Book of Contemporary Latin American Short Stories*. London: Faber and Faber, 1989.

Cohen, J.M., ed. *Latin American Writing Today*. Baltimore: Penguin Books, 1967.

Correas de Zapata, Celia, ed. *Short Stories by Latin American Women: The Magic and the Real*. Houston: Arte Publico Press, 1990.

Donoso, Jose and William A. Henken, eds. *The Tri-Quarterly Anthology of Contemporary Latin American Literature*. New York: Dutton, 1969.

Flakoll, Darwin, and Claribel Alegría, eds. *New Voices of Hispanic America: An Anthology*. Boston: Beacon Press, 1962.

Garfield, Evelyn Picon, trans. and ed. *Women's Fiction from Latin America*. Detroit: Wayne State University Press, 1985.

Grossman, William L., trans. and ed. *Modern Brazilian Short Stories*. Berkeley: University of California Press, 1967.

Howes, Barbara, ed. *The Eye of the Heart: Short Stories from Latin America*. Indianapolis and New York: Bobbs-Merrill, 1973; repr. Avon Books, 1983.

Jones, Willis Knapp, ed. *Spanish American Literature in Translation*. Vol. 2. New York: Frederick Ungar, 1963.

Lewald, H. Ernest, trans. and ed. *The Web: Stories by Argentine Women*. Washington, DC: Three Continents Press, 1983.

Luby, Barry J. and Wayne H. Finke, eds. *Anthology of Contemporary Latin American Literature: 1960–1984*. Rutherford, NJ: Fairleigh Dickinson University Press, 1986.

Mancini, Pat McNees, ed. *Contemporary Latin American Short Stories*. New York: Fawcett Premier, 1974.

Manguel, Alberto, ed. *Other Fires: Short Fiction by Latin American Women:* New York: Clarkson N. Potter, 1986.

Meyer, Doris and Margarite Fernandez Olmos, eds. *Contemporary Women Authors of Latin America: New Translations*. Brooklyn, NY: Brooklyn College Press, 1983.

Paschke, Barbara and David Volpendesta, eds. *Clamor of Innocence: Central American Short Stories*. San Francisco: City Lights Books, 1988.

Santos, Rosario, ed. *And We Sold the Rain. Contemporary Fiction from Central America*. New York: Four Walls Eight Windows, 1988.

Swanson, Philip, ed. *Landmarks in Modern Latin American Fiction*. London and New York: Routledge, 1990.

Torres-Ríoseco, Arturo, ed. *Short Stories of Latin America*. New York: Las Americas Publ. Co., 1963.

Yates, Donald A., ed. *Latin Blood: The Best Crime and Detective Stories of South America*. New York: Herder and Herder, 1972.